Training for Change

Alisha Moreland-Capuia

Training for Change

Transforming Systems to be Trauma-Informed, Culturally Responsive, and Neuroscientifically Focused

With contributions from Audrey A. Tran

Springer

Alisha Moreland-Capuia
Oregon Health & Science University
(OHSU)
Avel Gordly Center for Healing
Portland, OR, USA

ISBN 978-3-030-19207-5 ISBN 978-3-030-19208-2 (eBook)
https://doi.org/10.1007/978-3-030-19208-2

This Springer imprint is published by the registered company Springer Nature Switzerland AG
The registered company address is: Gewerbestrasse 11, 6330 Cham, Switzerland

I have a robust, loving and supportive network in my husband Daniel and children Julia, Daniel Jr. and Olivia. They gave me over 375 h of uninterrupted time to write this textbook—I could not have completed the task absent their encouragement and selflessness. They believe in me and the ideas shared in this textbook. They, like me, believe that this textbook provides a fresh perspective on tough issues and has the capacity to positively impact systems for change. I say to my beloved husband and children, thank you, thank you, thank you! I hope I make you proud.

Acknowledgements

My gratitude runs deep and wide. I wish to start by thanking the Multnomah County Department of Community Justice (DCJ) Parole/Probation Officers and Junior Court Counselors (JCC's) who welcomed, learned from and with me and who ultimately made major positive changes for the system in which they serve. Thank you Keith Murphy, Brie Murphy, Silvia Gomez, Dennis Moore, Erik Zilz, Kate Desmond, Erika Preuitt, and the research and planning team at Multnomah County DCJ in Portland, Oregon.

I've had the privilege of working with some of the best human beings at Oregon Health & Science University (OHSU). John Hunter, thank you for encouraging me to write and helping me make important connections. Charles Thomas, I appreciate the time you spent editing many of my publications and inspiring me to "just write." To the Psychiatry Department at OHSU—thank you for your provision. To every OHSU medical student I've had the honor to teach and learn from—thank you.

To my family, sisters, brothers, mother, grandmother, uncles, and aunts—thank you for your unwavering love.

To every teacher, professor, community member, and mentor that touched my life and saw greatness in me (you know who you are)—thank you.

Finally, a big thank you to Audrey Tran! Audrey is the illustrator for this textbook and is currently a second year medical student at OHSU. Audrey is known for advocating for health policy and employing music and writing as tools to optimize patient communication. She is a leader. I am honored to share this moment with her and look forward to a continued partnership.

Contents

About the Author

Dr. Alisha Moreland-Capuia grew up in Portland, Oregon. She graduated from Stanford University in 2002 with a B.S. in biological sciences and a minor in urban studies. She earned her Doctor of Medicine from the George Washington University School of Medicine in 2007. She completed four years of psychiatry residency and an addiction fellowship at Oregon Health and Science University. She is double board certified in addiction and general adult psychiatry.

She has trained judges, parole officers, school teachers, community members, and faith-based institutions in the areas of cultural responsivity, brain development, and trauma-informed approaches and practices. She built a program entitled Healing Hurt People Portland—a hospital-based, trauma-informed, community-focused youth violence prevention program that serves young males of color between the ages of 15 and 33 who've been stabbed, shot, and or assaulted.

She has committed her professional career to changing systems to optimally serve youth. Dr. Alisha is also the Co-Founder of The Capuia Foundation and believes in serving the global community. Through the Foundation, she and her family built a primary care clinic in Angola, Africa, which provides subsidized primary and preventative care services for Angolans. Annually, she travels to Angola, Africa to serve patients in the family-built clinic. The establishment of the clinic inspired the construction of roads and improved access to water, lights, and jobs for the surrounding Angolan community. Dr. Alisha has a history of building "with" people and community.

Her working motto is that systems change when people change and people change when they "feel" something. Dr. Alisha has passionately committed herself to working at the people level (getting them to connect with their "feeling space", also known as the birthplace for change) as a means of systems change.

She's had the privilege of bearing witness to people and systems changing.

This textbook is most about "people-individual work and change" that results in "system work and change". Changed people change systems.

About the Illustrator

Audrey A. Tran is a second year medical student at the Oregon Health and Science University School of Medicine.

She received her B.A. at Wellesley College, magna cum laude, in Biochemistry with a minor in Music. In college, her passion for exploring the sciences was coupled with a passion in sharing what she had learned through formal peer tutoring. She spent two years post-grad continuing stem cell and genome editing research in Boston, MA, where she worked along with brilliant scientific minds. It was in Boston where she learned about the importance of advocacy at the intersection of science, racial justice, and women's rights.

In medical school, her interest in medical education led to a style of tutoring that incorporates intuitive, illustrative, and color-coded study guides. This style is observed, appreciated, and thoughtfully integrated throughout this textbook. To stay creative, she is in a medical school rock band, writes music, and can likely be found harmonizing to popular songs.

Chapter 1
The Developing Brain and Trauma

Introduction

It is important to preface the introduction to this book with two critical points:

1. Change is constant, inevitable, and inspires considerable resistance.
2. Many systems recognize the need for change but are not always certain how to approach the change process.

"Systems" can be impersonal, colossal entities and at times can feel insurmountable and unchangeable. This book redefines systems by challenging the reader to consider this sentiment:

"**Systems are intimately attached to people. Systems don't change, if people don't change. People don't change if they don't feel something**". In other words, change must be targeted toward and happen at the "people" level and requires getting into what I call "the feeling space". The "feeling space" is the birthplace for genuine, sustained change. The concept of systems change through people change is a common thread throughout this text.

To this end, criminal justice is one of the primary systems based foci. A young person's entanglement with the criminal justice system is generally indicative of the culmination of multiple systems prior that have ineffectively served them (education, health care, family, and community). The criminal justice system powerfully epitomizes structural and historical disparities in our society. The criminal justice system represents both the pitfalls of and opportunities for other systems to change. This is why my work has centered on impacting it (the criminal justice system) for change by thoughtfully integrating training and coaching on brain development, cultural responsivity, and trauma-informed practices. If the criminal justice system can change, so can other systems that serve youth. The model and approaches outlined in this textbook have implications for multiple systems that serve youth.

Disproportionately, young males of color between the ages of 15 and 25 have been overrepresented in the criminal judicial system under the guise of rehabilitation, which readily assumes that these young males of color had preexisting skills and tools—a misguided assumption. The more appropriate frame is **habilitation** (also known as skill not will)—as this concept checks underlying assumptions and leaves

A. Moreland-Capuia, *Training for Change*,
https://doi.org/10.1007/978-3-030-19208-2_1

room for strong consideration of other factors that may impede the healing process and increase recidivism rates in young people, especially young men of color.

The Office of Juvenile Justice and Delinquency Prevention (OJJDP) produced a report that concluded a 15-month research project examining the role that minority status (African-American, Hispanic, Asian/Pacific Islander, and Native American) plays in the processing of youth by the juvenile justice system.

According to the OJJDP report by **Pope et al.**, the processing decisions in many State and local juvenile justice systems are not racially neutral: Minority youth are more likely than majority youth to become involved in the system. The effects of race may be felt at various decision points, they may be direct or indirect, and they may accumulate as youth continue through the system (Pope et al. 1995).

- In 2010, 4,828 young people of ages 10–24 were victims of homicide—an average of 13 each day.
- Homicide is the second leading cause of death for young people of ages 15–24 years old.
- Among homicide victims, 10–24 years old in 2010, 86% (4,171) were male and 14% (657) were female.
- Among homicide victims, ages 10–24 years old in 2010, 82.8% were killed with a firearm.
- Each year, youth homicides and assault-related injuries result in an estimated $16 billion in combined medical and work loss costs.
- Among 10–24-year olds, homicide is the leading cause of death for African-Americans; the second leading cause of death for Hispanics; and the third leading cause of death American Indians and Alaska Natives.
- Juveniles (<18 years) accounted for 13.7% of all violent crime arrests and 22.5% of all property crime arrests in 2010.
- In 2010, 784 juveniles (<18 years) were arrested for murder, 2,198 for forcible rape, and 35,001 for aggravated assault.

Young males of color between the age of 18 and 25 are more likely to have an Adverse Childhood Experience (ACE) Score of >4 increasing risk for the adoption of unhealthy behaviors, higher proclivity for aggression, chronic health conditions, cognitive distractions, and early death. A study by Soares and colleagues investigated ACEs in the Brazilian community and highlighted that several socioeconomic, demographic, and family-related characteristics were associated with the occurrence of ACEs, e.g., non-white skin color, low family income, low maternal schooling, and absence of mother's partner, maternal smoking, and poor maternal mental health (Soares et al. 2016).

Young people who become entangled with the law are more likely to have a history of trauma, toxic shame, and substance use—all factors that can negatively impact brain development. In the case of systems of care that impact children, adolescents, and families (criminal justice, health care, education, for example), with a history of trauma and substance use, there was keen recognition that the former way of proceeding toward impacting change has not been effective. The urgent underlying question is, what conditions must be set in order to achieve the type of change that systems desperately seek? One potential answer is—in order to facilitate change in young people who are entangled with the system, ***the system itself must change which meant that individuals who make up the system had to change***.

In this vein, this textbook focuses on active-intentional training, coaching, and supervising for change. The overarching themes of this book span three specific categories:

- Brain development—Rationale: If the system (individuals) that serves youth understands how the brain develops, functions, and potential threats to a normal developmental process, perhaps they (the system) can better understand behavior and actions of justice-involved youth of color and adjust the approach in serving them accordingly. When we know better, the hope is that we can do better.
- Cultural responsivity—Rationale: If the system (individuals) that serves youth understands the role that the powerful social construct of racism, discrimination, unconscious bias, labeling, prejudice played in driving behavior and shaping assumptions, perhaps they would be willing to check their own underlying assumptions, adjust behavior and beliefs, and re-envision their approach, the possibility of facilitating the change they seek in justice-involved youth can increase exponentially.
- Trauma-informed practices and approaches—Rationale: If the system (individuals) that serves youth understands the impact of trauma on brain development and how it can compromise cognition, decision-making, and behavior, perhaps they could secure improved targeted interventions that more effectively support healing and habilitation.

This textbook lays out the science, helps the reader see themselves in and through it, allows the reader to consistently employ practical examples, exercises, and honors repetition as a means of solidifying learning throughout. Each chapter builds on the other as there is a very clear beginning, middle, and end.

Training, teaching, and checking for comprehension are critical. Establishing a framework for practical application in the system is a key to sustained change.

When people intimately attached to systems change, they are more likely to facilitate change in the youth they are serving. In order to facilitate change, you must be the change. This book provides a framework for the process of individual change that impacts system change = effective change in youth.

Each chapter begins with a set of objectives, contains interactive exercises, and offers practical ways to employ the information gleaned from the respective chapter. Each chapter taps into the "feeling space". The sole objective is transformative system change. The final chapter offers a detailed (real-life) case study on a system I helped to change by employing the methods outlined in this textbook—these concepts, methods, practices, and approaches have the potential to transform other systems that serve youth.

According to Maya Angelou: "When you get, give and when you learn, teach". This textbook adheres to this rationale.

Understanding brain development and potential insults to normal, healthy development give a window to understanding behavior.

The brain develops from the bottom-up and the inside-out—see Fig. 1.1.

The lower and midbrain help to mediate the "fear response" and include the following structures:

Brain stem (bottom brain structure) is responsible for important body functions like breathing, heart rate, blood pressure, ability to swallow, wakefulness versus sleepiness, and has a role in consciousness. When someone is in a coma (nonresponsive and unconscious), the brain stem is the part of the brain that is implicated in this process. The brain stem also has a role in the fear response. When we are born, the brain stem is the most developed part of the brain. It is deemed "the primitive brain" because it is what allows for **survival**. If our hearts aren't beating and we aren't breathing, then we aren't living.

Amygdala (middle brain, almond-like structure) is responsible for emotions like anger, drives like sex and hunger, and plays a very important role in detecting fear and seeking safety to protect from a perceived and/or real threat. The amygdala is also part of an emotion/behavior network termed the limbic system granting it a casting role in emotion, memory, and reward/pleasure pathways in the brain as well.

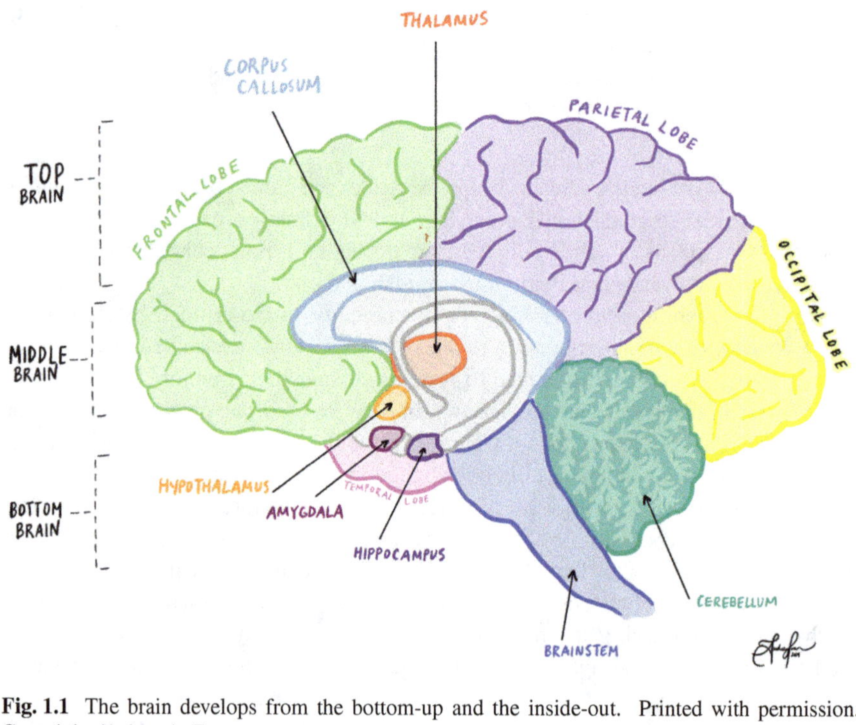

Fig. 1.1 The brain develops from the bottom-up and the inside-out. Printed with permission. Copyright Audrey A. Tran

Thalamus is a near midbrain structure and has a role in motor and sensory signal relay, sleep, and consciousness. Basal ganglia (subcortical structures responsible for intentional movements) are part of the limbic system and basal ganglia are located near the thalamus.

Hypothalamus (middle brain structure that can be found between the pituitary and thalamus) works closely with the pituitary, affectionately referred to as the hypothalamic–pituitary–adrenal axis (HPA axis). It is responsible for the release of hormones, regulates body temperature, mediating the fear/stress response in fight/flight and/or freeze.

Hippocampus (a middle brain, seahorse-like structure) is part of the limbic system and plays a critical role in memory, emotion regulation, and is involved in a process called fear conditioning.

Limbic system—the amygdala, hippocampus, thalamus, hypothalamus, cingulate gyrus, and basal ganglia make up the limbic system. The limbic system is where "emotions" live.

Cortex (frontal and parietal lobes, top brain structure) is the most sophisticated part of the brain, it has four different lobes and each lobe has a sophisticated function. All four lobes are considered to be a part of the "higher brain" and are responsible for sophisticated, complex thinking. Personality expression, empathy, regulate emotion, control impulses, the ability to problem-solve, perceive, understand, exercise good judgment, plan and produce comes from the cortex.

Again, the brain develops from the bottom-up and the inside-out. From sophisticated research techniques developed over the past three decades, we are now able to better understand the brain development process as early as conception. The developmental process is both miraculous and tenuous. There are conditions (i.e., early in utero exposure to trauma, poor nutrition, toxic stress, poverty, racism, adverse childhood experiences, and substance use) that force some to live in the bottom (survival) part of their brain at the expense of living in the top.

Understanding this phenomenon helps you to better manage expectations and know how to create the conditions that support greater access to the top part of the brain.

By the end of this chapter, you should be able to

- Be familiar with current theories and studies on brain development.
- Identify the **six** major stages of brain development in the gestational period (in utero).
- Understand the brain developmental stages from the age of 1–3.
- Understand the brain development from the age of 4 to adulthood.
- Name **three** major aspects of the brain and their function.
- Name **three** key neurotransmitters in brain development.
- Apply aspects of your newfound brain development knowledge into your practice.

When does brain development begin?
Brain development begins at the point of conception (when sperm meets egg) and continues to develop until around the age of 26. This means that the cortex (a top brain structure is the last to develop and be myelinated)—this will be repeated and

Fig. 1.2 Brain development begins at the point of conception (when sperm meets egg) Printed with permission. Copyright Audrey A. Tran.

reiterated multiple times throughout this book as it has profound implications for behavior and practice (Fig. 1.2).

Why is folic acid (Vitamin B9) important in development?

Folic acid is important because it plays a critical role in the folding of the neural tube, which is the blueprint for the brain and spinal cord (Fig. 1.3).

From the point of conception to up to about 4 weeks of gestation (in utero) (Schoenwolf et al. 2015), the makings of the brain begin. The first step in brain development is the process called neurulation.

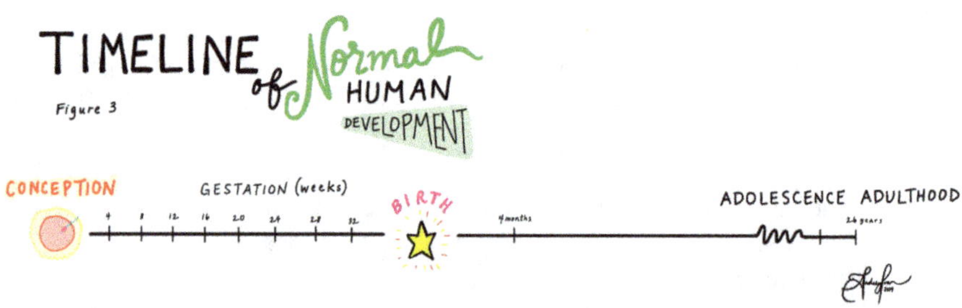

Fig. 1.3 Timeline of normal human brain development from the point of conception to about the age of 26. Printed with permission. Copyright Audrey A. Tran

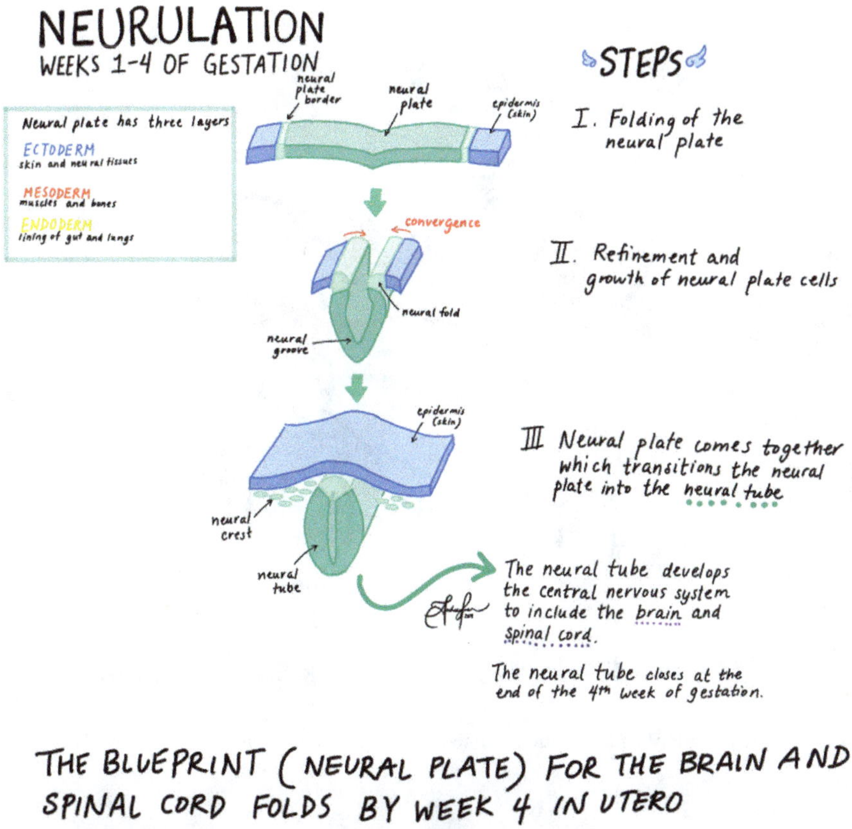

Fig. 1.4 Neurulation. Printed with permission. Copyright Audrey A. Tran

Neurulation phase of brain development (Fig. 1.4)

Approximately 2 weeks after conception, the developing embryo arranges into a three-layered structure (see Fig. 1.4). One part of this structure becomes the neural plate. Through the process of sophisticated neural signaling, the neural plate folds into what is called the "neural tube." The neural tube closes at the bottom first and then the top. The neural tube has inner cells and outer cells. The neural tube's inner cells are the blueprint for and will become the brain and the spinal cord also known as the central nervous system. The neural tube's outer cells are the blueprint for the nervous system outside of the brain and the spinal cord, termed the autonomic nervous system.

Neuronal proliferation to include segmentation, regionalization, new neuronal cell growth (neurogenesis), and early-stage migration phase of brain development (Fig. 1.5)

Once the blueprint for the brain is complete (represented by the folding of the neural plate to become the neural tube), the sophisticated process of cells growing, migrat-

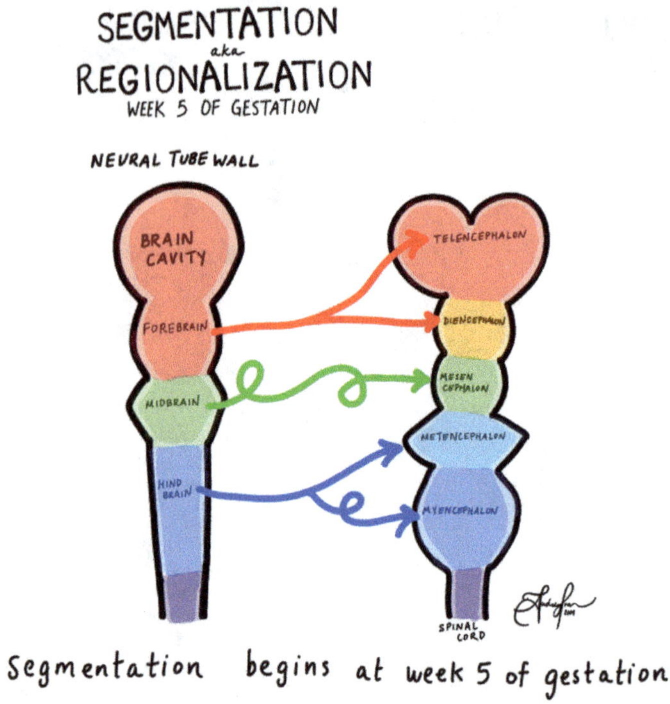

Fig. 1.5 Segmentation/regionalization. Printed with permission. Copyright Audrey A. Tran

ing, segmenting, and regionalizing begins. Again, the brain develops from the bottom-up and the inside-out. The brain stem (a bottom brain structure) is distinct from the amygdala (a middle brain structure) which is distinct from the orbitofrontal cortex (a top brain structure)—segmentation, regionalization, new neuronal cell growth (neurogenesis), and early-stage neuronal migration are the processes by which the bottom, middle, and top parts of the brain form and eventually develop with specificity in function and process.

At *7 weeks* of gestation, the following happens:

- Neurons and synapses begin to form in the spinal cord.
- Early neural connections allow the fetus to make its **first movements**, which can be detected by ultrasound and MRI (in most cases).
- **These movements**, in turn, provide the brain with sensory input that spurs on its development.
- More coordinated movements develop over the next several weeks (Kerjak et al. 2005) (Figs. 1.6 and 1.7).

Migration phase of brain development

As neurons are developing (neurogenesis) during 8–10 weeks of gestation, they are also being directed to where they will eventually live. For instance, the cerebral cortex

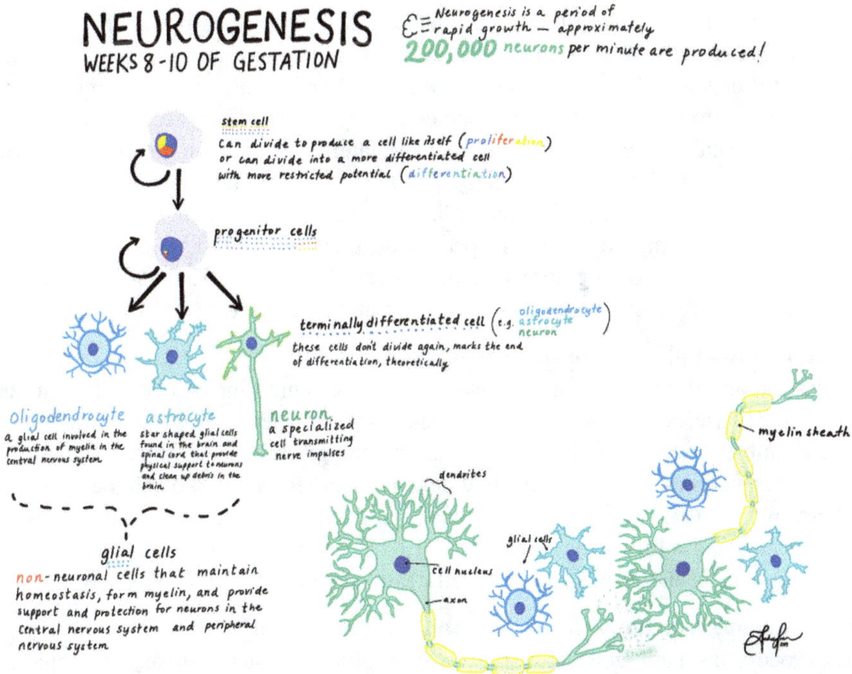

Fig. 1.6 Neurogenesis at 8–10 weeks of gestation. Printed with permission. Copyright Audrey A. Tran

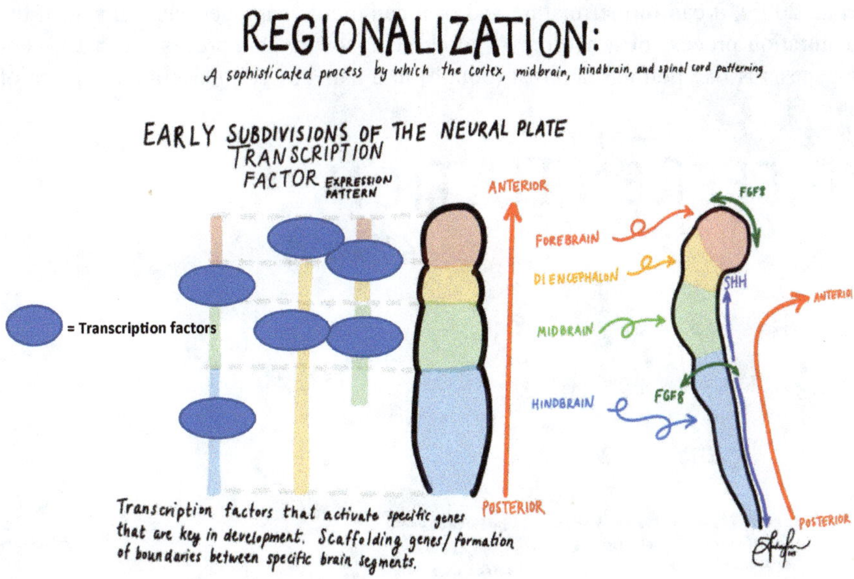

Fig. 1.7 Regionalization/segmental identity. Printed with permission. Copyright Audrey A. Tran

is very thick and is composed of many layers. The cortex (top brain structure and the last theoretically form in the brain development process) migration pattern is as follows: it develops from inside-out movement of cells. This inside-out movement creates zones to include the inside zone called the ventricular zone, then the quasi-middle zone called the intermediate zone and fatefully end up on the outside of the developing brain. There are ultimately six layers to the cortex, they are all formed through the inside-out migration patter described above. Each cell, in every layer of the cortex, has to migrate to their respective destinations for functionality sake.

Inside-out pattern of migration = radial migration represents 70–80% of migrating neurons most of which are pyramidal neurons and glia (see Fig. 1.6).

Differentiation phase of brain development

Migration and differentiation are happening at the same time. As described in the migration phase, neurons are generated and directed to where they will eventually live (for example, there are hippocampal neurons, amygdala neurons, cortical neurons, etc.); once neurons arrive at their final destination, there are two paths they can go. These two paths include further neuronal maturation (as defined by axon growth, guidance, synapse formation) seen in Fig. 1.8 or they die off (as defined by a process called apoptosis and/or programmed cell death) seen in Fig. 1.9 (Fig. 1.10).

Synaptogenesis (synapse formation and rearrangement)

The process of synaptogenesis overlaps with myelination and apoptosis, which makes sense. Synapse formation is a part of the maturation process of the developing neuron (in the developing brain), as indicated in the differentiation stage of neuronal development—there are two pathways for a neuron that finds its resting place (Strominger et al. 2005), it can further mature and/or it can die. Synaptogenesis is a part of the maturation process of a neuron. A good metaphor for this process is that synaptogenesis is like putting pie crust (dough) in a pan—as you place a large piece of

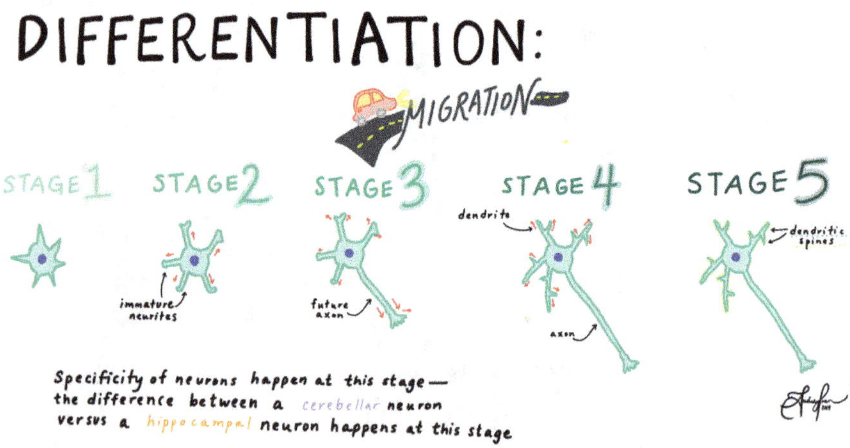

Fig. 1.8 Differentiation. Printed with permission. Copyright Audrey A. Tran

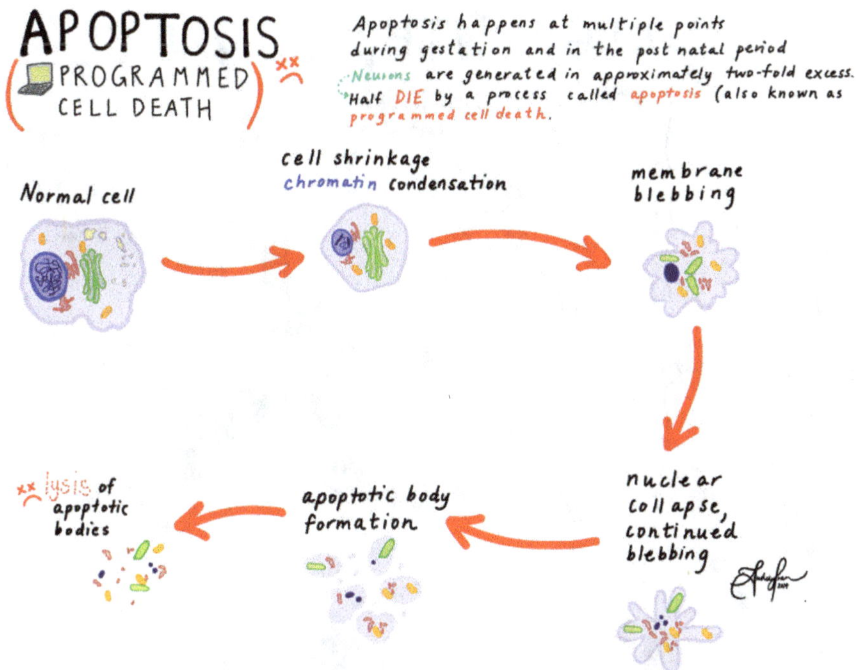

Fig. 1.9 Apoptosis. Printed with permission. Copyright Audrey A. Tran

rolled dough into a pan, you realize that parts of the dough are hanging over the side, so cuts have to be made in order to perfect the pie crust and its edges. If you can imagine the perfecting of a pie crust, then it would not be too difficult to understand that synapses form, sometimes to many and a process called pruning (like cutting the overhanging pieces of pie crust) happens to perfect the neuron. There is also the process of rearranging of synapses as well (Fig. 1.11). Synapses (connections) either thrive or die with environmental and genetic cues. In the end, it is all about fit, which subsequently determines functionality.

Synaptogenesis has its peak activity at 18 weeks of gestation and continues to maintain higher levels of activity into childhood. Although the activity tapers off with age, activity-dependent synaptic plasticity (changes in neuronal volume and connectivity) continues throughout life (Tau and Peterson 2010).

Myelination phase of brain development

Myelination begins in the second trimester (13–27 weeks in utero) and continues into adulthood. Myelin begins to appear on the axons of some neurons during the second trimester (Kagan and Herschkowitz 2005; Lenroot et al. 2007). During myelination, the axons (the communication aspect of the neuron) are insulated in fatty cells, insulation helps the axons to move electrical signals more efficiently and faster. Myelination is ordered like the brain development process—the brain develops from the bottom-up and the inside-out, so goes myelination. Sensory and motor aspects

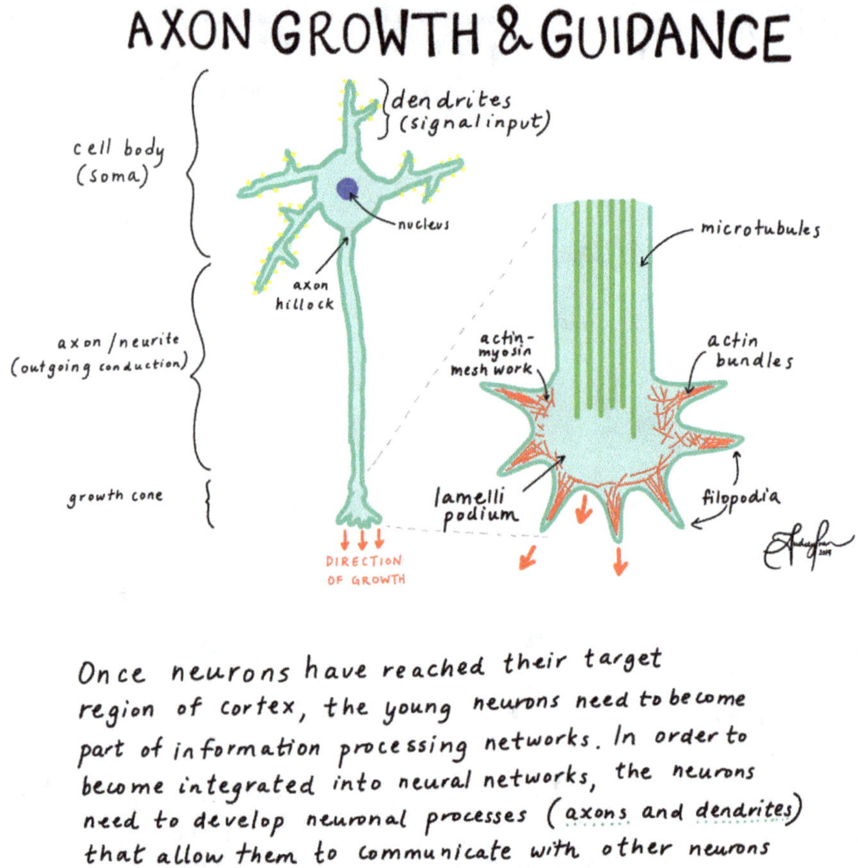

Fig. 1.10 Axon growth and guidance. Printed with permission. Copyright Audrey A. Tran

of the brain are myelinated (insulated by fatty cells) first and the cerebral cortex (top brain) is covered during adolescence into early adulthood (Fig. 1.12).

Third trimester brain development

The early weeks of the third trimester **(weeks 27–40 of gestation)** are a transitional period during which the cerebral cortex begins to assume many duties formerly carried out by the more primitive brain stem.

For example, reflexes such as fetal breathing and responses to external stimuli become more regular. The cerebral cortex also supports early learning which develops around this time (Dirix et al. 2009).

Between conception and the age of 3, a child's brain sustains colossal change. At birth, the brain contains about all of the neurons it will ever have (Gilmore et al. 2007; Nowakowski 2006). Synapses are formed at a faster rate during these years than at any other time. In fact, the brain creates many more of them than it needs: at age 2

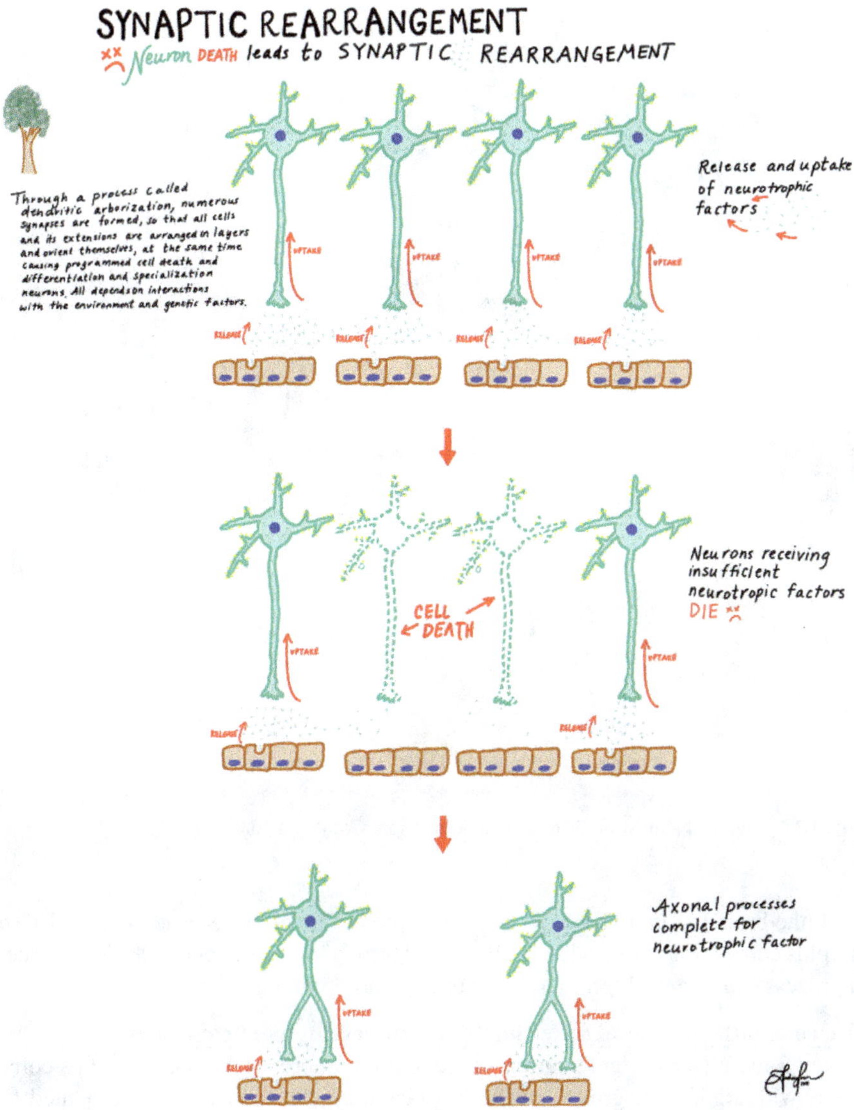

Fig. 1.11 Synaptic rearrangement/synaptogenesis. Printed with permission. Copyright Audrey A. Tran

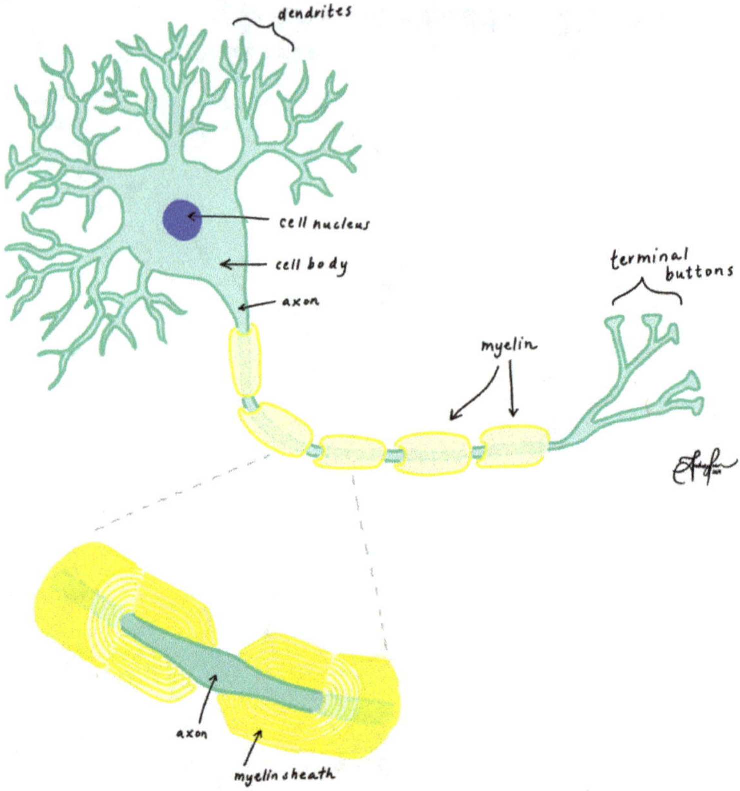

Fig. 1.12 Myelinated neuron. Printed with permission. Copyright Audrey A. Tran

or 3, the brain has up to twice as many synapses as it will have in adulthood. These surplus connections are gradually eliminated throughout childhood and adolescence, a process sometimes referred to as blooming and pruning (Corel 1975).

Three months postnatal (after birth), brain development continues

About 3 months, an infant's power of recognition improves dramatically; this coincides with significant growth in the hippocampus, the limbic structure related to recognition memory.

Language circuits in the frontal and temporal lobes become consolidated in the first year, influenced strongly by the language an infant hears. The first year of life is key in terms of language solidification—the brain becomes hardwired for one language over another.

The brain doubles in size in the first year of life (Gilmore et al. 2007).

By the age of 3, the brain has reached >80% of its adult volume (Nowakowski 2006).

The first year of life—Adulthood, brain development

In year one of life: the cerebellum triples in size, which appears to be related to the rapid development of motor skills that occurs during this period.

The visual areas of the cortex grow in the first year and the infant's initially dim and limited sight develops into full binocular vision (Knickmeyer et al. 2008; Coch et al. 2007).

During the second year of life, there is a major increase in the rate of myelination, which helps the brain to perform more complex tasks. Higher order cognitive abilities like self-awareness are developing (Kagan and Herschkowitz 2005).

During the third year of life, synaptic density in the prefrontal cortex probably reaches its peak during the third year, up to 200% of its adult level. This region also continues to create and strengthen networks with other areas. Complex cognitive abilities are being improved and consolidated (Tierney and Neslon 2009).

During the fifth year of life, the brain begins to prune away synapses. The decline continues before the onset of puberty.

During the 6th–12th year of life, the brain is primed for learning. Learning is easy at this stage. There are notable increases in the temporal and parietal lobes = increased language and understanding of spatial relationships.

During adolescence (the 12th–14th year of life), myelination occurs in the prefrontal cortex. Full myelination is not reached until age 26 and maybe later, but it starts at this point. The emotional (responsive, impulsive) mind develops before wise (measured, think before you act) mind.

Central nervous system gray and white matter

The central nervous system (the brain and spinal cord) has both gray and white matter (Fig. 1.13).

Gray matter contains most of the brain's neuronal cell bodies. The gray matter includes regions of the brain involved in the following:

- Muscle control,
- Sensory perception such as seeing and hearing memory,
- Emotions,
- Speech,
- Decision-making, and
- Self-control.

White matter is composed of bundles of myelinated nerve cell projections (or axons), which connect various gray matter areas (the locations of nerve cell bodies) of the brain to each other and carry nerve impulses between neurons. Myelin acts as an insulator, increasing the speed of transmission of all nerve signals (Fig. 1.14).

Figure 1.14 summarizes Chap. 2 of John Nolte's "The Human Brain"; Magnetic Resonance Image (MRI) of a 5-month old is compared (represented by image labeled A) to an MRI of a 2-year old (represented by image labeled B). They were looking for notable differences in myelination between the two. In the image, adapted from

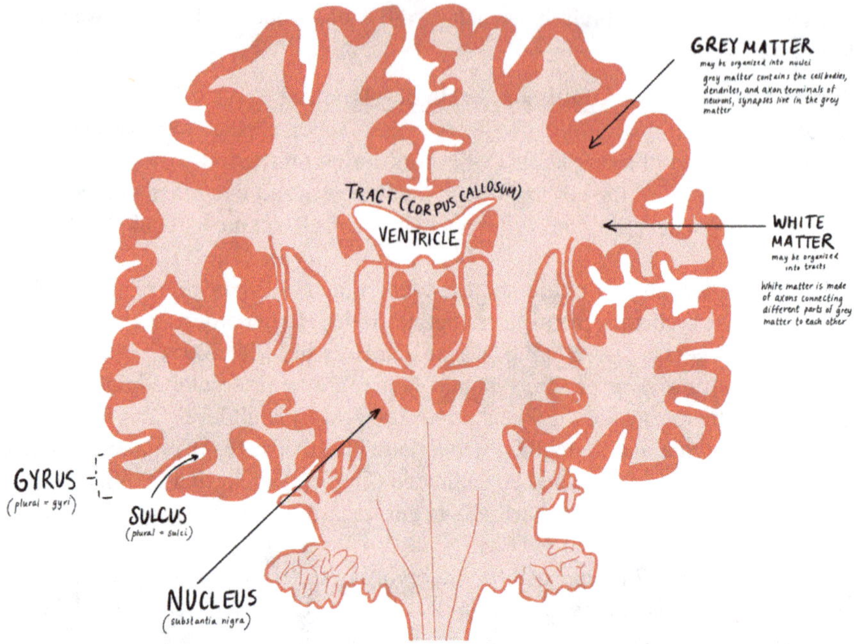

Fig. 1.13 Central nervous system gray and white matter. Printed with permission. Copyright Audrey A. Tran

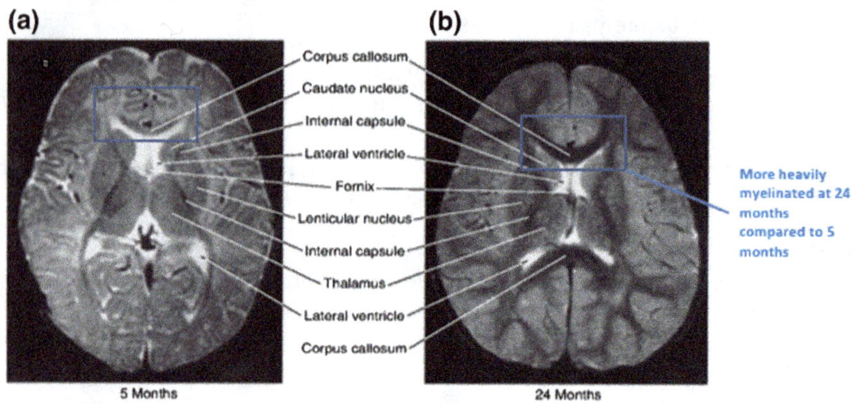

Fig. 1.14 Nolte (2008). The Human Brain: An Introduction to Its Functional Anatomy, Fifth Edition. Elsevier, Mosby, pp 1–60

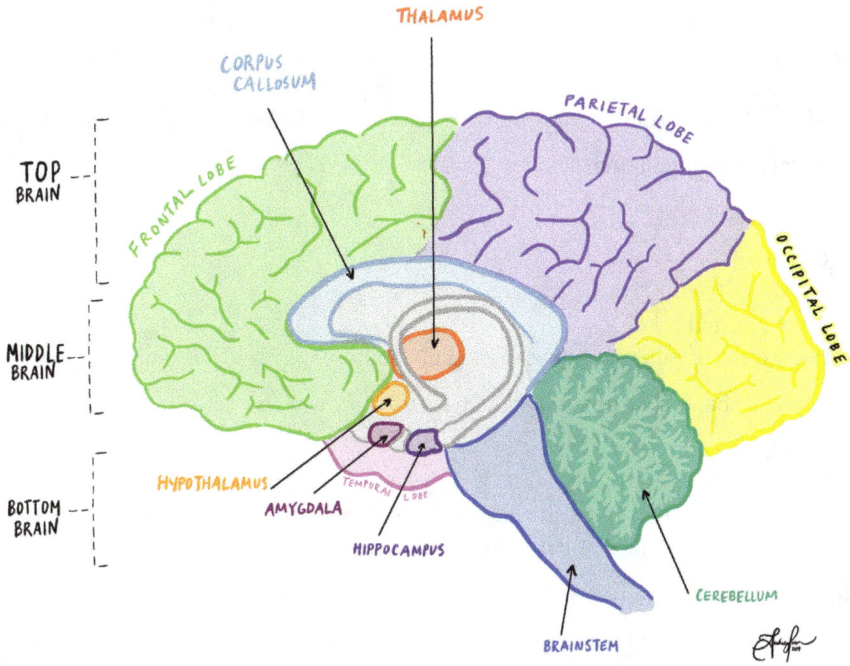

Fig. 1.15 The cortex. Printed with permission. Copyright Audrey A. Tran

Nolte, the dark areas represent myelination. Note the corpus callosum in the 5-month old versus the corpus callosum in the 2-year old. This illustrates the augmentation of the myelination process over time, in a tangible way, in real brains (versus theoretical and/or rat brains).

The cortex (Fig. 1.15)

The cortex, top portion of the brain, the last aspect to be myelinated and develop, is the gray matter of the brain and accounts for 75% of the brains weight (Noback et al. 1996).

The back of the cortex (near the cerebellum) makes up what is called the occipital lobes, responsible for primary processing for visual stimuli.

Temporal lobes are a part of the cerebral cortex and regulate primary processes for auditory stimuli.

Parietal lobes are a part of the cerebral cortex. The anterior parietal lobe = somatosensory.

The posterior parietal lobe = spatial awareness.

Frontal lobes are a part of the cerebral cortex = executive functioning, motor cortex, sensorimotor process, and cognition.

Critical aspects of the brain that we will come back to again and again throughout this book include the following structures:

Hypothalamus, a section of the brain responsible for the production of many of the body's essential hormones, chemical substances that help control different cells and organs.

The hormones from the hypothalamus govern physiologic functions to include

- Temperature regulation,
- Thirst,
- Hunger,
- Sleep,
- Mood,
- Sex drive, and
- The release of other hormones within the body.

Amygdala, shaped like an almond, plays a primary role in

- Decision-making,
- Memory,
- Emotional reactions (fear, anxiety, sadness, rage),
- Is considered as a part of the limbic system.

Hippocampus, shaped like a seahorse, plays a key role in

- Consolidation of short-term memory to long-term memory,
- Spatial navigation,
- Also, a part of the limbic system,
- Has a role in autonomic nervous system, and
- Has a role in emotion.

Caudate nucleus, part of the basal ganglia = primary motor cortex. Figure 1.16

- Caudate nucleus has been implicated in voluntary movement,
- Learning,
- Memory,
- Sleep,
- Social behavior, and
- Caudate has a prominent level of dopaminergic neurons.

Putamen, part of the basal ganglia = primary motor cortex

- The main function of the putamen is to regulate movements and to influence distinct types of learning to include implicit (passive) learning.

Important neurotransmitters of the brain

Lastly, there is an entire neurochemical network that works in tandem with the cortex and other brain structures to control and maintain consciousness. These same neurochemicals facilitate communication between neurons.

- Acetylcholine, a neurotransmitter that works in the central and peripheral nervous system. It operates at the neuromuscular junction. Muscles are activated when motor neurons release acetylcholine.

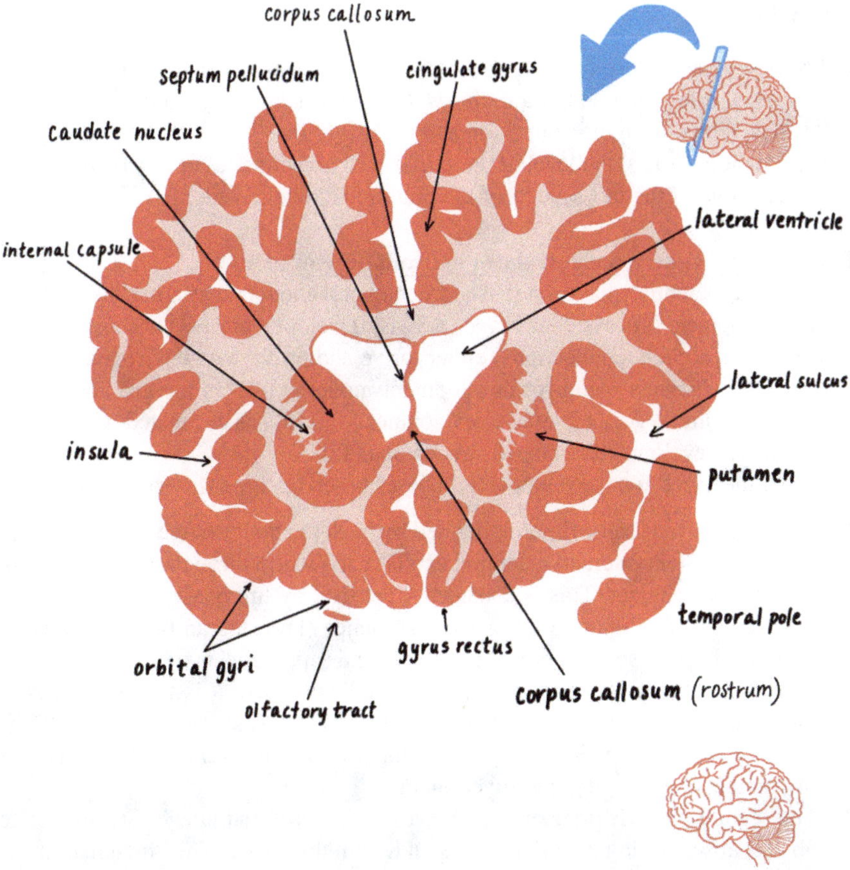

Fig. 1.16 Adapted from Nolte's "The Human Brain" Nolte (2008). The Human Brain: An Introduction to Its Functional Anatomy, Fifth Edition. Elsevier, Mosby, pp 1–60. Printed with permission. Copyright Audrey A. Tran

- Norepinephrine, a neurotransmitter and hormone that plays a key role in the stress, fear, andanxiety response. It impacts the entire body.
- Serotonin, a neurotransmitter theorized to have a role in memory, sex drive, appetite, modulation of mood and social behavior, and some implications in sleep. Correlated with depression and also involved in the reward pathway.
- Dopamine, a neurotransmitter that is involved in the experience of pleasure, reward, and motivation. Implicated in psychosis, disorganized thinking.
- Glutamate, an excitatory neurotransmitter that plays a role in memory and learning.
- GABA, an inhibitory neurotransmitter theorized to play a role in anxiety, vision, and motor control.
- Orexin, a neurotransmitter involved in sleep and appetite.

Key points

- The first year of development of the brain is due to additional glial cells which play a key role in the fetal brain, this is deemed a "sensitive period".
- Brain develops from the bottom-up and the inside-out.
- Myelination starts at the level of the spinal cord and migrates upward—prefrontal cortex is one of the last aspects of the brain to be myelinated.

Behavior and functional correlates to brain development

Many social scientists have established behavioral models that correlate with the brain development process. Jean Piaget, a Swiss developmental psychologist demonstrated that synapses (connections) either thrive and/or die with environmental and genetic cues. Piaget's cognitive development model considers a regressive phase, which represents selective synapse development and loss as correlated with behavior/cognitive developmental phases (Imada et al. 2006).

Piaget theorized four developmental phases based on age (Marwala et al. 2017).

1. The first phase is sensorimotor, defined by birth to about the age of 2 (2). In this phase, the infant interacts with and explores the world through the direct motor and sensory contact. This is considered the trial by fire phase. Two prominent highlights of this phase are object permanence (knowing an object still exists even if you can't see it and/or it is hidden) and separation anxiety.
   Imagine children who live in grim surroundings where it is too dangerous to touch and explore. What might you make of their developmental process? The interaction of children in their environment impacts the developing brain in terms of volume, connectivity, and functionality.
2. The second phase is preoperational, ages 2–6, words and images are applied to objects absent of logic and/or understanding in this phase. The "imagination" is developing at this stage and most children are self-centered or "egocentric".
3. The third phase is concrete operational, ages 7–12, concrete and logical thinking is further solidified and the concept of conservation (the logic that a certain quantity will remain the same in lieu of a change to the container that it is placed in). Sophisticated, higher thinking is developing in this phase. The ability to problem-solving is strengthened in this phase.
4. The fourth phase is formal operational, ages 12–adulthood, and the ability to think abstractly and establish hypotheticals are developed in this phase. This stage represents an iterative process of learning, knowledge that builds on itself through time and experience.

Piaget employed the concept of schemas to explain how individuals build on knowledge as a means of transitioning through the respective cognitive phases (Scott and Cogburn 2018). Three schemas in particular:

- Assimilation is the use of an existing schema that is applied to a new situation and/or object.
- Accommodation is a change in approach when an existing schema isn't helpful and/or effective in a situation.

- Equilibration is the integration of life lessons and experiences to inform/shape the cognitive developmental process.

Connecting important dots, brain development starts from the point of conception (when the sperm hits egg). At 4 weeks, the neural plate folds to become the neural tube, which is the blueprint for the brain and the spinal cord. The brain develops from the bottom-up and inside-out—the most prominent and well-developed aspect of our brain is the bottom brain (known for its role in survival), then the middle brain (clear role in emotion, pleasure, aggressive, drives), and then the top cortical part of the brain (the sophisticated part of the brain responsible for complex, logical thinking, motor function, and behavior). Myelination patterns, which is literally the wrapping of fat cells around the axons of neurons help them to function and communicate more efficiently, follow the same pattern of brain development. The brain develops from less sophisticated into more sophisticated. Piaget's model describes the behavioral correlates to the neurodevelopment of the brain.

Relatively normal brain development has been discussed in this chapter. The word "relative" is used loosely here to suggest the developing brain was not subject to neglect. The process by which the brain develops is both magical and tenuous, subject to myriad potential threats. These threats can compromise development and profoundly impact behavior, ability to learn, regulate emotions, and express empathy, which will be more widely explored in subsequent chapters.

Epigenetics made easy and potential threats to brain development

When the brain is ready to develop in a certain area, but the needed stimulus is not present, then normal development does not happen. Several emerging studies have demonstrated the impact that the external environment, experienced as stress, can have on genes, brain development and behavior—this new area of study is deemed epigenetics. Studies are now confirming what has been known intuitively, the external spaces and places one occupy can impact the internal milieu right down to turning certain genes on and off, right down to deoxyribonucleic acid (DNA).

DNA is found in every living thing and carries the genetic code (a road map) for development and growth.

Histones (proteins) help to fold DNA up and pack into packed units called nucleosomes. Nucleosomes form chromatin. Chromatin consolidates to form chromosomes.

DNA is double stranded and has base pairs adenine to thymine and cytosine to guanine.

Ribonucleic acid (RNA) is single stranded and helps DNA with translating the genetic code into proteins. RNA has base pairs: adenine to uracil and guanine to cytosine.

Not every gene is turned on. Like everything in the body, there is an on and off switch. DNA (and the turning on of genes) is regulated by a process called methylation. DNA methylation refers to the addition of a methyl (CH_3) group to the DNA strand itself, often to the fifth carbon atom of a cytosine ring. This is important to note because of the discussion around the environment impacting genes, protein, hormone expression, etc.. An environmental trigger can turn genes on and off through demethylation and/or methylation of DNA, this is the essence of epigenetics.

Genes operating in specific neurons govern the appearance of specific, biologically crucial behaviors. Neural systems are designed to respond to the environment because the strengths of their synaptic connections are activity dependent. Recall Piaget's cognitive developmental model, namely, sensorimotor which requires a motor and sensory interaction with the environment to compel neuronal development (from birth to age 2) and the fourth stage which is formal operational, an iterative stage of learning and forming new connections on the top of existing ones.

Cortical neurons require a capacity to reprogram by demethylation/methylation throughout adult life. Demethylation occurs during the process of hippocampal learning and memory (Levenson et al. 2006) and during adult neurogenesis (Keverne et al. 2015). Learning and memory require neuronal activity, which can strengthen synaptic connections and weaken other synaptic connection strengths through a process of synaptic plasticity. Once a signal has been sent from one neuron to another, they (neurons) carry out their duties through second messengers like calcium channels. The signaling events triggered by synaptic activity involve Ca^{2+} entry to the neuron via a range of neural receptors (N-methyl-D-aspartate receptor and GABA receptors featuring predominantly), leading to changes in neurotransmitter release and epigenetic changes to DNA methylation, acetylation, and hydroxymethylation. Through these epigenetic changes, neurons gain high plasticity to integrate and store the latest information (Colquitt et al. 2013).

Inhibition of DNA methyltransferases disrupts long-term potentiation in the hippocampus and alters methylation within hippocampal genes engaged with synaptic plasticity and the ability to accommodate new learning is compromised (Levenson et al. 2006).

Inflammation and brain development

In humans, the process is not well understood, but Ginsberg and team reviewed 10 years of studies, namely, of rat models to better understand the role of inflammation on the developing brain. Most of the studies summarized used local models of inflammation over systemic to better mimic the local inflammatory milieu in utero.

While early insult is associated with structural brain abnormalities such as neural tube defects (primary neurulation), later insults may disrupt the migration process of post-mitotic neurons and lead to aberrant cortical development (Burd et al. 2012). Late-gestation insults have been found to associate more with cognitive, behavioral, and psychiatric disorders, such as schizophrenia, autism, and obsessive–compulsive disorders (Burd et al. 2010; Cordeiro et al. 2015; Meyer et al. 2006).

Maternal inflammation (through infection and other stress-related insults) and inflammatory factors can damage neurons and negatively impact myelination. Further, MRI results on babies exposed to maternal inflammation demonstrated significant changes in the brain (gray and white matter) that are strongly associated with learning and memory (Ginsberg et al. 2017).

Inflammation is directly proportional to cortisol, when inflammation is high cortisol levels are typically high as well. This is an important association as current studies are highlighting the deleterious impact of inflammation and cortisol (stress hormone) on the developing brain. Of note, controlled experiments in rodents and to some extent in nonhuman primates demonstrate that exposure to chronic stressors and the resulting corticosterone/cortisol increase from the prenatal period through adulthood are associated with changes in amygdala volume, decrease in hippocampal volume, and decrease in volume of pyramidal dendrites, neurons that are integral to prefrontal cortex function and communication between prefrontal cortex and numerous regions throughout the brain, including limbic structures that modulate the stress response (Huzink et al. 2004; Holmes and Wellman 2009; Liston et al. 2006).

Toxic stress of poverty and brain development

There are several studies that demonstrate the impact of social stressors like poverty on the developing brain. In a study on poverty, stress, and brain development, Blair et al. highlight two prominent reports that demonstrated that poverty's impact on the developmental trajectory in children is profound. One study examined a cross-sectional sample of 389 children aged 4–22 years and found that children in families in poverty had reduced gray matter volumes in the frontal and temporal cortex and the hippocampus, note these are areas of the brain that mediate learning and higher level thinking. When families were at 150% of poverty, these reductions were 3–4% below developmental norms. For children in families at 100% of poverty or below, reductions in these regions were 8–9% below developmental norms (Blair and Raver 2016). Given the association of these regions with school readiness and school achievement, this analysis further examined the extent to which these gray matter reductions account for the well-known effect of poverty on academic outcomes. Changes in the gray matter from poverty accounted for up to 20% of the achievement gap based on an analysis of the standardized test. Poor academic outcomes were also attached to parental education and income. In instances where education and income are low, stress is higher and exposure to stress for the developing brain is much higher, which impacts cortical gray matter, compromising learning (Hair et al. 2015).

Blair et al's meta-analysis on poverty and brain highlighted the fact that the impact starts in utero and is seen in infancy. The National Institutes of Health MRI Study of Normal Brain Development had 77 children between the early postnatal period and 4 years of age participating in longitudinal analysis, and those in low-income or poor families were found to have total gray matter volumes that were nearly half a standard deviation smaller than their better-off counterparts. Poverty is experienced as stress and impacts brain development negatively. Cortisol (stress hormone) levels have been shown to be higher in children living in poverty (Blair and Raver 2016).

Past research on child development in the context of poverty has focused on reduced stimulation and limited opportunity for learning relative to children in higher income homes. Emerging research in a variety of disciplines is converging on the idea that in addition to the abridged opportunity for types of stimulation that affect development positively, like rich and varied language environment (Fernald et al. 2013) poverty is also defined by an excess of types of stimulation that negatively affect development. Key mechanisms that link children's exposure to poverty-related adversity and brain development include the presence of chronic stressors such as noise, including background noise such as that associated with ongoing and unmonitored television, household chaos, and conflict among family members that alter the physiologic response to stress, leading to potentially teratogenic effects of stress-related hormones on the developing brain and to a series of negative cognitive, emotional, and behavioral sequelae (Coley et al. 2015; Deater-Deckard et al. 2010).

Rasmussen et al.'s study on maternal inflammation via Interleukin-6 (IL-6) concentration during pregnancy, employed mother–child dyads as part of an ongoing, longitudinal study, conducted at the University of California, Irvine. 147 mothers were recruited during the first trimester of pregnancy. Magnetic resonance imaging was successfully performed shortly after birth in 86 offspring with gestational age 34.6–41.8 weeks. After birth scans were done at 0.7–8.2 weeks and repeated 12 months with 32 participant's of ages 51.3–56.1 weeks. There were no significant differences in demographic variables between the samples of mother–child pairs enrolled in the study. Socio-emotional and cognitive developmental status at 12-mo age was available for all but two children. Measurement of maternal IL-6 concentration during pregnancy was obtained via maternal antecubital venous blood samples, collected in serum tubes in the first, second, and third trimesters. The study highlighted the relationship between inflammation in pregnant mothers and its subsequent impact on the developing brain in utero and long-term sequelae after birth is highlighted. In specific, there is compelling, supporting evidence that the maternal inflammatory state during pregnancy is prospectively associated with offspring frontolimbic white matter microstructural properties and these changes are associated with early cognitive development (Rasmussen et al. 2018).

Some conclusions to draw for this study, early and protracted exposure to inflammation (from obesity, stress, and infection) do impact the developing brain and there are long-term cognitive and behavioral consequences.

In utero substance use and the developing brain

There are several animal models that demonstrate the negative impact of cocaine and nicotine on the brain, secondary to dangerous increases in serotonin and dopamine. Liu et al. (2013) set out to investigate the impact of cocaine and/or tobacco on the human brain status post prenatal/in utero exposure. Liu and his team secured 40 adolescents between the ages of 13–15. Half of the participants have prenatal cocaine and/or tobacco exposure and the other half did not have prenatal cocaine and/or tobacco exposure. Each participant was matched for head circumference, gestational age, maternal alcohol use, age, sex, race/ethnicity, IQ, family poverty, and socioeconomic status. MRIs were performed, and behavioral data were obtained.

In adolescents with prenatal cocaine exposure, cortical thickness of the right dorsolateral prefrontal cortex was significantly thinner compared to controls.

In adolescents with prenatal tobacco exposure, pallidum volume was smaller compared to controls. Impulsivity was measured as higher in adolescents with prenatal cocaine and tobacco exposure, which was correlated with thalamic volume (Liu et al. 2013).

This is not a surprising finding as multiple epidemiological and animal studies have demonstrated how well drugs of abuse pass from mother to child in utero. We've learned at the very beginning of this chapter how tenuous the brain development process is with the neural plate eventually folding into the neural tube at 4 weeks in utero and how it serves as the blueprint for the brain and spinal cord. Brain development is miraculous and tenuous, there are many potential threats to normal development to include but not limited to in prenatal and in utero exposure to toxic stress, inflammation, poverty, and substance use.

Poor nutrition and vitamin deficiency pose a threat to the developing brain

A review by Dr. Barker illustrates the connection between limited maternal nutrition, its impact on fetal nutrition, and predictability of chronic disease later in life. Barker explained that the fetus's primary response to limited nutrients or oxygen is to slow the rate of cell division—particularly in tissues that are in critical developmental stages at that time. The slowing of cell division is considered a direct effect of undernutrition on the cell or through altered concentrations of growth factor and/or hormones (Barker 1997).

Various animal studies demonstrated that the supply of nutrients and oxygen is the part of the intrauterine environment that compromises fetal growth. Additionally, many animal studies show that poor nutrition/oxygen may both impair growth and development during critical periods of fetal life and permanently affect the structure and physiology of organs and tissues. In the case of human beings, low birth weight and disproportion in head circumference, length, and weight are indicators of limited nutrients at specific stages of gestation (Barker 1997).

In a systematic review on nutrition and development in the Lancet, several vitamin deficiencies were noted to impact brain development. The importance of folic acid and the role it plays in facilitating the folding of the neural plate to become the neural tube (the blueprint for brain and spinal cord) has been discussed. This systematic review summarizes current studies on the role of Vitamin D in brain development. In the case of the mother and the internal fetal milieu, Vitamin D helps to certain that the developing fetus gains sufficient access to calcium for bone development. Vitamin D also has a starring role in helping the immune system adjust to maintain a normal pregnancy, reducing the risk of miscarriage and supporting normal brain development. Highlighted is the fact that three trials of Vitamin D in pregnancy demonstrated a correlation with a reduction in low birth weight and the use of Vitamin D (Black et al. 2013).

Early exposure to child abuse during critical and sensitive brain developmental phases

Susan L. Andersen and colleagues investigated the impact of childhood abuse (namely sexual trauma) on brain development. As has been discussed in this chapter, there are heightened sensitive periods of development (periods and stages of development where the risk for the threat to healthy development is heightened). Andersen et al. performed and analyzed MRI scans on adults, who were subject to abuse at critical brain development stages during their childhood. The study revealed decreased hippocampal volume associated with individuals who experienced sexual abuse at ages 3–5 and ages 11–3. Further, they found that the corpus callosum was reduced with childhood sexual abuse at ages 9–10 years, and frontal cortex was attenuated in subjects with childhood sexual abuse at ages 14–16 years. The study concluded that brain regions have distinctive windows of susceptibility to the effects of traumatic stress (Andersen et al. 2008).

Let's remind ourselves of the underlying subtext. Systems that currently serve youth (children and adolescents) must be keenly aware of the brain development process and potential threats to it because it helps to adjust practices, approaches, and policies. If the goal is to strengthen systems that serve youth so that they can be better served—then a deeper understanding of what might have happened to them should be considered and profoundly change a systems' perspective, behavior, and the means by which it (the system) pursues change and/or outcomes. Systems include but are not limited to education, health care, criminal justice, employment, family, and community.

While the focus is on youth, this book has implications for adults and systems that serve adults as well. After all, adults subconsciously reflect the child that hasn't completely healed from what happened to them as children. This topic will be addressed in subsequent chapters.

To solidify the learning in this chapter, there is a brain exercise to complete. Keep in mind that many of the systems that serve youth consciously and subconsciously require them to engage cognitively (in the top part of their brain). A few things to reiterate, in adolescents the top part of the brain is still developing (which can manifest as impulsivity and poor judgment) and there are many prenatal, in utero, and environmental stressors that can negatively impact the development of the top part of the brain. Therefore, it is important to appropriately assess whether or not youth can sufficiently access the top part of their brain or if a skill building, more intentional approach is required before significant cognitive expectations are placed on them. Imagine chaos, distraction, fear, anxiety, and stress—do these conditions make it more likely or less likely to engage the top part of the brain (the cortex)?

Potential threats to developing brain, upstream, midstream, and downstream—quick summary

1. Environmental exposures can impact genes—epigenetics (upstream), disrupting normal brain development.
2. In utero exposures can impact the folding of the neural tube and contribute to structural brain changes (midstream), disrupting normal brain development.
3. After birth, exposure to toxic stress can impact brain connectivity and volume, impacting behavior and emotion regulation (downstream), disrupting normal brain development.

Brain exercise 1.1

BRAIN GAMES: BUDDY UP—You have 2 min to complete the exercise, for both participants to complete #1 and #2

First—Spell your first and last name backward.

Second—Now spell your first and last name backward, while your partner holds a full conversation with you.

- Were you able to execute #1?
- Were you able to execute #2?
- If so, what helped you to accomplish the task?
- If not, what were potential barriers?
- Did you find #2 to be more challenging than #2?
- What part(s) of the brain do you think were being engaged in this task?
- What was the purpose of this exercise?

In 2010, Patricia Wolfe wrote a book entitled "Brain Matters": Translating research into Classroom Practice. In the book, she outlined four important ways that learning takes place.

Matching instruction to how the brain learns best (in relatively normal brain development) (Wolfe 2010):

- The more elaborative information is rehearsed at the time of learning, the stronger the memory becomes.
- The more modalities used to rehearse, the more paths that are established for retrieval.
- The more real-world examples given for a concept, the more likely it is that the concept will be understood and remembered.
- The more information that is linked to previous learning, the stronger the memory will become.

The goal, in engaging youth for change in any system, should include considering what is developmentally appropriate in the context of potential exposure to trauma.

Case example and practical application

Young person who has been in and out of foster care, father was chronically in prison and mother struggles with substance use issues. This young person became entangled with the law and is on probation and supervision.

Standard practice for most community supervision models is centered on cognitive behavioral interventions. The cognitive model typically involves a check-in, review, a cognitive intervention, practice, and homework. The model relies heavily on the ability to pay attention, read, learn, comprehend, and be mindful enough to complete and bring back some form of homework.

A few weeks into supervision, the parole officer notes that the youth has not completed the assigned homework assignments and struggled to remember the things that had been discussed in prior sessions.

Parole officer notes that the client is "noncompliant" and "unmotivated" with the expectations of supervision and reports to the youth that a violation is imminent.

Is this an appropriate response from the parole officer?

What other factors should be considered in working with this youth?

Is the parole officer's expectation developmentally appropriate in the context of this youth's potential exposure to trauma?

What part of the brain is this youth in, top or bottom?

Integrating key concepts

1. **Inquire about any issues at birth.**

   – Are you aware of any issues or complications you had at birth?

2. **Ask about difficulty with remembering things in the past or recalling recent information (you want to know if there are issues with memory or better understand how they best receive information).**

   – Do you struggle, or have you struggled with remembering things in the past?
   – Do you struggle, or have you struggled with remembering or recalling new information?

3. **Ask about the best learning experience in the past and present.**

   – How do you learn best?
   – Do you mind sharing a time when you enjoyed learning something new?

4. **Assess cognitive capacity** by using a valid screening tool (Montreal Cognitive Assessment).
5. **Assist** with a referral for more formal testing if warranted. In the interim, use the information from the screening to readjust expectations. For example, if attentional and delayed recall challenges have been identified, instead of calling on the young person to operate in a strict structural cognitive behavioral frame, this would be the time to go back to their answer on their best learning experience and employ it. This may deviate from traditional learning. Some clients learn best with music and/or drawing. Find other ways to support youth in actively participating in the change process.

3A's

ASK (gain permission) to better understand young people's capacity for learning.

ASSESS learning capacity and if the systems expectations are reasonable and developmentally appropriate.

ASSIST with creating safety and increasing the likelihood that young people can meaningfully participate in the change process.

Discussion and questions

1. When does brain development start?
2. At what stage does the neural tube close? Why is this important? What are the implications of this on brain development?
3. Why is understanding brain development important in serving youth?

4. Why is understanding brain development so vital changing systems that serve youth for the better?

As mentioned in the introduction, understanding normal brain development and potential threats to have myriad implications to include but not limited to

Education—current education is set up to accommodate youth who are cognitively intact, poised, and safe to learn. The education system assumes that youth have and/or can readily develop skills required for knowledge acquisition and/or retrieval. This assumption is and has historically been harmful to youth who have been exposed to toxic stress, poverty, and in utero exposures (mostly experienced as trauma). What would the education system look like if it always considered these potential factors?

Policy—legislators are beginning to seek and understand brain development and the potential threats to it. This is starting to shape and change the way we treat and help justice-involved youth. The system should seek to move away from further traumatizing a group that has been disproportionately traumatized but rather move toward healing and habilitation.

Public health—if every system that served youth from the pediatrician's office, schools, churches, etc. provided consistent education and narrative about healthy brain development, it could powerfully change and shape behavior. If the brain health was given the same amount of respect as physical body health in the total wellness discussion, behavior and practices could be powerfully impacted. Public service announcements like: "give the brain a fighting chance" should be placed in every system that serves youth. The message must be consistent, insistent, and persistent. Brain health must be prioritized, especially in the case of youth.

Many systems that serve youth lean heavily on cognitive ability

Appreciating brain development and functionality helps to better shape our understanding of human behavior, cognitive capacity. If change is what is sought, then the approach is everything. There are specific approaches that can be applied to increase the efficiency and effectiveness of the behavior change process.

References

Andersen, S. L., Tomada, A., Vincow, E. S., Valente, E., Polcari, A., & Teicher, M. H. (2008). Preliminary evidence for sensitive periods in the effect of childhood sexual abuse on regional brain development. *The Journal of Neuropsychiatry and Clinical Neurosciences, 20*(3), 292–301.

Barker, D. (1997). Maternal nutrition, fetal nutrition, and disease in later life. *Nutrition, 13*(9).

Black, et al. (2013, 3–9 August) Maternal and child undernutrition and overweight in low-income and middle-income countries. *The Lancet, 382*(9890), 427–451.

Blair, C., & Raver, C. C. (2016). Poverty, stress, and brain development: new directions for prevention and intervention. *Academic Pediatrics, 16*(3 Suppl), S30–S36. https://doi.org/10.1016/j.acap.2016.01.010.

Burd, I., Bentz, A. I., Chai, J., & et al. (2010). Inflammation-induced preterm birth alters neuronal morphology in the mouse fetal brain. *Journal of Neuroscience Research, 88,* 1872–81. https://doi.org/10.1002/jnr.22368.

Burd, I., Balakrishnan, B., & Kannan, S. (2012). Models of fetal brain injury, intrauterine inflammation, and preterm birth. *American Journal of Reproductive Immunology, 67,* 287–94. https://doi.org/10.1111/j.1600-0897.2012.01110.x.

Coch, D., Fischer, K. W., & Dawson, G. (eds.). (2007). *Human behavior, learning, and the developing brain: Typical development* (pp. 50–73). New York, NY: Guilford Press.

Coley, R. L., Lynch, A. D., & Kull, M. (2015). Early exposure to environmental chaos and children's physical and mental health. *Early Childhood Research Quarterly, 32,* 94–104.

Colquitt, et al. (2013). Alteration of genic 5-hydroxymethylcytosine patterning in olfactory neurons correlates with changes in gene expression and cell identity. *Proceedings of the National Academy of Sciences of the United States of America, 110*(36), 14682–14687.

Cordeiro, C. N., Tsimis, M., & Burd, I. (2015). Infections and brain development. *Obstetrical & Gynecological Survey, 70,* 644–55. https://doi.org/10.1097/OGX.0000000000000236.

Corel, J. L. (1975). *The postnatal development of the human cerebral cortex.* Cambridge, MA: Harvard University Press.

Deater-Deckard, K., Sewell, M. D., Petrill, S. A., et al. (2010). Maternal working memory and reactive negativity in parenting. *Psychological Science, 21,* 75–79.

Dirix, C. E. H., Nijhuis, J. G., Jongsma, H. W., et al. (2009). Aspects of fetal learning and memory. *Child Development, 80*(4), 1251–1258.

Fernald, A., Marchman, V. A., & Weisleder, A. (2013). SES differences in language processing skill and vocabulary are evident at 18 months. *Dev Sci., 16,* 234–248.

Gilmore, J. H., Lin, W., Prasatwa, M. W., et al. (2007). Regional gray matter growth, sexual dimorphism, and cerebral asymmetry in the neonatal brain. *Journal of Neuroscience, 27*(6), 1255–1260.

Ginsberg, Y., Khatib, N., Weiner, Z., & Beloosesky, R. (2017). Maternal inflammation, fetal brain implications and suggested neuroprotection: A summary of 10 years of research in animal models. *Rambam Maimonides Medical Journal, 8*(2), e0028. https://doi.org/10.5041/RMMJ.10305.

Hair, N. L., Hanson, J. L., Wolfe, B. L., et al. (2015). Association of child poverty, brain development, and academic achievement. *JAMA Pediatrics, 169,* 822–829.

Holmes, A., & Wellman, C. L. (2009). Stress-induced prefrontal reorganization and executive dysfunction in rodents. *Neuroscience and Biobehavioral Reviews, 33,* 773–783.

Huizink, A. C., Mulder, E. J., & Buitelaar, J. K. (2004). Prenatal stress and risk for psychopathology: Specific effects or induction of general susceptibility? *Psychological Bulletin, 130,* 115.

Imada, T., Zhang, Y., Cheour, M., et al. (2006). Infant speech perception activates Broca's area: A developmental magnetoencephalography study. *NeuroReport, 17*(10), 957–962.

Kagan, J., & Herschkowitz, N. (2005). *A young mind in a growing brain.* Mahwah, NJ: Lawrence Erlbaum Associates Inc. In: Kahn, C. A., Kelly, P. C., &Walker, W. O. (1995). Lead screening in children with attention deficit hyperactivity disorder and developmental delay. *Clinical Pediatrics, 34*(9), 498–501. Kandel, ER. (2001).

Keverne, et al. (2015, June) Epigenetic changes in the developing brain. *Proceedings of the National Academy of Sciences, 112*(22), 6789–6795. https://doi.org/10.1073/pnas.1501482112.

Knickmeyer, R. C., Gouttard, S., Kang, C., et al. (2008). A structural MRI study of human brain development from birth to 2 years. *Journal of Neuroscience, 28*(47), 12176–12182.

Kurjak, A., Pooh, R. K., Merce, L. T., et al. (2005). Structural and functional early human development assessed by three-dimensional and four-dimensional sonography. *Fertility and Sterility, 84*(5), 1285–1299.

Lenroot, R. K., Gogtay, N., Greenstein, D. K., Wells, E. M., Wallace, G. L., Clasen, L. S., et al. (2007). Sexual dimorphism of brain developmental trajectories during childhood and adolescence. *NeuroImage, 36,* 1065–1073.

Levenson, et al. (2006). Evidence that DNA (cytosine-5) methyltransferase regulates synaptic plasticity in the hippocampus. *Journal of Biological Chemistry, 281*(23), 15763–15773.

Liston, C., Miller, M. M., Goldwater, D. S., et al. (2006). Stress-induced alterations in prefrontal cortical dendritic morphology predict selective impairments in perceptual attentional set-shifting. *Journal of Neuroscience, 26,* 7870–7874.

Liu, J., et al. (2013). Regional Brain Morphometry and Impulsivity in Adolescents Following Prenatal Exposure to Cocaine and Tobacco. *JAMA Pediatrics, 167*(4), 348–354.

Marwaha, S., Goswami, M., & Vashist, B. (2017). Prevalence of principles of Piaget's theory among 4–7-year-old children and their correlation with IQ. *Journal of clinical and diagnostic research: JCDR, 11*(8), ZC111–ZC115.

Meyer, U., Feldon, J., Schedlowski, M., & Yee, B. K. (2006). Immunological stress at the maternal—foetal interface: A link between neurodevelopment and adult psychopathology. *Brain, Behavior, and Immunity, 20,* 378–88. https://doi.org/10.1016/j.bbi.2005.11.003.

Noback, C. R., Strominger, N. L., & Demarest, R. J. (1996). *The human nervous system: Structure and function*. Baltimore: Williams & Wilkins.

Nolte, John. (2008). *The human brain: An introduction to its functional anatomy* (5th ed., pp. 1–60). Mosby: Elsevier.

Nowakowski, R. S. (2006). Stable neuron numbers from cradle to grave. *Proceedings of the National Academy of Sciences of the United States of America, 103*(33), 12219–12220.

Pope, C. E., & Feyerherm, W. (1995, July). *Minorities and the Juvenile justice system*. US Department of Justice Office of Justice Programs. A Publication of the Office of Juvenile Justice and Delinquency Prevention.

Rasmussen, et al. (2018, April 11). Maternal Interleukin-6 concentration during pregnancy is associated with variation in frontolimbic white matter and cognitive development in early life. Neuroimage. pii: S1053-8119(18)30316-1. https://doi.org/10.1016/j.neuroimage.2018.04.020.

Schoenwolf, G. C., Bleyl, S. B., Brauer, P. R., & Francis-West, P. H. (2015). *Larson's human embryology* (5th ed., pp. 1–519). Copyright @2105 by Churchill Livingstone, an imprint of Elsevier Inc.

Scott, H. K., & Cogburn, M. (2018, January). *Piaget* [Updated 2017 Oct 9]. In: StatPearls [Internet]. Treasure Island (FL): StatPearls Publishing.

Soares, A. L., Howe, L. D., Matijasevich, A., Wehrmeister, F. C., Menezes, A. M., & Gonçalves, H. (2016). Adverse childhood experiences: Prevalence and related factors in adolescents of a Brazilian birth cohort. *Child Abuse and Neglect, 51,* 21–30.

Strominger, N. L., Demarest, R., & Laemle, L. B. (2005). *Noback's human nervous system: Structure and function* (7th ed., pp. 39–141). Humana Press.

Tau, G. Z., & Peterson, B. S. (2010). Normal development of brain circuits. *Neuropsychopharmacology, 35,* 147–168.

Tierney, A. L., & Nelson, C. A. (2009). Brain development and the role of experience in the early years. *Zero to Three, 30*(2), 9–13.

Wolfe, P. (2010). *Brain matters: Translating research into classroom practice* (2nd ed., pp. 1–221). ACSD.

Chapter 2
Cultural Responsivity

All human beings exist within a culture.
Culture must be inquired about, understood, and appreciated when working with youth.

"Culture makes people understand each other better. And if they understand each other better in their soul, it is easier to overcome the economic and political barriers. But first they have to understand that their neighbor is, in the end, just like them, with the same problems, the same questions"—Paulo Coelho.

By the end of this chapter, you should be able to

- Identify all three tiers of Schein's Organizational Culture Model.
- Understand the basic neurobiology of fear and its intersection with trauma.
- Better recognize the relationship between trauma-informed practices and improved cultural responsivity.
- Appreciate the impact of underlying assumptions.
- Understand the concept of "stereotype threat."
- Demonstrate greater empathy for the clients you serve by being keenly aware/intentionally conscious of your underlying assumptions and the impact it may have on client care/interaction/engagement.

If change is desired in youth, then the systems that serve youth must change. Change is a parallel process. The former way of doing things has not rendered the rate and/or type of change hoped for. Considering culture (and what it means) is critical in constructing conditions for real sustained change. Culture must be placed in context. The subtext of the introductory quote by Paulo Coehlo challenges the reader to see culture as a gathering place that draws out the best of our humanity, calls us to our higher selves.

What is culture?

In 2014, Joshua Rothman published a piece in the New Yorker entitled "The Meaning of Culture." Rothman contends that the definitions for culture are myriad. He writes

"The problem is that "culture" is more than the sum of its definitions. If anything, its value as a word depends on the tension between them (the sum of its definitions).

A. Moreland-Capuia, *Training for Change*,
https://doi.org/10.1007/978-3-030-19208-2_2

The critic Raymond Williams, in his souped-up dictionary, "Keywords," writes that "culture" has three divergent meanings: there's culture as a process of individual enrichment, as when we say that someone is "cultured"; culture as a group's "particular way of life,"...company culture, or multiculturalism; and culture as an activity, pursued by means of the museums, concerts, books, and movies... These three senses of culture are actually quite different, and, Williams writes, they compete with one another. Each time we use the word "culture," we incline toward one or another of its aspects: toward the "culture" that's imbibed through osmosis or the "culture" that's learned at museums, toward the "culture" that makes you a better person or the "culture" that just inducts you into a group" (Rothman 2014).

Rothman further explains the meaning of culture from a historical sense as well, which he contends is controversial as culture was opposed to civilization. "Civilization, the thinking went, was a homogenizing system of efficient, rational rules, designed to encourage discipline and progress." Culture was the opposite: an unpredictable expression of human potential for its own sake. No comparable "culture" term has been invoked in relation to the deaths of Michael Brown, Eric Garner, and the other African-Americans killed, recently, in encounters with the police. But those events have also pushed us to think about "culture" as an "inhumane, malevolent force."

What can be concluded is that culture must be placed in context (and is attached to a set of experiences, underlying assumptions, and core beliefs). Rothman captures the unattractive, complex, very real elements of culture–"an inhumane, malevolent force" that is derived from "osmosis (what is in the environment and around us)."

Culture is intimately attached to core beliefs, underlying assumptions, and bias.

Cultural responsivity is used heavily in the academic literature as a euphemism and antidote for racism, discrimination, prejudice, and preconceived notions.

What culture are we talking about? We are talking the culture of an individual and the culture of a system.

How is cultural responsivity possible if culture isn't clearly defined?

Cultural responsivity should flow from respect and is defined as the ability to learn from and relate humbly to people from your own and other cultures. Culture shapes the lens from which the world is viewed, perceived, experienced, and engaged. Culture has an influence on underlying assumptions, behavior, and actions. Change is accelerated when the drivers of culture are clearly highlighted and worked on and when humanity is at the center of what we do.

The culture of systems (which are intimately attached to the culture of people) must be thoughtfully confronted and challenged to get to change. Culture shift happens when core beliefs, bias, and underlying assumptions are addressed.

Dr. Maya Angelou said it best: "I am human; therefore nothing human can be alien to me."

Exercise 2A—Imagine

It is circa 1970, Midwest. Imagine a grainy, old black and white photo. Centered in this photo is a young (7- or 8-year-old boy) with a half-smile revealing a gap in the top row of his teeth. His eyes are partially closed and tired. He is wearing a light colored suit. In the backdrop is an old 1920s house.

Take 5 min to discuss the following:

- What are your (immediate) initial thoughts when you consider the description of the individual given?
- Consider why you are being asked to make judgments based on so little information and a limited description?

The purpose of this exercise was to test your automatic thoughts and assumptions—we all have them.

In this case:

- Were your assumptions positive or negative?
- How do you think your assumptions impact your behavior (how you act)?

The description given is of a very young Benjamin Carson—an image captured early in his childhood. In brief, Dr. Benjamin Carson grew up in very difficult conditions—his father left, he was raised by his mother who only had a third-grade education.

Young Benjamin was a very angry kid. He was not great at math and was often teased.

His anger got the best of him one day when he lunged at a child on the playground with a sharp object. Lucky for young Benjamin, the sharp object hit the kid's belt buckle and no physical harm was done.

It was at this point that Benjamin realized he was going to be in real trouble, if anger was the predominant emotion he operated from.

Benjamin's mother decided that she was going to have him start reading a few books a week at the library instead of being idle with his time.

Benjamin took an interest in rocks.

Meanwhile, Benjamin continued to be challenged by mathematics.

One of his teachers took note of the fact that Benjamin had a strong interest in rocks.

The astute teacher used his interest in rocks as a foundation to help improve his interest and skills in other subjects.

Long story short, Benjamin quickly went from failing to top of his class.

He graduated high school.

He went to college.

Eventually went to medical school.

He became the chief of pediatric neurosurgery at the age of 33 at Johns Hopkins University.

He became a world-renowned pediatric neurosurgeon after performing a once thought impossible procedure on a set of twins who were connected by tortuous vasculature.

Why the story?

- Benjamin is no different from most youth systems desire to serve.

- One individual (a teacher in his case) saw one good thing in Benjamin and it changed the trajectory of his life.
  Everybody has the capacity to see one good thing in a youth and help to change their trajectory.
- One person seeing one good thing in every youth is well within everyone's reach.
- Can you imagine if the assumptions about young Benjamin would have been applied by every adult in his life?
- Let's recognize and acknowledge the good in our youth and develop it. Remember, just one good thing.

Exercise 2B

In 1993, Toni Morrison was on the infamous Charlie Rose Show (no longer on air). Charlie asked Toni to describe her thoughts on White supremacy. Toni responded with several poignant points:

- Toni poses this question about racism: "Don't you understand that people who practice racism are bereft. There is something distorted about the psyche. It (racism) is like a profound neurosis."
- Racism, when practiced, negatively impacts White individuals as it does those who are subject to racism.
- Toni points out that she is only talking to White individuals who "do not examine themselves."
- She highlights that every race to include "White" is a powerful social construct that has a serviceability element to it.
- She goes on to pose a question to dominant culture—"what would you be if we took your race away? Would you be strong? Would still feel smart? Are you any good?"
- Toni concludes by stating: "If you can only be tall if someone is on their knees then you have a serious problem. White individuals have a serious issue and they must figure out what they will do about it. Take me out of it."

Toni makes a few powerful points to include

- There is a difference between the person who examines themselves versus the one who does not.
- She poses an important question when she asks dominant culture to consider that they are a "race" as well. Further, she asks "what would you be if your race were taken away?" Would you be strong, still smart?
- If the only way you can feel tall is when someone is on their knees, then there is a serious problem.

How do you resonate with Toni Morrison's words?

Does reading her words regarding White supremacy and racism changes how you view the world and race as a powerful social construct?

System change = change in culture

Change is what is sought; changing the culture of a system requires a deep dive into the elements that make up culture…

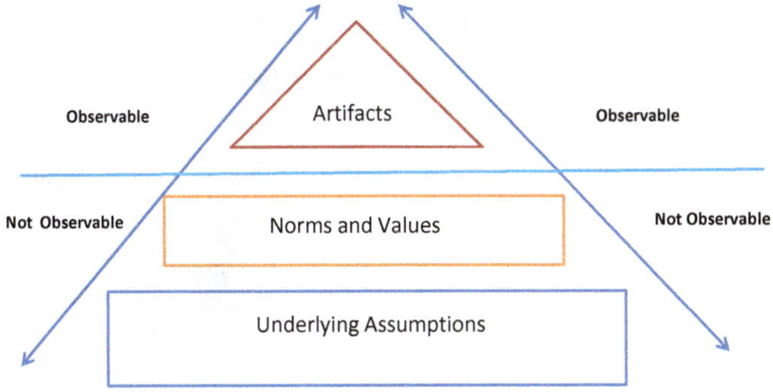

Fig. 2.1 E. Schein's three levels of culture. Organizational culture model

Psychologist Edgar Schein made an indelible mark on the field of organizational/system development and is well known for his work on the organizational culture model, providing a framework for organizational change. According to Schein:

- Cultures surround us all.
- Cultures are deep seated and rooted in complex structures.
- Cultures are pervasive and complex.

System learning, developmental and planned change cannot be understood without considering culture as a primary source of resistance to change. He further contends that if individuals who make up the system do not become conscious of the culture that surrounds and defines them, the culture will predominate, increasing the risk that the culture will overwhelm, dominate, and manage them.

Schein presents three levels of culture change from top to bottom to include visible, norms, and values and underlying assumptions (Fig. 2.1).

First level of culture, artifacts

- Visible,
- Undecipherable physical, behavioral, and verbal manifestations of the culture, and
- Can be observed by anyone.

Represent the most accessible elements of culture to include

- dress and appearance (physical manifestations),
- ceremonies, reward, and punishments (behavioral manifestations), and
- stories and jargon.

Second level of culture, norms, and values

- Typically not observed,
- More conscious than basic assumptions but are not usually at the forefront of member's minds, and
- Norms are closely associated with values (unwritten rules that allow members of a culture to know what is expected of them in a wide variety of situations).

Third level of culture, underlying assumptions

- Underlying assumptions, drive the norms and values, and
- Underlying assumptions shape the artifacts.

One example: If we assume that all purple people are bad, how might this shape behavior, norms, language, etc.?

- According to Schein, organizational members hold values and conform to norms because their underlying assumptions nurture and support the norms.

One of the many conclusions from this model:
Unless organizations/systems of care dig down to the deepest level of basic underlying assumptions, change is less likely to occur.

Schein contends that organizations/systems don't change unless they address

1. What they think they see (artifacts),
2. What they don't see, but think they know (norms and values), and
3. What they don't see, but often feel (underlying assumptions).

The "observable" aspect (artifacts) of Schein's model is similar to explicit bias. Judgment is given and/or value is placed on a person, place, or thing based on what one thinks and/or perceives they see or in this case, observe. Theoretically, there is a conscious element at play in this process and what is conscious has a greater possibility of being managed.

The "not observable" aspects of Schein's model (norms and values, underlying assumptions) are similar to implicit bias. In other words, there is a subconscious application of firmly held beliefs. Norms and values are typically not openly verbally shared, but lived out. In the same way that underlying assumptions, a strong driver and predictor of behavior and actions, cannot be seen, but is often felt in its application.

When we place this model in the context of changing systems that impact youth—what is often observed (shaped by bias and preconceived notions) drives and reinforces underlying assumptions and values and norms. What is observed is attached to bias, preconceived notions, and socialization. A very conscious process (observing with the naked eye) influences the subconscious (norms, values, and underlying assumptions) and heavily impacts behavior and culture. Again, understanding culture and what constitutes culture is critical in moving toward cultural responsivity.

Schein's model indirectly highlights structural elements that make up culture that must be highlighted in order to shift culture and create the conditions for change.

Bias, preconceived notions, prejudice, discrimination, racism, and every other "ism" show up in systems and must be confronted immediately and appropriately. Bias and the "isms' are undergirded by fear.

Greenwald et al. wrote about the implicit association test (IAT), which catapulted research on implicit bias. The IAT's methods were designed to be adapted across a wide variety of groups and group trait associations attached to stereotypes and attitudes. The most commonly used IAT measure assesses implicit attitudes toward African-Americans and European Americans, termed the Race IAT. Respondents were initially asked to classify who was African-American versus European American based on faces. Second, respondents were asked to classify pleasant words from unpleasant words. In a random order, all four categories were given to include African-American, European American, unpleasant, and pleasant. Implicit attitude measure birthed from the Race IAT was based on relative speeds of responding in a set of four category tasks. The outcome of the Race IA, in the case of American respondents—response speed was faster when European Americans were paired with pleasant words (much higher than when African-Americans were paired with pleasant words). Consistently and overwhelmingly European Americans were associated with pleasant words at a significantly higher rate than their African-American counterparts (Greenwald et al. 2009).

As indicated in the introduction to this textbook, the criminal justice system represents the culmination of many prior failed systems in the case of youth. The culture of the criminal justice system is shaped by biases, preconceived notions, and "ism-s"—because of this, the youth of color are disproportionately and negatively crushed by the system (and by most systems that preceded the criminal justice system).

Connecting systems to people

Systems (which are made up of people) internalize attitudes and are socialized to think and react in a certain way. A system is so colossal and often times feels too overwhelming to tackle and/or deconstruct. One way to approach a system is through approaching the people attached to them. In the case of people attached to systems designed to serve youth, a fundamental reevaluation, and analysis and checking of norms, values, and underlying assumptions are keys in jump-starting the change process. While data are presented throughout this text, data have not moved the needle for change—tapping into the "feeling" space has traditionally moved individuals. Real time, take the opioid epidemic, for instance. Back in the 1960s, when communities of color were caught in its grips, it was deemed a public safety issue. People of color were thrown in jail and/or died secondary to addiction. However, in the late 90s and early 2000s, prescription opioid OxyContin came on the scene. Physiological and addictive tendencies developed in Caucasian Americans—when they could no longer access prescription opioids, they turned to heroin. A precipitous increase in opioid-related deaths in dominant culture and the opioid epidemic intentionally shifted from being a public safety matter to public health matter. This shift in framing the issue changed the approach and the kind of resources dedicated to remedying the issue. What happened? Why the shift? Notable politicians and actors/actresses were personally affected by death from an opioid overdose, it hit home, it was personal, and it was felt. As a consequence, change was imminent.

Bottom line: When the "feeling" space is reached, change is more likely to occur.

Exercise 2B

- There are names of individuals.
- You have 60 s to articulate your automatic impressions of the names you read below.
- What are the first thoughts that come to mind when you read the names below?

- Timothy McVeigh,
- James Holmes,
- Dzhokhar Tsarnaev,
- Eric Harris and Dylan Klebold,
- Treyvon Martin,
- Michael Brown,
- Freddie Gray,
- Sandra Bland, and
- Eric Garner.

The power of word and names

The power of names/words: context and subtext: Conscious expression, subconscious application, and race as the powerful social construct

What can underlying assumptions lead to?

Conscious denial, subconscious application

Column 1	Column 2
Timothy McVeigh—Oklahoma	Treyvon Martin—Florida
James Holmes—Colorado	Michael Brown—Missouri
Dzhokhar Tsarnaev—Boston	Freddie Gray—Baltimore
Eric Harris and Dylan Klebold—Colorado	Sandra Bland—Texas
	Eric Garner—New York

- What do the individuals in Column 1 have in common?
- What do the individuals in Column 2 have in common?
- Is there a pattern? (Try not to focus on exceptions)—identify the pattern.
- If you note a pattern, what might you conclude?

Of note regarding Column 1, the majority of these individuals were identified as Caucasian males and/or perceived less of a threat based on complexion; they all were involved in and/or accused of killing people.

Timothy McVeigh (now dead)—was involved in the Oklahoma bombing injuring and killing many, the police managed to capture him alive.

James Holmes—was involved in shooting individuals in a Colorado movie theater. He was captured by police, alive.

Dzhokhar Tsarnaev (not White, but it was referred to as a young kid who made mistakes in media and was deemed less of threat because of how he looked)—was involved in the Boston marathon bombing. He was captured by police alive.

Eric Harris and Dylan Klebold—were involved in one of the deadliest school shootings in American history, Columbine. They, too, were captured by police, alive.

This list is not exhaustive by any means. There is also Dylan Roof (not pictured), involved in shooting nine African-Americans in a church in Charleston, South Carolina. Not only was he safely taken by the police, but he was treated to Burger King before being taken to jail. This list was designed to start the conversation.

Of note regarding Column 2, they consist of African-Americans who were killed by people and/or the police for "being suspicious."

Treyvon Martin—killed in his father's Florida neighborhood by a man who found him suspicious for wearing a hoodie, carrying skittles, ice tea, and being Black. Stand your ground laws in Florida protected the individual who killed Trayvon.

Michael Brown—a Black boy deemed a thug and a threat in Ferguson, Missouri. He was killed by police. This killing sparked the #BlackLivesMatter movement.

Freddie Gray—a Black man in Baltimore, Maryland was accused by the police of having a knife. The altercation was so rough that Freddie's neck was broken, he was near lifeless when was thrown in the back of a police wagon. His lifeless body swayed back and forth with each turn and twist of the vehicle. Eventually, Freddie fell into a coma and died.

Sandra Bland—a Black woman in Texas who challenged what she felt like was an inappropriate police stop. You cannot be Black, no your rights and challenge authority. She ended up dead.

Eric Garner—an unarmed Black man choked to death by police on a New York street.

What were their (Black boys, men, and women in Images 2) crimes? Many would content that being Black in America and subject to bias, preconceived notions, racism, and prejudice. This is a real public health crisis. The criminal justice system, as it exists, is disproportionately harmful to people of color.

This is not an exhaustive list either, but meant to spark a wider conversation.

Some readers may feel challenged by Images 1 and 2 and/or by the analysis. It is critical to note that nothing in history has ever changed among comfort and convenience. Change often comes at the feet of controversy and discomfort. If individuals can honestly, openly, and genuinely engage in this exercise and appreciate the pattern, the capacity for change is widened.

Getting into the "feeling space"

Every single person mentioned in this exercise can be deemed a tragedy for various reasons. However, one of the most unforgettable images of loss and tragedy is a picture of Treyvon Martin's father sitting in front of his son's casket with family surrounding him as he is looking up to the sky, crying with his mouth open consumed with agony. Most human beings could relate to this image of Trayvon's father because of how it made them "feel." The anguish, pain, hurt, loss, and grief are palpable. The emotionality and hurt of two parents who have lost a child is felt. Somehow, human beings are able to look past color, gender, socioeconomic status, and see the raw emotion because at some point down the line it (pain, anguish, and loss) has been and/or will be experienced by many. Individuals may not readily be able to wrap their mind around and/or relate to racism, but can understand deep emotional pain. This is a "point of convergence." Point of convergence is a shared experience among many that possess the power to tap into the best of the human spirit and inspires change. It (point of convergence) will be referred to often in this textbook as it represents change points.

Mostly every parent and mostly every human can understand loss, but might find it difficult to process senseless, needless loss. In the case of Trayvon Martin, his untimely death was motivated by deep bias/racism and was preventable. The logic goes like this, if the emotion can be understood, then all that contributed to the emotion perhaps can be understood (the bias/racism), then the fact that it was a needless death and could have been prevented is more likely to be understood, then the proclivity toward changing it is greater. If it can be understood, it can be changed.

Racism, a powerful social construct, driver of culture

Harrell defines racism as a system of dominance, power, and privilege based on racial group designations…where members of the dominant group create or accept their societal privilege by maintaining structures, ideology, values, and behavior that have the intent or effect of leaving nondominant group members relatively excluded from power, esteem, status, and/or equal access to societal resources (Harrell 2000).

Schein articulates that the culture of systems cannot be changed until the system deals with their underlying assumptions (implicit bias). Further systems are attached to people, systems don't change if people don't change, people don't change if they don't feel something. Getting into the "feeling" space requires moving an individual along a road of better understanding. If it can be understood, it increases the likelihood that it can be changed.

Culture of people and the culture of systems (organizations) too are connected to social and economic systems that structurally strengthen and reinforce racism as a powerful social construct, underlying assumptions, implicit bias—see Fig. 2.2.

Intersectionality, an important lens applied to cultural responsivity

Intersectionality is a framework established by Kimberle Williams Crenshaw (activist and legal scholar) in the 1980s, birthed from Black feminism to explore the intersection of race and gender. The framework has since been extended to include the intersection and interplay of class, sexuality, class, disability, age, and other identities.

In an article written about intersectionality as a feminist praxis, Evans explains the following:

- Intersectionality is understood as a mutually constitutive relationship among social identities.
- Intersectionality is the recognition of multiple and overlapping points of oppression.
- Intersectionality theories have allowed scholars to explore the matrices of oppression impacting power dynamics in individuals and groups.
- Identities can only be understood within the narratives of other identities.
- Intersectionality as a concept is difficult because identity markers like gender, race, and sexuality are open to individual interpretation and construction.
- Intersectionality speaks directly to questions of power: how it is used, and by whom, to marginalize and exclude groups of people through the intersecting domains of racism and sexism (Evans 2016).

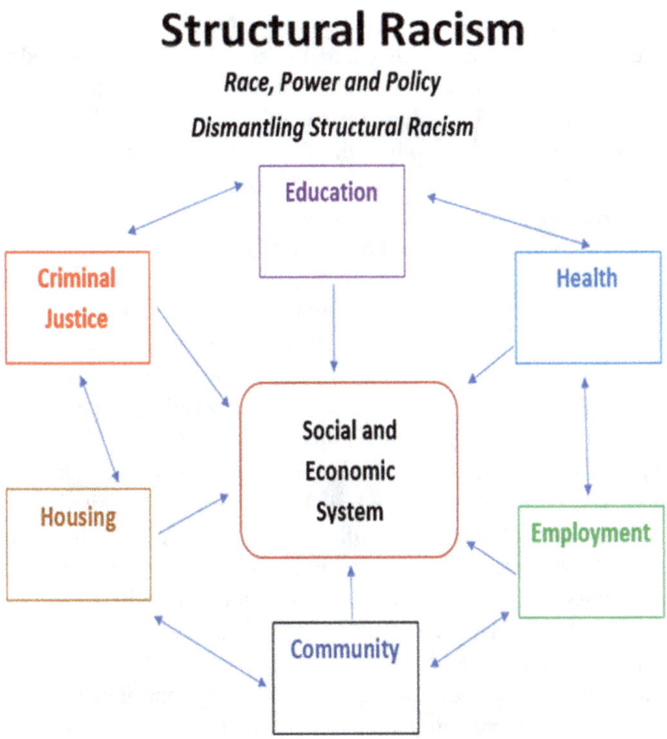

Fig. 2.2 Recreated from Race, Power, and Policy, Dismantling Structural Racism (Hinson et al. 2018)

An article by Rosenthal on intersectionality highlighted the following (Rosenthal 2016):

- Critical aspect of intersectionality is its focus on interlocking systems of oppression and the need for broad structural level change to promote social justice and equity.
- Multiple systems of oppression must ***be both understood and struggled against simultaneously***.
- As a consequence of intersections, people are at the same time members of many different social groups and have unique experiences with privilege and disadvantage.

Intersectionality as a theory cannot be ignored in the discussion and/or practice of culture responsivity. A genuine attempt to understand, appreciate, and respect that intersection of identities in youth is critical in optimally serving them.

Exercise 2C: Discuss the two quotes below. What do they mean to you?

1. "If we aren't intersectional, some of us, the most vulnerable, are going to fall through the cracks."—Crenshaw
2. "There is no such thing as a single-issue struggle because we do not live single-issue lives."—Audre Lorde

The history, power, and impact of racism on systems

The powerful social construct of racism and strategic exclusion formed the culture of America. Some historians would contend that the United States of America was birthed from the American Revolutionary War. A critical founding document that emerged from the country's inception, the Declaration of Independence, makes an impactful proclamation—"All men are created equal." The first question that arises is who is **not** included in this proclamation? Women and people of color certainly aren't. Legal and strategic exclusion stained the making of a nation. That stain profoundly permeated the fabric of this country shortly after the Civil War (which ended in 1865) and, according to many historians, molded the culture of the United States of America. The Civil War wasn't just about preserving the Union, but it was also about ending slavery. Consequently, constitutional amendments 13, 14, and 15 emerged to end slavery, equal protection under the law and voting rights, respectively. The 13th amendment has had the most pervasive impact as it reads:

"Neither slavery nor involuntary servitude, except as a punishment for crime whereof the party shall have been duly convicted, shall exist within the United States, nor any place subject to their jurisdiction." While the 13th amendment theoretically freed slaves, it offered a very critical clause that jump-started a new form of slavery—disproportionate mass incarceration of people of color. Michelle Alexander refers to the phenomenon as "The New Jim Crow" or the beginning of the prison industrial complex (Alexander 2010).

This country was found, built off the backs of free labor of African-Americans, birthed from strategic exclusion and shaped by racism. The very inception of the country and every single system established was built for the purpose of maintaining an economic base and social order. The center of these structures to include education, prison, health care, employment, and housing cannot hold in absence of deep-seated exclusionary, discriminatory practices fueled by a very intentional and powerful social construct, racism.

The Times writes about James Baldwin's "I am Not Your Negro": At the heart of Baldwin's argument was the question of who is responsible for the problem of racism, a point the film makes with Baldwin's use of language. Never one to mince words, he wrote and spoke what Toni Morrison called in a 1987 remembrance of her friend the "undecorated truth" about the American illusion, which juxtaposed whiteness as American innocence with blackness as sullying American purity, hence "the Negro Problem" (Magnolia Home Entertainment Firm, Jackson, Baldwin).

Baldwin contends that history is not the past, it is the present as we carry it with us (Baldwin 1924). It is this unfortunate truth that has resulted in a persistent and pervasive psychological burden on Black people in America.

The Reconstruction era followed the Civil War (1865–1877)—the country was likened to the new frontier. A very select few individuals were able to seize economic opportunities during this era such as JP Morgan, Ford, Carnegie, Vanderbilt, and Rockefeller. Economic upward mobility was restricted and like Martin Luther King Jr. astutely pointed out in a speech in 1968 in reference to the peculiar institution: slaves were freed but they weren't given land or economic opportunity like our White fellow citizens of the Republic. King's argument was that economic freedom was critical in the achievement of ultimate freedom. Freed slaves were not uniquely suited and/or provided with the tools to productively exploit a new economic opportunity.

Shortly after the Reconstruction era, Jim Crowism (1877–mid-1960s) emerged, a racial caste system developed in the South that perpetuated multigenerational segregation and inequitable treatment of African-Americans. This era was marked by myriad lynchings of black bodies and lives. The most prominent lynching is that of Emmett Till, a young 14-year-old Black male child who was lynched in the South in 1955 upon being accused of offending White women in a grocery store. The question of whether or not Black lives matter has been a tenacious one? We all know that it is easier to be cruel toward something and/or someone that is not considered human, that is perceived to not have a soul and is without feeling. Historically, Blacks have been painted as soulless, non-feeling individuals of subhuman existence.

If we are incredibly honest—this underscores the real issue; lack of humanity and tremendous fear.

We cannot get to the resolution of the matter, until we can agree on what the underlying driver of its persistence is.

Many movements rose up to fight against the tyranny of racism and discrimination and exclusion. The Harlem Renaissance of the 1920s, arguably, was one such movement and served as a prelude to the civil rights movement of the 1950s and 1960s. Langston Hughes, a key figure during the Renaissance wrote a memorable poem entitled, "I, too, Sing America." In this poem, Hughes highlights the struggle of invisibility and the plea of the Negro for inclusion, to be seen:

> I, too, sing America.
>
> I am the darker brother.
> They send me to eat in the kitchen
> When company comes,
> But I laugh,
> And eat well,
> And grow strong.
>
> Tomorrow,
> I'll be at the table
> When company comes.
> Nobody'll dare
> Say to me,
> "Eat in the kitchen,"
> Then.
>
> Besides,
> They'll see how beautiful I am
> And be ashamed—
>
> I, too, am America.

Hughes is imploring America to acknowledge and *see* him, a plea that is further developed decades later in Ralph Ellison's classic The Invisible Man. Part of the motivation for the civil rights movement of the 1960s was about inclusion and visibility (asking a country to see, honor, acknowledge, and respect the very existence of Blacks).

President Lyndon B Johnson signed important Civil Rights legislation in 1964, but it turns out that the fight for liberation, acceptance, and inclusion remained/remains a persistent battle for Black and brown people in present-day America.

Fast forward to the present day (twenty-first century) and African-American lives are still undervalued. The relationship between Police and the Black community remains volatile and now that we are in the era of cell phones, cameras, and social media, the disproportionate violence is being captured. Trayvon Martin's fatal death at the hands of a White man in the south who was later acquitted by under the guise of "fearing for his life," supported by Stand Your Ground Laws in Florida, is an example of the evolution of excuses that are gaining legitimacy for the killing of black and brown bodies. The fear (racial fear) is rooted in history and perpetuated on a daily basis through social interactions and the soft bigotry of limited consideration and consistent degradation. There are several laws (local and federal) that widen the gaps of inequity, discrimination, and racism—like the aforementioned Stand Your Ground (self-defense) law in Florida. If I fear you, I can kill you and it is justified. The challenge with this logic is that fear undergirds racism. Fear is the foundation for the powerful structure that is racism. Fear has resulted in needless death. This is unacceptable and, quite frankly, unsustainable, as the current state of affairs jeopardizes the continued existence of our democracy.

Modern-day lynching, inexplicably, of young Black males reflects a continuation of the underlying sentiment that Black lives don't matter. Shortly after George Zimmerman was acquitted for taking the life of Trayvon Martin, the #BlackLivesMatter movement was initiated.

Interestingly, back in the 1920s, Langston Hughes shared a similar sentiment to the #BlackLivesMatter movement when he wrote: "I, too, am America." Blacks in America are on the chronic offensive trying to demonstrate and tell America that we, too, matter.

The murder of young Black males continued in mass with Eric Garner in New York, Michael Brown in Ferguson, Freddie Gray in Baltimore, Tamir Rice in Cleveland, and the list goes on.

The political milieu changed in 2008. The hope of racial reconciliation and healing was on the table, or so a significant swath of America thought. When President Obama took office in early 2009, the nation was shocked and excited; shocked that America voted for a person of African descent to serve in the highest office in the most powerful country in the history of the world. The White House was built by slaves and now a man of African heritage would occupy it. President Obama, a Harvard-educated constitutional law professor, married to a Princeton-educated lawyer (who also is Black), was called every racial name in the book and some. During a State of the Union address, a congressman yelled out "liar" to him. The opposition party made it clear from day one that their main job would be to block and stall with the goal of rendering him the most "ineffective President" in our nation's history. They worked so hard, but with Obama's steadfast efforts, the Affordable Care Act was passed—many administrations prior had attempted to accomplish a semblance of universal health care with little success. A man of African descent got in office and got the job done in the context of great opposition—this has also been our history, achieving in the presence of great resistance.

Eric Michael Dyson addressed the constraints of the politics of race in the era of President Obama as "The First Black President" in his book The Black Presidency. President Obama's hands were tied because if he did too much for Blacks, it would be viewed as welfare, favoritism, and reverse racism, so he had to operate under White supremacy expectations in order to get the little bit accomplished that he did (Dyson 2016).

During his Presidency, he was met with such hateful accusations from then Donald Trump. Trump questioned Obama's citizenship and demanded that he show his birth certificate. Trump's irresponsible birther narrative unleashed deep-seated racial hate and tension in America.

After 8 years of Obama, our White counterparts had seen enough of people of color and foreign countries being considered, they wanted to "make America great again" and overwhelmingly did so by voting in Donald Trump as President of the United States. Trump ran on hate, bigotry, and exclusion—he reminded the country of values that it was found on to include strategic exclusion. There was a precipitous rise in violence toward marginalized communities under his influence and leadership.

In the Trump era, children have been separated from their parents at the border, communities of colored are pinged as violent and useless, health care is being dismantled, and prisons/jails are being filled disproportionately by people of color.

In this Trump era, if you are Black, you can get the police called on you for studying in the Yale library, sitting at Starbucks, barbecuing in a public park, and being 8-year old selling water on the sidewalk without a permit.

Unfortunately, the country feels like it is regressing. All things must evolve in order to improve except if you are not interested in improvement and only interested in maintaining the status quo.

The reality though is that maintaining the status quo has significantly increased the psychological burden of Black people in this country (Steele and Aronson 1995).

This gets back to Baldwin who contends that *history is not the past; it is the present as we carry it with us* (Baldwin 1963).

History must be reconciled or a whole entire generation of Black Americans will be crushed under its unyielding pressure. Again, this is unacceptable.

Why has it been so difficult to tackle racism in this country?

Every single system is held up by racist principles that by their very nature discriminate and create inequitable outcomes because they offer inequitable opportunity to thrive. Every system from education, health care, prison, housing, and employment is held up by racist infrastructure.

Changing this dynamic would require taking each structure down to its base and rebuilding. The task feels daunting to folks, so metaphorical hands are thrown up and people don't try.

We cannot afford another day of being impacted by racism; it is making African-Americans sick and literally killing us.

Eventually, the entire nation will die if the issue is not resolved. Racism is a pervasive process that will eventually destroy everything in its path. We are getting to a point where the perpetrators of it will also be consumed, if they don't make a commitment to retreat from this path of self-destruction.

History has shaped the psyche, driven unconscious thoughts and processes, which has impacted bad behavior. The subliminal, historical message has been: "Black lives **don't** matter."

Baldwin contends that history is not the past; it is the present as we carry it with us (Baldwin).

How do we shift this dynamic? We must revisit and reconcile history.

The psychological impact of racism on Black lives is heavy, significant.

Current research demonstrates the deadly psychological, physiologic, and physical impact of chronic stress from conditions like racism. African-Americans disproportionately are contracting and dying from chronic diseases at a higher rate than our White counterparts.

Desantis et al. took adolescents in two racially diverse High Schools, one in Chicago suburbs and Los Angeles. The following measures were utilized in the study (a) a demographic questionnaire, (b) the Structured Clinical Interview for DSM-IV-TR (SCID)], (c) a Life Stress Interview, (d) salivary cortisol samples, collected six times per day on three consecutive weekdays during the school year, (e) momentary diary reports of negative emotion at the time of cortisol sampling, and (f) health questionnaires. Participants were classified into racial/ethnic categories based upon their responses on the demographic questionnaire. The study concluded that African-American and Hispanic adolescents had significantly flatter daytime cortisol slopes compared to their White counterparts. Cortisol is supposed to be high in the morning and lower at night (DeSantis et al. 2006). *Lower daytime cortisol is related to negative health consequences.* The stress is literally killing us.

Stereotype threat

In a study by Steele and Aronson, stereotype threat is defined as a situational predicament in which people are or feel themselves to be at risk of conforming to stereotypes about their social group.

The threat of stereotype threat on academic performance; African-American and European American college students took the difficult portion of the GRE Exam. Students were split into three groups: (1) stereotype threat (test was described as being "diagnostic of intellectual ability"), (2) non-stereotype threat (test was described as a laboratory problem-solving task that was nondiagnostic of ability), (3) third condition was "Nondiagnostic of ability"—students were told that it was just a test. Based on national averages, the African-American students did not perform as well on the test compared to their White counterparts. Placement in the diagnostic condition (test was described as being diagnostic of intellectual ability) significantly, negatively impacted African-Americans compared to European Americans. Also of significance:

- African-American students who regarded the test as a measure of intelligence had more thoughts related to negative stereotypes of their group.
- Steele and Aronson measured this through a word completion task.
- African-Americans who thought the test measured intelligence were more likely to complete word fragments using words associated with relevant negative stereotypes (e.g., completing "__mb" as "dumb" rather than as "numb").

The stereotype threat study is an example of how culture is shaped by preconceived notions, bias, and underlying assumptions. Further, demonstrates how the culture of systems can and has negatively impacted individuals of color. Again, as indicated by Rothman culture can be seen "as an inhumane, malevolent force" that is derived from osmosis (what is in the environment and around us)." Systems that serve youth, and in specific, youth of color must, at the very least acknowledge the ways in which they (the systems) have judged, mistreated, and hurt them, conscious and unconscious. Cultural responsivity must include this acknowledgment.

Toni Morris was very involved in the discussions around the O. J. Simpson trial in the 1990s. As a matter of fact, she co-authored a book entitled "The Birth of a Nation 'hood: Gaze, Script and Spectacle in the O. J. Simpson case." There is a YouTube clip of Toni Morrison discussing her co-authored book on race, racism, and powerful social constructs that have influenced systems like the police and criminal justice system. This further highlights the complexity of systems and the need for change (Morrison et al. 1997).

Think It Over

Toni Morrison calls out the racist association of blackness with criminality, 1997 Charlie Rose Show

- Context: the conversation between Toni Morrison and Charlie Rose was happening at the height of the OJ Simpson case. America was torn across racial lines. Generally, African-Americans saw him as innocent and White Americans deemed him guilty.
- TIME Magazine hosted OJ Simpson on its cover and made certain to make his photo reminiscent of that of a mug shot. The background was dark and the lighting of OJ's face was very dark.
- Toni Morrison made the argument that blackness and criminality are merged in the minds of most White Americans.
- Toni pointed out the TIME magazine image, contending that there was intentionality in constructing an image that triggered a conditioned response of fear and conjured up thoughts of violence in reference to a Black man in America.

- What is the impact of pairing blackness with criminality?
- How might stereotype threat be applied?
- How might perceptions and preconceived notions shape behavior?

Racism as toxic stress; experienced as trauma and its impact on the brain

A meta-analysis by Busse et al. (2017), on discrimination the hypothalamic–pituitary–adrenal axis (HPA axis) to include 27 studies (10 experimental, 17 observational), suggests that discrimination is associated with alterations in HPA axis activity and that the direction of this association depends on the timing and length of exposure of the discrimination experience (Busse et al. 2017). In other words, discrimination is experienced as a prolonged stress response, a form of trauma. Cortisol levels are impacted and as demonstrated in Chap. 1 of this textbook, stress and changes in cortisol levels can result in changes in the developing and developed brain.

Within this meta-analysis, the work of Gunnar and Quevedo is cited. Their work indicates that adolescents may be more susceptible to the toxic effects of stress (extended cortisol responses) which affects underlying mechanisms of emotional and cognitive processing (Gunnar and Quevedo 2007; Lupien et al. 2009).

Underneath bias, racism, discrimination is "fear." Comprehending the intersection of fear and trauma opens up the possibility for healing and change in people, attached to systems, shaped by culture.

Moving toward cultural responsivity: making the connection between fear and trauma

One approach to changing/managing underlying assumptions, changing culture: Employing a trauma-informed approach

- Involves understanding the physiology of "fear."
- Every single human being on this earth has been afraid (in a state of fear) at some point in their lives.
- If you can identify with your own fear (how it felt, what it prevented you from doing etc.), then it becomes easier to understand the fear of youth and others.

Fear plays a vital role in the lives of human beings. It helps humans to appropriately manage threats (perceived or real) and seek safety. Fear has a role in survival. As indicated in Chap. 1, the brain develops from the bottom-up and the inside-out. The most developed part of the brain when each of us was born was the brain stem, seen in Fig. 2.3. The brain stem, primitive brain is known as the survival center and is involved in mediating the "fear" response. Without it, we wouldn't breathe nor would our hearts beat.

Figure 2.4 outlines the aspects of the brain involved in fear. "Fear" is a full-body response, involving multiple aspects of the brain and body. The brain on fear involves multiple elements of the brain introduced in Chap. 1 of this textbook.

In the case of fear—there is first a threat **sensed** (seen, heard, felt, etc.) externally and it is matched with the internal response of "fear" as means of seeking safety, to flee danger and move away from threat.

In the fear response:

Thalamus (bottom, midbrain) operates as a switchboard, directing traffic in the brain, alerting nearby systems that there is a threat and represents the *sensory aspect of fear*.

Hippocampus and amygdala (midbrain structures) help with giving emotional context to the fear process and represents the *emotional aspect of fear*.

The frontal and temporal lobes (the cortex, top brain) are what help to make one aware and/or conscious of the dread experienced from the fear process and represent the *cognitive aspect of fear*.

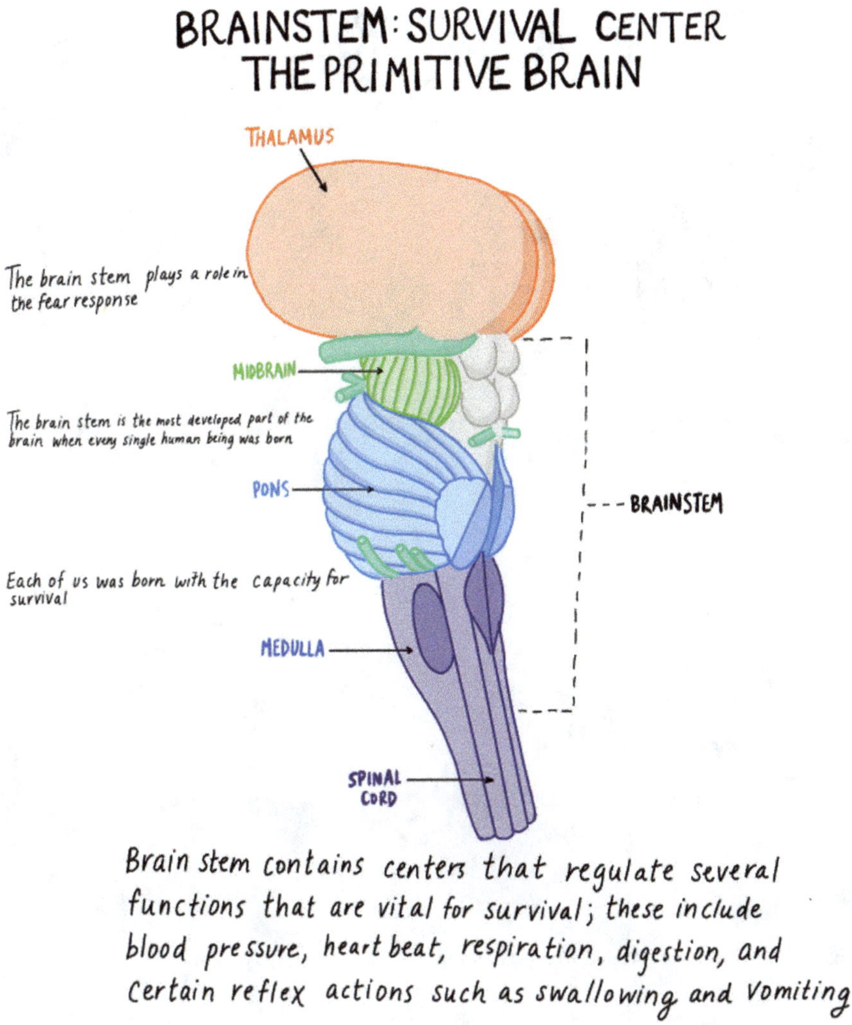

Fig. 2.3 Brain stem as the survival center mediates the fear response. Printed with permission. Copyright Audrey A. Tran

The hypothalamus mediates the fight, flight, and/or freeze response, impacts the release of the stress hormone cortisol from the adrenal gland (which sits on top of the kidney) along with several other stress-related neurohormones, and represents the *physiologic aspect of fear* (See Fig. 2.5).

The Fear response

- Is designed to help us "seek safety" in the face of threat.
- When the threat leaves, theoretically, we should no longer be "seeking safety."

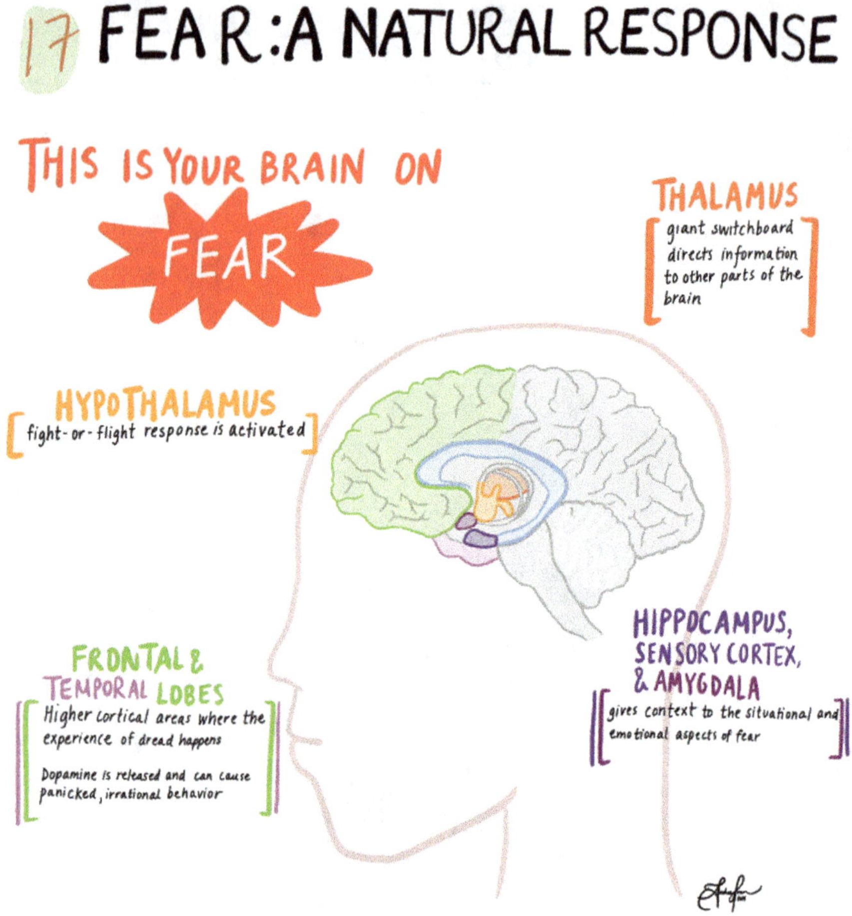

Fig. 2.4 Brain on fear. Printed with permission. Copyright Audrey A. Tran

- However, there are some among us who remain in a constant state of fear and always "seeking safety" = trauma.

Natural fear response unchecked = traumatization.

"Traumatization occurs when both internal and external resources are inadequate to cope with external threat." (Van der Kolk 1989)

In the neurobiology of violence, Siever outlines various risk factors that increase the possibility of violence. Trauma history was noted as a significant risk factor. Traumatization unchecked can lead to aggression.

Neurobiology of trauma, employing a trauma-informed approach as a path to healing

One potential way to begin the process of deconstructing the very powerful social construct, that is, racism is to understand the intersection of fear (which undergirds

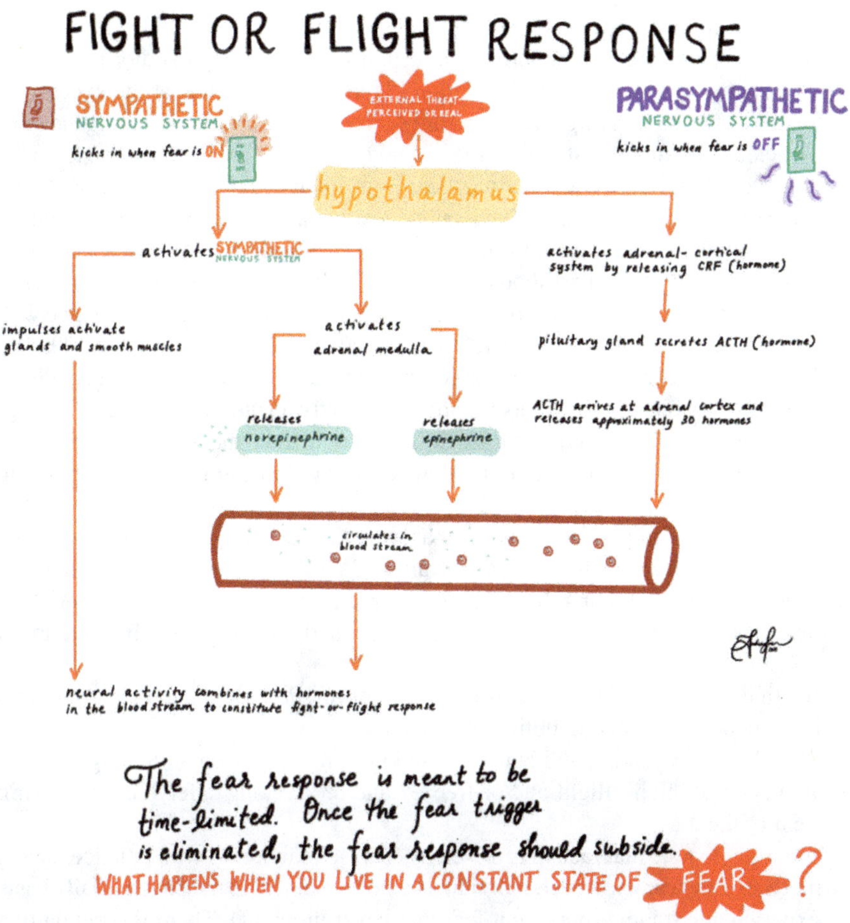

Fig. 2.5 Fight or flight or freeze: the hypothalamus in focus. Printed with permission. Copyright Audrey A. Tran

and gives life to racism, bias) and trauma. Once this is understood, we can more clearly begin constructing the path to healing.

The science made easy. Understanding the fears role in trauma and racism. The argument is that if you can relate to fear because we have all experienced it, then maybe we can move toward releasing the powerful grip of racism and the structures that reinforce it.

We've all been afraid at some point in our lives. Fear is a natural, appropriate response to a perceived and/or real threat. There are physical (body breaks down sugar stores to gain access to the energy you will need to fight, flee, and/or freeze), psychological (the doom that is experienced mediated by the brain), and physiologic (increased heart rate, breathing, sweating, stress hormones like cortisol are released, etc.) manifestations of fear. If(fear) is designed to drive us to seek safety—then fear and all of its parts is an appropriate response to a perceived and/or real threat. When in fear and seeking safety, the brain is focused on survival at the expense of reasonable, rational thinking. When you are surviving, you are not executing the most sophisticated thinking. Most of the time, the body and mind are in action mode. In the true spirit of physics, for every action, there is an equal and opposite reaction. Logic would have it that once the perceived and/or real threat dissipates, the fear response should be quelled, and the mind, body, and spirit should go back to a particular baseline—the body and mind should no longer be on high alert. Breathing and heart rate should go back to baseline, cortisol levels should decrease, and all should be well (Brown and Ryan 2003; Douglas Bremner 2006; Lanius et al. 2010; Siever 2008).

The brain's role in fear—the top part of the brain, also known as the cortex, allows us to exercise good judgment, think before we act, and execute sophisticated thinking. The mid and bottom part of the brain is designed to mediate the fear response. When we are in fear, we are in the mid to bottom part of our brain at the expense of being in the top.

The process and impact of fear is one that every human being has experienced—we know the feeling because we've been afraid and in a state of fear at some point in our lives. Recall that feeling, how uncomfortable fear was and is, how powerless it can make you feel while you are experiencing it and how unproductive you are in the midst of it.

Imagine if the natural fear response never turns off. Persistent fear that never turns off is the neurobiological definition of trauma.

Consider the psychological burden of living in fear every day—feeling like you are in a state of "fight, flight and/or freeze" and/or "seeking safety" every waking moment of the day.

Important to note that racism is driven by fear, so individuals who practice racism are motivated by fear. However, individuals who are subject to racism on a daily basis are experiencing trauma (persistent fear that never turns off). There is essentially a fear on fear response. Now that we know what it is, we can work on remedying it. There must be a willingness to change.

The bottom line: racism is experienced as a form of trauma (as fear with persistent psychological, physiological, and physical consequences).

Employing a trauma-informed approach considers trauma at every level and seeks to reduce triggering trauma and creating safety. I contend that this approach places humanity at the center of all we do. It is much harder to disrespect and/or disregard something when you've had personal experience with it. Again, we have all experienced fear and know the hardship that it creates on the body. We all know the powerlessness of being in a state of survival. It is like the Freddy Cougar movies of the 1980s and the quintessential character running from Freddy with a set of keys in their hands. We all know how it ends, the character gets to the door with keys in hand and attempts to unlock the door, instead of accomplishing the task, they drop the keys. Why? Why do they drop the keys? Because they are in an utter state of fear, survival mode, mid to bottom part of the brain. It turns out that the motor control required to get the key into the lock is mostly a top brain function. When we are in survival mode, we are not actively engaging the top part (cortical) part of our brains, but the bottom (Douglas Bremner 2006).

What approaches can be employed to begin the process of deconstructing the very powerful social construct of racism?

One potential answer is to employ a trauma-informed approached. Ask every human being and every system to be/become trauma informed (Felitti et al. 1998; Schein 1990).

- The real Gestalt of being trauma informed =
  coming to grips with your own humanity and proclivity toward trauma and managing it daily and intentionally.
- Minimizing creating and/or triggering trauma in others.
- Increase efforts toward creating and preserving peace.
- Creating safety—safe spaces, places, environments, communities, offices, and workspaces.
- Being kind, considerate, and mindful of others.
- A desire to see others and yourself healed.

History shows us that individuals are compelled to change when they can relate to a struggle. We must meaningfully connect others to our struggle, because our struggle really is their struggle.

Hopefully by connecting a universal emotion (fear) to an unbearable phenomenon (trauma perpetuated by racism) compels change in behavior and practice.

The golden rule is applicable: Care for others as you would like to be cared for. These are fundamental, critical steps in dismantling racism and reducing its profound psychological, physical, and physiologic grip on Black people. A genuine trauma-informed frame will assist individuals, who've been in a persistent state of fear in transitioning from the bottom part of their brain to the top and the conditions for healing can be established.

History hasn't changed behavior; science and data have been limited in its ability to impact lasting change; so perhaps appealing to humanity, common feelings, and emotions we've all experienced will help the wider community appreciate the impact of racism and the shared responsibility to change it.

If we can care for one another free of judgment.

If we consider our history and are conscious of the fact that we carry it with us, we are more poised to realize our power to reconcile it (history).

If consider our own relationship to fear, then we are more likely to avoid triggering this response in others.

If we do these things, we are drawn closer to our collective humanity and seek to protect it.

If we do these things, we can start the process of deconstructing the very powerful social construct of racism and begin our collective healing—one person at a time, one system at a time.

Practical application—Think it through

Being trauma informed builds a greater capacity for empathy.

Empathy = improved cultural responsivity.

Profound lesson in developing a greater capacity for empathy: "A Time to Kill"—Imagine

In 1988, John Grisham wrote a book entitled "A Time to Kill"—In 1996, this book was adapted to a movie starring Samuel L. Jackson and Matthew McConaughey. In brief, the setting was the south, Confederate flags and deep-seated racism. A young Black girl is minding her own business walking home one day and is confronted with two White Men in a truck marked with a Confederate flag. These two White men rape this little girl, urinate on her, and attempt to hang her from a tree near a deep ravine. The branch could not hold her weight, so she fell into the ravine where she was left to recover.

In the movie, the father of this little Black girl was Samuel L. Jackson—when he learned that the two men that brutally assaulted his daughter were two White men, he became enraged. He (Samuel L. Jackson's character as the father) did not have faith that the system would hold these two White men accountable, so he took the law into his own hands and murdered them (a Black man killed two White men in the south to avenge his wounded young daughter).

Samuel L. Jackson's character ends up in prison. He seeks legal counsel in an attempt for liberation. The lawyer who came to his defense was a young Matt McConaughey. Samuel L. Jackson's character had to persuade Matt to get the jury (who was an all-White Jury in the south) to see him as a human being who acted out of rage as any father would in the context of his child being hurt. Sam wanted Matt to convince the jury to see him as a human being as opposed to a Black man.

The most powerful scene of the movie came during closing arguments during the trial of Sam. Matt, in an effort to accomplish the goal of getting the jury to see Sam as a human, as a father, constructed a very compelling argument.

Matt asked the jury to close their eyes and then asked them to imagine. With their eyes closed, Matt described a young, innocent girl who was violently violated by two men to the point of not being able to have children. He described this little girl left alone by the roadside to die. There was a palpable shift in the room as tears rolled down the cheeks of the jurors. After a dramatic pause, while Matt allowed the tears of the jurors to flow (so they could really feel the moment), he asked them to now imagine that this little girl was White.

This was a very powerful scene. It demonstrated what empathy looks like.

Empathy is about the capacity to imagine, to feel, and to make a demonstrable shift as a result of that feeling.

Keen reminder on behalf of Dr. Maya Angelou: "I am human; therefore nothing human can be alien to me."

Systems change when people change.

The overarching goal of this chapter: Impacting people by getting them into the "feeling space" to impact systems for change.

Checking for understanding

- What is the relationship between fear and trauma? (this is a theme that will be repeated throughout this textbook)
- What is the most important aspect of E. Schein's organizational model of change?
- Why is it important to put "culture" in the context?
- How does bias, preconceptions, racism, and discrimination shape culture, behavior?
- How might checking underlying assumptions motivate change in a system?
- Why is cultural responsivity important?
- Racism, bias, and discrimination are experienced as toxic stress, trauma and impacts the developing and developed brain? True or False.

References

Alexander, M. (2010). *The new Jim Crow: Mass incarceration in the age of colorblindness*. New York: New Press.

Baldwin, J. 1924–1987. (1963). *The fire next time*. New York: Dial Press.

Brown, K. W., & Ryan, R. M. (2003). The benefits of being present: Mindfulness and its role in psychological well-being. *Journal of Personality and Social Psychology, 84*(4), 822–848.

Busse, D., Yim, I. S., Campos, B., et al. (2017). *Journal of Behavioral Medicine, 40,* 539. https://doi.org/10.1007/s10865-017-9830-6.

DeSantis, A. S., et al. (2006). *Racial/Ethnic Differences in Cortisol in Diurnal Rhythms in a Community Sample of Adolescents*. Program on Human Development and Social Policy, School of Education and Social Policy and the Cells to Society Center, Institute for Policy Research, Northwestern University, Evanston, Illinois Department of Psychology, Northwestern University, Evanston, Illinois, Department of Psychology, University of California at Los Angeles, Los Angeles, California. Received 18 December 2006, Accepted 23 March 2007, Available online 16 June 2007.

Douglas Bremner, J. (2006). Traumatic stress: Effects on the brain. *Dialogues in Clinical Neuroscience 8*, 445–461.

Dyson, M. E. (2016). *The Black presidency: Barack Obama and the politics of race in America.*

Evans, E. (2016). Intersectionality as feminist praxis in UK. *Women's Studies International Forum, 59,* 67–75.

Felitti, V. J., Anda, R. F., Nordenberg, D., Williamson, D. F., Spitz, A. M., Edwards, V., et al. (1998). The relationship of adult health status to childhood abuse and household dysfunction. *American Journal of Preventive Medicine, 14,* 245–258.

Greenwald, A. G., et al. (2009). Understanding and using the Implicit Association Test: III. Meta-analysis of predictive validity. *Journal of Personality and Social Psychology, 97*(1), 17–41.

Gunnar, M., & Quevedo, K. (2007). The neurobiology of stress and development. *Annual Review of Psychology 58*, 145–73.

Harrell, S. P. (2000). A multidimensional conceptualization of racism-related stress: Implications for the well-being of people of color. *American Journal of Orthopsychiatry, 70,* 42–57.

Hinson, S., et al. (2018, October 24). *Race, Power and Policy: Dismantling Structural Racism*, Workbook. Grassroots Policy Project. https://www.racialequitytools.org/resourcefiles/race_power_policy_workbook.pdf.

Hughes, L. 1902–1967. (1994). *The collected poems of Langston Hughes*. New York: Knopf: Distributed by Random H.
Lanius, R. A., Frewen, P. A., Vermetten, E., & Yehuda, R. (2010). Fear conditioning and early life vulnerabilities: two distinct pathways of emotional dysregulation and brain dysfunction in PTSD. *European Journal of Psychotraumatology, 1*. https://doi.org/10.3402/ejpt.v1i0.5467.
Lupien, S. J., McEwen, B. S., Gunnar, M. R., Heim, C. (2009). Effects of stress throughout the lifespan on the brain, behaviour and cognition. *Nature Reviews Neuroscience, 10*, 434–445.
Magnolia Home Entertainment (Firm), Jackson, S. L., Baldwin, J., & Peck, R. (2017). *I am not your negro [DVD videorecording]* (Widescreen format). Los Angeles, CA: Magnolia Home Entertainment.
Morrison, T., & Lacor, C. B. (Eds.). (1997). *Birth of a nation'hood: Gaze, script, and spectacle in the O. J. Simpson case*. New York: Pantheon.
Rosenthal, L. (2016). Incorporating intersectionality into psychology: An opportunity to promote social justice and equity. *American Psychologist, 71*(6), 474–485.
Rothman, J. (2014, December). The meaning of culture. *The New Yorker*. Retrieved from https://www.newyorker.com/books/joshua-rothman/meaning-culture.
Schein, E. H. (1990). Organizational culture: What it is and how to change it. In P. Evans, Y. Doz, & A. Laurent (Eds.), *Human resource management in international firms*. London: Palgrave Macmillan.
Siever, L. J. (2008, April). The neurobiology of aggression and violence. *The American Journal of Psychiatry, 165*(4), 429–442.
Steele, C. M., & Aronson, J. (1995). Stereotype threat and the intellectual test performance of African Americans. *Journal of Personality and Social Psychology, 69*(5), 797–811. Copyright 1995 by the American Psychological Association, Inc. 0022-3514/95.
van der Kolk, B. A. (1989). The compulsion to repeat the trauma: Re-enactment, re-victimization and masochism. *Psychiatric Clinics of North America, 12*(2), 389–411.

Chapter 3
Trauma Informed: The Intersection of Fear, Trauma, Aggression, and a Path to Healing

A few important reminders as we get deeper into fear and trauma.

Fear that does not turn off = neurobiological trauma.

Trauma = bottom brain, survival predominant functioning.

Applying trauma-informed practices and approaches can assist youth with moving from the bottom (survival, impulsive) part of their brain to more actively engage in the top part of the brain (helps with exercising good judgment, impulse control, emotion regulation, etc.). Trauma-informed approaches and practices help to create safety and make healing more likely. This chapter will consider the intersection of fear and trauma and offer practical means for moving down a path that leads to healing.

By the end of this chapter, you should be able to

- Comprehend the physiology of fear.
- Define trauma.
- Understand the intersection between fear, trauma, and violence.
- Appreciate fear conditioning and stress sensitization.
- Recognize adverse childhood experiences
- Appreciate the relationship between trauma-informed practices and empathy.

Exercise 3A—Rocky and Adrian: Everything you need to know about trauma-informed care in one scene (described)

The Rocky movie series was wildly popular in the 1980s (the continued sequel is now represented in the movie Creed). There is a specific scene between Rocky (the main character, a boxer with a robustly muscular build) and his partner (Adrian)—they were on the beach and held an intense exchange around Rocky's proclaimed fear. The scene included Rocky admitting to Adrian that he was afraid. Actually, he yelled "I am afraid alright." Adrian met his intensity, stating that she knew that he was afraid. She continued to encourage him that being afraid is okay as long as we can try and find our way to the other side of it. As Adrian is talking to Rocky, he visibly calms down, and his voice lowers as he was able to appreciate the validation, support, and safety that Adrian created.

What trauma-informed elements do you note in scene description?

A. Moreland-Capuia, *Training for Change*,
https://doi.org/10.1007/978-3-030-19208-2_3

Notables from this scene description:

- Rocky is the quintessential strong man and is communicating that he is afraid.
- Rocky is emotionally elevated (as evidenced by his raised voice and body language).
- Adrian meets Rocky where he is.
- Adrian listens to Rocky.
- Adrian validates Rocky's fear, she doesn't try to change it, she just works with it and eventually through it.
- Rocky eventually calms down and is able to listen to Adrian.
- They are on a beach (which for many represent a place of peace, solace).

Piecing it together

- Adrian created safety.
- In the midst of safety, Rocky felt validated, heard, and understood.
- When youth feel validated, heard, and understood (which is trauma informed), they are more likely to open themselves to change.
- When individuals in a system feel validated, heard, and understood (which is trauma informed), they are more likely to open themselves up to change. Further, the system (attached to people) is more apt to change.

Rocky, metaphorically speaking, is like the youth systems seek to serve. Youth may not come into the system yelling that they are afraid, but the fear is manifested in other ways like attitude.

This chapter respectfully challenges systems that serve youth to be like Adrian (metaphorically speaking)—create safety, validate, listen, and seek to understand.

On creating safety—in this scene description, Rocky and Adrian are at the beach. It is recognized that systems will not be on a beach; the goal is to encourage systems to create a beach-like experience that represents calm, solace, respect, kindness, and dignity.

The key elements of being trauma informed are found in this clip.

If the youth we serve are like Rocky, then system shall be Adrian.

Reminder of the connection between fear and trauma

Most human beings can relate to fear and/or being afraid.

Some may recall being afraid of the dark as children and actually still might be.

To all reading this textbook, question: have you or anyone around you **never** been afraid?

If the question is answered truthfully, every human being, at some point in their life either has and/or will be afraid. In this sense, fear and being afraid is a "point of convergence." Remember the point of convergence as a theme from Chap. 2 as it is defined in a shared experience among many that possess the power to tap into the best of the human spirit and inspire change. If an individual can relate to it then they can understand it, if they can understand it then they are more likely to change it.

As outlined in Chap. 2 of this text, fear is a natural response shared by all human beings. The fear response stems from all human's natural proclivity toward survival.

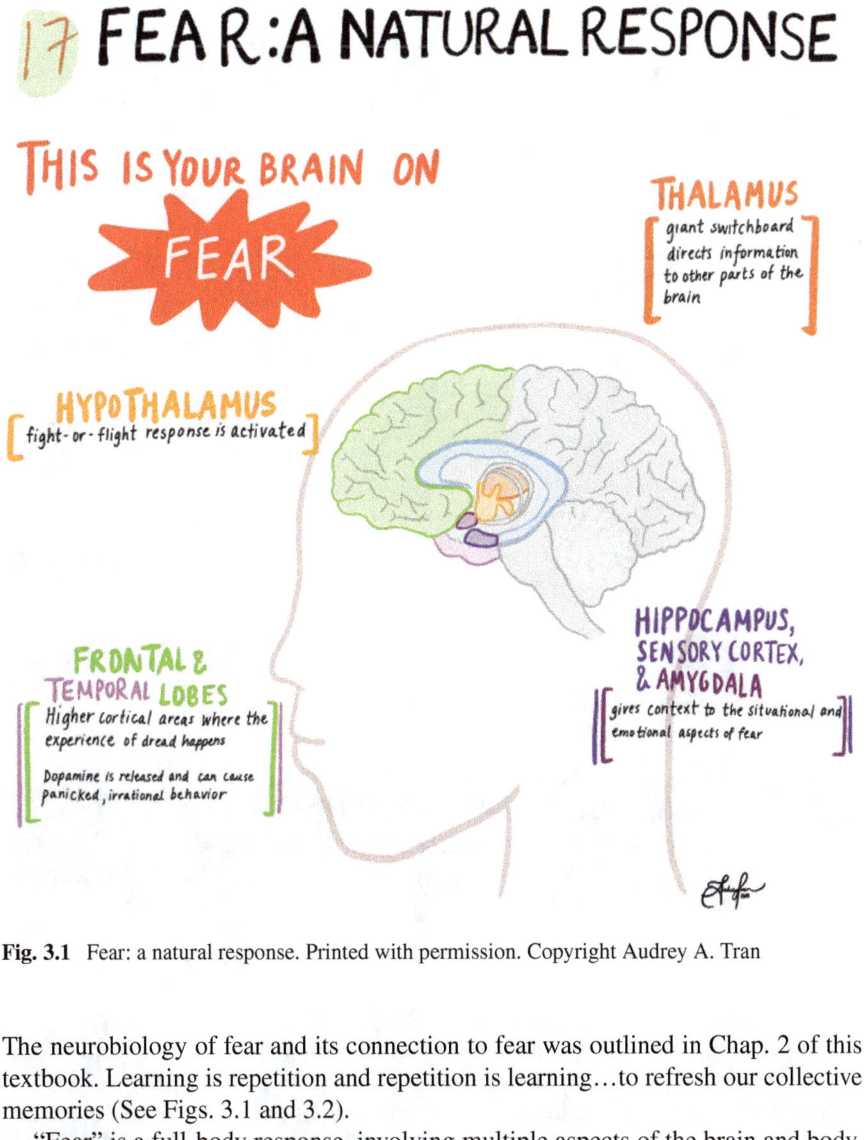

Fig. 3.1 Fear: a natural response. Printed with permission. Copyright Audrey A. Tran

The neurobiology of fear and its connection to fear was outlined in Chap. 2 of this textbook. Learning is repetition and repetition is learning…to refresh our collective memories (See Figs. 3.1 and 3.2).

"Fear" is a full-body response, involving multiple aspects of the brain and body. The brain on fear involves multiple elements of the brain introduced in Chap. 1 of this textbook.

In the case of fear—there is first a threat **sensed** (seen, heard, felt, etc.) externally and it is matched with the internal response of "fear" as means of seeking safety, to flee danger, and move away from threat.

Thalamus (bottom, midbrain) in the fear response operates as a switchboard, directing traffic in the brain, alerting nearby systems that there is a threat, and represents the *sensory aspect of fear*.

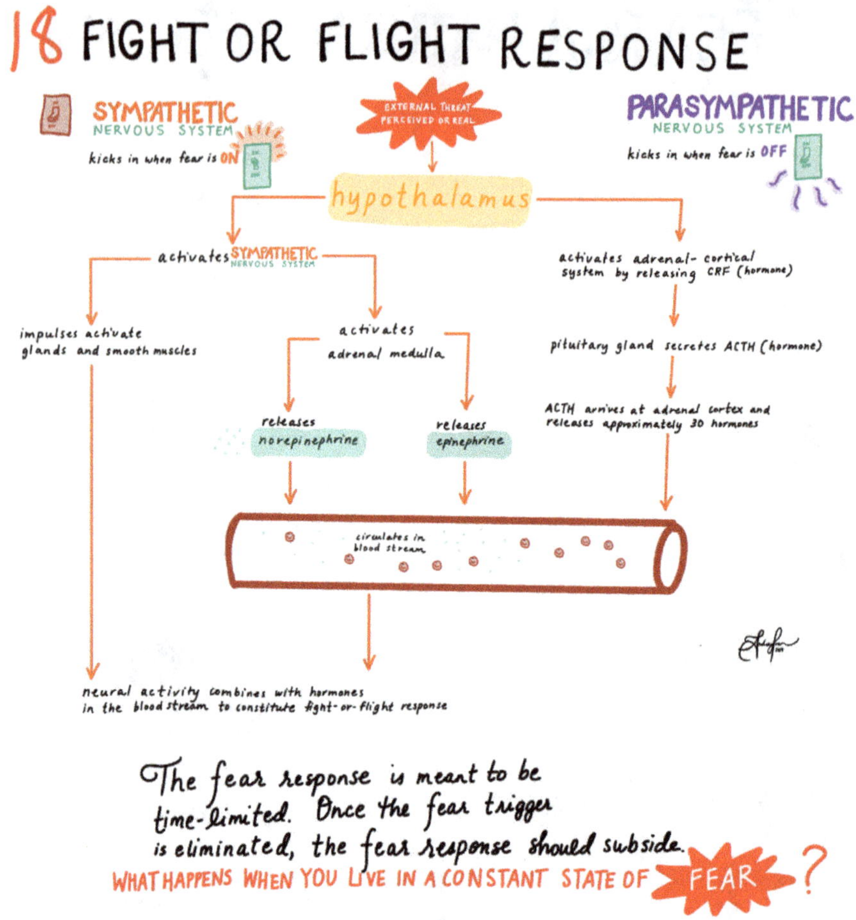

Fig. 3.2 Hypothalamus in detail. Printed with permission. Copyright Audrey A. Tran

Hippocampus and amygdala (midbrain structures) help with giving emotional context to the fear process and represent the *emotional aspect of fear*.

The frontal and temporal lobes (the cortex, top brain) are what help to make one aware and/or conscious of the dread experienced from the fear process and represent the *cognitive aspect of fear*.

The hypothalamus mediates the fight, flight, and/or freeze response, impacts the release of the stress hormone cortisol from the adrenal gland (which sits on top of the kidney) along with several other stress-related neurohormones, and represents the *physiologic aspect of fear*.

The hypothalamus is the physiological aspect of fear and activates the entire body to participate in the fear response. This schematic shows the hypothalamus's part in triggering Corticotrophin-Releasing Factor (CRF) leading to adrenocorticotropin

(ACTH) hormone release, which impacts the adrenal cortex resulting in the release of several stress hormones into the bloodstream to include cortisol, norepinephrine. The release of hormones into the bloodstream creates the fight or flight response. For example, during the fear response, adrenaline (norepinephrine) inspires the breakdown of glycogen stores. In order to access the energy needed to run and/or fight. During a fear-led response, blood flow to the brain (the brain's access to oxygen is limited in a fear response, an individual is literally not thinking straight, but literally surviving in this state) and intestines is reduced, heart rate and breathing picks up—these changes in the body are attached to the neurohormones to include but not limited to cortisol and norepinephrine. In a study by Yehuda, it is postulated that there is a reduced cortisol response after a traumatic event, this is thought to trigger the release of CRF and norepinephrine which prolongs the stress response. Norepinephrine and cortisol are thought to influence learning (consolidation of memory and retrieval of the trauma) and extinction (turning off) of the fear response (Yehuda 2006).

According to Newton's third law in physics: for every action, there is an equal and opposite reaction. The body and the brain are amazing—if there is a path to turn a function on, then there is also a path to turn it off. In the case of fear, the sympathetic nervous system is the "accelerator or on switch" and the parasympathetic nervous system is the "brake system and/or off switch."

Sympathetic nervous system = getting the fear (stress, anxiety) response to go in the presence of a threat, perceived and/or real.

Parasympathetic nervous system = when the threat (perceived and/or real disappears) kicks in and restores the brain and body back to baseline. Breathing and heart rate theoretically go back to normal, blood flow to brain increases, and the ability to think straight improves.

The routine response to "fear" has been described above. In other words, the body and brains of mostly every human being have undergone this process in the fear response. Again, a point of convergence—a shared human experience.

What happens when fear is unwoven?

What happens when fear is "on" all of the time?

In Chap. 2, the metaphor of Freddy Cougar was given. What happens when it feels like Freddy Cougar is running after you all the time, 24–7, 365 days out of the year? What might it feel like if everyone encountered in any system looked like and/or perceived as Freddy Cougar, 24–7, 365 days per year?

From a neurobiological perspective, fear that never turns off = trauma.

Lanius et al. (2010a, b) addresses fear conditioning and early life vulnerabilities and provides one potential answer to the question of what happens when fear is on all the time. The article suggests that there are two pathways that can lead to emotion dysregulation and eventually posttraumatic stress disorder (fear that never turns off). The first pathway suggests that emotion dysregulation as a result of the constant fear is strengthened and augmented (also known as fear conditioning). The second pathway considers "the things that might happen to individuals" to include childhood trauma, poverty, etc. (the potential threats to brain development discussed in Chap. 1 of this textbook) and the development of emotion dysregulation. Both

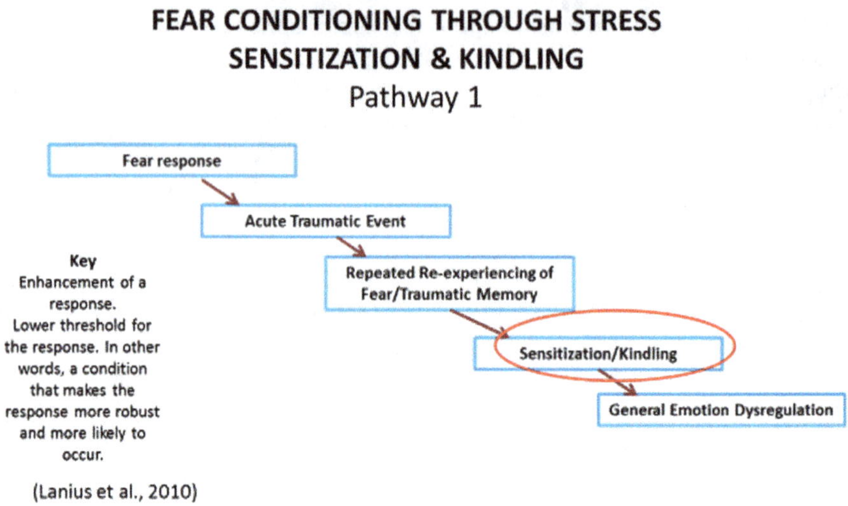

Fig. 3.3 Lanius et al. (2010a, b). Fear conditioning—pathway 1

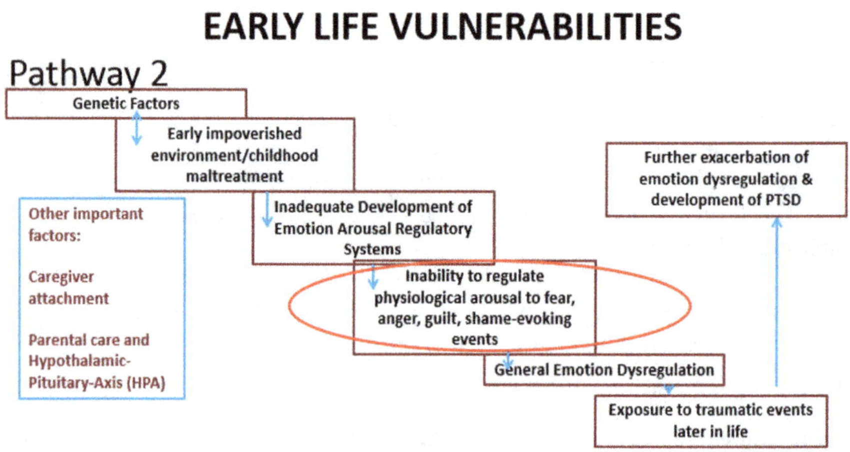

Fig. 3.4 Lanius et al. (2010a, b). Fear conditioning—pathway 2

paths as outlined by Lanius et al. result in emotion dysregulation and long-term effects of trauma. In understanding these early vulnerabilities and their impact has led to greater consideration for prevention. If early exposure to trauma is limited, then the risk of emotion dysregulation might decrease (Figs. 3.3 and 3.4).

Three key brain areas involved in the fear conditioning response according to Lanius et al. (2010a):

1. Medial Prefrontal Cortex (mPFC)—cortical aspect of the brain, top brain.
2. Amygdala—midbrain.
3. Anterior Cingulate Cortex (ACC)—cortical aspect of the brain, top brain.

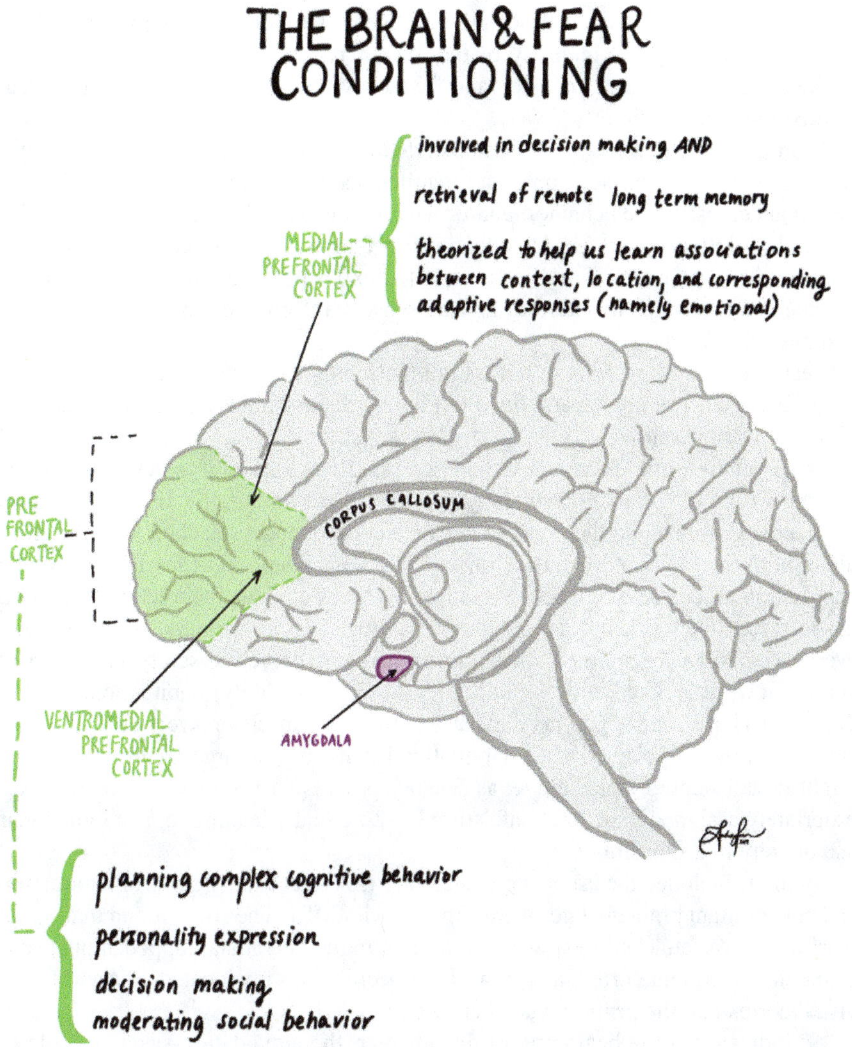

Fig. 3.5 Fear conditioning and the medial prefrontal cortex, amygdala, and anterior cingulate cortex. Printed with permission. Copyright Audrey A. Tran

These three areas of the brain (make up the fear circuitry) mediate and strengthen the "fear response" in the fear conditioning process (Fig. 3.5).

Fear acquisition = fear is acquired and is a form of conditioning.

In 1977, Rachman wrote the following about fear acquisition as a form of conditioning. Fears are acquired and that the process of acquisition is a form of conditioning. Neutral stimuli which are associated with a fear or pain-producing state of affairs develop fearful qualities. The strength of the fear is determined by the number of repetitions of the association between the pain/fear experience and the stimuli and also by the intensity of the fear or pain experienced in the presence of the stimuli. Exposure, intensity, and frequency are all essential elements in fear acquisition/conditioning.

Multiple studies were able to demonstrate the fear response generated in animals (mostly by use of electric shock) and manifest as avoidance behavior, physiologic disturbance, disruptive behavior, and/or the combination of the three.

Fear Habituation—refers to reductions in **fear** over time/repeated exposure, a decrease in response to stimuli over repeated exposures. Habituation is a learning mechanism that helps to filter out myriad sensory information that comes our way (Ramaswami 2014).

Fear is triggered by what is sensed (all the senses to include sight, touch, smell, taste, feel). Sensory input as outlined in Fig. 3.1 demonstrates how fear is mediated based on what is sensed.

When a new stimulus emerges, the brain rapidly processes it to determine if it is dealing with a threat and/or reward (Avery and Blackford 2016). If the stimulus is not deemed a threat and there are no negative consequences attached to it (the stimulus), both the brain and behavior of human beings adapt accordingly—this is the habituation process in a nutshell. An article by Avery et al. on the role of habituation in social fear, the following is highlighted: habituation is a core human process; however, variation has been noted in fast (associated with perceived safety and security) and/or slow (associated with unfamiliarity and lack of safety) habituation. Further differences have been appreciated in early in infancy. Article of Avery et al. accentuates the following point: as rapid habituation is adaptive, failure to habituate rapidly might be considered maladaptive, as sensory processing resources are being inappropriately assigned to neutral, safe stimuli—potentially leading to misaligned fear and anxiety in a safe situation.

Methods included the use of a repeated face task to cue the process of habituation and concomitant brain changes were captured via fMRI. The study found that social fearfulness was attached to slower habituation in the amygdala, hippocampus, ventromedial prefrontal cortex, a region of the occipital cortex located adjacent to the visual cortex and the primary visual cortex.

As indicated at the beginning of this chapter, the amygdala plays a key role in mediating and interpreting the fear response, and is part of the limbic system and connected to various other parts of the brain in its response to the threat perceived and/or real. The study conducted by Avery and colleagues highlighted that differences in habituation may lie within the relationship between the amygdala and the visual cortex.

Some of the conclusions have further implications for how early exposure to trauma and stress, insecure versus secure attachments as a child may contribute heavily to variation in habituation capacity. This study serves as another compelling example of how early exposure to trauma impacts the thinking parts of the developing brain and can effectively change "how" threat is perceived and interpreted.

Fear extinction—learned inhibition of retrieval of previously acquired memories (Furini et al. 2014).

In Furini's review, extinction is viewed as one more form of learning with multiple paths of which one could lead to forgetting. Additionally, the review explains that fear extinction is initiated and maintained by interactions between the hippocampus, basolateral amygdala, and ventromedial prefrontal cortex.

Protracted exposure to fear (fear that does not turn off) not only gets stronger, but it can transform into posttraumatic stress disorder (PTSD). In the article entitled Emotion Modulation in PTSD: Clinical and Neurobiological Evidence for a Dissociative subtype, Lanius et al. go into greater detail about the impact and outcome of prolonged fear on brain function and behavioral manifestations. The article highlights two forms of PTSD to include classic non-dissociative and dissociative. Classic PTSD is characterized by re-experiencing, avoidance, and a constant sense of seeking safety and/or being on watch. From the brain perspective, classic PTSD symptoms can be explained as a failure of corticolimbic inhibition or undermodulation—which means that the top part of the brain (the cortex responsible for impulse control, exercising good judgment, etc.) loses its ability to modulate and/or control the limbic system (the part of the brain responsible for drives, emotions, reward). In the absence of top-down control from the cortex, the emotional side of the brain is left to run wild. Aggression, impulse control, and exercising good judgment may be compromised in the context of prolonged exposure to fear (Siever 2008). The amygdala overrides the cortex (bottom brain overrides the top brain) = trauma. Keep this concept in mind as it is a common theme that will be referred to throughout this textbook.

Lanius and colleagues also make a compelling argument for the dissociative form of PTSD.

"Fear on all the time" can lead to posttraumatic stress disorder

Dissociation includes fragmentation of memory (remember the role of the hippocampus in the fear response) and fragmented consciousness, identity, body awareness, and perception of self and external surroundings. From a brain perspective, dissociation is theorized to occur in the context of overmodulation or what is deemed corticolimbic inhibition. The cortex's top-down control of the limbic system (amygdala and other structures) is too strong. Many have theorized that dissociation as an immediate response to trauma may seem protective as it allows for detachment from overwhelming emotional content. Limited ability to retrieve memory and/or alterations in memory as indicated above not only involves the cortex over controlling the limbic system, but it too is theorized to involve cortisol and norepinephrine. The article also consolidated the findings of several studies on dissociation, which suggested that persons with chronic psychological, sexual, and physical trauma as well as neglect (including parental unavailability) were more likely to experience dissociation.

Science has advanced to the point of being able to move beyond animal models to be able to physically study the human brain via functional Magnetic Resonance Imaging (fMRI). In a few studies, the neural circuitry of dissociative versus non-dissociative PTSD was investigated with fMRI and script-driven imagery. In script-driven imagery, patients develop a narrative of their traumatic experience and are then asked to read it when they are in the scanner. While reading, they are asked to try and recall the traumatic memory as best and as clearly as they can while simultaneously the MRI scanner measures oxygen use in distinct parts of the brain. The results of these studies demonstrated that different responses can occur in recalling traumatic memories for persons with chronic PTSD. In the case of chronic PTSD to include re-experiencing, hyperarousal, fMRI imaging confirmed undermodulation—the cortex's loss of control over the limbic system. In the case of the dissociative form of PTSD, fMRI confirmed overmodulation—the cortex's excessive control of the limbic system. The implications of Lanius's studies are many, to include changing the treatment approach for persons experiencing dissociation.

For the purpose of this textbook, understanding the neurobiology of trauma should compel systems that serve youth to rethink their strategies of engagement. There is legitimate evidence that trauma changes how the brain works. Systems must respond to this (Lanius et al. 2010b; Kean 2008; Orr et al. 2000).

Stress created in mouse models and the use of dexamethasone as a potential treatment to prevent progression to PTSD after a traumatic event

In one of the many animal models on fear acquisition and extinction, T. Sawamura et al. demonstrated the dexamethasone changes Fkbp5 regulation and fear extinction. FKBP5 gene encodes for the protein FK506 binding protein 5 (FKBP5), which regulates the sensitivity of the glucocorticoid receptor (GR) (Binder 2009), and is involved in hypothalamic–pituitary–adrenal axis (HPA axis) activity during the stress response. The GR is an important element of the mammalian stress response system and a primary binding site for cortisol (corticosterone in rodents).

In this study, they created stressful traumatic conditions (similar to stressful traumatic conditions in humans that impact the HPA axis) in mice through a process called immobilization stress with fear conditioning a week later. Mice were tested for levels of conditioned fear expression/EXT in standard rodent modular test chamber.

For mice exposed to stress through immobilization = higher levels of corticosterone after fear conditioning compared to controls (in this case mice who were not exposed to immobilization stress).

Dexamethasone has been shown to modulate stress responses and cortisol levels in human subjects. In this study, when dexamethasone was administered to mice, there appeared to be a dose-dependent impact on cortisol levels.

Equally, dexamethasone appeared to have some epigenetic impact on stress pathways via methylation of the FBKB5 gene, which has implications for how to prevent or reduce the long-term sequel of trauma (Binder 2009).

Why is this important?

The study highlights several key points to include

- Stress can lead to trauma (fear that never turns off) and is mediated through the hypothalamic axis.
- The salience of epigenetics (the environmental impact on genes) demonstrated by dexamethasone modulating genes through methylation.

Fear conditioning = the fear threshold lowered

Fear conditioning might be better understood in the context of building muscles. To build up muscles (protracted exposure to lifting weights and/or weight resistance training), they must first be broken down and they emerge stronger.

Muscle-building process is like fear conditioning, the longer the brain is exposed to fear, there is a breakdown and the fear response augmented (or comes back stronger). The threshold for a fear response is effectively lowered—fear becomes the predominant response.

Natural fear response unchecked = traumatization

"Traumatization occurs when both internal and external resources are inadequate to cope with external threat."—Van der Kolk, 1989

Fear unchecked = Trauma.

Trauma unmanaged increases the risk for aggression and violence. In Siever's article, the neurobiology of aggression and violence—aggression and violence are described as the failure of "top-down" control systems in the prefrontal cortex to modulate the limbic system, namely, the amygdala.

Bremner's (2006) article reviews traumatic stress and the effects on the brain. One of the studies highlighted in this review included 19 healthy women. Eight of the 19 women had a history of severe childhood abuse and a diagnosis of PTSD and 11 of the 19 women did not have a history of childhood abuse nor did they have PTSD. Participants were told that they were going to be subject to electric shocks and viewing images on a screen (considered the conditioned stimulus) during the collection of PET scan (measurement of cerebral blood flow) and psychophysiology (measurement of heart rate and skin conductance) data. Their participants had data collected in three phases to include habituation, acquisition, and extinction conditions.

In the habituation phase, subjects were exposed to a blue square on screen (noted as the conditioned response) for 4 s, followed by 6 s of a blank screen. This process was repeated eight times over 80 s in two separate blocks (separated by 8 min). A PET image was obtained at the beginning of each of the blocks.

In the fear acquisition phase, the blue square (conditioned stimulus) was paired with an electric shock to the forearm (unconditioned stimulus). There were eight pairs of conditioned and unconditioned stimulus presentations, at 10 s intervals for each of the two blocks.

In the extinction phase, subjects had electric shocks delivered randomly in the absence of the blue square as opposed to intervals.

The results of this study, PTSD subjects compared to controls had higher levels of anxiety, fear, dissociation, distress, and substance use disorders. Acquisition of fear was associated with increased skin conductance responses to conditioned stimulus conditions.

In PET imaging, PTSD subjects showed activation of the bilateral amygdala during fear acquisition compared to controls. Non-PTSD subjects showed an area of activation in the region of the left amygdala. In PTSD subjects, there was decreased orbitofrontal cortical blood flow during the extinction phase. Of note, when PTSD versus non-PTSD subjects were compared directly, PTSD subjects had greater activation of the left amygdala during fear conditioning compared to the control.

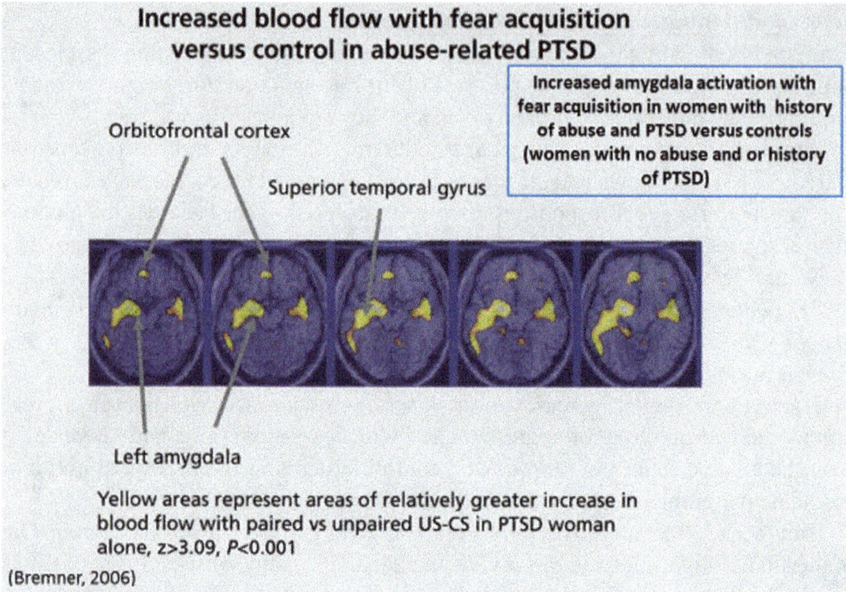

Fig. 3.6 Increased blood flow and activity in the amgydala and less blood flow in the orbitofrontal cortex in acute and chronic stress. Imaging proof of real human brains to support the working theory that "bottom brain" survival overwhelms "top-down" control in acute and prolonged stress

Orbitofrontal cortex had limited blood flow in the PET scan. The finding of decreased activity in the orbitofrontal cortex during extinction and increased activity of the limbic system during the fear acquisition phase is consistent with the undermodulation theory in various other studies on fear—which translates into a fear response that doesn't turn off resulting in PTSD. All accelerator and no brakes. Again, human imaging (PET and fMRI) is now able to confirm the findings from animal model neural circuits on fear (Fig. 3.6).

Early and prolonged exposure to stress and brain changes

Bruce Perry's study on altered brain development following global neglect highlighted the consequences of sensory deprivation *(defined by minimal exposure to language, touch, and/or social interactions)* on neurodevelopment in neglected children. In this study, children of ages 0–17 were referred to a trauma specialty clinic for evaluation by Child Protective Services and/or other agencies serving children following abuse and/or neglect.

For the purpose of appropriate placement, treatment planning, and service provision, the following evaluations were completed during the assessment of the young people in this study to include physical, developmental, neuropsychiatric, ample *pre and perinatal history was obtained* to include growth measurements, and charts were reviewed for prenatal drug exposure.

In this study, neglect was considered global with sensory deprivation as defined above.

Then there was chaotic neglect which was defined as physical, emotional, social, or cognitive neglect.

Number of neglected children = 122.
122 participants were divided into four groups.
Global neglect = 40.
Global neglect with prenatal drug exposure = 18.
Chaotic neglect = 36.
Chaotic neglect with prenatal drug exposure = 28.

Some neuroimaging was done in some of the evaluations, and these images were reviewed in retrospect.
Results
In the area of growth, in specific comparing Frontal-Occipital Circumference (FOC)—for children who were globally neglected, decreased brain growth was appreciated compared to global neglect with prenatal drug exposure, chaotic neglect, and chaotic neglect with prenatal drug exposure.

In the area of neuroimaging, 3 of 26 scans were deemed abnormal in the chaotic neglect group. Whereas 11 of the 17 in the global neglect group had significant brain changes.

Most of the readings demonstrated enlarged ventricles (a sign of decreased cortical brain volume) and/or cortical atrophy (volume of the cortex, top brain significantly decreased).

Perry also infamously compares CT scans of a normal 3-year-old brain (absent of neglect) versus a 3-year-old brain, who experienced extreme neglect as defined by this study. The significant decrease in cortical brain volume and increased ventricle size in the brain of the extreme neglect child is striking compared to the brain of the child who did not experience neglect.

This 1997 study established that early exposure to trauma and/or toxic stress in the form of neglect or poor nutrition had deleterious effects on the developing brain.

Why might the youth be more likely to experience this phenomenon?

Adverse Childhood Experiences

Felitti and Anda's adverse childhood experiences (ACE) study revealed a strong correlation between childhood trauma and behavioral and physical health. The ACE study grew from an obesity study through Kaiser Permanente in the 1980s. Felitti, a preventative medicine physician at Kaiser at the time, noted a cohort that began to precipitously drop out of the study after they had lost a certain amount of weight. He suspected that there was more to the weight gain than the original obesity study failed to consider. In follow up with the study drop out cohort, there were higher rates of depression, anxiety, and trauma noted. As the investigatory process progressed in the mid-1990s, Felitti joined forces with Anda (who worked at the Centers for Disease Control) to survey a larger group, to gain a deeper understanding of their childhood experiences. They assessed over 17,000 participants with the following demographics: majority Caucasian, middle class, insured, educated, and employed. Ten specific areas were assessed through what is now called the ACE Survey;

Physical/sexual/emotional abuse, physical/emotional neglect, exposure to domestic violence, household mental illness/substance use, divorce, and/or separation of parents and household member incarcerated. The ACE survey is designed as "yes" or "no"—for the ten questions spanning the ten subject areas mentioned above, a "yes" = a score of 1 and a "no" = 0 points, there is a total of 10 points possible. Over 87% of participants had one adverse childhood experience. An ACE score of 4 or more translated into increased risk for chronic behavioral and physical health conditions (Felitti et al. 1998).

Felitti and Anda contend adverse childhood experiences influence health and well-being throughout the life span from conception to death in the form of a pyramid, the factors on the pyramid from *bottom to top*:

At the base of the pyramid is early and prolonged exposure to toxic stress and trauma (divorce, poverty, poor nutrition, abandonment) called ***adverse childhood experiences***.

Just above adverse childhood experiences, second from the base is ***disrupted neurodevelopment***—early exposure to toxic stress and trauma has a direct impact on how the brain develops. Recall Chap. 1 of this textbook and all of the potential threats to normal development, namely, cortical development (top brain which impacts early learning, emotion regulation, and impulse control).

Just above disrupted neurodevelopment is ***social, emotional, and cognitive impairment.*** When the brain does not develop normally, there are behavioral, emotional, and cognitive consequences.

Just above social, emotional, and cognitive impairment is ***adoption of health risk behaviors***, poor judgement, and impulse control.

Just above adoption of health risk behaviors are disease, ***disability, and social problems***.

At the top of the pyramid (above disability and social problems) is an ***early death***.

Recall that adverse childhood experiences were birthed from the following demographic, majority Caucasian, educated, insured, employed, and middle class. The ACE scores were significant in this demographic, with a concomitant increase in the adoption of high-risk behaviors that lead to chronic health conditions, which impact social functioning, leading to an early death. Now imagine applying the ACE survey to a wider demographic to include traditionally marginalized communities with higher instances of poverty, food insecurity, discrimination, and racism. There have been several spin-off ACE studies that do add the aforementioned demographics and it was noted, overwhelmingly, that ACE scores were much higher under these conditions with a more intense negative impact on physical and mental health.

The original ACE survey was performed in persons >18. Given the nature of the questions asked in the survey would avoid employing the ACE survey with youth under the age of 16. As a clinician whose focus is on trauma, a notable trend is that ACE surveys are administered, very intense memories and feeling emerge and there is no structure in place to help contain what is unearthed. This results in the significant emotional disruption. Many systems have come to appreciate ACEs and are trying to integrate them, which is wonderful. The management process is lacking. To alleviate the phenomenon of unearthing without support would recommend other methods to get at some of the information an ACE survey would provide. Identifying an active adult/guardian in a young person's life <16 to inquire about past trauma history is warranted and asking to administer the ACE survey to that identified adult is optimal. In engaging responsible adults and/or family attached to youth, be careful not to come off as accusatory and/or judgmental. Often systems inadvertently blame and shame adults for what they believe is less than good parenting or guardianship. The goal is to move far away from blame, shame, judgment, and guilt and move to understanding openness, partnering, and serving. Often, youth are managed in a vacuum with very little consideration for the fact that someone loves them and wants to wholeheartedly participate in seeing them get better. This will be addressed in subsequent chapters.

Chapter 2 of this textbook is wrestled with defining culture, a major step in moving toward cultural responsivity. Additionally, Chap. 2 discusses the culture of a system, which is influenced by social and economic conditions. Different systems (education, health care, community, criminal justice) discriminate disproportionately and with varying levels of intensity depending on the demographic it involves. In the case of youth, some systems designed to help end up contributing to greater exposure to toxic stress and trauma. Every system that serves youth should operate with the following presupposition: at some point, something happened in this youth's life that might have been stressful and/or traumatic. With this knowledge, the system then has a responsibility to behave and engage youth accordingly. Most systems ultimately want change. For example, in education, the goal is to decrease the achievement gap; in criminal justice, the goal is to reduce recidivism; in community, the goal is reduced instances of violence, house-lessness, and substance use. If the system seeks change from individuals that utilize it, then the system must change. What has been done in the past has not resulted in the change hoped for.

Step by step

- Presupposition is that something stressful, harmful, and/or traumatic may be happening or has happened in the life of a youth. This should automatically change approach.
- A responsible caring adult and/or guardian should be identified for youth.
- Be careful not to shame, blame, and/or judge the adult/guardian attached to the youth.
- One approach is respecting the adult/guardian as the expert on their child. As an expert, they have something to offer in the partnership of supporting their youth for change.
- There should be a clear and transparent explanation as to why they (adult/guardian) are being asked a set of questions and they should know what the information they are giving will be used for.
- Asking open-ended, nonjudgmental questions.
- Avoid assumptions.
- Practice reflective listening.
- Reiterate with great frequency that the goal is partnership for good, establishment for a coalition, and network of support to assist them and their child.

Exercise 3.1

Case example: A 16-year-old girl enrolled in an alternative high school. Counselors and teachers are concerned about poor academic performance and aggressive behavior toward peers. Her teacher would mostly redirect and remind her to be kind, but because of the number of students in the class couldn't give more than that. Four weeks into the new semester, her behavior intensified and upgraded to consistent bullying. The teacher wrote her up and sent her to Principal's office with this note: "I have reached a point where I don't know what to do. She is usually re-directable, but she started bullying other students and I cannot allow such behavior. Something must be done, but I am not sure what."

Consider all that you've read and learned so far about brain development and threats to its process in Chap. 1; cultural responsivity and the social and economic drivers of culture in Chap. 2; and the connection of fear, trauma, aggression, and adverse childhood experiences (and their impact on the brain) in this chapter and answer the following questions related to this case example:

- If you were the Principal, what is the first question you ask this youth?
- What factors should you consider in managing, helping, partnering?
- Who should you involve in the care of this youth?
- Given this youth's age, where are they in terms of brain development?
- What are the potential threats to brain development both now and in childhood?

This youth would typically get detention and even considered for suspension.

- Is detention and/or suspension an appropriate response? Why or why not?
- What is the alternative?
- How might the system (in this case, the education system) help this youth heal?

Applying Trauma-Informed Approaches and Practices as a path to healing

Trauma- informed approaches are one way to help get youth out of the bottom part of their brain (brain stem–limbic area that oversees emotional, unconscious, irrational, impulsive, lacking judgment) to the top part of their brain (cortex; oversees impulse control, thinking before you act, exercising good judgment, sophisticated cognitive task, emotion regulation).

This chapter outlined the neurobiology of fear and connected "fear that never turns off" to trauma (fear acquisition through fear conditioning). Further, it was highlighted that fear conditioning (fear that does not turn off) can lead to conditions like posttraumatic stress disorder.

The parts of the brain involved in fear (a natural response until it is not) include the thalamus (represents the sensory aspect of fear), amygdala (emotional aspect of fear), hippocampus (memory aspect of fear), and frontal and temporal cortex (cognitive aspect of fear).

Fear conditioning (fear acquisition) involves the following parts of the brain: medial prefrontal cortex, anterior cingulate cortex, and the amygdala.

Posttraumatic stress disorder impacts the brain in the following way: failure of corticolimbic inhibition, which means that the cortex (rational sophisticated brain) doesn't impose its regulatory top-down control on the limbic system (irrational, emotional brain).

Brain development happens from the bottom-up and the inside-out. Brain development happens from conception to about the age of 26, which means that the sophisticated, rational brain is the last to cement. Even in "normal" development, society can anticipate a young person who at times acts impulsively without much thinking and is intermittently irrational and developmentally appropriate.

However, if you superimpose early and protracted exposure to stress and trauma on the already developing brain, it is easier to understand emotional dysregulation, aggression, compromised cognition, and learning. This is the level of understanding that systems must move to in order to optimally serve youth. Systems must accommodate this knowledge and change if they expect to facilitate change in youth.

What does it mean to be trauma informed?

- Understanding the neurobiological, social, physical, and psychological aspects of trauma.
  These elements have been outlined in this chapter.
  Neurobiological: fear as a natural response to responding to threat (perceived or real) that can transition to "fear that never turns off" = trauma.
  Physical: as outlined by the ACE's study, protracted toxic stress and trauma can lead to decreased immunity and a higher metabolic profile.
  Social: the impact of poverty, racism, poor nutrition, poor access to health, limited educational system, disproportionate involvement in the criminal judicial system.
  Psychological: emotion dysregulation, posttraumatic stress disorder.
- Changing the way questions are posed: instead of "what's wrong?" ask "what happened?"—changes the way we engage one another.
  If we consider the way in which systems were designed and maintained, the (systems) have historically been built from a deficit (what's wrong) perspective. For example, schools were built with detention and suspension (the unspoken expectation that some youth will require it as opposed); youth juvenile justice system was constructed with the expectation that some youth would require and further terms like felon, offender, and deviant are employed to describe them.
  What is the difference between being called a "felon" versus a person who has made a mistake? Narrative therapy provides a framework for answering this question. Narrative therapy is a method of therapy that separates a person from their problem (Etchison 2000). In other words, if a youth is called a felon, it becomes difficult to separate the act from the good that still remains within youth—rendering the motivation and capacity for change limited. However, if youth are deemed individuals who made a mistake, there is room for them to see themselves as capable of good and making a change.
  The language used to engage youth is critical. You can cut off and/or expand a conversation based on how you ask questions. To further illustrate this point, consider the example of several young children playing in a room upstairs. All of a sudden, the adult hears "boom, bang" and then a loud cry. The adult rushes upstairs to assess the situation and finds a broken closet door and several young

children looking sheepishly at them. The first question that most adults ask when they get to the room of chaos is "what did you do?" The reply that is typically given from all young children in the room is "I don't know." They don't know how the closet door got broken or why one of their colleagues is in tears. What is realized at this moment is that the answer was influenced by the question. Underneath the question "what did you do?" is judgment, blame, and fault. Young people do what most human beings would do to avoid trouble and/or blame (which for most is unbearable feeling)—they lie and say, "I don't know." Now the adult and young children have reached an impasse in terms of communication and resolution.

Let's take the same scenario of an adult responding to "boom, bang," a crying child among children and an observed broken closet door. Now the adult reaches the room of young children and instead of asking "what did you do" the adult asks, "is everyone safe?" There is a fundamental difference in tone with the question of safety first. Once safety is established, it can then be followed up with "what happened?' Children in the room begin explaining that they were playing and on accident, one child fell into the closet door breaking it and apologize because they didn't mean it. This is a real scenario by the way. Try asking if everyone is safe the next time there is a room full of children and chaos. Asking a judgment/shame/blame-free question opened up the conversation for greater bidirectional exchange. Children felt safe to respond.

Turns out that this same principle can be applied to youth and adults. Youth can be more thoughtfully engaged when safety is prioritized. Words matter and how we use them (words) matters even more.

- Check underlying assumptions

  In Chap. 2, Schein's work on organizational culture change was highlighted and emphasized checking underlying assumptions as critical in the process of changing systems. However, checking underlying assumptions is a trauma-informed approach because it calls on individuals attached to systems to examine themselves (it compels individuals to shift unconscious processes to conscious awareness); it motivates behavior change.

  If someone made the following blanket statement: "All purple people are bad," what would be the visceral reaction?

  Most folks would probably think why a person would make such a blanket statement. Some people might think, I've never met a purple person, so the statement loses relevance.

  Three hours later, you are on your way home and you spot a purple person. What do you think? Honestly. If honesty is operating, the response likely would be that you would go back to the comment that you heard earlier in the day that "purple people are bad." It would cross your mind and result in some type of behavioral adaption (feeling a little unsafe, questioning in your head). Whether or not you believe that purple people or bad or not, the general blanket statement made earlier

in the day called this idea/thought to question (brought it to consciousness) where it had not prior (you weren't thinking about purple people being bad until it was stated out loud).
This is an example of how narrative can influence assumptions and change behavior.
Being trauma informed implores individuals/systems to check their narratives, check their underlying assumptions as a means of modulating behavior.

- Building greater capacity for empathy (increases one's capacity to mentalize)
Humans are born with the capacity for empathy (to consider what it might be like to walk in someone else's shoes)—in the anterior cingulate cortex. However, empathy is something that must be developed over time. Language acquisition and development is marked in the first 3 years of life. Recall some of the first words uttered from toddlers, words like "mine" predominant. As developing human beings, the goal is to transition from a self-centered, ego-centric approach to become more self-less and consider others. The procurement of empathy happens more efficiently when it is modeled and practiced.
Although there has been controversy over mirror neurons, even the critics agree that they be associated with the process of imitation of behavior. Mirror neurons live in the supplementary motor area, premotor cortex, and primary somatosensory and inferior parietal cortex. The ability to model behavior (and in this case, to see caring for others and model it) improves as the brain develops.
Bringing it home: the more youth observe and experience kindness, selflessness, compassion, love, the greater the chances are that they will model it (mirror neurons get fired up and help facilitate this process).
- Placing humanity at the center, considering points of convergence
This book chapter started out by posing a question: "Is there anyone who has never been afraid?" The predominant response to this question is "no." If you are a human being with a beating heart and a conscious, you have and/or will at some point in your life be afraid and/or experience fear. This reality (that all human beings have and/or will experience fear) was deemed a point of convergence (an experience shared by most). A racing heart, the feeling of suffocation and doom, and the inability to think straight in a state fear is understood because most human beings have experienced it. It supports the idea that if it has been experienced then it can be understood. This point of convergence, shared experience, puts our collective humanity on display.
Being trauma informed places humanity at the center of narrative, behavior, and action. Being trauma informed calls on the system to actively and intentionally seek out points of convergence.
In the case of youth, if "fear" can be understood as a shared human phenomenon, then "fear that doesn't turn off" also known as trauma can be understood.
- Inherently supports culturally responsivity
Trauma informed includes being sensitive to narrative, checking underlying assumptions, building greater capacity for empathy, placing humanity at the center, and considering points of convergence. When trauma-informed approaches are employed as described it does the work of deconstructing powerful social

constructs so that the system might more clearly see, acknowledge, and serve youth—this is ultimate cultural responsivity.

Exercise 3.2 Remember the Rocky description at the beginning of this chapter?
Why the Rocky moment?
What are the implications for systems that serve youth?

- Rocky is just like…. most youth who enter a system anticipating service. They, like Rocky, are yelling out (metaphorically speaking) "I am afraid, alright".
- If young people are represented as Rocky. The system (that would be you) should respond and be like Adrian.
- Adrian validated Rocky, created safety, de-escalated, and helped him to more effectively process his fear.
- Without intervention: fear-laden, traumatized, aggressive Youth become fear-laden, traumatized, aggressive Adults.

Practical application(s)
Build Trauma-Informed ***people*** in order to ….

- Build trauma-informed systems of care.
- Change the way systems engage youth—being concerned with "what happened?" instead of "what is wrong."
- Create safe environments for youth by establishing trauma-informed spaces. Trauma-Informed Oregon (TIO), an organization committed to disseminating the latest research on trauma-informed practices and approaches and inspiring systems to learn about and adopt these practices, has thoughtful assessments that can be accessed online by visiting the Trauma-Informed Oregon website. Several self-assessment and planning protocol assessments can be found that contains the types of questions that should be considered in establishing safe, trauma-informed spaces and organizational culture.
  The spaces in which we engage youth should be safe and inspire fear, stress, and trauma reduction. These assessments (one for inpatient and one for outpatient) are thoughtful and help organizations/systems think through how they reimagine their space to promote healing and reduce trauma.
- Mindfulness as a trauma-informed practice for youth and for systems.
  I trained and coached a cohort of Multnomah County Department of Community Justice Parole Officer (POs) and Junior Court Counselors (JCCs) to employ and practice mindfulness before they engage youth in supervision. The results have been phenomenal as the youth, POs and JCCs endorse that the use of mindfulness helps to effectively bring the temperature down, reduce anxiety, and create safety. All parties involved benefit.

Mindfulness, what the research says
The simplistic version of how mindfulness positively impacts the brain. There is a healthy shift from unconscious-amygdala-mid/bottom brain predominant responses to improved conscious-cortex-top brain rational responses. The prefrontal cortex is strengthened in its ability to exert appropriate top-down control of the amygdala = calm, emotional regulation, rational thinking (Fig. 3.7).

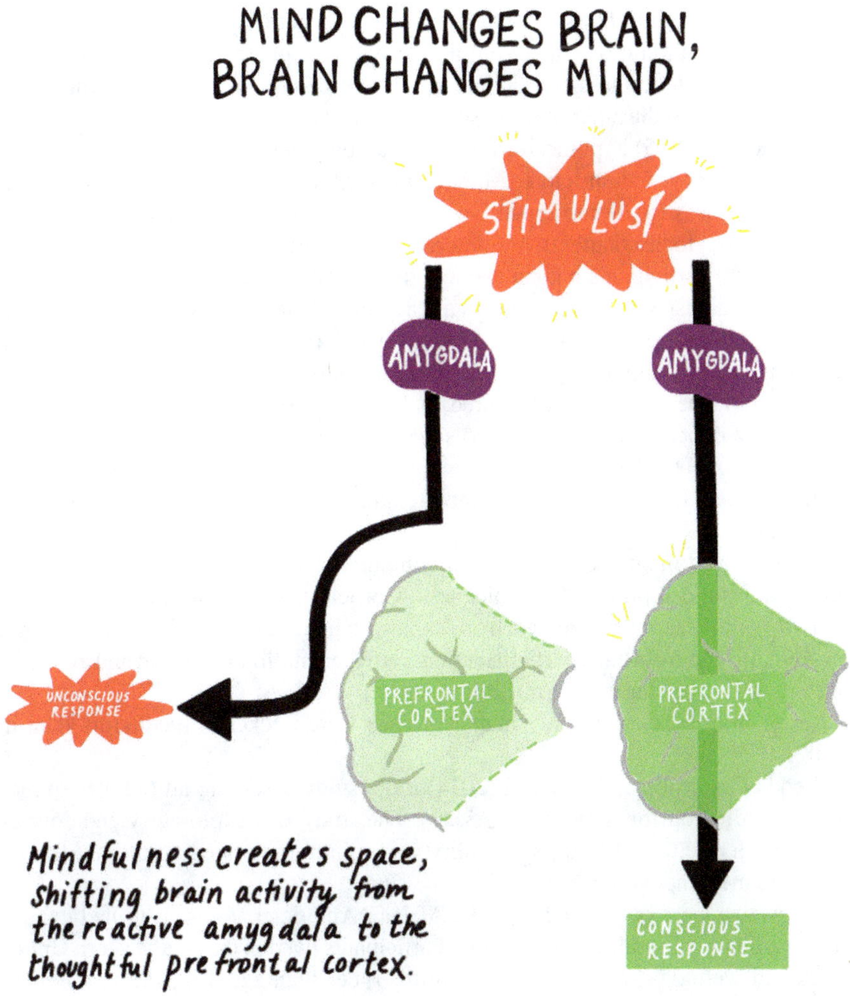

Fig. 3.7 Mindfulness, when practiced consistently, helps to heal the brain from trauma. Printed with permission. Copyright Audrey A. Tran

Mindfulness studies show…

- Lowered intensity and frequency of negative affect, ability to control emotions (Brown and Ryan 2003; Chambers et al. 2008).
- Reduced anxiety (Shapiro et al. 1998).
- More adaptive responding to stress (Davidson et al. 2003).
- Decreases in difficulties regulating emotions (Robins et al. 2011).
- Less prolonged physiological reactivity to emotional stimuli, in the form of decreased autonomic arousal (skin conductance response) (Ortner et al. 2007).

How long must mindfulness be practiced and with what frequency?

There is not a ton of literature out that provides a specific length of time and/or frequency for mindfulness to start the process of changing and healing the brain. There are some studies that offer a useful framework.

Lazar et al. (2005) hypothesized that meditation practice might result in changes in the brain's physical structure. Magnetic resonance imaging was used to assess cortical thickness in 20 participants with extensive insight meditation experience, which involves focused attention to internal experiences.

Lazar's 20 participants had an average range of 2–16 years of employing meditation/mindfulness with an average frequency of 2–10 h per week. All participants in the study were required to do at least a 1-week insight meditation retreat (with involved 10 h of meditation per day, high dose meditation).

The treatment group was compared to 15 control participants with no meditation or yoga experience noted. Controls were matched for age, sex, race, and years of education. Both the treatment and control group were deemed physically and psychologically healthy. All participants (treatment group and controls) were 100% Caucasian.

Sophisticated magnetic imaging and computational approaches were employed to measure the cerebral cortical thickness. Cortical thickness was estimated from the two magnetizations prepared from rapid gradient echo (MPRAGE) structural images collected from each participant that were then motion-corrected and averaged together to form a single high-resolution image.

Result in brief, cortical gray matter regions were thicker in meditators than in controls.

Woods-Giscombe and Gaylord (2014) did a study assessing attitudes on mindfulness meditation for African-Americans. The study was exploratory and considered the intersection of faith, spirituality, and mindfulness meditation in African-American men and women (N = 15) in the study.

Interviews were completed with 15 African-American adults, who had experience practicing mindfulness meditation. Participants lived in the southeastern United States and were 24–57 years old (two-thirds older than age 40). The sample was composed of 12 females and 3 males. Religious backgrounds represented include Christian ($n = 6$), Buddhist ($n = 3$), and nondenominational ($n = 1$). One participant reported an affiliation with "Religious Sciences" and described this as a belief system based on the science of metaphysics. Three reported that they were not affiliated with any particular religious faith. One participant did not respond to the question about religious affiliation. All participants were college educated. Overall, participants had an average of 9 years of experience practicing mindfulness meditation (range 1–30).

Many conclusions were drawn and suggestions for further areas of study provided. Notable was that African-American adults who practice mindfulness meditation were generally enthusiastic about the potential for mindfulness practice among their fellow African-American friends and family to promote health and well-being.

Woods-Giscombe et al. study included the work of Kerrigan et al. (2011) and Sibinga et al. (2011) outlining their qualitative assessment of mindfulness meditation among African-American youth age of 13–21 years (Kerrigan et al. 2011; Sibinga et al. 2011). The punch line is that participants perceived improvements in interpersonal relationships, academic achievement, physical health, and stress reduction (Sibinga et al. 2011). Equally, quantitative data from that study revealed reductions in hostility, general discomfort, and emotional discomfort (Sibinga et al. 2011).

Summary of the impact of mindfulness/meditation from myriad studies
Increased gray matter/cortical thickness in the following key areas:

Prefrontal Cortex—plays a key role in executive functioning such as planning, problem-solving, and emotion regulation.
Anterior Cingulate Cortex (ACC) volume increases—ACC is involved in the fear response, personality expression, empathy, early learning, and attention.
Hippocampus volume increases with mindfulness. The hippocampus plays a role in memory, learning, and fear response.
Amygdala decreases in size, volume.

- Research has demonstrated that the amygdala, which plays a key role in our fear response decreases in brain cell volume after mindfulness practice.

Mindfulness calms areas of the brain that are also associated with fear and trauma
In the introduction to this text, the idea of parallel processes in considering "other" and "self" was mentioned. Mindfulness is an exercise that everyone can benefit from. Individuals within systems are encouraged to practice mindfulness and model it for the youth they seek to serve. Further systems are encouraged to educate youth on the benefits of mindfulness and encourage the practice of it.

There are multiple ways to be mindful and to meditate. Suggest starting out with 1–2 min per day. There are a number of online resources. You can literally google mindfulness and meditation exercises. Here is one tip to get you started working with youth who've experienced trauma:

Start with observational mindfulness—pick an object in the room or in your office to focus your attention on. Look at it directly for 2 min. During that 2-minute window, be conscious of your breathing and your thoughts. Many thoughts will come through your mind, just let them pass, don't entertain them, just allow them to go in and out of your mind. Note the sounds around you. Note your breathing patterns and note your posture and body as you observe.

It may seem awkward at first, but the more you do, the more comfortable you get, the better you begin to feel. Observational mindfulness is one clever way to start the process because it doesn't require you to close your eyes—for many starting the process, safety and trust are issues (making the closing of the eyes a bit more tenuous).

Consider integrating mindfulness into your daily routine.

The practice of mindfulness will benefit you and youth.

Exercise 3.3—Coach Carter moment

At the end of the day, we all want to facilitate change and save lives.

If there is an intentional, genuine commitment to employing trauma-informed practices and approaches, then you might experience what I call "A Coach Carter moment."

In 1999, the movie "Coach Carter" starring Samuel L. Jackson emerged. It is the story of a coach who works for a high school boys' basketball team. The team consisted mainly of males of color. The teams had won several championships and were amazing on the court. However, their life off the court was not as stellar. Coach Carter, played by Samuel L. Jackson, employed drastic measures to get the team to be as concerned with their academics as they had been with sports. The coach ended up locking the gym doors—the team, parents, and the community were all upset, but Coach Carter was determined to help these young men shine and excel. Many of the young men on the basketball team had emerged from adverse childhood experiences and no one had ever expected greatness from them, until Coach Carter came along. The coach's tactics were met with great resistance, but once everyone saw that he wasn't going to budge—things started to shift. The basketball players started to show up to class and began completing homework.

One of the most poignant scenes takes place in the basketball gym when one of the players who hated Coach Carter for forcing him to be great, stood up and thanked the Coach in the end.

This young man stood up and said: (paraphrase) "I want to thank you, Sir. Our greatest fear is not that we are inadequate, but that we are powerful beyond measure…When we let our lights shine, we unconsciously give others permission to do the same. I want to thank you Sir, you saved my life."

Highlights of this scene are the following:

- Young people will respond to environmental cues of and expectations for greatness.
- Young people are looking for adults to see one good thing in them—to see one good thing and develop it.
- Saving someone's life is a result of believing in them **until** they can believe in themselves.

This is quintessential trauma informed—creating the conditions for hope and change.

Questions and discussion

- What is the connection between fear and trauma?
- Name one impact that trauma can have on the brain?
- Can you identify one practice that helps to heal the brain?

References

Avery, S. N., & Blackford, J. U. (2016). Slow to warm up: The role of habituation in social fear. *Social Cognitive and Affective Neuroscience, 11*(11), 1832–1840.

Binder, E. B. (2009). The role of FKBP5, a co-chaperone of the glucocorticoid receptor in the pathogenesis and therapy of affective and anxiety disorders. *Psychoneuroendocrinology, 34,* S186–S195.

Bremner, J. D. (2006). Traumatic stress: Effects on the brain. *Dialogues in Clinical Neuroscience, 8*(4), 445–461.

Brown, K. W., & Ryan, R. M. (2003). The benefits of being present: Mindfulness and its role in psychological well-being. *Journal of Personality and Social Psychology, 84*(4), 822–848.

Chambers, R., et al. (2008). The impact of intensive mindfulness training on attentional control, cognitive style, and affect. *Cognitive Therapy and Research, 32,* 303–322.

Davidson, R. J., Kabat-Zinn, J., Schumacher, J., Rosenkranz, M., Muller, D., Santorelli, S. F., et al. (2003). Alterations in brain and immune function produced by mindfulness meditation. *Psychosomatic Medicine, 65*(4), 564–570.

Etchison, M., et al. (2000). *Review of narrative therapy: Research and utility.* First Published January 1, 2000. Review Article retrieved from: https://doi.org/10.1177/1066480700081009/.

Felitti, V. J., Anda, R. F., Nordenberg, D., Williamson, D. F., Spitz, A. M., Edwards, V., et al. (1998). The relationship of adult health status to childhood abuse and household dysfunction. *American Journal of Preventive Medicine, 14,* 245–258.

Furini, C., et al. (2014). The learning of fear extinction. *Neuroscience and Biobehavioral Reviews, 47,* 670–683.

Keane, T. M. (2008). Posttraumatic stress disorder: Future directions in science and practice. *Journal of Rehabilitation Research and Development, 45,* vii–vix.

Kerrigan, D., Johnson, K., Stewart, M., Magyari, T., Hutton, N., Ellen, J. M., et al. (2011). Perceptions, experiences, and shifts in perspective occurring among urban youth participating in a mindfulness-based stress reduction program. *Complementary Therapies in Clinical Practice, 17,* 96–101.

Lanius, R. A., et al. (2010a, June). Emotion modulation in PTSD: Clinical and neurobiological evidence for dissociative subtype. *American Journal of Psychiatry, 167*(6), 640–647. https://doi.org/10.1176/appi.ajp.2009.09081168.

Lanius, R. A., Frewen, P. A., Vermetten, E., & Yehuda, R. (2010b). Fear conditioning and early life vulnerabilities: Two distinct pathways of emotional dysregulation and brain dysfunction in PTSD. *European Journal of Psychotraumatology, 1.* https://doi.org/10.3402/ejpt.v1i0.5467.

Lazar, S. W., Kerr, C. E., Wasserman, R. H., Gray, J. R., Greve, D. N., Treadway, M. T., et al. (2005). Meditation experience is associated with increased cortical thickness. *Neuroreport, 16*(17), 1893–1897.

Orr, S. P., et al. (2000). Psychophysiological assessment: Clinical applications for PTSD. *Journal of Affective Disorders, 61,* 225–240. [PubMed: 11163424].

Ortner, et al. (2007). Mindulness meditation and reduced emotional interference on cognitive task. *Motivation and Emotion, 31*(4), 271–283.

Rachman, S. (1977). The conditioning theory of fear-acquisition: A critical examination. *Behaviour Research and Therapy, 15,* 375–378 (Pergamon Press. Printed in Great Britain).

Ramaswami, M. (2014). Network plasticity in adaptive filtering and behavioral habituation. *Neuron, 82,* 1216–1229.

Robins, C. J. et al. (2011, December 5). Effects of mindfulness-based stress reduction on emotional experience and expression: A randomized controlled trial. *Journal of Clinical Psychology.*

Sawamura, T., et al. (2016, February). Dexamethasone treatment leads to enhanced fear extinction and dynamic Fkbp5 regulation in Amygdala. *Neuropsychopharmacology: Official Publication of the American College of Neuropsychopharmacology, 41*(3).

Shapiro, S. L., Schwartz, G. E., & Bonner, G. (1998). Effects of mindfulness-based stress reduction on medical and premedical students. *Journal of Behavioral Medicine, 21*(6), 581–599.

Sibinga, E. M., Kerrigan, D., Stewart, M., Johnson, K., Magyari, T., & Ellen, J. M. (2011). Mindfulness-based stress reduction for urban youth. *Journal of Alternative and Complementary Medicine*, *17*, 213–218 [PMC free article] [PubMed].

Siever, L. J. (2008). Neurobiology of aggression and violence. *American Journal of Psychiatry*, *165*, 429–442.

Woods-Giscombé, C. L., & Gaylord, S. A. (2014). The cultural relevance of mindfulness meditation as a health intervention for African Americans: Implications for reducing stress-related health disparities. *Journal of Holistic Nursing: Official Journal of the American Holistic Nurses' Association*, *32*(3), 147–160.

Yehuda, R. (2006). Advances in understanding neuroendocrine alterations in PTSD and their therapeutic implications. *Annals of the New York Academy of Sciences*, *1071*, 137–166.

Chapter 4
Substances of Abuse and the Brain

As mentioned in the first chapter of this textbook, substances of abuse pose a profound public health challenge, especially to the developing brain. "Give the brain a fighting chance" is an appropriate slogan for this chapter. Chapters 1–3 outlined the effects of toxic stress, poor nutrition, limited access to folic acid and Vitamin D, poverty, racism, and discrimination on the developing brain. These types of insults on the body and brain are a form of trauma. Substances of abuse pose a threat to the developing and developed brain and the impact on the brain is similar to trauma. Substances of abuse can limit an individual's access to the top (cortical thinking, compromising cognition, impulse control, exercising good judgement, and emotion regulation) part of the brain, leaving them mostly in the bottom survival part of the brain (poor impulse control, emotional dysregulation, increased proclivity for aggression, and fight/flight or freeze).

In the case of working to impact change in youth, understanding the depth and width of substances of abuse on the brain is key. This chapter is dedicated to outlining the impact of the various substances of abuse on and at critical stages of brain development and making the connection between compromised cognition in the context of substance use. The capacity to change (behavior namely) relies heavily on the cortex (top part of the brain) being functional. Most of the behavior change work in youth is heavily geared toward cognitive behavioral processes. To this end, assessment of cognitive capacity should happen early in the work with youth in order to appropriately manage expectations and support the change process.

By the end of this chapter, you should be able to

- Understand the reward pathway and the developing brain
- Understand the impact of substances on ova, sperm, and developing fetus,
- Distinguish physical dependence from addiction,
- Appreciate cocaine/amphetamine and its impact on the developing brain,
- Comprehend nicotine and its impact on the developing brain
- Know cannabis and its impact on the developing brain,
- Recognize alcohol and its impact on the developing brain
- Realize opioids and its impact on the developing brain

A. Moreland-Capuia, *Training for Change*,
https://doi.org/10.1007/978-3-030-19208-2_4

- Consider hallucinogen's impact on the developing brain
- Appreciate the current understanding of social media and smartphones on the developing brain
- Understand new trends in nonmedical use of benzos and energy drinks,
- Consider a brief exploration of nonmedical use: a worldwide public health threat,
- Pharmacologic management of primary substances of abuse
- Appreciate the importance of cognitive assessment in the case of substance use

Reward Pathway and the Developing Brain

The brain has a pleasure center from which all drives emerge, named the reward center. Scientific literature has made the connection between the pleasure/reward center and substance use. Further, the reward/pleasure center and its connection to novelty-seeking behavior in adolescence have been noted as well. When a pleasurable experience happens (sex, good food), the brain is set up to want to re-experience that feeling of pleasure. The experience is both remembered and desired. There are specific parts of the brain that mediate the pleasure process to include structures like

- Prefrontal cortex (top brain responsible for exercising good judgement, emotion regulation, etc.).
- Nucleus accumbens (active in reward pathway).
- Striatum = caudate, putamen, and ventral striatum. Ventral striatum includes the nucleus accumbens.
- Ventral tegmental area (works with the nucleus accumbens to create feeling of pleasure).
- Amygdala, which imparts agreeable or disagreeable affective colorations to perceptions.
- Hippocampus which facilitates memory of the pleasurable experience.
- Insula gets sensory input from the thalamus and sends signals to several structures found in the limbic system (amygdala, ventral striatum) and the orbitofrontal cortex. The insula is also part of the limbic system theorized to be essential in active pleasure-seeking associated with substances and food.
- Substantia nigra, midbrain structure involved in reward and movement.
- Locus coeruleus (found on the pons of the brain stem) which produces norepinephrine (NE) and is involved in the drive to seek pleasure again and again. *Also involved in responses related to fear and anxiety.*
- Raphe nucleus (cluster of nuclei) in the brain stem which produces serotonin (5HT) and sends to various parts of the brain.

There are specific neurotransmitters responsible for mediating the pleasure response/reward pathway in the context of substance use:

- Dopamine is released from the nucleus accumbens to the prefrontal cortex—dopamine increases pleasure drive.
- Serotonin is also released and is thought to serve as a way to modulate or dampen the pleasure drive. Again, for every action, there is an equal and opposite reaction.

- Glutamate (excitatory neurotransmitter) receptors play a key role in learning, memory, and communication between neurons. Glutamate also regulates dopamine release in the nucleus accumbens.
- GABA (inhibitory neurotransmitter) receptors mediate stress and anxiety response. GABA also modulates dopamine in the reward/pleasure pathway (Fig. 4.1).

Dopamine projections in reward

- Ventral tegmental area (VTA) has dopaminergic projections to the brain stem, limbic area, and prefrontal cortex.
- Substantia nigra has dopaminergic projections to the striatum.

Serotonin projections in reward

- Raphe nucleus projects to the cortex (prefrontal to occipital), limbic structures, and striatum.

Worthy of repeating is that the brain develops from the bottom-up and inside-out. Parts of the brain responsible for good decision-making, planning, and impulse control are still in development in youth and adolescence compared to midbrain/bottom brain structures like the limbic system and the reward pathway that are more developed. This leaves youth more susceptible to being driven by midbrain structure and limbic system (more impulsive, greater desire for pleasurable and new experiences, poor planning, etc.). The top part of the brain, prefrontal cortex, is responsible for keeping the mid and bottom part of the brain in check. The prefrontal cortex and other cortical structures help individuals to stop at one piece of cake (impulse control), etc. When the prefrontal cortex is not optimally functioning as the top-down control (brake), the drive for pleasure and impulse can dominate. It turns into a discussion of the top brain being limited in its ability to modulate the bottom brain.

Making the connection, the parts of the brain implicated in fear and trauma are implicated in the reward pathway too.

The desire for pleasurable experiences is associated with novelty-seeking/risk-taking behaviors in adolescence. Several studies have made the connection between the two, and a quick review increases understanding of the neurobiological underpinnings of adolescent behavior and perhaps offers a means of better managing expectations and more meaningfully constructing supportive environments for youth.

In an article by Walker et al. on adolescence and reward, the following was asserted, changes in the reward pathway (mesolimbic pathway) is a part of adolescent development and increases sensitivity to increased risk-taking behaviors like substance use. Additionally, the article points out that changes in the reward pathways in adolescence are influenced by neural pathways, endocrine (hormonal), and environmental cues. The article highlights the fact that the medical prefrontal cortex plays an important role in reward-directed behaviors and more than likely contributes to cognitive development during adolescence. Of note, a key brain change in adolescence is dopamine projections in the prefrontal cortex and dopamine receptor expression in the mesocorticolimbic system (dopamine projections from the VTA to the cortex and limbic system). Rat studies have demonstrated the impact of puberty

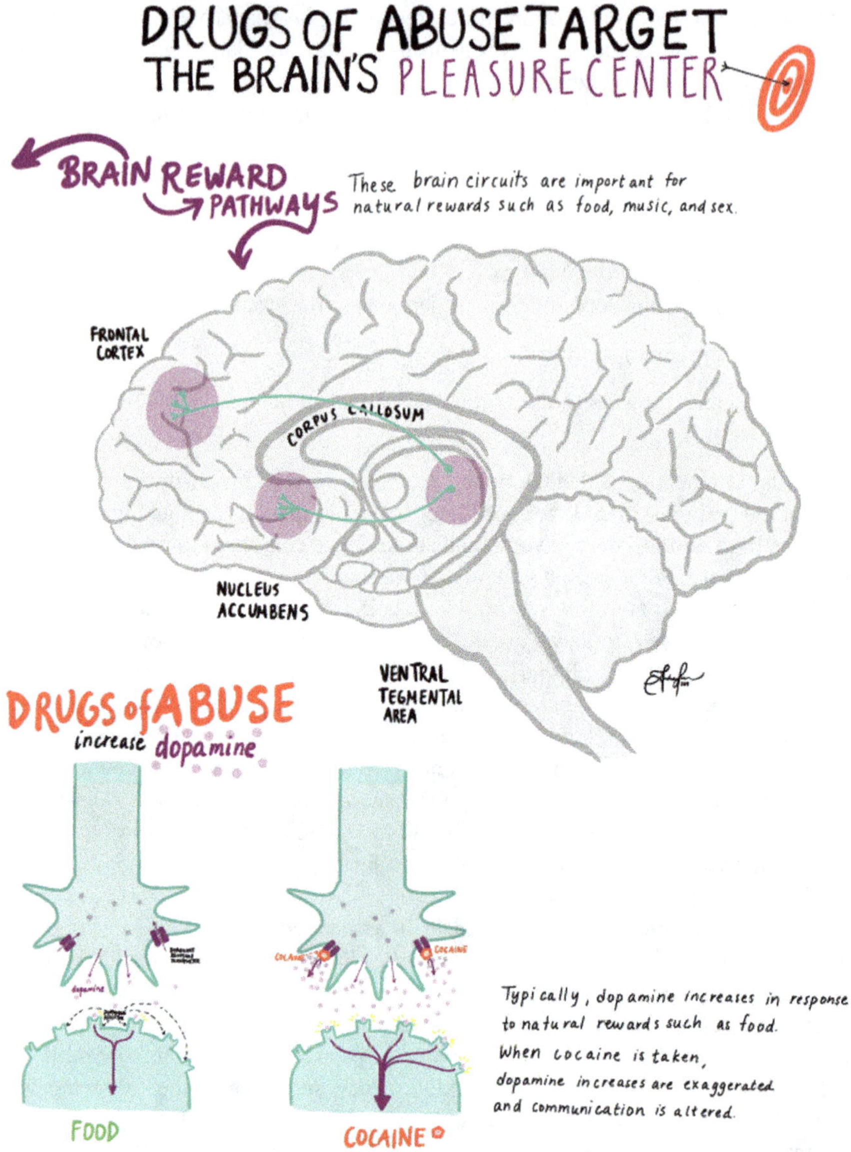

Fig. 4.1 Reward Pathway (also known as the mesolimbic pathway) with a focus on dopamine and serotonin. Printed with permission. Copyright Audrey A. Tran

(hormones) on neuronal loss, changes in dendritic complexity, and synapse number. The review points out that substance use disorders are described as maladaptive or compromised decision-making and reward learning. The limbic system is described as the regulator of social interaction and reward, specifically the amygdala and its role in the integration and regulating emotion and motivation (Walker et al. 2017).

Increased reward-seeking behavior is a notable feature in adolescent development (Crews et al. 2007). Many animal and human studies have demonstrated changes in the brain's reward network during adolescence. As indicated in Chap. 1 of this textbook, there are points in the brain development process that are more susceptible to environmental and/or social threats. A study on adolescent development of reward sought to better understand two working theories on increased reward, novelty seeking (1) the striatum is under-responsive to rewards during adolescence to the point that increased reward-seeking behavior is required to obtain the same level of activation/excitement seen in adults and (2) the striatum is over-responsive and therefore leads to heightened increased reward-seeking behavior. The review points to research suggests that during the neuronal pruning process in adolescent brain development, there is dopamine receptor overproduction (Teicher et al. 1995). Upon thorough review of the literature, there was strong support for the hypothesis that the dopamine system is over-responsive and over-engaged in response to the reward pathway in adolescence.

These findings are consistent with how the brain develops, again, from bottom-up to inside-out. The regulatory part of the brain (top brain) is still developing and is more prone to being overridden by the emotion-driven (mid-bottom part of the brain) (Figs. 4.2, 4.3 and 4.4).

Substances Use Impact on Ova, Sperm, and Fetus

In a review on the epigenetic mechanisms of drug addiction, Nestler explains that addiction possibly entails lifelong behavioral abnormalities in vulnerable populations as a consequence of repeated exposure to a drug of exposure. We are learning that early exposure can change gene expression at the level of the sperm and ova, well before conception.

Nestler points out that the doggedness of these behaviors suggests lasting changes in gene expression, within particular parts of the brain, which might contribute greatly to the addiction phenotype. As indicated in Chap. 1 of this textbook, epigenetics as a study has evolved over the last 10 years to include various studies on animal models of drugs of abuse. Particularly, these animal models of drugs of abuse have demonstrated consistent negative and profound impact on the epigenetics of brain development. In careful review, Nestler highlights strong evidence that consistent, repeated exposure to drugs of abuse result in epigenetic changes to the brain's reward pathway in three specific ways: (1) histone modifications like acetylation and methylation, (2) DNA methylation, and (3) noncoding RNAs.

Further, it is suggested (while controversial) that there is the possibility that drugs or other environmental exposures induce epigenetic changes in sperm or ova, which are then passed on to offspring and alter their vulnerability to addiction, deemed a transgenerational epigenetic inheritance of addiction (Nestler 2013).

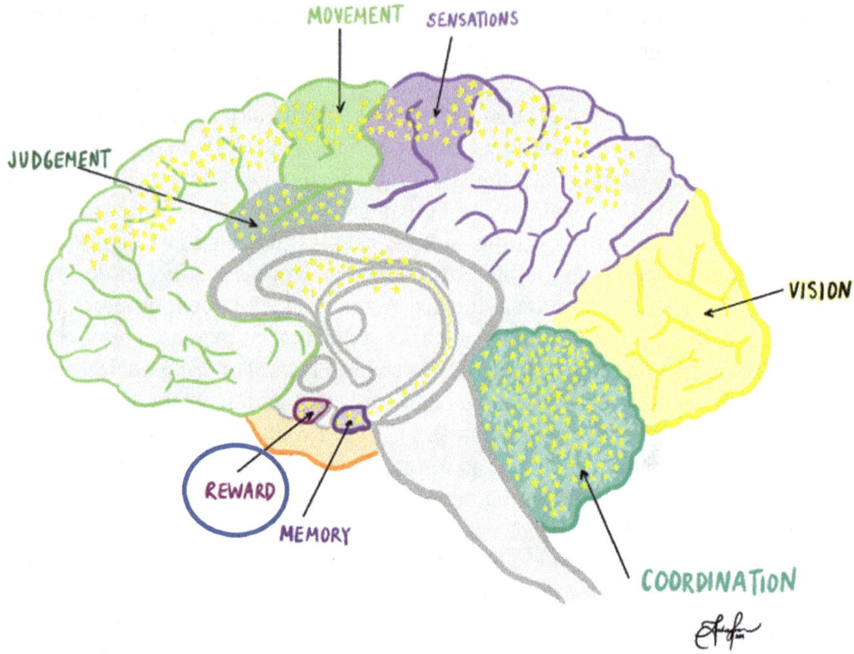

Fig. 4.2 Substances of abuse impact the brain's reward pathway. Printed with permission. Copyright Audrey A. Tran

According to Heard et al., epigenetic inheritance is relatively common in plants. The plant germ line arises from somatic cells exposed to developmental and environmental cues, first demonstrated by botanist Jean-Baptiste Lamarck. Implications for epigenetic inheritance for mammalian development have been highlighted when it comes to intergenerational inheritance versus transgenerational. In the intergenerational studies, DNA sequence changes have been implicated as the underlying driver of heritability. Maternal effects (considered intergenerational effects) do occur in mammals, the degree to which these intergenerational effects are passed down without an initial trigger is unclear. Heard points out that in mammals, efficient reprogramming happens in the early embryo and in the germ line (Heard and Martienssen 2014).

In Heard et al. review, it is explained that epigenetic changes in mammals can happen intermittently or can be influenced by the environment (toxins, poor nutrition, stress, and trauma). To further illustrate the difference between intergenerational effects versus transgenerational effects, Heard highlights a hypothetical pregnant female mouse model (exposed to environmental stressors. A stressed, pregnant female mouse will directly impact the fetus (in utero)—called F1 in this model. Further, the germ line of the fetus (from original stressed, pregnant female mouse) called future F2 can also be impacted. F1 and Future F2 impacts are considered parental effects that contribute to intergenerational epigenetic inheritance. Heard

Addiction	Physical dependence
▪ Compulsive use despite negative consequences ▪ Inability to stop use (loss of control) ▪ Failure to meet family obligations ▪ Failure to meet work obligations ▪ Failure to meet social obligations ▪ Need for more of the drug to get a high and or effect (tolerance) ▪ Physical or behavioral symptoms if the drug is stopped (withdrawal)	▪ Physical dependence can lead to addiction but must be distinguished by two key features: ▪ Need for more of the drug to get a high and or effect (tolerance) ▪ Physical or behavioral symptoms if the drug is stopped (withdrawal)

Fig. 4.3 Addition versus Physical dependence

contends that true transgenerational epigenetic inheritance would occur if F3 (future F3)—demonstrated gene changes similar to F1 and F2 in the absence of exposure (Heard and Martienssen 2014).

While the mechanism of transgenerational inheritance is not well documented in mammals, it does not fully eliminate the possibility that it may indeed occur. Transgenerational inheritance has been appreciated in plants, fruit flies, and some animals like roundworms.

Nestler's review endorses that repeated exposure to a drug of abuse in adolescence or adulthood causes addiction in vulnerable individuals by inducing stable changes in gene expression through epigenetic regulation of those specific genes.

In a review by Burdge et al., induction of stable changes in gene expression through epigenetic regulation is demonstrated in the role of changes in the epigenetic regulation of transcription, specifically DNA methylation and modification of histones in the context of nutritional limitations early in life and changed observable characteristics of an individual. There is overwhelming evidence for genes and observable characteristics in an individual being heavily influenced by early life environment, including nutrition, risk of disease, and a process called fetal programming (the concept that the development of the fetus and embryo is impacted by environmental factors like nutrition or the lack thereof).

There are several studies which have investigated the effect of maternal nutrition during pregnancy and/ or lactation on gene expression in the offspring in animal mod-

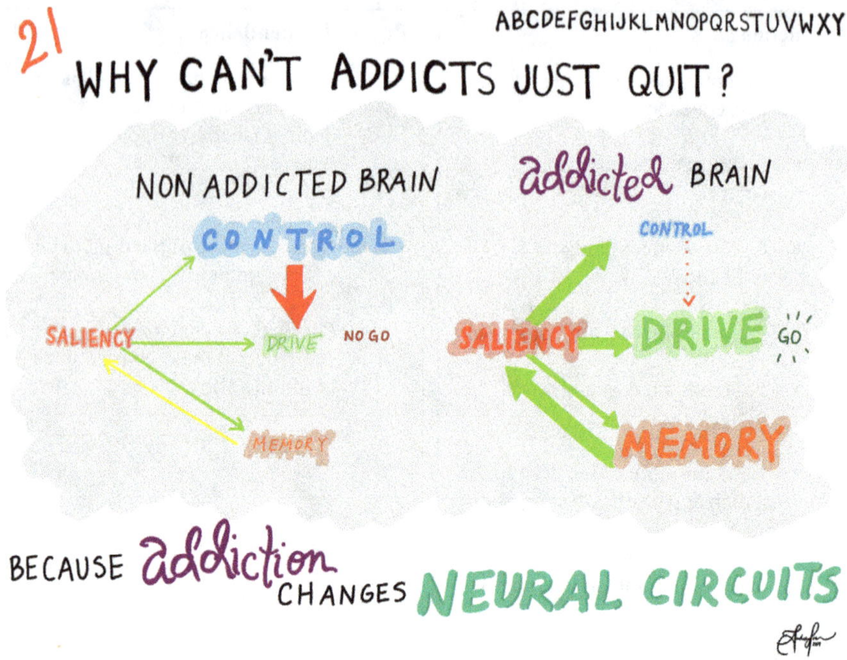

Fig. 4.4 **Control** in this image = cortex (top part of brain)
Salience in this image = amygdala/ventral tegmental area (midbrain/limbic structures)
Memory in this image = hippocampus
Basic summation: addiction happens when the cortex loses its ability to modulate and regulate amygdala/ventral tegmental area. ***There is a loss of top-down control = less control of impulses and compulsions***. Printed with permission. Copyright Audrey A. Tran

els. These studies have used a candidate gene approach to identifying the molecular basis for changes in activities of metabolic and endocrine pathways, with a specific focus on corticosteroid activity, and carbohydrate and lipid metabolism. Restricting maternal protein intake during pregnancy and/or lactation in rats also alters the expression of genes involved in lipid homeostasis (Burdge et al. 2007).

Epigenetic regulation mediates changes in steady-state gene expression or inducibility of genes that occur throughout an individual's lifetime in response to a host of environmental exposures, which help determine that individual's vulnerability to drug exposure and addiction later in life (Hiroi and Agatsuma 2005).

Neonatal Abstinence Syndrome

Several studies have demonstrated that substance use during pregnancy may contribute to higher instances of miscarriage, prematurity, low birth weight, and challenges with emotion regulation. Some babies are also born dependent on a substance, given mother's use patterns during pregnancy, resulting in a withdrawal syndrome when babies are born. In the literature, this withdrawal syndrome is referred to as neonatal abstinence syndrome (NAS).

NAS is a phenomenon characterized by complex, variable behavioral and physiologic challenges that a baby experiences upon protracted exposure to substances in utero. Much of the literature describes NAS associated with maternal use of opioids. Opioids refer to a class of drugs that include the illegal drug heroin, synthetic opioids such as fentanyl, and pain relievers available legally by prescription, such as oxycodone (OxyContin), hydrocodone (Vicodin), codeine, morphine, and many others (NIDA, Opioids).

Opioid use and overdose-related deaths have increased considerably in the past 15 years. This uptick in opioid use appears to correlate with increases in prescription opioid prescribing for chronic pain in the early 2000s. When pronounced morbidity and mortality were more directly associated to prescribed opioids, a shift in prescribing practices was inspired. This meant that individuals who were getting opioids for chronic pain were encouraged to secure new means of managing pain. Opioids very positively and robustly activate the reward pathway (and dopamine paths) and as such contribute physical dependence. This means that when individuals aren't appropriately tapered off of opioids, they experience uncomfortable withdrawal. Withdrawal is dangerous in pregnancy because it can increase the risk of spontaneous abortion. In order to avoid uncomfortable withdrawal, a significant proportion of individuals (who were previously prescribed opioids and prescriptions were significantly reduced) turned to heroin because it was easily accessible and cheaper than prescription opioids and some individuals found a way to continue to purchase prescription opioids off the street and for nonmedical use. Now, opioid use is deemed a public health crisis, and many states and the federal government have allocated funding for treatment and research. While methadone is the most studied (and considered gold standard treatment in pregnant women), newer studies on subutex (buprenorphine alone) have demonstrated sufficient treatment for opioid use disorder in pregnant women and have been shown to lessen the impact of neonatal withdrawal. Pharmacologic treatment for substances of abuse will be covered in greater detail later in this chapter.

Much of the research on NAS stems from maternal opioid use (and more specifically referred to as Neonatal Opioid Withdrawal Syndrome, NOWS) during pregnancy. Here is what is understood thus far:

- It is theorized that altered levels of neurotransmitters such as norepinephrine, dopamine, and serotonin are presumed to play a significant role (Kocherlakota 2014).
- Genetic variations of the mu-opioid receptor (*OPRM1*) and the catechol-o-methyltransferase (*COMT*; encodes an enzyme that metabolizes neurotransmitters like epinephrine and dopamine) genes appear to impact pharmacotherapy needs and length of stay in neonates with prenatal opioid exposure (Wachman et al. 2013).

The most common clinical findings in NOWS negatively and disproportionately impact four main areas to include motor and tone control (unconscious regulation of the heart rate, digestion, respiratory rate, etc.), sensory integration (response to sound, touch, and other senses), autonomic functioning, and state control and attention (ability to shift attention, ability to respond to multiple tasks).

These impacts are manifested as

- Irritability and high-pitched crying,
- Trouble with feeding (uncoordinated suck–swallow capacity),
- Hyperactive primitive reflexes like the startle reflex,
- Increase in muscle tone,
- Tremors,
- Vomiting, gassiness/flatulence/loose stools,
- Autonomic disturbances include things like sneezing, nasal stuffiness, sweating, and yawning—symptoms seen in adults in opioid withdrawal,
- Disturbances to the sleep/wake cycle, and
- Disrupted physical growth and development also known in the literature as failure to thrive.

Primary treatment for NOWS is supportive management.

Babies born with NOWS also experience longer hospital stays that often involve NICU support compared to babies without NOWS.

The MOTHER's study demonstrated that opioid-dependent mothers on medication-assisted treatment (MAT) with subutex (buprenorphine alone) versus methadone gave birth to babies with less severe withdrawal symptoms and decreased the length of stay in the hospital (Jones et al. 2012).

Further, subutex (buprenorphine alone) is excreted in low concentrations into breast milk and appears to be safe for the infant of a breastfeeding mother maintained on buprenorphine (Jansson 2016).

Although little is known about the long-term impact of NOWS, there have been strong correlations and associations between NOWS and impact overall development and functionality (Fig. 4.5).

A study done in New South Wales Australia linked analysis of health- and curriculum-based test data for all children born in the state of New South Wales (NSW), Australia, between 2000 and 2006. Children with NAS ($n = 2234$) were compared with a control group matched for gestation, socioeconomic status, and gender ($n = 4330$, control) and with other NSW children ($n = 598\ 265$, population) for results on the National Assessment Program: Literacy and Numeracy, in grades 3, 5, and 7 (Oei et al. 2017).

- Mean test scores for children with NAS were significantly lower in third grade.
- NAS score of 359 versus control score of 410 (a 50 point difference).
- This study demonstrated that the deficits appeared to be progressive. By seventh grade, children with NAS scored lower than children in the fifth grade.
- The risk of not meeting minimum standards was independently associated with NAS, indigenous status, male gender, and low parental education—all were statistically significant (Oei et al. 2017).

The study concluded that a neonatal diagnostic code of NAS was strongly associated with poor and deteriorating school performance (Oei et al. 2017).

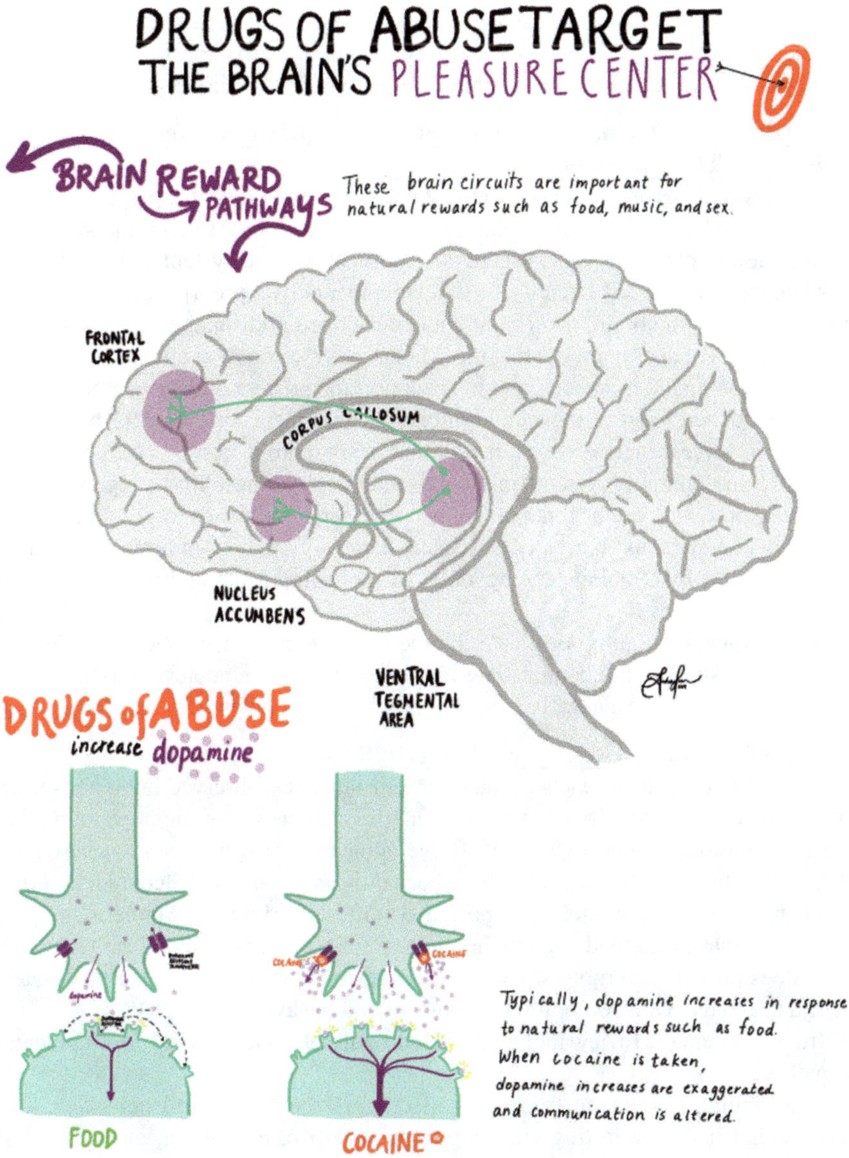

Fig. 4.5 Cocaine acts at the dopamine transporter by blocking the uptake of dopamine. Blocking uptake markedly increases concentration of dopamine which positively reinforces the reward pathway in the brain. Printed with permission. Copyright Audrey A. Tran

It is known that association and correlation don't equal causation. It is important to note that both NOWS, NAS and early-persistent in utero exposure to substances is a form of trauma and has been demonstrated to impact brain development.

The Adolescent Brain, Developmentally Appropriate to Want to Try New Things, but There Are Consequences

It is understood that adolescence, behaviorally and socially mark the pursuit of autonomy, independence shaped by an increase in risk-taking, prone to act impulsively and explore new experiences (Adolescent development Reward system 2010). Much of this behavior, which has been deemed developmentally appropriate, does correlate with changes in the brain, namely, an underdeveloped prefrontal cortex. Social scientists like L.P. Spear point out that these behaviors are common among adolescents of diverse mammalians species and may support the process of drug use. Spear also highlights puberty and changes in hormones as an impetus or driver for behavioral changes in adolescence as well (an area that bears more research). Spear contends that shifts in dopamine systems in the mesocortical and mesolimbic regions of the brain also powerfully contribute to the incentive for adolescence to use drugs.

It is also understood that in adolescence, there is more bottom brain functioning than top brain functioning lending itself to more impulsive and novelty-seeking behaviors (Casey et al. 2010).

While **Spears** is highlighting a developmental phenomenon, we should not deviate too far from studies that demonstrate that substance use in adolescence holds real consequences and has a negative impact on brain development (Spear 2000).

Impact of Substance Use on the Adolescent Brain

Irner breaks down the impacts of maternal substance use observed in both research and clinical experience. Irner's review highlights various studies demonstrating that preschool children hold a higher risk of developing cognitive, behavioral, and socioemotional difficulties. Many studies have been done in the arena of alcohol use during pregnancy—both the in utero and postnatal (after birth impact). While the impact of opiates, marijuana, and cocaine in pregnancy have not been as robustly studied, Irner does provide emerging studies and evidence regarding the impact of opiates, marijuana, and cocaine on brain development and behavior (Irner 2012).

Irner's systematic review included 25 studies on substance use and developmental sequelae.

The running conclusion from the collective of the studies in Irner's review is that alcohol had long-lasting and long-term cognitive, behavioral, and emotional development consequences. The depth of the consequences was dependent upon the timing during in utero exposure and the amount of substance used. Irner also points out new studies that powerfully demonstrate the impact of substances like opiates, marijuana, and cocaine on the brain through functional magnetic resonance imaging, which will be highlighted further in this chapter. Additionally, studies have shown an association between early, in utero exposure to substances of abuse and deficits to areas of the brain responsible for language, attention, cognitive performance, and impulse control in adolescents (Irner 2012).

The brain develops from the bottom-up and the inside-out. Brain development starts at conception and nears completion around the age of 26. An adolescent, defined from around the age of 12–25, marks a very interesting period as far as brain development is concerned. By way of quick summary from Chap. 1, the developing brain during adolescent (the twelfth through fourteenth year of life), myelination occurs in the prefrontal cortex. Full myelination is not reached until age 26 and maybe later, but it starts at this point. The emotional (responsive, impulsive) mind develops before wise (measured, think before you act) mind (Squeglia et al. 2009).

Squeglia et al., in an article on the influence of substance use on adolescent brain development, highlight recent research indicating that adolescent substance users show abnormalities on measures of brain functioning linked to changes in cognition over time. Of note, in adolescence, alcohol and marijuana are common (Squeglia et al. 2009).

Youth with as little as 1–2 years of heavy drinking and use levels of 20 drinks per month or binge drinking (defined as more than 4–5 drinks in one setting) had brain abnormalities in the following: structure, volume, white matter quality, and response to cognitive tasks. The article asserts that adolescence may be a period of heightened vulnerability for alcohol's effect on the brain (Clark et al. 2008; Spear 2005).

Youth with heavy marijuana use also demonstrated some brain changes.

Squelia and colleagues summarize literature findings on the impact of adolescent heavy drinking in the following manner: while impact is subtle, it is poignant as there are negative impacts on working memory, speed and information processing, attention, and ability to plan, organize, and complete tasks—deficits mostly associated with top brain, cortical function (prefrontal, orbitofrontal cortex).

Adolescents who regularly smoke marijuana performed poorer on performance tests of learning, cognitive flexibility, visual scanning, error commission, and working memory (Medina et al. 2007a, b).

In Squeglia's review, several studies used functional magnetic resonance imaging (fMRI) through measurement of changes in blood oxygen levels/signals in the brain to track changes in the hippocampus (the part of the brain implicated in memory), prefrontal cortex (responsible for planning, executive function, exercising good judgement), white matter volume (important for neuronal transmission between connecting brain regions), and spatial working memory. While there were notable differences in heavy versus light users of alcohol and marijuana, respectively, the studies overwhelming demonstrate that alcohol and marijuana use in adolescents (during critical brain development phases) does have a negative impact (Squeglia et al. 2009).

As an addiction psychiatrist who works with adolescents in the community, I would contend that alcohol and marijuana should be avoided or minimized at best (harm reduction model) in the developing brain. "Give the brain a fighting chance."

Physical Dependence Versus Addiction

There are distinct differences between addiction and physical dependence. Addiction is a complex disease that involves compulsive use despite consequences; inability to stop use; failure to meet obligations at work; failure to meet obligations at home; failure to meet social obligations; a need for more of the drug to get a high and/or effect (tolerance); and physical and behavioral symptoms if the drug is stopped (withdrawal) (Ruiz and Lowinson 2011).

Physical dependence can lead to addiction, but should be distinguished in the following way: there are only two real criteria, a need for more of the drug to get an effect (tolerance) physical and/or behavioral symptoms if the drug is stopped (withdrawal).

An example of physical dependence: after surgery, an individual is prescribed Vicodin for 1 month. The individual uses the Vicodin daily and consistently for the entire month to control surgical-related pain. Once the patient goes off, they experience some withdrawal symptoms. Withdrawal, in this case, does indicate physical dependence and the bodies' adaptation to the use of the substance (Ruiz and Lowinson 2011).

Note: appropriate tapering of the Vicodin can significantly reduce withdrawal.

Classical and Operant Conditioning as a Theoretical Framework for Understanding Addiction

The historical framework for learned behaviors can be found in the concepts of classical and operant conditioning. Ivan Pavlov, Russian physiologist and Nobel Prize winner, stumbled upon the concept of classical conditioning. Pavlov is well known for his work with dogs, specifically investigation digestion in dogs. During his investigative process, he noted that the dogs would start to salivate when an assistant would enter the room. Of note, behavior changes in dogs were seemingly associated with an external stimulus (the assistant). In Pavlov's desire to better understand this phenomenon, he designed the following study (Brembs et al. 2000):

- Assistants provided appetizing and less appetizing objects,
- Saliva production was measured with appetizing and less appetizing objects,
- Salivation was deemed a reflexive process, and
- Salivation happened automatically and unconsciously to a specific stimulus and salivation also happened when there was no specific stimulus.

From these observations and associations with dog's salivation tendencies in the presence and absence of stimulus, Pavlov concluded

- Salivation was not automatic, and
- Salivation was learned (conditioned).

Unconditioned reflex = salivation at the sight of food

Conditioned reflex = salivation with the expectation of food

To further understand the mechanism behind unconditioned and conditioned processes, Pavlov conducted several experiments that attached a conditioned response with a neutral stimulus (like food). The sight and smell of food automatically and naturally inspire salivation, and hence Pavlov's decision is to use it as a neutral stimulus.

A second neutral stimulus was presented in the form of the sound of a metronome.

1st—dogs would hear the metronome

2nd—dog would immediately be shown food

The dogs were exposed to several iterations of first hearing the metronome and then immediately being shown food.

From this trial, Pavlov observed that the dogs would salivate upon hearing the metronome, confirming that the metronome as a neutral stimulus was transformed into the conditioned stimulus which inspired salivation (a conditioned response).

Operant conditioning: a way to modulate behavior

- Uses reinforcement and/or punishment to increase and/or decrease a behavior.
- Association between behavior and consequences is established through the operant conditioning process.

Drugs of abuse (very much like the science behind neutral stimuli and food with Pavlov's dogs) represent a specific type of stimulus that invokes a specific type of response, the reward/pleasure pathway.

Pavlov's work is influential in shaping the understanding of learned behavior. Addiction is understood from the framework of the theory of classical conditioning (associating an involuntary response and a stimulus) and operant conditioning (associating a voluntary behavior and a consequence) (Brembs et al. 2000).

Cocaine and the Developing Brain

What is cocaine?

Cocaine, an addictive stimulant drug derived from the leaves of the coca plant native to South America.

2017 Monitoring the Future data shows a steady decline in cocaine use among adolescents.

How is it used?

- Cocaine can be snorted,
- Cocaine can be rubbed into gums,
- Cocaine powder can be dissolved in water and injected into the bloodstream,
- Cocaine can be processed into rock crystal termed "crack-cocaine" and smoked, and
- Given the powerful way that cocaine impacts the brain, most individuals who use it, often binge, and use more frequently at higher doses to get and stay high.

What are the short- and long-term effects of cocaine on the body?

Short-term effects of Cocaine:

- extreme happiness and energy,
- mental alertness,
- hypersensitivity to sight, sound, and touch,
- irritability, and
- *paranoia*—extreme and irrational distrust of others.

Some long-term health effects of cocaine depend on the method of use and include the following:

- *snorting*: loss of sense of smell, nosebleeds, frequent runny nose, and swallowing issues.
- *consuming by mouth*: severe bowel decay from reduced blood flow.

- *needle injection*: higher risk for contracting HIV, hepatitis C, and other blood-borne diseases.
- Heart attack and stroke.

Cocaine's neurobiological impact on the brain

Cocaine has multiple targets and impacts, and in the pre-synapse, cocaine binds differently to several transporters to include the dopamine, norepinephrine, and serotonin transporters. When humans experience a pleasurable experience, there are neurochemicals that facilitate communication between certain neurons to mediate the pleasure response. The neurochemicals like dopamine, serotonin, and norepinephrine are designed to increase during pleasurable, rewarding experiences. The pleasure–reward response turns down once the pleasure is gone. It turns down by reabsorbing and/or taking back up the neurotransmitters floating in the synapse—the transporters assist with the process of reabsorption/reuptake.

Cocaine binds to these transporters, blocking the ability for them to reuptake—this results in markedly increased amounts of the neurotransmitters in the synapse, which reinforces the pleasure pathways.

In the case of cocaine, it is more robust and targeted in its blockage of the dopamine transporter.

The ventral tegmental area has dopaminergic projections to the striatum (which consist of the nucleus accumbens and caudate nucleus). The striatum has several dopaminergic receptors with receptors D1 and D2 predominating in the reward pathway. In a review article by Hummel et al. (2002), D1 receptors are implicated in cocaine signaling and mediate behavior. Hummel summarized cocaine research literature by highlighting significant advances in cocaine research which has seemingly inspired a better understanding of the D_1 dopamine receptor and its associated signaling pathway. Some of the experimental paradigms directed at further clarifying a role for the D_1 receptor in cocaine-induced behaviors include studies on the discriminative stimulus, reinforcing, and locomotor-activating effects of cocaine. In several studies, the discriminative stimulus effects of drugs of abuse in animals are maintained to model those subjective effects often experienced by human as they assist in predicting mechanisms for reward, well-being, and a greater understanding of the underlying neurobiological underpinnings of the desire for repetitive use of a drug. Various studies suggest that cocaine is a discriminative stimulus in animals (Woolverton and Trost 1978). Several landmark studies have confirmed a prominent role for dopamine (McKenna and Ho 1980) and a supportive role for D_1 dopamine receptors in mediating the discriminative stimulus effect of cocaine.

What is discriminative stimulus?

A discriminative stimulus is a term used in classical conditioning as a part of the process known as operant conditioning. A discriminative stimulus is a type of stimulus that is used consistently to gain a specific response and that increases the possibility that the desired response will occur.

Cocaine's epigenetic impact

A review by Nielsen et al. (2012) considered the role of epigenetics in response to drugs of abuse and epigenetic changes witnessed in drug addiction and withdrawal.

The article set out to more deeply explore if epigenetic alterations increased vulnerability to develop a drug addiction, or if addiction itself created an epigenetic response to certain drugs of abuse. Nielsen et al. reviewed myriad studies on cocaine, opioids, and alcohol.

The review highlighted the following:

- Chromatin remodeling has been implicated as a factor in long-term development of cocaine addiction. Accumulation of the transcription factor subunit ΔlFosB, a truncated splice variant of FosB, in the striatum of the brain is a characteristic of the administration of several stimulants (like cocaine, meth, ecstasy), narcotics and depressants, and demonstrates gene activation (Nielsen et al. 2012).
- Several studies (animal and human) have focussed on the 5-HTTLPR variation in the promoter of the serotonin transporter—which is a notable target for cocaine and ecstasy (3,4-methylenedioxy-N-methylamphetamine)—(Han and Gu 2006).
- Serotonin transporter expression and uptake are decreased by the short 5-HTTLPR allele (Lesch et al. 1996).
- A study of adolescents revealed that the rate of substance abuse initiation in subjects with one or two copies of the short allele was moderated by exposure to supportive parenting or membership in community-building initiative demonstrating that environmental conditions can regulate, or fully reduce, genetic predispositions to psychiatric conditions such as addiction vulnerability (Brody et al. 2009).
- Studies on short- and long-term cocaine administration revealed immediate and chronic gene expression changes via epigenetic modifications.
- In rodent studies, both *c-fos* (also referred to as *cFos* or *Fos*) and Δ*FosB* expression is activated by cocaine (McClung et al. 2003; Graybiel et al. 1990).
- In the nucleus accumbens, a single acute cocaine injection rapidly increases immediate early gene expression, including expression of *c-fos*, indicating a role for c-fos in mediating the initial response to psychostimulants (Hope et al. 1992).
- Acute and chronic cocaine has been shown to cause hypomethylation of the *FosB* promoter, decreased MeCP2 binding, and upregulated *FosB* expression in the nucleus accumbens (Anier et al. 2010).
- Mouse hippocampus demonstrated changes in expression of a gene called Bdnf with cocaine withdrawal (Filip et al. 2006).

Current studies and literature suggest that drugs of abuse like cocaine can result in changes in chromatin structure that alter gene expression. These epigenetic factors may alter initial response to a drug, continued response, the development of tolerance leading to addiction, as well as withdrawal and relapse.

Cocaine's impact on the developing brain
In a systematic review, Vassoler et al. examine the effects of parental exposure to drugs of abuse prior to conception on the development of subsequent generations. The review looks at five major substances which include cocaine, cannabis, alcohol, opioids, and nicotine (Vassoler et al. 2013).

To avoid the confounding factor of maternal in utero exposure of cocaine, most of the animal studies investigated cocaine's impact on sperm.

In the case of cocaine, Vassoler et al. review highlights clinical and preclinical literature on parental cocaine administration, which have focused primarily on the developmental impact of prenatal cocaine exposure. Preclinical studies have consistently demonstrated disrupted cortical and hippocampal development in the offspring as well as compromised executive function and memory following in utero cocaine exposure (Dow-Edwards 2011; Lidow 2003; Malanga and Kosofsky 2003).

The environmental impact on genes (epigenetic forces) appears to play a role in these changes in which male mice exposed to cocaine prenatally had altered patterns of DNA methylation in hippocampal pyramidal neurons (Novikova et al. 2008), which could contribute to impaired sustained attention and spatial working memory observed in these offsprings (He et al. 2006).

Human studies by Mule et al. and Yazigi et al. have demonstrated the fact that cocaine concentrates in the testes because of specific binding sites on spermatozoa (Yazigi et al. 1991; Mule et al. 1977). Several animal studies have also demonstrated that protracted cocaine use impairs sperm production (George et al. 1996.).

Much of the studies on cocaine use in adolescent have highlighted its negative impact on cognition, impulse control, and ability to modulate emotions.

Cocaine can impact the brain at every stage of development epigenetic, from conception, in utero, and adolescents and even into adulthood. Dr. Karen Ersche, a neuroscientist, demonstrated cocaine's impact on the frontal cortex, specifically through magnetic resonance imaging (MRI) of chronic cocaine users that showed decreased gray matter in the frontal cortex (the rational, impulse control, exercising good judgment portion of the brain).

Dr. Ershe's lab had 60 cocaine-dependent individuals who undergo an MRI and was able to compare the MRI images with 60 individuals who were not cocaine dependent. In this comparative analysis, the following was discovered:

- Gray matter in the orbitofrontal cortex was significantly decreased in cocaine-dependent subjects. Again, this is the area of the brain associated with exercising good judgment, impulse control, decision-making, etc.
- The insula (part of the brain associated with learning and feedback processing) was negatively impacted in cocaine-dependent individuals.
- Anterior cingulate (associated with the processing of emotions, attention, etc.) gray matter was decreased.
- Areas of the brain associated with the reward pathway, motor, and movement were increased in volume to include the caudate nucleus in cocaine-dependent subjects.

While the results of Ersche's studies were not conclusive, they were consistent with what has been seen clinically and behaviorally in individuals with prolonged cocaine use.

Cocaine is not benign and it does appear to change genes, negatively impact sperm, and compromise brain development and function (Ersche et al. 2011).

How does cocaine use lead to addiction?

- Repetitive and continued use of cocaine can cause long-term changes in the brain's reward circuit and other brain systems, which can lead to addiction. The reward circuit (over time) adjusts to the high levels of dopamine created by cocaine's action of blocking the dopamine transporter. The dopamine response is so robust and powerfully activates the reward pathway resulting in individuals requiring more of the drug at frequent doses to get high and to avoid withdrawal.

Withdrawal symptoms include

- depression,
- fatigue,
- increased appetite,
- unpleasant dreams and insomnia, and
- slowed thinking.

Methamphetamine and the Developing Brain

What is methamphetamine?

Methamphetamine (also called meth, crystal, chalk, and ice, among other terms) is a stimulant drug (very addictive) that is chemically similar to amphetamine. Methamphetamine is a white, odorless, bitter-tasting crystalline powder.

Methamphetamine can be taken in the following forms:

- Orally,
- Smoked—delivers drug quickly to the brain,
- Snorted,
- Can be quickly delivered to the brain if dissolved in water or alcohol and injected, and
- Meth has a long half-life, up to 10–12 h, the longer the substance is in the system, the greater its propensity to damage the brain and other organs.

Long-term use of methamphetamine might experience the following mood behavior symptoms:

- Anxiety (excessive worry),
- Confusion,
- Sleeping difficulty,
- Changes in mood,
- Increased risks of behaving violently,
- Paranoia, visual, and auditory hallucinations—forms of psychosis, and
- Delusions (fixed, false beliefs).

Physical consequences of methamphetamine use may include

- Increased risk of HIV and Hepatitis C with intravenous use (IV),
- Severe tooth decay and abscesses which increases the risk of bacterial infections in the heart, and
- Severe muscle wasting, where an observer can appreciate bone demarcations of an individual.

Methamphetamines neurobiological impact on the brain

- Similar to cocaine, methamphetamine causes the release of the neurotransmitters dopamine, norepinephrine, and serotonin.
- Methamphetamine disproportionately and powerfully increases the concentration of the neurotransmitter dopamine in two important ways: (1) it blocks the reuptake of dopamine and (2) increases the release of dopamine into the synapse. The dopamine response in methamphetamine use is way more robust than the dopamine response in cocaine use. This very strong dopamine surge renders methamphetamine more addictive compared to other substances of abuse and other stimulants like cocaine.
- Dopamine has a starring role in reward, motivation, pleasure, and motor function.
- Studies of chronic methamphetamine users reveal severe structural and functional changes have been found in areas of the brain associated with emotion and memory, motivation, and reward (Volkow et al. 2001) (Canadian Medical Association 2008).

Methamphetamine epigenetic impact
Limanaqi et al. (2018) review revealed some evidence that epigentic changes happen in presynaptic dopamine receptors in the striatum of the brain—these changes are what lead to some of the behaviors seen in methamphetamine use. In specific, the review highlights epigenetic changes in DR1-DR5 dopamine-like, G-protein-coupled receptors.

Methamphetamine has been noted to modify certain subtypes of glutamate receptors. To further understand this phenomenon (epigenetic changes to glutamate signaling in the brain), Cadet (2013) gave rats increased doses of meth over time—four times/day over a 2-week period. They found a significant decrease in mRNA and protein levels of glutamate in the striatum. This study supports a growing body of evidence that substances of abuse like methamphetamine can alter genes and gene expression, impacting brain function and structure.

A study by Volkow et al. took methamphetamine abusers and comparison subjects without a history of drug abuse underwent positron emission tomography (PET) scans following administration of a substance that binds the dopamine transporter ⁽C]*d-threo*-methylphenidate (a dopamine transporter ligand) to measure dopamine transporters, which serve as a marker for dopamine cell terminals. Equally, they administered a series of neuropsychological tests to evaluate the impact of methamphetamine abuse on motor activity and cognition. This study found changes in the dopamine system, namely, a notable decrease in dopamine transporters in methamphetamine abusers—these changes have been attached to compromised verbal learning and decreased motor skills (Volkow et al. 2001).

Methamphetamine's impact on the developing brain (adolescent and adult)
It is important to point out that methamphetamine use among adolescents is lower compared to other substances of abuse and there are more studies on the impact of methamphetamine on adults compared to adolescents. The studies regarding adolescent methamphetamine use provide information on risks factors for use, specific conditions that may increase the likelihood that an adolescent would use methamphetamine. A review article by Buck and Siegel (2015) summarizes the current

literature on the impact of methamphetamine on adolescent brain and behavior in the following manner:

- Adolescents who were being treated for methamphetamine abuse were more likely to have a psychiatric (higher rates of depression and suicidal ideation) and family history of drug misuse.
- Adolescents using methamphetamine were more likely female (Gonzalez et al. 2010) (Miura et al. 2006) (Rawson et al. 2005).
- Methamphetamine use in adolescent was associated with increased incidence of risk sexual behavior, increased risk of pregnancy, and behavioral disturbances (Zapata et al. 2008; Embry et al. 2009).
- With adolescent use of methamphetamine, psychological and behavioral changes seen with use continued well after they stopped using. This was evidenced by heightened depression and anxiety scores and higher physiological stress response in stressful situations with 4–11 months of no meth use (King et al. 2010b).
- 4–11 months of no methamphetamine use in adolescents also demonstrated impairment in executive functioning (prefrontal cortex disruption) when matched and compared with non-methamphetamine using adolescents (King et al. 2010a).
- Methamphetamines impact on the adolescent brain is similar to adults in that there are executive function and memory disruptions and higher incidences of depression and anxiety (Scott et al. 2007; Zweben et al. 2004; Salo et al. 2011; Li et al. 2013).

Methamphetamine use in youth is also not benign as it has a direct, disproportionate, and negative impact on decision-making, exercising good judgment, impulse control, cognitive agility, and it increases the risk for lasting changes in affect (i.e., depression, anxiety, and psychosis).

Nicotine and the developing brain

Tobacco use is the leading preventable cause of disease, disability, and death in the United States. According to the Centers for Disease Control and Prevention (CDC), cigarette smoking results in more than 480,000 premature deaths in the United States each year—about 1 in every 5 U.S. deaths—and an additional 16 million people suffer from a serious illness caused by smoking **(NIDA)**.

Cigarettes and tobacco-based products like cigars, pipe tobacco, snuff, and chewing tobacco contain the addictive drug nicotine.

Nicotine's neurobiological impact on the brain

- Nicotine is readily absorbed into the bloodstream when a tobacco product is chewed, inhaled, or smoked. A typical smoker will take 10 puffs on a cigarette over a period of about 5 min that the cigarette is lit (NIDA).
- Thus, a person who smokes about 1 pack (25 cigarettes) daily gets 250 "hits" of nicotine each day (NIDA).
- Upon entering the bloodstream, nicotine immediately stimulates the adrenal glands to release the hormone epinephrine (adrenaline) (NIDA).
- Epinephrine stimulates the central nervous system and increases blood pressure, respiration, and heart rate (NIDA).

- Nicotine/tobacco suppresses monoamine oxidase inhibitor (MAOI), leaving more Dopamine in the system. MOAI is responsible for the cleanup of dopamine (NIDA).
- Nicotine (primary addictive substance in tobacco smoke) influences continued and compulsive use of the tobacco (Benowitz 2009).
- Nicotine goes into the brain's circulation and binds to neuronal nicotinic acetylcholine receptors (nAChR) when a cigarette is puffed. nAChR are attached to ligand-gated ion channels that give way to sodium, potassium, and calcium ions.
- Most nAChR in the brain are presynaptically located and regulate the release of acetylcholine (Ach), dopamine, serotonin, glutamate, gama-aminobutyric acid (GABA), and norepinephrine (Dani et al. 2007).
- nAChR can also be postsynaptically located, such as on the dopamine-producing neurons in the ventral tegmental area (VTA). Nicotinic acetylcholine receptors in the brain are α4β2 and α7nAChR which are the two most commonly expressed receptors (Dani et al. 2007).
- Stimulation of the α4β2 nAChR located on the dopamine cell bodies in the ventral tegmental area shifts these cells from less active to more active resulting in increased dopamine release in both the nucleus accumbens and the prefrontal cortex (Herman et al. 2014).
- Similar to other drugs of abuse, increased dopamine release in the nucleus accumbens facilitates the rewarding and pleasurable effects of nicotine and is theorized to play an important role in the starting and continuing of nicotine addiction. Increased dopamine release in the prefrontal cortex is thought to be critical in mediating the cognitive-enhancing effects of nicotine (Herman et al. 2014).
- The nucleus accumbens also contains GABA and glutamate synapses (along with dopamine synapses), which inhibit and stimulate nicotine-induced dopamine release, respectively. Prolonged exposure to nicotine is associated with desensitization and upregulation of nAChRs and the rates of these changes vary across nAChR subtypes (Mansvelder et al. 2009).
- A relative deficiency of GABA over glutamate may lead to an enhanced dopamine release in the nucleus accumbens and this may be a crucial mechanism that propagates nicotine addiction (Mansvedler et al. 2009).

Nicotine's epigenetic impact

As mentioned earlier in this chapter, there are multiple sensitive periods (that impact cognition and emotion) of brain development from conception to adolescence and early adulthood (around age 26), which are easily disrupted in the context of substance use. Several studies on substances of abuse highlight the fact that adolescence (as a critical developmental phase) also appears to be a critical period for maturation of the mesocortical dopamine system, during which it is vulnerable to gene–environment interactions (Yuan et al. 2015). Dopamine neurons of the ventral tegmental area only begin to express the netrin-1 receptor UNC5C during adolescence (Manitt et al. 2010; Auger et al. 2013). While the other netrin-1 receptor, DCC (deleted in colorectal cancer), is expressed earlier, adolescence is a period in which it exerts unique effects on the organization of mesocortical dopamine circuitry (Grant et al. 2007, 2009;

Manitt et al. 2011). Numerous studies have demonstrated nicotine's neurotoxicity (damage to brain cells, neurons) at multiple stages of brain development.

Yaun et al. review of myriad animal and human studies on nicotine's impact on the developing brain suggests that rapidly maturing dopamine systems may be especially sensitive to disruption by environmental influences during adolescence, with long-term consequences on behavior and associated psychopathologies such as drug abuse or schizophrenia (Yuan et al. 2015).

Equally, both human epidemiological and preclinical research models have demonstrated that exposure to tobacco smoke in utero is harmful to development and can result in low birth weight, sudden infant death syndrome, and serious behavioral issues in the offspring (Abbott and Winzer-Serhan 2012).

The literature perpetually articulates the challenge in distinguishing indirect epigenetic effects of paternal and/or maternal nicotine abuse on the offspring from potential in utero or postnatal second-hand smoke exposure. Some studies have shown increased risk of spontaneous abortion associated with paternal smoking (Blanco-Munoz et al. 2009; Venners et al. 2004).

Various studies have secured evidence that male smoking affects multiple fertility factors in the male in the form of defects in the tail of the spermatozoon (Ozgur et al. 2005) and decreases in sperm density, motility, and morphology (Sofikitis et al. 1995). Some studies have demonstrated decreased semen volume (Pasqualotto et al. 2006).

Nicotine has been demonstrated to alter genes, impact sperm, and negatively impact brain development.

Nicotine's impact on the adolescent brain

During adolescence, the brain does not mature by increasing in size, but brain development is refined by the reorganization of gray matter, white matter, and neurochemical systems (Yuan, et al. 2015). Changes in cognition in adolescence correspond with a decrease in cortical gray matter thickness, resulting from both losses of certain neuronal connections and strengthening of others (Ostby et al. 2009; Gogtay et al. 2010; Paus 2010). These changes (brain refined by reorganization) are connected to greater neuronal efficiency and capacity for sharper, more sophisticated cognition.

The following structural brain changes have been noted during adolescence:

- Gray matter volume and density decrease in the prefrontal cortex (important for impulse control, executive functioning)—(Giedd et al. 1999).
- Gray matter volume and density decreases in parietal cortex and basal ganglia (responsible for sensory procession and motivated behaviors)—(Sowell et al. 1999, 2001).
- Increase in white matter, which is thought to reflect increased myelination and axonal diameter, resulting in increased efficiency of impulse transduction (Paus 2010).

Protracted nicotine exposure during adolescence is also shown to contribute to changes in the neurochemistry of the brain and behavior. The following has been noted:

- Changes to the serotonin system—changes in serotonin receptor function manifest as decreased serotonin receptor binding (namely 5-HT2 receptor binding) and changes in serotonin signaling (Xu et al. 2002).
- Some studies have demonstrated that chronic nicotine exposure during adolescence has a negative impact on serotonin systems into adulthood (Slotkin et al. 2009, 2014).
- Chronic high dose nicotine exposure has been theorized to result in age-specific decrease in striatal serotonin transporter densities (Collins et al. 2004).
- Changes in serotonin indirectly impact several other neurochemicals like dopamine, GABA, and glutamate.
- Changes in serotonin binding, signaling, and transporters have implications for increased risk for depression, anxiety, and other mood components in adolescence.

Adolescence and vaping
According to the National Institute on Drug Abuse (NIDA), e-cigarettes are popular among teens and are now the most commonly used form of tobacco among youth in the United States.

In 2017, the Monitoring the Future survey (MTF) queried high school students about vaping specific substances ever, in the past year and in the past month.

MTF is a long-term epidemiological study that assesses trends in illicit and legal drug use among American adolescents and adults. Equally, it assesses perceived risk and disapproval for each drug.

According to 2017 MTF results:

- Vaping among 8th graders was 13.3%.
- Vaping among 10th graders was 23.9%.
- Vaping among 12th graders was 27.8%.
- Vaping was the third most common form of substance use in high school seniors and 10th graders (after alcohol and marijuana) and the second most common among 8th graders (after alcohol) **(NIDA, MTF)**.

Tobacco use is decreasing secondary to tighter government regulation (Farrelly et al. 2013; US Dept of Health and Human services 2014). As demonstrated by the MTF results, the use of e-cigs and vaping is steadily increasing and these products have been marketed as a smoking cessation aid and a safer alternative to smoking (Paradise 2014).

The Food and Drug Administration (FDA) now regulates manufacturing, importing, packaging, labeling, advertising, promotion, sale, and distribution of e-cigarettes. Under U.S. FDA regulations, minors can no longer buy e-cigarettes in stores or online—for the protection of the health of young Americans **(NIDA, E-cigs)**.

Electronic cigarettes, known as e-cigarettes and e-vaporizers, or electronic nicotine delivery systems, are battery-operated devices that people use to inhale an aerosol, which typically contains nicotine (though not always), flavorings, and other chemicals (Camenga et al. 2014). They take on the form of pipes, pens, and some even look like USB memory sticks **(E-cigarettes, NIDA)**.

While e-cigarettes are new and little is understood about their long-term sequele, early studies suggest that e-cigarette use may serve as an introductory product for preteens and teens who then go on to use other tobacco products, including cigarettes, which are known to cause disease and premature death. Other early studies suggest that e-cigarettes are a gateway drug given the high nicotine content that hijacks the reward pathways of the brain **(E-cigarettes, NIDA)**.

According to the CDC and US Department of Health and Human Services, e-cigarettes, neurobiologically, impact the brain's dopamine and reward pathways similar to other drugs. This means that e-cigarettes, a form of nicotine, also affect the development of brain circuits that control attention and learning. Other risks include mood disorders and permanent problems with impulse control—failure to fight an urge or impulse that may harm oneself or others (Executive summary US DH 2016).

Cannabis and the developing brain

In this section, cannabis will be briefly discussed as Chap. 5 goes into greater detail about the history, epidemiology, and societal, psychological, and legal and physical impact.

Marijuana should be compared to other substances of abuse in terms of its impact on the developing brain.

Marijuana refers to the dried leaves, flowers, stems, and seeds from the hemp plant, *Cannabis sativa.*

The plant contains the mind-altering chemical *delta-9-tetrahydrocannabinol* (THC) and other related compounds—NIDA

Marijuana is the most commonly used illicit (legal in some states) drug in the United States.

Marijuana use is widespread among young people.

Marijuana is used in several ways:

- Smoked marijuana in hand-rolled cigarettes (*joints*),
- In pipes or water pipes (*bongs*) or blunts—emptied cigars partly filled with marijuana,
- Edibles (i.e., brownies, cookies, candy, and brew tea),
- Smoking and/or eating different forms of THC-rich resins,
- Vaporizers (these units pull THC primarily from marijuana and concentrate vapor in a storage unit, then the vapor is inhaled, not the smoke),
- Tinctures, and
- Oils.

Neurobiological impact on the brain

THC acts on specific brain cell receptors that ordinarily react to natural THC-like chemicals in the brain. These natural chemicals play a role in normal brain development and function, more details on this phenomenon will be provided in Chap. 5.

Marijuana over activates parts of the brain that contain the highest number of THC-like receptors, activates the reward pathway, and stimulates dopamine release—contributing to the "high" that users feel.

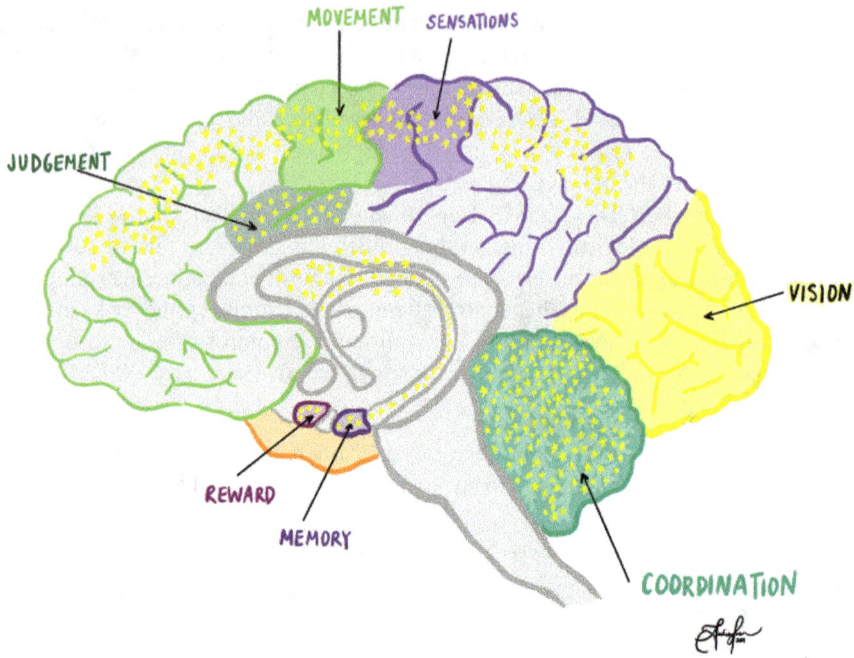

Fig. 4.6 Marijuana impacts reward (ventral tegmental area, amygdala, striatum), memory (hippocampus), judgement (cerebral cortex), movement (motor cortex), sensation, vision (occipital cortex), and coordination (cerebellum). Printed with permission. Copyright Audrey A. Tran

Other effects include

- Altered senses (for example, seeing brighter colors),
- Altered sense of time,
- Changes in mood,
- Impaired body movement,
- Difficulty with thinking and problem-solving, and
- Impaired memory (Fig. 4.6).

Cannabis's epigenetics impact
Various studies in human and animal models reveal irregular epigenetic modifications in the brain and periphery linked to cannabis exposure.

DNA methylation marks at specific gene loci have been shown to even persist during the maturation of germ cells (egg and sperm) (Szyf 2013, 2015) and thus are interesting candidates for the propagation of the long-term effects of cannabis throughout multiple generations.

Histone lysine methylation is known to maintain stable gene expression alterations, and it is also the nucleosomal modification that has been associated with the long-term effects of marijuana and different cannabinoids in neurons and other cell types (Aguado et al. 2007; DiNieri 2017; Tomasiewicz et al. 2012; Yang et al. 2014).

Noncoding RNAs (ncRNAs) regulate gene expression at the transcriptional and posttranscriptional level. Changes in miRNA (one of three different noncoding RNA) profiles have been associated with cannabinoid exposure in the mammalian brain, peripheral blood cells, and the gut (Chandra et al. 2015; Hedge et al. 2013; Jackson et al. 2014; Molina et al. 2011).

Studies have demonstrated cannabis's ability to change genes and expression of specific proteins. As discussed at the beginning of this chapter, cannabis use has transgenerational implications.

Cannabis's impact on the developing brain

Cannabis use is such a controversial topic. Some studies demonstrate severe cognitive, attentional, and behavioral impact and others don't. Individuals are divided in two powerful ways, those who do not believe cannabis has harmful impact on humans and those who do not believe it is benign. In the case of the youth and from my clinical experience as a double board certified addiction psychiatrist, I believe it is critical to consider the fact that brain is still developing and the brain must be given a fighting chance to develop to its full potential. I contend (and some may vehemently disagree) that many substances should be avoided until brain development is near complete (around the age of 26). The impact of cannabis on the developing brain will be covered more thoroughly in Chap. 5. This textbook is about transforming systems that serve youth, which also requires facilitating powerful transformation in and of youth. We can all agree that what we've been doing has not been effective. I encourage an open mind with a focus on solutions and healing moving forward. The trend for vaping and marijuana use is increasing according to the Monitoring the Future Survey for 2017, and this should be concerning for multiple reasons.

Alcohol and the developing brain

According to the 2017 Monitoring the Future Survey, alcohol use and binge drinking continued to show a significant 5-year decline among all grades.

Daily alcohol use and binge drinking (defined as consuming five or more drinks sometime in the past 2 weeks) also decreased significantly among all grades between 2012 and 2017.

Monitoring the Future Survey: High School and Youth Trends. December 2017. Retrieved from https://www.drugabuse.gov/publications/drugfacts/monitoring-future-survey-high-school-youth-trends.

Neurobiological impact on the brain.

I hope that the pattern is noted here as alcohol impacts the brain similar to cocaine, methamphetamine, nicotine, and cannabis.

Alcohol modulates several neurotransmitters to include dopamine (robustly), GABA, glutamate, and serotonin. Specifically:

- Alcohol activates the reward pathway in the limbic system (dopamine-rich pathway). Dopamine is released in the ventral tegmental area and projects to the nucleus accumbens.

- Alcohol decreases glutamate (excitatory neurotransmitter) in the nucleus accumbens and limits glutamate-supported signal transmission in the amygdala (specifically in the central nucleus of the amygdala).
- Alcohol changes N-Methyl-D-aspartic acid (NMDA) and glutamate receptors, disrupting glutamate transmission.
- Alcohol increases the release of GABA (inhibitory neurotransmitter), enhancing GABA receptor action in the post-synapse.
- There is an association with alcohol use and reduction in serotonin (Ruiz et al. 2011).

Alcohol's epigenetic impact
Chronic alcohol exposure produces changes in DNA and histone methylation, histone acetylation, and microRNA expression that affect expression of multiple genes in various types of brain cells (i.e., neurons and glia) and contribute to brain pathology and brain plasticity associated with alcohol abuse and dependence.

DNA methylation generally is associated with transcriptional repression.

Multiple studies on alcohol's impact on the brain highlight various epigenetic processes in controlling alcohol-induced changes in brain gene expression and behavior, which may play an important part in the development of alcohol addiction.

Alcohol's impact on the developing brain
Alcohol interferes with the brain's communication pathways and can affect the way the brain looks and works. These disruptions can change mood and behavior, and make it harder to think clearly and move with coordination.

Research indicates that alcohol use during the teenage years could interfere with normal adolescent brain development and increase the risk of developing AUD. In addition, underage drinking contributes to a range of acute consequences, including injuries, sexual assaults, and even deaths—including those from car crashes (NIAA 2006).

Several studies on alcohol and the adolescent population reveal that the prefrontal cortex may be more vulnerable to the effects of alcohol than other brain regions as it continues to develop throughout adolescence and young adulthood—(Squelia et al. 2014).

The cerebral cortex (namely the prefrontal cortex), limbic system, cerebellum, and other parts of the cortex (all parts of the brain that are still developing), have been identified as being vulnerable to the effects of alcohol use during adolescence (Squeglia et al. 2009a).

A study by De Bellis et al. revealed that adolescents and young adults (ages 13–21) diagnosed with alcohol use disorders had smaller bilateral hippocampal volumes than demographically matched controls; those who started drinking at a younger age and who had a longer duration of alcohol use disorder had even smaller hippocampal volume (De Bellis et al. 2000).

Cortical thickness in adolescent's age 16–19 that were identified as heavy episodic drinkers was reviewed. Gender interactions were considered with binge drinking in four left frontal brain regions in a study by Squeglia et al. 2011. Female binge drinkers had thicker cortices compared to female controls in the four left frontal regions. Male binge drinkers had thinner cortices compared to male controls. In this case, thicker cortices = less mature. Less mature, thicker cortices correlated with poorer visuospatial, inhibition, and attention performances for female bingers and worse attention for male bingers. Squeglia and colleagues (Squeglia et al. 2011).

White matter allows for efficient information processing and quick communication between cortical regions. White matter continues to increase linearly in volume until late adolescence and early adulthood (Lebel and Beaulieu 2011). Several structural MRI studies have found smaller overall white matter volumes in adolescents with alcohol use disorders compared to matched controls, particularly prefrontal cortex white matter (De Bellis et al. 2005).

Various studies suggest that heavy drinking during adolescence has a subtle but significant deleterious effect on adolescent neurocognitive functioning and working memory (Squeglia et al. 2014).

Alcohol withdrawal

Alcohol use can lead to addiction, which includes loss of control, continued use despite consequences, brain changes in the reward pathway, a need for more of substance to get a high and withdrawal from the substance when you don't have it. As mentioned earlier, alcohol is not a benign drug not solely because of its impact on the developing brain, but it is also dangerous in withdrawal. Alcohol withdrawal can lead and has led to death.

Opioid withdrawal is uncomfortable and unpleasant and begins to pose threat to life in the context of severe dehydration, electrolyte imbalance, and fluid loss (unreplaced). Alcohol withdrawal can result in autonomic changes (heart rate and blood pressure changes) and can lead to seizure—alcohol withdrawal is serious and can lead to death.

Opioids and the developing brain

As described earlier in this chapter, opioid abuse, misuse, dependence, and overdose related deaths have increased significantly. It is now deemed a public health crisis in America and as such the government has appropriated funds for research, intervention, prevention, and treatment.

A recent article regarding trends of medical (prescribed by a licensed medical provider for a medical purpose like postsurgical) versus nonmedical (i.e., use of a parents prescription or purchase off the street) concluded that prescription opioid exposure is common among US adolescents. Long-term trends indicate that one-fourth of high school seniors self-reported medical or nonmedical use of prescription opioids. Medical and nonmedical use of prescription opioids has declined recently and remained highly correlated over the past 4 decades. The decrease may be attributed to the public health policy approach to include but not limited to psychoeducation of licensed medical providers on the addictive capacity of prescription opioids; educating patients about the risks of long-term opioid use and offering alternatives to short- and long-term pain management; the recognition that opioids have contributed to increased, unnecessary death; implementation of prescription drug monitoring programs nationally to track all scripts that may be controlled substances; and improved access to treatment services (like medication-assisted treatment) for individuals who have become dependent (McCabe et al. 2017).

Neurobiological impact on the brain

In the 1990s, research highlighted the fact that human beings have what is called an endogenous (endogenous is naturally occurring) opioid system in the form of three major opioid receptors to include the mu-opioid receptor, kappa-opioid receptor, and the delta-opioid receptor. These internal receptors help to manage pain. These opioid receptors are activated by endogenous peptides like enkephalins, dynorphins, and endorphin, which are released by neurons. The endogenous opioid system is a primitive system that naturally aids in tempering pain in the human body.

Several studies have demonstrated a number of external substances (also called exogenous opioids) like morphine (which is similarly structured like endogenous opioids enkephalins, dynorphins, and endorphin) can activate the endogenous opioid system and modulate pain as well. While exogenous opioids like morphine can and do activate the endogenous opioid system, it has very different and dire consequences. Exogenous opioids like heroin (modified and structured to act on the naturally occurring receptor, not natural to the body) mimic endogenous opioids (i.e., enkephalins) and disrupt how neurons send, receive, and process signals through neurotransmitters—a familiar theme throughout this chapter. When substances like heroin (an exogenous, not naturally occurring opioid) attaches to an endogenous opioid receptor (mu, kappa and/or delta), it activates the neuron, driving a series of miscommunicated, confused signals throughout the brain and body.

Opioids undermine brain circuitry and disrupt the dopaminergic pathway in two very important ways: (1) Interrupts the frontal cortex, the area of the brain responsible for goal setting, motivation, and control of impulses and planning and (2) Heightens limbic negative affect, impulsivity, anxiety. Namely, the hippocampus and amygdala are impacted (Feng et al. 2012).

Opioids also work at the level of the brain stem (bottom, primitive brain), which is responsible for controlling breathing, heart rate, and impacting sleep. This level of activity, quite frankly, is what has rendered exogenous opioids (prescription drugs like morphine/oxycodone/fentanyl and illegal substances like heroin) so incredibly dangerous in overdose—they have the powerful ability to compromise breathing and have contributed to disproportionate death in the United States of America and beyond. More complicated is when opioids are combined with other substances that powerfully suppress ability to breath (lung capacity) to include alcohol and benzodiazepines.

Opioids epigenetic impact

Neonatal opioid withdrawal syndrome was addressed earlier in this chapter and demonstrates the impact that in utero exposure can have on the developing brain and body. There is a body of emerging literature that suggests epigenetic changes with opioid use—like the other substances outlined in this chapter. Recall that epigenetic is a fancy word for environmental impact on gene expression. Do recall the various epigenetic methods by which gene expression can be changed (i.e., DNA methylation, acetylation, histone changes, etc.). The μ-opioid receptor is expressed in sperm cells and β-endorfin, an endogenous opioid, is produced locally in the male reproductive tract (Albrizio et al. 2006). Expression of all opioid receptors is also detected in oocytes and, interestingly, the pattern of μ- and κ-opioid receptors is changing during oocyte maturation, which points to a possible role of endorphins in this process (Agirregoitia et al. 2012; Gilard et al. 2018).

Some of the epigenetic changes noted in the literature with opioid use

- The presence of opioid receptors in both gamete types is suggestive of possible epigenetic effects triggered by opioids on these cells that, in turn, could be transmitted to subsequent generations.
- Some studies suggest opioid addiction increased DNA methylation at specific sites of the *OPRM* gene (gene provides directives for making a protein called the mu (μ) opioid receptor) promoter in several cells, including sperm (Nielsen et al. 2010; Chorbov et al. 2011; Ebrahimi et al. 2018).

An article by Gilardi et al. asserts that converging evidence suggests that opioids can induce long-lasting transgenerational changes in subsequent generations, particularly concerning drug sensitivity and tolerance, with possible implications for drug abuse vulnerability (Gilardi et al. 2018).

Of note, a prospective observational cohort study was conducted in 133 adolescents with idiopathic scoliosis undergoing spine fusion under standard protocols demonstrated DNA methylation at the mu-1 opioid receptor gene (*OPRM1*) promoter predicts preoperative, acute, and chronic postsurgical pain after spine fusion. Changes in the OPRM1 gene that were likely passed along from mother and/or father in an intergenerational fashion further suggesting that the environment (with prior exposure to a substance) can impact genes and gene expression (Chidambaran et al. 2017).

Methamphetamines, cocaine, alcohol, nicotine, cannabis, and opioids all impact the developing brain similarly. Studies on each of these substances have demonstrated a deleterious impact on brain development at multiple stages. An epigenetic impact has been demonstrated, meaning that substances of abuse can and have changed the gene expression and impacted the passing of those changes in genes from one generation to the next known as intergenerational transmission and to some extent, transgenerationally. Myriad studies on substances of abuse and developing brain have also pointed to the negative impact in the form of considerable compromise of cognition, memory, impulse control, attention, and ability to exercise good judgment. By way of reminder, the brain develops from the bottom-up and the inside-out, this means that the top part of the brain is near the last to develop, leaving it vulnerable and susceptible to threats like trauma and substances. Think of the brain as a moving wheel, what happens when you put a cog in that wheel? We know the answer, a cog in a wheel results in arrested and disrupted motion of that wheel. Substances and trauma are very much like a cog in the brain's developmental wheel. To this end, it is important to refresh the memory and make the connection between trauma and substances of abuse as posing similar threats to brain development. The impact of substances on the developing brain should be strongly considered when working with youth and adults alike (as adults were youth who may or may not have had early exposure to substances as well).

Hallucinogens

Hallucinogens are set of drugs that profoundly change perception, thoughts, and behavior. Their use has the potential to cause long-term perceptual disturbances (hallucinations, psychosis).

Side effects of hallucinogens and dissociative drugs (drugs that have individuals feeling disconnected from their body or outside of their own body, detached) are dose dependent.

At lower doses, an individual can experience numbness, confusion, loss of coordination, dizziness, nausea, vomiting, perceptual disturbances, dissociation, and autonomic instability (heart rate, blood pressure, breathing, and body temperature changes).

At higher doses risk of memory loss is high. When hallucinogens and dissociative drugs are combined with other substances like alcohol or benzodiazepines, they can lead to death (hallucinogens and dissociative drugs 2019).

While the national data suggest that hallucinogen use among youth and adolescents remains at a steady low, experimentation of these drugs typically happens in adolescence. It is important to know what hallucinogens are as class of drugs and what the current literature reveals on their individual and collective impact on the developing brain.

LSD, Psilocybin (mushrooms), and the developing brain

Lysergic acid diethylamide (LSD) is a known hallucinogen. LSD is odorless, clear, and white substance derived from fungus that grows on rye and other grains. Data about its use are controversial, and some studies suggest that the therapeutic index is high and others indicate it is low. LSD has been described as a substance that creates bliss, connectedness, happiness, and psychosis—it is theorized to modulate the release of hormones like oxytocin. In Australia, LSD is used in a therapeutic setting, but it is not used in the United States in such context. Youth are experimenting more with this substance, so it is important to know its physiological and behavioral impact. My sole public service announcement: give the brain a fighting chance. As you review this section on LSD, consider Chap. 1 on the developing brain.

Carhart-Harris and colleagues investigated how LSD acts on the brain through functional brain imaging. LSD acts on serotonin receptors and is deemed a serotonergic hallucinogen. LSD activity at the serotonin receptor (there are multiple serotonin receptor subtypes, LSD works mainly at 5HT2A) (Halberstadt 2015) is theorized t impact cognition and play a role in hallucinations by an ill-understood mechanism. The study highlighted the following changes in the brain in the context of LSD use: (Carhart-Harris et al. 2016)

- Blood flow,
- Electrical activity, and
- Network communication patterns—postulated to be connected with LSD's hallucination-producing and consciousness-altering component.

Hallucinations related to LSD were characterized by

- Increased visual cortex cerebral blood flow (CBF), decreased visual cortex alpha power, and a greatly expanded primary visual cortex (V1) functional connectivity profile.
- LSD appears to have a significant impact on visual processing.

LSD's impact on the brain was demonstrated as follows (Carhart-Harris et al. 2016):

- Right middle temporal gyrus (main part of the brain responsible for hearing),
- Superior/middle/inferior/frontal gyrus (part of the brain involved in speech production and understanding),
- Anterior cingulate cortex (plays a role in cognition and emotion, involved in fear conditioning),
- Left superior frontal and postcentral gyrus (plays a role in language), and
- Cerebellum (plays a role in speech, movement, coordination, and balance).

Other areas activated in producing the visual images experienced with LSD use (Carhart-Harrris et al. 2016)

- Changes in thalamus functioning (sensory),
- Increased activity in the paralimbic structures (emotions), and
- Increased activity in the frontal cortex (cognition).

A review by Liechti (2017) on the latest clinical research on LSD highlighted the following:

- Plasma concentration of cortisol is acutely increased with cortisol (Strajhar et al. 2016).
- Increased concentrations of prolactin, oxytocin, and epinephrine (Schmid et al. 2015).
- Blissful psychosis—as increased delusional thinking and cognitive disorganization are noted with LSD intoxication (Carhart-Harris et al. 2016).
- Impaired an individual to recognize certain facial emotions like fear and/or sadness (Dolder et al. 2016).
- This may seem contradictory (after I just wrote above that a study stated LSD's capacity to decrease empathy by impairing emotion recognition on the face), LDS has been noted to also increase emotional empathy (Dolder et al. 2016).

There are physical effects of LSD too, and it can lead to

- Autonomic instability (blood pressure changes, increased heart rate, and rhythm changes) and
- Metabolic changes—increase in blood sugar.

Psilocybin (mushrooms)

Psilocybin (mushrooms) like LSD make their psychedelic impact through acting on pathways in the brain that use serotonin. Psilocybin is derived from various types of mushrooms found in tropical and subtropical parts of Mexico, US, and South America. Mushrooms mainly impact the prefrontal cortex, the part of the brain that is responsible for planning, organizing, exercising good judgment, impulse control, and emotion regulation.

3,4-Methylenedioxymethamphetamine (MDMA) AKA *Ecstasy and the developing brain*

Most of the studies on Ecstasy have been done in animal models. Ecstasy effects are mediated by central serotonin networks (Battaglia et al. 1987). Serotonin plays a critical role in higher level cognitive processes, memory, emotion regulation, sleep, and pain. One of the few human studies on the impact of Ecstasy on the brain confirmed disturbances in serotonin uptake sites (Ricuarte et al. 2000). A study on the developing brain and MDMA's impact on serotonin pathways varied based on age of exposure (Klomp et al. 2012). The following is understood about ecstasy thus far regarding ecstasy (Kelly 2000):

- Studies demonstrating the cognitive and mood disturbances, and increased risk of strokes with Ecstasy (Cohen and Cocores 1997; Curran and Travill 1997; Davison and Parrott 1997).
- Neurotoxicity secondary to increased disruption to certain hormone production (McCann et al. 1999).
- Insufficiencies in verbal memory and reasoning (Reneman et al. 2000).
- Shortfalls in short memory and semantic recognition (McCann et al. 1999).
- Shortages in visual memory (Bolla et al. 1998).

Phencyclidine (PCP) and developing brain

Phencyclidine (PCP) is classified a hallucinogen as it alters the mental state similar to LSD. PCP is found in the following forms: tablets, capsules, white crystal powder, and liquid. The mechanism by which PCP exerts its action differs from LSD in that its main target is the excitatory neurotransmitter glutamate and NMDA receptors. According to a study by Lindahl and colleagues, manipulation of glutamate concentrations and receptors is theorized to play a role in changes in brain glial cells responsible for myelination of neurons in the central nervous system (also known as oligodendrocytes). The study used rat models to better understand the relationship between glutamate and oligodendrocytes. Lindahl et al. blocked NMDA receptors with PCP in the prenatal phase and then examined different stages of oligodendrocyte development in the postnatal phase. Results in rat brains with prenatal exposure to PCP revealed the following (Lindahl et al. 2008):

- Oligodendrocyte progenitor cell markers are decreased.
- Immature cells were increased.
- Late stage markers for oligodendrocytes were decreased.

Lindahl et al. study suggests that PCP impacts the development of brain cell (neurons and in this case neurons responsible for myelination). In a study by Harris and colleagues, blockade of NMDA receptors in neonatal rats was reported to increase neuronal cell death (Harris et al. 2003; Lindahl et al. 2008).

Ketamine

Ketamine is an N-methyl-D-aspartate (NMDA) receptor ion channel blocker that is being widely used in obstetric and pediatric anesthesia. It is used because of the following characteristics, it is short acting and provides quick dissociative anesthesia and is associated with quick recovery. Ketamine is being sold on the street, being diverted from veterinary offices. It is sold in pill, powder, and injectable liquid form on the streets. Nonmedical uses of ketamine can profoundly impact the brain. Most studies on its impact have been demonstrated in animal models (mostly rats and rat pups).

In adolescent rat models, ketamine was found to induce the learning and memory impairment and damage to neurons. The cerebral cortex and hippocampus were noted for marked neuronal damage (Wang et al. 2014).

Studies in rats demonstrated Ketamine's deleterious effects on the developing brain as NMDA-receptor antagonists may also have direct neurotoxic effects. Ketamine appears to impact synaptogenesis (Zou et al. 2009; Liu et al. 2011) **and** gene expression in rat brain development according to a study by Liu and colleagues (Liu et al. 2011).

Addictive potential of hallucinogens and dissociative drugs is mixed. There is evidence of cross tolerance, in other words use of one hallucinogen can result in tolerance to similar drugs. In the case of the developing brain, studies suggest that nonmedical use of hallucinogens and dissociative drugs can exert significant harm to the developing and developed brain.

Emerging trend (honorable mention): Social media, smartphones, and the developing brain

Emerging studies highlight how susceptible the developing brain is to social media. A review by Crone and Konijn summarizes literature on behavioral trends (the need to be accepted and sensitivity to feedback of their peers) and critical brain development milestones/stages in adolescents (ages 10–22 mostly) to include emotion regulation, ability to reflect on and make sense of how we view ourselves and how we view others also known as mentalization (mostly frontal cortex functions) and social reward processing (involving parts of the prefrontal cortex and limbic structures like the amygdala) (Meshi et al. 2015) and social media's capacity to disrupt these brain developmental milestones (Crone and Konijn 2018).

Cyberbullying, increase in depression and anxiety from comparing oneself to images on social media, and changes in the reward circuits of the developing brain have all been mentioned in association with the rising prominence of smartphone use and social media engagement.

Depending on the input from social media, brain development and behavior in adolescents can be positive and/or less than ideal. What should be noted here is that trending and emerging studies suggest that social media can impact brain development. A trend worthy of close observation.

Increased nonmedical benzo use in adolescents

There has been a recent trend in adolescents using benzodiazepines that have not been prescribed to them or used for a purpose that the medication was not envisioned for, in the literature, this is called nonmedical use.

Benzodiazepines have street names **benzos, downers, nerve pills, and tranks. They** are a class of drugs that can depress the central nervous system. Benzos are usually prescribed to treat sleep issues and anxiety. Dependence potential is high as benzos do possess a tolerance and withdrawal phenomenon. Historically, risk for abuse has been higher in individual with a history of prior substance use. According to the DEA, the most commonly prescribed and misused (used on the street for nonmedical purposes) benzos include Alprazolam (e.g., Xanax), lorazepam (e.g., Ativan), clonazepam (e.g., Klonopin), diazepam (e.g., Valium), and temazepam (e.g., Restoril).Benzos have different rates of onset, meaning how fast they act in the system and how fast they leave the system. Benzos are Schedule IV depressants under controlled substances as defined by the Drug Enforcement Agency (DEA) (Drug Enforcement Administration Office of Diversion Control).

Benzodiazepines with rapid onset are more likely to be abused to produce a euphoric effect. The following trends have been noted:

- Diazepam and alprazolam are used in combination with methadone to potentiate methadone's euphoric effects.
- Cocaine addicts use benzodiazepines to relieve the side effects (e.g., irritability and agitation) associated with cocaine binges.
- Benzodiazepines are also used to augment alcohol's effects and modulate withdrawal states.
- Benzodiazepines have been used to facilitate sexual assault.
- Persons who abuse benzos, typically use them in higher doses than are safe and/or indicated.

According to this same DEA report, The American Association of Poison Control Centers reported over 80,000 case mentions, over 31,000 exposures, 11 deaths, of great significance, an estimated 345,691 emergency department visits attributed to benzodiazepines in 2010 (New DAWN ED) with alprazolam, clonazepam, lorazepam, and diazepam being predominant.

Benzodiazepines activate the gamma amino butyric acid (GABA)-A receptor. The GABA-A receptor is a ligand-gated chloride-selective ion channel. GABA is the most common neurotransmitter in the central nervous system, found in high concentrations in the cortex and limbic system (Griffin et al. 2013).

There are not many studies on this uptick in the nonmedical use of benzodiazepines in adolescence. Boyd et al. conducted the first longitudinal, prospective study to survey the association between an adolescent having a legally prescribed prescription for an anxiolytic or sleep medication and their long-term risk of using another person's prescription for these classes of medication.

The prospective study had three hypotheses (Boyd et al. 2014):

1. A recent prescription would be associated with a higher incidence of nonmedical use was supported. By medication class, the study demonstrated that adolescents

with a recent prescription were 6–9 times more likely to engage in nonmedical use of the class of medication they were recently prescribed.
2. Once exposed to a prescribed anxiolytic or sleep medication, some adolescents would begin using them for sensation-seeking motivations, in contrast to self-treating motivations. This was determined to be an accurate prediction.
3. Predicted that acquiring more cumulative experience medically would be associated with an increased incidence of nonmedical use.

There were 2745 participants. They were divided into three groups based on responses to a questionnaire administered regarding lifetime and recent use of anxiety reduction and sleep medication.

1. Never prescribed anxiolytic or sleep medication in their lifetime
2. Prescribed anxiolytic or sleep medication in their lifetime, but not during the 3-year study; or
3. Prescribed anxiolytic or sleep medication during the 3-year study. Each time the SSLS was administered, the respondents were asked about their medical use and nonmedical use (i.e., using someone else's prescription) and their motivations to engage in nonmedical use were assessed.

Participants prescribed sleep medication during the study demonstrated higher incidence of nonmedical use for sensation-seeking motivations. Participants prescribed anxiolytic medication during the study were 3–14 times more likely to engage in nonmedical use for self-treating or sensation-seeking motivations, respectively (Boyd et al. 2014).

Benzo withdrawal is very dangerous and can result in death.

Petursson described the benzodiazapene withdrawal syndrome in the following way:

- Sleep disturbance.
- Irritability.
- Increased tension and anxiety, panic attacks.
- Hand tremor.
- Sweating.
- Difficulty in concentration.
- Dry wrenching and nausea.
- Some weight loss.
- Palpitations.
- Headache.
- Muscular pain and stiffness.
- Perceptual changes and disturbances.
- High-dosage category = increased risk of seizure activity and psychosis in withdrawal.
- Common is a short-lived "rebound" anxiety and insomnia, coming on within 1-4 days of discontinuation, depending on the half-life of the particular drug.
- Second pattern is the full-blown withdrawal syndrome, usually lasting 10–14 days.

- Third pattern may represent the return of anxiety symptoms which then persist until some form of treatment is instituted.
- Physiological dependence on benzodiazepines can occur following prolonged treatment, still not clear what proportion of patients are likely to experience a withdrawal syndrome, but its withdrawal is possible and can be dangerous.
- Of note, it is also unknown to what extent the risk of physiological dependence is dependent upon a minimum duration of exposure or dosage of these drugs.
- Withdrawal phenomena appear to be more severe following withdrawal from high doses or short-acting benzodiazepines (Petursson 1994).

According to an article by Steward, benzos long-term impact on cognition is controversial. Long-term treatment with benzodiazepines has been described as causing impairment in several cognitive domains, such as visuospatial ability, speed of processing, and verbal learning. Conversely, long-term benzodiazepine use has also been described as causing no chronic cognitive impairment, with any cognitive dysfunction in patients ascribed to sedation or inattention or considered temporary and associated with peak plasma levels (Stewart 2005).

Benzos limit ability to breathe among other things, but they become more dangerous when they are combined with substances like alcohol and opioids (also depressants that compromise ability to breathe), increasing the risk of overdose and death. Benzos have been known (with long-term use) to impact cognition. In the case of medical use and prescription, long-term benzo use should be avoided in youth. In terms of nonmedical use of benzos, use should be avoided completely, especially in the case of the developing brain.

Energy drinks and health consequences in adolescents
Energy drinks contain high levels of caffeine and are marketed as way for people to get more energy to be more attentive. Energy drink consumption has increased among adolescents with notable trends in the association of cardiac arrest and consumption of energy drinks; increased mortality when energy drinks are combined with alcohol and an association between executive function changes and use of energy drinks. While there is not a ton of research on the impact of excessive caffeine exposure through energy drink consumption and its impact on adolescence, it is worthy of being highlighted in this chapter.

A 2017 editorial was written about unexplained cardiac arrest in some young individuals developed after consuming energy drinks, particularly simultaneously with alcohol intake. The editorial read: "The concern is that these beverages could easily lead to severe cardiovascular events in young and older individuals who have underlying silent cardiovascular disease. Because of their high amounts of caffeine and other substrates, dangerous arrhythmias can easily develop in the hearts of individuals who consume them." (2017, Sports energy drinks).

This editorial, other commentary, and limited studies all highlight concern regarding high caffeine concentrations on both the body and the brain.

A study by Van Batenburg-Eddes et al. sought to investigate the impact of energy drinks on brain development in young people. Noting that young adolescents are in a critical stage in development and endorsing caution when it comes to regular use of energy drinks (excessive caffeine). There were 509 participants between the ages 11 and 16; they were required to report their caffeine (like coffee) and energy drink consumption for every day of the week. Each participant was also asked to give information on their sleeping patterns and quality. Parents (parents offered their perspective on how high caffeine intake impacted their youth's ability to organize, plan, be attentive, etc.) and participants completed the Behavior Rating Inventory of Executive Function (BRIEF). The study found the following (Van Batenburg-Eddes et al. 2014):

- One or more energy drinks per day were associated with more problems in self-reported behavior regulation and cognitive function.
- One or more energy drink per day was also associated with more parents noting cognitive changes in their youth.
- High caffeine use, defined as two or more cups per day was associated with parent-reported issues with cognition.
- Caffeine (coffee) + energy drink consumption was associated with greater self-reported cognitive issues and parent-reported challenges with regulating behavior. The following adjustments were made in the study: adjusted for pubertal status, gender, educational level. When these adjustments were made, the number of sleeping problems and hours of sleep did not change the effect estimates substantially (Van Batenburg-Eddes et al. 2014).

The study concluded that there is an observed association between energy drink use in adolescents and disruption in executive function. It is well known that association doesn't equate to causation; however, it is important to keep in mind that the brain develops from the bottom-up and the inside-out, starts from conception and is near completion around the age of 26. One of the main objectives should be to protect this developmental phase as best we can.

Nonmedical use: a worldwide public health threat
The rate of nonmedical use has peaked and is a threat to public health around the world as noted in review article by Martins et al. The article highlights the rise in prescription opioid and stimulant-related morbidity and calls us to consider the consequences. Martins et al. thoughtfully write: "The greater 'social acceptance' for using these medications (versus illegal substances) and the misconception that they are 'safe' may be contributing factors to their misuse. Hence, a major target for intervention is the general public, including parents and youth, who must be better informed about the negative consequences of sharing with others medications prescribed for their own ailments" (Martins and Ghandour 2017).

Pharmacologic management of primary substances of abuse
While there is controversy over treating primary substance use disorders in adolescents (and adults too), studies have powerfully demonstrated the fact that treatment can and has saved lives. For example, the American Academy of Pediatrics recently recommended that pediatricians consider medication-assisted treatment (MAT) for adolescents with severe opioid use disorders (Feder et al. 2017). Every system serv-

ing youth should, at minimum, be aware of current treatment options to make certain that youth have every tool available to them for their healing.

Brief review of how substances of abuse affect the brain's reward pathway

- In the brain, dopamine helps to regulate reward and body movement.
- As part of the reward pathway, dopamine is produced by neurons in the ventral tegmental area (VTA) and released in the nucleus accumbens and the prefrontal cortex, leading to the feeling of pleasure. The pleasure/reward pathway is hijacked in addiction leading to brain changes, compulsive use despite consequences, and loss of control, tolerance, and withdrawal.

Pharmacologic treatment of alcohol use disorders

Action of alcohol: binds to GABA-A receptors, which is an ionotropic receptor and ligand-gated chloride ion channel.

Treatment for alcohol dependence involves agonizing and/or antagonizing GABA-A and sometimes GABA-B receptors.

Pharmacologic treatment options for alcohol include

- Disulfuram—FDA approved in 1951,
- Naltrexone (Oral, Intramuscular and now implantable—designed to block opiate effects for 8–10 weeks)—FDA approved in 1994,
- Acamprosate—FDA approved in 2004,
- Gabapentin,
- Baclofen,
- SSRIs, and
- Nalmefene.

NALTREXONE in the treatment of alcohol use disorders: Opioid receptor antagonist

FDA approved in 1994 for treatment of alcohol dependence, approval was inspired by two 1992 randomized controlled trials that demonstrated its efficacy in reducing frequency and severity of relapse to drinking.

Mechanism of action: Naltrexone and its active metabolite 6-β-naltrexol are competitive antagonists at μ- and κ-opioid receptors, and to a lesser extent at δ-opioid receptors plasma half-life of naltrexone is about 4 h and for 6-β-naltrexol 13 h. Postulated to involve modulation of the dopaminergic mesolimbic pathway.

Forms: Oral formulation is Revia and Depade.

Once-monthly extended-release injectable formulation is Vivitrol.

Common SE's: Gastrointestinal, diarrhea, and abdominal cramping. When given at high doses (beyond 50 mg, there is increased risk for liver damage).

Multicenter COMBINE study showed the usefulness of naltrexone in a primary care setting, without adjunct psychotherapy (Pettinati et al. 2006).

Standard oral dosing is 50 mg per day.

Standard intramuscular IM dosing is 380 mg IM gluteal injection every 4 weeks or once a month.

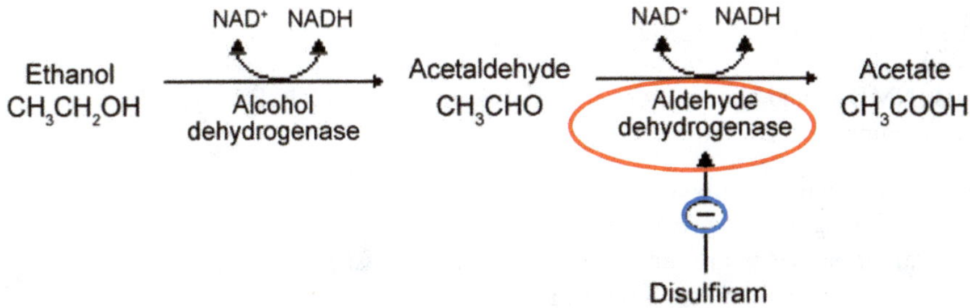

Fig. 4.7 Disulfiram inhibits acetaldehyde dehydrogenase

Disulfiram (Antabuse) in the treatment of alcohol use disorders

DISULFIRAM (Antabuse): inhibitor of ***acetaldehyde dehydrogenase***

Normal metabolism of alcohol: broken down in the liver by the enzyme alcohol dehydrogenase TO acetaldehyde. Acetaldehyde is then converted to less innocuous acetic acid BY acetaldehyde dehydrogenase. Disulfiram blocks this metabolic process (Fig. 4.7).

Total daily dosage of Disulfiram should not exceed 500 mg.

Expect a severe reaction within 10 min of alcohol intake. Symptoms are reminiscent of a severe hangover to include

- Flushing of the skin,
- accelerated heart rate,
- shortness of breath,
- nausea/vomiting,
- throbbing headache,
- visual disturbance,
- mental confusion,
- postural syncope, and
- circulatory collapse.

Disulfiram (Antabuse) side effects:

- Drowsiness (Tryptophol formation),
- Headaches,
- Garlic taste in mouth,
- Rare cases of extrapyramidal symptoms,
- Interaction with acetaminophen, caffeine, and theophylline (occurred in 20–40% and was mild), and
- Liver problems.

It is considered aversion therapy.

It doesn't reduce cravings, so adherence is an issue.

Acamprosate in Treatment of Alcohol Use Disorder

ACAMPROSATE: Theorized to work by antagonizing N-methyl-D-aspartate receptors (NMDA) and agonizing gamma-aminobutyric acid (GABA) type A receptors.

Acamprosate is

- Effective when combined with CBT-based treatment,
- Oral dosing: 666 mg (two 333 mg tabs),
- Acamprosate is poorly absorbed after oral administration,
- Average bioavailability of only 11%,
- Time to reach steady state occurs within 5 days of dosing, and
- Steady-state peak plasma concentrations are reached within 3–8 h following dosing.

Side effects are

- Diarrhea,
- Allergic reactions, and
- Irregular heartbeats and low or high blood pressure.

Acamprosate does not undergo metabolism.

Acamprosate is primarily excreted unchanged through the kidneys; avoid in persons with kidney disease.

No significant drug–drug interactions.

A study by Feeney et al. (2006) found no significant difference between Naltrexone and Acamprosate in terms of average days of abstinence and days until the first breach of abstinence.

Gabapentin in the Treatment of Alcohol Use Disorder

GABAPENTIN: GABA analog

- Side effects:
- Dizziness,
- Fatigue,
- Weight gain,
- Drowsiness, and
- Peripheral edema.

Gabapentin is

- Associated with high risk of suicide and violent deaths,
- Excreted primarily unchanged from the kidney, so avoid in persons with kidney disease,
- Limited drug–drug interactions, and
- Not FDA approved, but study published in JAMA shows Gabapentin as a promising treatment option.

A randomized clinical trial on Gabapentin treatment for alcohol dependence by Mason et al. (2013) suggests utility.

- 12-week randomized, double-blind, placebo-controlled study of 150 subjects with alcohol dependence.
- Oral gabapentin (dosages of 0 [placebo], 900 mg, or 1800 mg/d) and concomitant manual-guided counseling.
- Results: Gabapentin (particularly the 1800-mg dosage) was effective in treating alcohol dependence and relapse-related symptoms of insomnia, dysphoria, and craving, with a favorable safety profile.

Baclofen in the Treatment of Alcohol Use Disorder

Baclofen is a GABA-B agonist; not FDA approved but has demonstrated promise.

Nalmefene in the Treatment of Alcohol Use Disorder

NALMEFENE: opioid receptor modulator with increased relative potency for kappa opiate receptors compared to its potency at mu opiate receptors.

A randomized controlled trial on nalmafene's use in the treatment of alcohol use disorder was promising (Mann et al. 2013).

Study Design:

- Recruited 604 alcohol-dependent patients.
- Half of whom were randomized to receive Nalmefene.
- Other half received visually identical placebo pills.
- Neither patients nor their doctors knew which treatment they were receiving.
- Patients were instructed to take one tablet on each day they perceived a risk of drinking alcohol.
- Each participant was followed by the study investigators for 24 weeks.

Results: Promising.

- Nalmefene was significantly better than placebo in reducing alcohol consumption and it improved patients' clinical status and liver enzymes.
- Generally well-tolerated.

Most side effects characterized as mild or moderate and quickly resolved.

Selective Serotonin Reuptake Inhibitors (SSRIs) in the treatment of alcohol use disorder

SSRIs

- Shown to reduce cravings.
- Mostly helpful in the treatment of comorbid depression, and anxiety disorders.

Pharmacologic treatment of cocaine use disorder

Brief reminder about cocaine's mechanism of action in the brain:

Cocaine blocks reuptake of dopamine (powerfully), norepinephrine, and serotonin.

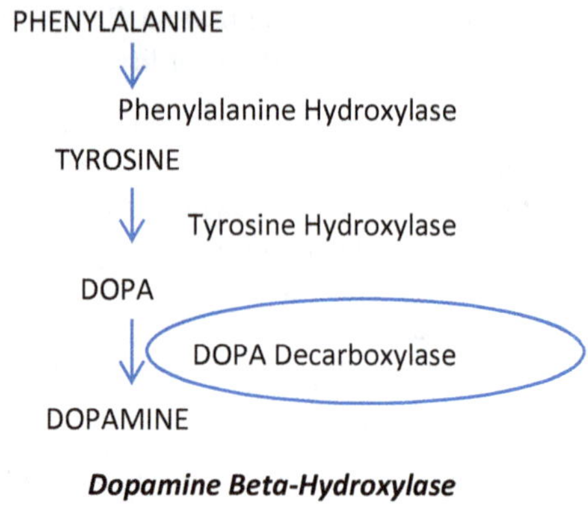

Fig. 4.8 Disulfiram inhibits dopamine beta-hydroxylase resulting in an excess of dopamine and decreased synthesis of norepinephrine

In the normal communication process, dopamine is released by a neuron into the synapse, where it can bind to dopamine receptors on neighboring neurons. Normally, dopamine is then recycled back into the transmitting neuron by a specialized protein called the dopamine transporter. If cocaine is present, it attaches to the dopamine transporter and blocks the normal recycling process, resulting in a buildup of dopamine in the synapse, which contributes to the pleasurable effects of cocaine.

No FDA-approved treatment for cocaine use disorder at this time, but several studies point to promising trends in treatment.

Studies implicate the use of

- Topiramate—a glutamate receptor antagonist and GABA agonist.
- Modafinil—elevates hypothalamic histamine levels.
- Naltrexone—reduces cravings by acting on mesocorticolimbic pathway.
- Disulfiram—inhibits dopamine beta-hydroxylase resulting in an excess of dopamine and decreased the synthesis of norepinephrine (Fig. 4.8).

Topiramate in the treatment of cocaine use disorder

Topiramate (Topomax)

Johnson et al. (2013) conducted a double-blind, randomized placebo-controlled, 12-week trial of 142 Cocaine-dependent adults in clinical research facilities at the University of Virginia between November 2005 and July 2011

INTERVENTIONS Topiramate (n = 71) or placebo (n = 71) in escalating doses from 50 mg/d to the target maintenance dose of 300 mg/d in weeks 6–12, combined with weekly cognitive behavioral.

OUTCOMES the primary outcome was the weekly difference from baseline in the proportion of cocaine nonuse days; the secondary outcome was urinary cocaine-free weeks, and exploratory outcomes included craving and self- and observer-rated global functioning on the Clinical Global Impression scales.

CONCLUSION Topiramate > Placebo in reducing use and cocaine cravings.

Disulfiram in the treatment of cocaine use disorder
Several studies on Disulfiram in cocaine use disorder demonstrate a positive trend

- Seven studies, 492 participants, met the inclusion criteria for Disulfiram versus placebo: no statistically significant results for dropouts but a **trend favoring disulfiram**, two studies, 87 participants, RR 0.82 (95% CI 0.66–1.03).
- One more study, 107 participants, **favoring disulfiram**, was excluded from meta-analysis due to high heterogeneity, RR 0.34 (95% CI 0.20–0.58).
- For cocaine use, it was not possible to pool together primary studies, results from single studies showed that 1 of 4 comparisons was in **favor of disulfiram** (number of weeks abstinence, 20 participants, WMD 4.50 (95% CI 2.93–6.07).
- Disulfiram versus naltrexone: no statistically significant results for dropouts but a **trend favoring disulfiram** (Pani et al. 2010).

Modafinil in the treatment of cocaine use disorder
A double-blind placebo-controlled study on Modafinil in cocaine use disorder by Anderson et al. (2009) showed reduction in cocaine use over time.

- 12 weeks of treatment and a 4-week follow-up.
- Six outpatient substance abuse treatment clinics participated in the study.
- 210 treatment seekers randomized, having a diagnosis of cocaine dependence.
- 72 participants were randomized to placebo.
- 69 to modafinil 200 mg, and 69 to modafinil 400 mg, taken once daily on awakening.
- Participants came to the clinic three times per week for assessments and urine drug screens, and had 1 h of individual psychotherapy weekly.
- The primary outcome measure was the weekly percentage of cocaine nonuse days.

Pharmacologic treatment of nicotine use disorder
FDA-Approved Pharmacotherapeutic Agents—treat cravings.

- Verinicline (Chantix),
- Buproprion (Wellbutrin).

FDA Nicotine Replacement Therapy—treats withdrawal symptoms, but does not treat/stop cravings.

FDA-Approved Nicotine Replacement Therapy (mainly to treat w/d sx's and should be distinguished from Verinicline and Buproprion that treat cravings).

- Nicotine Patch: Approved for 3–5 months of use, possible SEs include skin irritation, dizziness, racing heartbeat, **sleep problems**, headache, nausea, muscle aches, and stiffness.
- Nicotine Lozenges: Lozenge makers recommend using them as part of a 12-week program. Recommended dose is 1 lozenge every 1–2 h for 6 weeks, then 1 lozenge every 2–4 h for weeks 7–9, and finally 1 lozenge. SEs include trouble sleeping, nausea, hiccups, coughing, heartburn, headache, and flatulence.
- Nicotine Gum: Recommended for 6–12 weeks of use with the maximum being 6 months. SEs include nausea, bad taste, throat irritation, mouth sores, hiccups, jaw discomfort, and racing heartbeat.

- Nasal Spray: FDA recommends 3 month rx periods and no use longer than 6 months total. SEs include nasal irritation, runny nose, watery eyes, sneezing, throat irritation, and coughing.
- Inhalers: FDA recommends 3 month rx periods and no use longer than 6 months total. SEs include coughing, throat irritation, and upset stomach.

Pharmacologic treatment of Nicotine use Disorder with Varenicline
Varenicline (FDA Approved)

- The efficacy of CHANTIX in smoking cessation is believed to be the result of Varenicline's activity at **$\alpha_4\beta_2$ subtype of the nicotinic receptor**, where its binding produces agonist activity at a significantly lower level than nicotine while simultaneously preventing nicotine binding to these receptors.
- Varenicline also acts as an agonist at **5-HT3 receptors.**
- Due to its competitive binding on these receptors, varenicline blocks the ability of nicotine to bind and stimulate the mesolimbic dopamine system.
- Dosing: ½ tab BID for the first week, then increase to 1 mg BID. Recommended use for 3 months intervals, NTE 6 months of use.
- Side effects: increased SI risks, abdominal pain, nausea, vomiting, flatulence, abnormal dreams, and increased cardiovascular risks.

DESIGN
Rose et al. (2013) study is double-blind, parallel-arm adaptive treatment trial outlined in the following manner (Rose et al. 2013):

- A total of 606 cigarette smokers started open-label nicotine patch treatment 2 weeks before the quit date.
- Those whose ad lib smoking did not decrease by > 50% after 1 week were randomly assigned to one of three double-blind treatments.
- Nicotine patch alone (control condition).
- "Rescue" treatment with bupropion augmentation of the patch.
- Rescue treatment with varenicline alone.
- Participants whose pre-cessation smoking decreased > 50% but who lapsed after the quit date were also randomly assigned to the two rescue treatments or to nicotine patch alone.
- Logistic regression analyses compared each rescue treatment against the control condition in terms of abstinence at the end of treatment (weeks 8–11) and at 6 months.

Results

- Abstinence rates were higher with Buproprion + Patch.
- **Buproprion + patch (28%) > Verinicline (16.5%) > Patch Alone (6.6%).**

Pharmacologic treatment of Nicotine Use Disorder with Wellbutrin (Buproprion)
Bupropion (Wellbutrin)

SNRI that increases levels of dopamine and norepinephrine, and brain chemicals that are also boosted by nicotine.

DOSING

- Bupropion usually is started as 150 mg once daily for 3 days, and then the dose is increased if the patient tolerates the starting dose. Smoking is discontinued for 2 weeks after starting bupropion therapy.
- Wellbutrin SR is given as two daily doses.
- Wellbutrin XL is given as one dose daily.

Side effects: insomnia, headache, lower seizure threshold, alopecia, and anorexia.

Pharmacologic treatment of opioid use disorder

FDA approved pharmacological interventions for Opiate Substance Abuse Disorder

- Methadone: opioid agonist.
- Buprenorphine (subutex): mu agonist, kappa antagonist.
- Buprenorphine + Naloxone (suboxone) = oral, film, and sublingual (Zubsolv) formulation.
- Naltrexone (po form and IM form, Vivitrol): opioid antagonist.

Pharmacologic treatment of opioid use disorder with methadone

Methadone

- Opioid agonist.
- FDA Schedule II.
- Dosing: 80–125 mg.
- Rule of thumb: go low and go slow.
- Doses should be increased by no more than 5–10 mg on any day and the total weekly increase beyond the starting day's dose should not exceed 20 mg.
- Long acting.
- Several drug–drug interactions: enzymes CYP3A4, CYP2B6, and CYP2D6.
- Side effects: anxiety, sleep problems (insomnia), feeling weak or drowsy, dry mouth, nausea, vomiting, diarrhea, constipation, loss of appetite, decreased sex drive, impotence, or difficulty having an orgasm.

Notable side effects: QTc prolongation; affects testosterone and thyroid.

Pharmacologic treatment of opioid use disorder with buprenorphine

Buprenorphine

- DEA, Schedule III.
- Subutex (buprenorphine) = Suboxone (buprenorphine + naloxone) and both are > placebo.
- Naloxone = special narcotic drug that reverses the effects of other narcotic medicines (mu antagonist).
- Transdermal and injectable formulation is used primarily for chronic pain.
- Sublingual and oral used for treatment of opiate substance use disorder.
- Buprenorphine is metabolized by the liver, via CYP3A4; CYP2C8 isozymes of the cytochrome P450.
- Half-life: 20–73 h.

Methadone (M)	Buprenorphine (B)
Has the longest history of use for opioid use disorder	Used to treat opioid use disorder around 2002
Must be prescribed in a licensed setting	Can be prescribed in an office setting
Cost is low	Cost is higher than methadone
Has multiple drug-drug interactions	Has less drug-drug interactions compared to Methadone
There is no limit to dose – dosing effectiveness varies from person to person based on multiple factors.	There is a limit to dose – there is a limit to dosing effectiveness of buprenorphine, they call it a "ceiling effect"

Fig. 4.9 Methadone versus Buprenorphine, a quick comparison

PJ Whelan and colleagues compared Methadone to Buprenorphine which points to buprenorphine as more favorable treatment option (Whelan et al. 2012). For simplicity sake, I will only highlight a few key differences to include the following (Fig. 4.9).

Meaningful resource: screening, brief intervention, and referral to treatment (SBIRT)

SBIRT is an evidence-based practice employed to identify, reduce, and prevent problematic use, abuse, and dependence on alcohol and illicit drugs.

The SBIRT model was encouraged by set Institute of Medicine recommendations for community-based screening for health risk behaviors to include substance use.

- The "S" stands for screening—there are several screening tools that can be used in an outpatient and/or community setting to assess for risky substance use.
- The "B" stands for Brief Intervention—once risky behavior has been identified, a brief conversation about use should take place, feedback and advice are warranted.
- The "RT" stands for Referral to Treatment—refer for brief and/or long-term treatment for substance use is warranted.

To learn more about the SBIRT model and to access a host of resources, please visit the SAMHSA-HRSA website and search the site for integration and SBIRT as a clinical practice.

Helpful tips when engaging youth with potential substance use struggles—you don't have to be a healthcare expert to intervene

- Always assess for active substance use among youth—use SBIRT screening tools that can be found at the SAMHSA/HRSA website.
- Make appropriate referrals—you are not asked to be the expert, but you are expected to know when to refer.
- Depending on your level of comfort, you can share some of things you've learned from this chapter about substances of abuse and the developing brain that could potentially help to reduce use and overall risk.

Making the connection: the impact of substances of abuse on the brain is similar to the impact of prolonged fear and trauma

Recall Bruce Perry's study on neglected children outlined in Chap. 3 of this textbook. Perry was an early pioneer in demonstrating the impact that trauma had on the developing brain as he showed CT scans of 3-year-old children who had grown up in neglect (social, emotional, and language impoverished) versus children who did not grow up in neglect. In the case of neglected 3-year-old children, Perry's study highlighted prolonged exposure to trauma that triggered physiological changes in the brain (triggered the fear response); neural circuits that were interrupted resulting in changes to the hippocampus (the memory and emotion aspect of the brain); reduction in the size of the cortex resulting in compromise in learning, memory and behavior, difficulty regulating emotions, and greater risk of chronic disease and mental health burden in adulthood (Perry 1999).

When we are born, one could argue that the most developed part of our brain is the bottom and to a certain extent, the limbic (middle)—these are parts of the brain that help us to "survive." We are born with the natural proclivity for survival as we respond to threat, seek safety, and allow us to breath and our hearts to beat. The middle and bottom brain is where drives for sex, food, water, and other strong emotions like anger and other impulses live. From a developmental standpoint, it makes sense that youth are intermittently irrational and impulsive and exercise poor judgement—the middle and bottom parts of the brain that motivate this activity are MORE developed than the top part of the brain which helps to control and regulate this activity. See Fig. 4.10.

Consider the impact of substances of abuse superimposed on a history of trauma in a brain that is still developing. The capacity for disruption of the development process is evident. Substances of abuse powerfully reinforce middle and bottom brain living and disrupt the ability of the top brain to exert top-down control. Imagine the amygdala gone wild.

Survival can, at times, come at the expense of thriving (Fig. 4.11).

Exercise 4.1

The connection between fear and trauma was explained in the first three chapters.

1. In terms of the impact to the developing brain, can you make the connection between substance use and trauma?
2. What impact do substances have on cognition, judgment, impulse control, and early learning (or learning at all)?
3. Name two FDA-approved medications for alcohol use disorder.
4. Name two FDA-approved medications for opioid use disorder.
5. Name two FDA-approved medications for nicotine use disorder.

Youth of color disproportionately experience greater mental and substance use disorder burden

Racial and ethnic minorities currently make up about a third of the population of the nation and anticipated to become a majority by 2050. These diverse communities

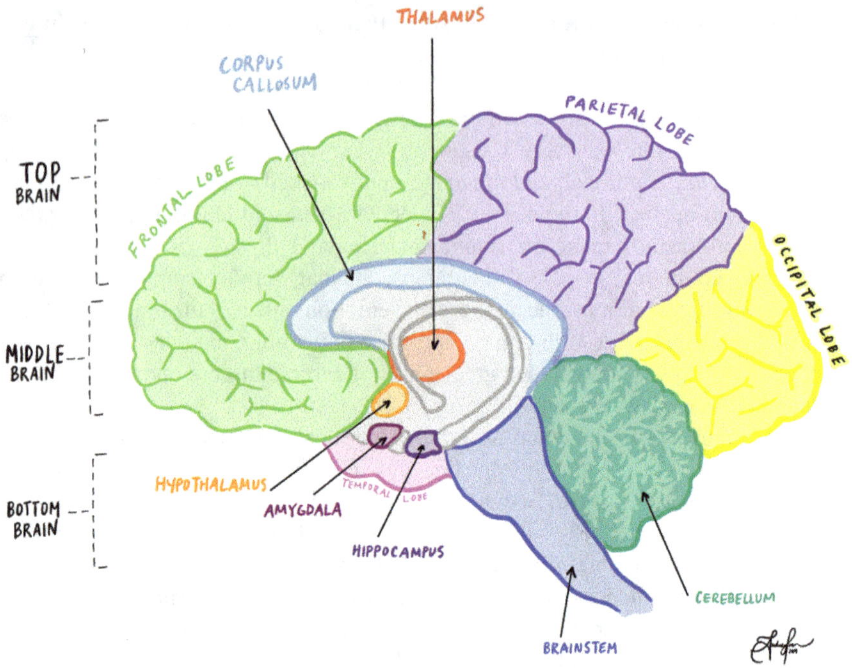

Fig. 4.10 Substances of abuse strengthen middle and bottom brain functioning at the expense of top brain development and functioning. Printed with permission. Copyright Audrey A. Tran

have unique behavioral health needs and experience different rates of mental and/or substance use disorders and treatment access (SAMHSA 2018).

Communities of color tend to experience greater burden of mental and substance use disorders often due to poorer access to care, inappropriate care, and higher social, environmental, and economic risk factors (SAMHSA 2018).

Summary

This textbook is about impacting systems for change. Systems are intimately attached to people; systems don't change if people don't change and people don't change when and if they don't feel something. The "feeling" space must be tapped to motivate change. This chapter on substances of abuse and the developing brain is an important one because it helps to explain how the brain is affected and how that translates into compromised behavior and cognition. Key takeaway is that substances of abuse are a form of trauma in terms of its impact to the brain.

Many systems that serve youth assume that cognition is intact (they assume that the top cortical part of the brain is engaged)—traditional education systems, places of employment, some adults in the lives of youth, juvenile justice institution, and their respective cognitive behavioral change supervision models, to name a few. The goal is to help youth be safe, learn, and thrive. It is more challenging to reach these goals in the absence of considering substance use and risk for substance; in

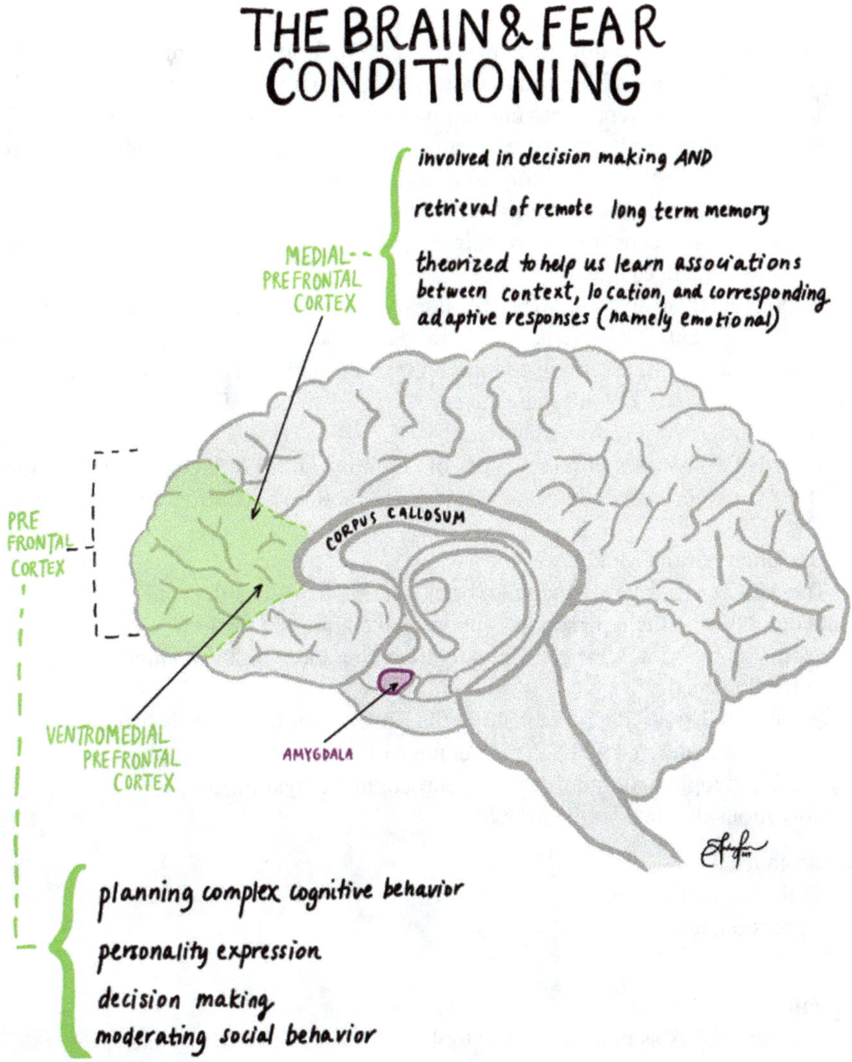

Fig. 4.11 Recall fear conditioning also known as "fear that doesn't turn off," also known as neurobiological trauma impacts the same areas of the brain that substances of abuse do. Printed with permission. Copyright Audrey A. Tran

the absence of considering history of trauma, risk of trauma, and/or active trauma. There are certain conditions that make it less likely that a young person is fully engaging the top part of their brain (adults, too, actually) and are in survival mode. This does not always represent noncompliance or inability to learn. More than likely it represents an opportunity to create safety, access for immediate needs, and adjust expectations accordingly. Inability to exercise good judgment today doesn't mean that in ability forever. As demonstrated in prior chapters, there are trauma-informed approaches that can heal the brain, helping youth more readily access the top part of their brain—practices like mindfulness.

Practically, there are ways to briefly assess cognitive capacity. The Montreal Cognitive Assessment (MOCA) is a well-validated tool to assess cognitive capacity. MOCA is one way of assessing cognitive function and has been used consistently in persons with a history of substance use.

What Does the MOCA evaluate?

The MoCA assesses different types of cognitive abilities, including orientation, short-term memory, executive function, language abilities, attention, and visuospatial ability.

Usefulness of the MoCA.

The MoCA is a relatively simple, brief test that helps health professionals determine quickly whether a person has suboptimal cognitive function.

Scores on the MoCA range from 0 to 30, with a score of 26 and higher generally considered normal.

In the initial study data establishing the MoCA, normal controls had an average score of 27.4, compared with 22.1 in people with Mild Cognitive Impairment (MCI), and 16.2 in people with more serious neurocognitive dysfunction.

Conditions that impact the MOCA:

- Substance use
- Medical conditions,
- Depression, and
- Anxiety.

Practical application

Use the MOCA as brief screening tool.

Brain areas assessed by the MOCA are also involved in the reward pathways in substance use.

Prefrontal cortex = attention, visual spatial, delayed recall.

Hippocampus = memory.

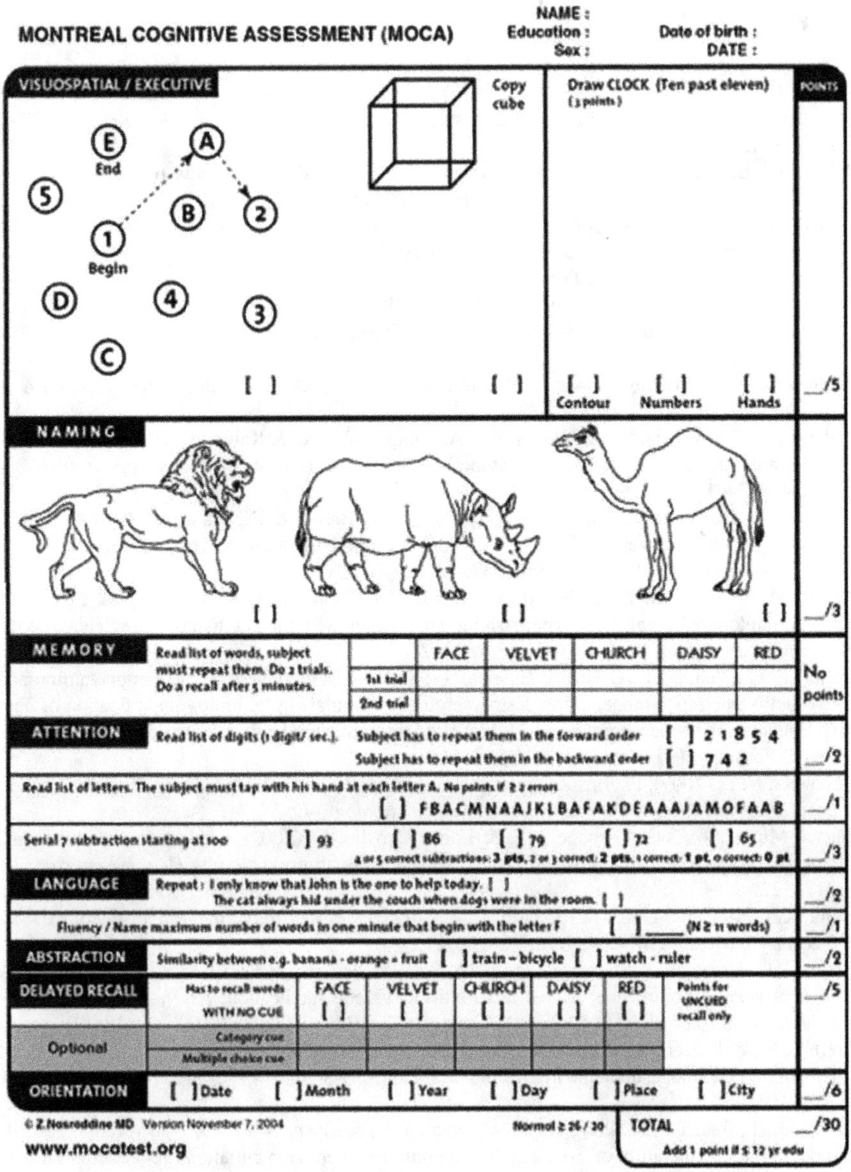

MONTREAL COGNITIVE ASSESSMENT (MOCA)

NAME :
Education :
Sex :
Date of birth :
DATE :

VISUOSPATIAL / EXECUTIVE			POINTS
E End, A, 5, B, 2, 1 Begin, D, 4, 3, C [ ]	Copy cube [ ]	Draw CLOCK (Ten past eleven) (3 points) [ ] Contour [ ] Numbers [ ] Hands	___/5

NAMING			
[ ]	[ ]	[ ]	___/3

MEMORY	Read list of words, subject must repeat them. Do 2 trials. Do a recall after 5 minutes.		FACE	VELVET	CHURCH	DAISY	RED	No points
		1st trial						
		2nd trial						

ATTENTION — Read list of digits (1 digit/ sec.). Subject has to repeat them in the forward order [ ] 2 1 8 5 4; Subject has to repeat them in the backward order [ ] 7 4 2 — ___/2

Read list of letters. The subject must tap with his hand at each letter A. No points if ≥ 2 errors
[ ] FBACMNAAJKLBAFAKDEAAAJAMOFAAB — ___/1

Serial 7 subtraction starting at 100 [ ] 93 [ ] 86 [ ] 79 [ ] 72 [ ] 65
4 or 5 correct subtractions: 3 pts, 2 or 3 correct: 2 pts, 1 correct: 1 pt, 0 correct: 0 pt — ___/3

LANGUAGE — Repeat : I only know that John is the one to help today. [ ]
The cat always hid under the couch when dogs were in the room. [ ] — ___/2

Fluency / Name maximum number of words in one minute that begin with the letter F [ ] ____ (N ≥ 11 words) — ___/1

ABSTRACTION — Similarity between e.g. banana - orange = fruit [ ] train – bicycle [ ] watch - ruler — ___/2

DELAYED RECALL	Has to recall words WITH NO CUE	FACE [ ]	VELVET [ ]	CHURCH [ ]	DAISY [ ]	RED [ ]	Points for UNCUED recall only	___/5
Optional	Category cue							
	Multiple choice cue							

ORIENTATION — [ ] Date [ ] Month [ ] Year [ ] Day [ ] Place [ ] City — ___/6

© Z.Nasreddine MD Version November 7, 2004
www.mocatest.org
Normal ≥ 26 / 30 — TOTAL ___/30
Add 1 point if ≤ 12 yr edu

Questions and Discussion

Change and capacity for change are attached to cognition.

1. Can change occur if cognition is compromised?
2. In what way might the MOCA be helpful in assisting you with managing your expectations for change in youth?

References

Abbott, L. C., & Winzer-Serhan, U. H. (2012). Smoking during pregnancy: lessons learned from epidemiological studies and experimental studies using animal models. *Critical Reviews in Toxicology, 42,* 279–303.

Adolescent development of the reward system. (2010). *Frontiers in Human Neuroscience, 4,* 6. Published February 12, 2010. https://doi.org/10.3389/neuro.09.006.2010.

Aguado, T., Carracedo, A., Julien, B., Velasco, G., Milman, G., Mechoulam, R., et al. (2007). Cannabinoids induce glioma stem-like cell differentiation and inhibit gliomagenesis. *The Journal of biological chemistry, 282,* 6854–6862.

Albrizio, M., Guaricci, A. C., Calamita, G., Zarrilli, A., & Minoia, P. (2006). Expression and immunolocalization of the mu-opioid receptor in human sperm cells. *Fertility and Sterility, 86,* 1776–1779.

Anderson et al. (2009, September 1). Modafinil for the treatment of cocaine dependence. *Drug & Alcohol Dependence, 104*(1–2), 133.

Anier, K., Malinovskaja, K., Aonurm-Helm, A., Zharkovsky, A., & Kalda, A. (2010). DNA methylation regulates cocaine-induced behavioral sensitization in mice. *Neuropsychopharmacology, 35,* 2450–2461.

Agirregoitia, E., Peralta, L., Mendoza, R., Exposito, A., Ereno, E. D., Matorras, R., et al. (2012). Expression and localization of opioid receptors during the maturation of human oocytes. *Reproductive Biomedicine Online, 24,* 550–557.

Auger, M. L., Schmidt, E. R., Manitt, C., Dal-Bo, G., Pasterkamp, R. J., & Flores, C. (2013). *unc5c* haploinsufficient phenotype: striking similarities with the *dcc* haploinsufficiency model. *European Journal of Neuroscience, 38,* 2853–2863.

Battaglia, G., Yeh, S. Y., O'Hearn, E., et al. (1987). 3,4-Methylenedioxymethamphetamine and 3,4-methylenedioxyamphetamine destroyserotonin terminals in rat brain: quantification of neurodegeneration by measurement of [3H]-labelled serotonin uptake sites. *Journal of Pharmacology and Experimental Therapeutics, 242,* 911–916.

Benowitz, N. L. (2009). Pharmacology of nicotine: Addiction, smoking-induced disease, and therapeutics. *Annual Review of Pharmacology and Toxicology, 49,* 57–71.

Blanco-Munoz, J., Torres-Sanchez, L., & Lopez-Carrillo, L. (2009). Exposure to maternal and paternal tobacco consumption and risk of spontaneous abortion. *Public Health Reports, 124,* 317–322.

Bolla, K. I., McCann, U. D., & Ricuarte, G. A. (1998). Memory impairment in abstinent MDMA ("ecstasy") users. *Neurology, 51,* 1532–1537.

Boyd, C. J., Austic, E., Epstein-Ngo, Q., Veliz, P. T., & McCabe, S. E. (2014). A prospective study of adolescents' nonmedical use of anxiolytic and sleep medication. *Psychology of addictive behaviors: journal of the Society of Psychologists in Addictive Behaviors, 29*(1), 184–191.

Brembs, B., & Heisenberg, M. (2000). The operant and the classical in conditioned orientation of Drosophila melanogaster at the flight simulator. *Learning & Memory (Cold Spring Harbor, N.Y.), 7*(2), 104–115.

Brody, G. H., Beach, S. R., Philibert, R. A., Chen, Y. F., & Murry, V. M. (2009). Prevention effects moderate the association of *5-HTTLPR* and youth risk behavior initiation: gene x environment hypotheses tested via a randomized prevention design. *Child Development, 80,* 645–661.

Buck, J. M., & Siegel, J. A. (2015). The effects of adolescent methamphetamine exposure. *Frontiers in Neuroscience, 9,* 151. https://doi.org/10.3389/fnins.2015.00151.

Burdge, G. C., Hanson, M. A., Slater-Jefferies, J. L., & Lillycrop, K. A. (2007). Epigenetic regulation of transcription: a mechanism for inducing variations in phenotype (fetal programming) by differences in nutrition during early life? *The British Journal of Nutrition, 97*(6), 1036–1046.

Cadet, L. J. (2013, January). Epigenetics of methamphetamine-induced changes in glutamate function. *Neuropsychopharmacology, 38*(1), 248–249. https://doi.org/10.1038/npp.2012.169.

Camenga, D. R., Delmerico, J., Kong, G., Cavallo, D., Hyland, A., Cummings, K. M., et al. (2014). Trends in use of electronic nicotine delivery systems by adolescents. *Addictive Behaviors, 39,* 338–340.

Carhart-Harris, R. L., Muthukumaraswamy, S., Roseman, L., Kaelen, M., Droog, W., Murphy, K., et al. (2016a). Neural correlates of the LSD experience revealed by multimodal neuroimaging. *Proceedings of the National Academy of Sciences of the United States of America, 113*(17), 4853–4858.

Carhart-Harris, R. L., Kaelen, M., Bolstridge, M., Williams, T. M., Williams, L. T., Underwood, R., et al. (2016b). The paradoxical psychological effects of lysergic acid diethylamide (LSD). *Psychological Medicine, 46,* 1379–1390.

Casey, B. J., et al. (2010). Neurobiology of the adolescent brain and behavior: Implications for substance use disorders. *Journal of the American Academy of Child and Adolescent Psychiatry, 49*(12), 1189–1201.

Centers for Disease Control and Prevention. (2013). Notes from the field: electronic cigarette use among middle and high school students—United States, 2011–2012. *MMWR. Morbidity and Mortality Weekly Report, 62,* 729–730.

Centers for Disease Control and Prevention. (2014). *Smoking and tobacco use: fast facts.* Retrieved December 12, 2014, from http://www.cdc.gov/tobacco/data_statistics/fact_sheets/fast_facts/index.htm#toll. Updated April 2014.

Chandra, L. C., Kumar, V., Torben, W., Vande Stouwe, C., Winsauer, P., Amedee, A., et al. (2015). Chronic administration of Delta9-tetrahydrocannabinol induces intestinal anti-inflammatory microRNA expression during acute simian immunodeficiency virus infection of rhesus macaques. *Journal of Virology, 89,* 1168–1181.

Chidambaran, V., Zhang, X., Martin, L. J., Ding, L., Weirauch, M. T., Geisler, K., et al. (2017). DNA methylation at the mu-1 opioid receptor gene (*OPRM1*) promoter predicts preoperative, acute, and chronic postsurgical pain after spine fusion. *Pharmacogenomics and Personalized Medicine, 10,* 157–168. https://doi.org/10.2147/pgpm.s132691.

Chorbov, V. M., Todorov, A. A., Lynskey, M. T., & Cicero, T. J. (2011). Elevated levels of DNA methylation at the OPRM1 promoter in blood and sperm from male opioid addicts. *Journal of Opioid Management, 7,* 258–264.

Clark, D. B., Thatcher, D. L., & Tapert, S. F. (2008). Alcohol, psychological dysregulation, and adolescent brain development. *Alcoholism, Clinical and Experimental Research, 32*(3), 375–385.

Cohen, R. S., & Cocores, J. (1997). Neuropsychiatric manifestations following the use of 3,4 methylenedioxymethamphetamine (MDMA; "ecstasy"). *Progress in Neuropsychopharmacology and Biological Psychiatry, 21,* 727–734.

Collins, S. L., Wade, D., Ledon, J., & Izenwasser, S. (2004). Neurochemical alterations produced by daily nicotine exposure in periadolescent versus adult male rats. *European Journal of Pharmacology, 502,* 75–85.

Crews, F., He, J., & Hodge, C. (2007). Adolescent cortical development: A critical period of vulnerability for addiction. *Pharmacology Biochemistry and Behavior, 86*(2), 189–199.

Crone, E. A., & Konijn, E. A. (2018). Media use and brain development during adolescence. *Nature Communications, 9*(1), 588. https://doi.org/10.1038/s41467-018-03126-x.

Curran, H. V., & Travill, R. A. (1997). Mood and cognitive effects of ±3,4-methylenedioxymethamphetamine (MDMA, "ecstasy"). *Addiction, 92,* 821–831.

Dani, J. A., & Bertrand, D. (2007). Nicotinic acetylcholine receptors and nicotinic cholinergic mechanisms of the central nervous system. *Annual Review of Pharmacology and Toxicology, 47,* 699–729.

Davison, D., & Parrott, A. C. (1997). Ecstasy (MDMA) in recreational users: Self-reported psychological and physiological effects. *Human Psychopharmacology, 12,* 221–226.

De Bellis, M. D., Clark, D. B., Beers, S. R., et al. (2000). Hippocampal volume in adolescent-onset alcohol use disorders. *American Journal of Psychiatry, 157,* 737–744.

De Bellis, M. D., Narasimhan, A., Thatcher, D. L., et al. (2005). Prefrontal cortex, thalamus, and cerebellar volumes in adolescents and young adults with adolescent-onset alcohol use disorders and comorbid mental disorders. *Alcoholism, Clinical and Experimental Research, 29,* 1590–1600.

DiNieri, J. A., Wang, X., Szutorisz, H., Spano, S. M., Kaur, J., Casaccia, P., et al. (2011). Maternal cannabis use alters ventral striatal dopamine D2 gene regulation in the offspring. *Biological Psychiatry, 70,* 763–769.

Dolder, P. C., Schmid, Y., Mueller, F., Borgwardt, S., & Liechti, M. E. (2016). LSD acutely impairs fear recognition and enhances emotional empathy and sociality. *Neuropsychopharmacology, 41,* 2638–2646.

Dow-Edwards, D. (2011). Translational issues for prenatal cocaine studies and the role of environment. *Neurotoxicology and Teratology, 33,* 9–16.

Drug Enforcement Administration Office of Diversion Control. *Drug & Chemical Evaluation Section.* BENZODIAZEPINES. Retrieved from https://www.deadiversion.usdoj.gov/drug_chem_info/benzo.pdf.

Ebrahimi, G., Asadikaram, G., Akbari, H., Nematollahi, M. H., Abolhassani, M., Shahabinejad, G., et al. (2018). Elevated levels of DNA methylation at the OPRM1 promoter region in men with opioid use disorder. *American Journal of Drug and Alcohol Abuse, 44,* 193–199.

Electronic Cigarettes (E-Cigarettes). (2018, June). Retrieved from https://www.drugabuse.gov/publications/drugfacts/electronic-cigarettes-e-cigarettes.

Embry, D., Hankins, M., Biglan, A., & Boles, S. (2009). Behavioral and social correlates of methamphetamine use in a population-based sample of early and later adolescents. *Addictive Behaviors, 34,* 343–351.

Ersche, K. D., Barnes, A., Jones, P. S., Morein-Zamir, S., Robbins, T. W., & Bullmore, E. T. (2011). Abnormal structure of frontostriatal brain systems is associated with aspects of impulsivity and compulsivity in cocaine dependence. *Brain: A Journal of Neurology, 134*(Pt 7), 2013–2024.

Farrelly, M. C., Loomis, B. R., Han, B., Gfroerer, J., Kuiper, N., Couzens, G. L., et al. (2013). A comprehensive examination of the influence of state tobacco control programs and policies on youth smoking. *American Journal of Public Health, 103,* 549–555.

Feder, K. A., Krawczyk, N., & Saloner, B. (2017). Medication-assisted treatment for adolescents in specialty treatment for opioid use disorder. *The Journal of Adolescent Health: Official Publication of the Society for Adolescent Medicine, 60*(6), 747–750.

Feeney, G. F., Connor, J. P., Young, R. M., Tucker, J., & McPherson, A. (2006). Combined acamprosate and naltrexone, with cognitive behavioural therapy is superior to either medication alone for alcohol abstinence: A single centre's experience with pharmacotherapy. *Alcohol and Alcoholism, 41*(3), 321–327.

Feng, Y., He, X., Yang, Y., Chao, D., Lazarus, L. H., & Xia, Y. (2012). Current research on opioid receptor function. *Current Drug Targets, 13*(2), 230–246.

Filip, M., Faron-Gorecka, A., Kusmider, M., et al. (2006). Alterations in *BDNF* and *trkB* mRNAs following acute or sensitizing cocaine treatments and withdrawal. *Brain Research, 1071,* 218–225.

George, V. K., Li, H., Teloken, C., Grignon, D. J., Lawrence, W. D., & Dhabuwala, C. B. (1996). Effects of long-term cocaine exposure on spermatogenesis and fertility in peripubertal male rats. *Journal of Urology, 155,* 327–331.

Giedd, J. N., Blumenthal, J., Jeffries, N. O., Castellanos, F. X., Liu, H., Zijdenbos, A., et al. (1999). Brain development during childhood and adolescence: A longitudinal MRI study. *Nature Neuroscience, 2,* 861–863.

Gilardi, F., Augsburger, M., & Thomas, A. (2018). Will widespread synthetic opioid consumption induce epigenetic consequences in future generations? *Frontiers in pharmacology, 9,* 702. https://doi.org/10.3389/fphar.2018.00702.

Gogtay, N., & Thompson, P. M. (2010). Mapping gray matter development: Implications for typical development and vulnerability to psychopathology. *Brain and Cognition, 72,* 6–15.

Gonzales, R., Mooney, L., & Rawson, R. A. (2010). The methamphetamine problem in the United States. *Annual Review of Public Health, 31,* 385–398. https://doi.org/10.1146/annurev.publhealth.012809.103600.

Grant, A., Hoops, D., Labelle-Dumais, C., Prevost, M., Rajabi, H., Kolb, B., et al. (2007). Netrin-1 receptor-deficient mice show enhanced mesocortical dopamine transmission and blunted behavioral responses to amphetamine. *European Journal of Neuroscience, 26,* 3215–3228.

Grant, A., Speed, Z., Labelle-Dumais, C., & Flores, C. (2009). Post-pubertal emergence of dopamine phenotype in netrin-1 receptor-deficient mice. *European Journal of Neuroscience, 30,* 1318–1328.

Graybiel, A. M., Moratalla, R., & Robertson, H. A. (1990). Amphetamine and cocaine induce drug-specific activation of the *c-fos* gene in striosome-matrix compartments and limbic subdivisions of the striatum. *Proceedings of the National Academy of Sciences of the United States of America, 87,* 6912–6916.

Griffin, C. E., Kaye, A. M., Bueno, F. R., & Kaye, A. D. (2013). Benzodiazepine pharmacology and central nervous system-mediated effects. *The Ochsner Journal, 13*(2), 214–223.

Halberstadt, A. L. (2015). Recent advances in the neuropsychopharmacology of serotonergic hallucinogens. *Behavioural Brain Research, 277,* 99–120.

Hallucinogens and Dissociative Drugs. Retrieved January 18, 2019, from https://www.drugabuse.gov/publications/research-reports/hallucinogens-dissociative-drugs/what-are-effects-common-dissociative-drugs-brain-body.

Han, D., & Gu, H. (2006). Comparison of the monoamine transporters from human and mouse in their sensitivities to psychostimulant drugs. *BMC Pharmacology, 6,* 6.

Harris, L. W., Sharp, T., Gartlon, J., Jones, D. N., & Harrison, P. J. (2003). Long-term behavioural, molecular and morphological effects of neonatal NMDA receptor antagonism. *European Journal of Neuroscience, 18,* 1706–1710.

He, F., Lidow, I. A., & Lidow, M. S. (2006). Inhalational model of cocaine exposure in mice: Neuroteratological effects. *Neurotoxicology and Teratology, 28,* 181–197.

Heard, E., & Martienssen, R. A. (2014). Transgenerational epigenetic inheritance: myths and mechanisms. *Cell, 157*(1), 95–109.

Hegde, V. L., Tomar, S., Jackson, A., Rao, R., Yang, X., Singh, U. P., et al. (2013). Distinct microRNA expression profile and targeted biological pathways in functional myeloid-derived suppressor cells induced by Delta9-tetrahydrocannabinol in vivo: regulation of CCAAT/enhancer-binding protein alpha by microRNA-690. *The Journal of Biological Chemistry, 288,* 36810–36826.

Herman, A. I., DeVito, E. E., Jensen, K. P., & Sofuoglu, M. (2014). Pharmacogenetics of nicotine addiction: Role of dopamine. *Pharmacogenomics, 15*(2), 221–234.

Hiroi, N., & Agatsuma, S. (2005). Genetic susceptibility to substance dependence. *Molecular Psychiatry, 10,* 336–344.

Hope, B., Kosofsky, B., Hyman, S. E., & Nestler, E. J. (1992). Regulation of immediate early gene expression and AP-1 binding in the rat nucleus accumbens by chronic cocaine. *Proceedings of the National Academy of Sciences of the United States of America, 89,* 5764–5768.

Hummel, M., et al. (2002). D_1 dopamine receptor: A putative neurochemical and behavioral link to cocaine action. *Journal of Cellular Physiology, 191*(1), 17–27.

Irner B. T. Substance exposure in utero developmental consequences in adolescence: A systematic review. Child Neuropsychology. Volume 18, 2012 - Issue 6.

Jackson, A. R., Nagarkatti, P., & Nagarkatti, M. (2014). Anandamide attenuates Th-17 cell-mediated delayed-type hypersensitivity response by triggering IL-10 production and consequent microRNA induction. *PLoS One, 9,* e93954.

Jansson, L. M., et al. (2016). Maternal buprenorphine maintenance and lactation. *Journal of Human Lactation, 32*(4), 675. Epub September 26, 2016.

Jones, H. E., et al. (2012). Maternal Opioid Treatment: Human Experimental Research (MOTHER)–approach, issues and lessons learned. *Addiction (Abingdon, England), 107 Suppl 1*(0 1), 28–35.

Johnson, B. A., et al. (2013, October 16). Topiramate for the treatment of cocaine addiction: A randomized clinical trial. *JAMA Psychiatry*.

Kaşıkçıoğlu, E. (2017). Sports, energy drinks, and sudden cardiac death: stimulant cardiac syndrome. *Anatolian Journal of Cardiology, 17*(2), 163–164.

Kelly, P. A. (2000). Does recreational ecstasy use cause long-term cognitive problems? *The Western Journal of Medicine, 173*(2), 129–130.

King, G., Alicata, D., Cloak, C., & Chang, L. (2010a). Neuropsychological deficits in adolescent methamphetamine abusers. *Psychopharmacology (Berl), 212,* 243–249.

King, G., Alicata, D., Cloak, C., & Chang, L. (2010b). Psychiatric symptoms and HPA axis function in adolescent methamphetamine users. *Journal of Neuroimmune Pharmacology, 5,* 582–591.

Klomp, A., den Hollander, B., de Bruin, K., Booij, J., & Reneman, L. (2012). The effects of ecstasy (MDMA) on brain serotonin transporters are dependent on age-of-first exposure in recreational users and animals. *PLoS One, 7*(10), e47524.

Kocherlakota, P. (2014). Neonatal abstinence syndrome. *Pediatrics, 134*(2), e547.

Lebel, C., & Beaulieu, C. (2011). Longitudinal development of human brain wiring continues from childhood into adulthood. *Journal of Neuroscience, 31,* 10937–10947.

Lesch, K. P., Bengel, D., Heils, A., et al. (1996). Association of anxiety-related traits with a polymorphism in the serotonin transporter gene regulatory region. *Science, 274,* 1527–1531.

Li, S. X., Yan, S. Y., Bao, Y. P., Lian, Z., Qu, Z., Wu, Y. P., et al. (2013). Depression and alterations in hypothalamic-pituitary-adrenal and hypothalamic-pituitary-thyroid axis function in male abstinent methamphetamine abusers. Human Psychopharmacology.

Lidow, M. S. (2003). Consequences of prenatal cocaine exposure in nonhuman primates. *Brain Research Developmental Brain Research, 147,* 23–36.

Liechti, M. E. (2017). Modern clinical research on LSD. *Neuropsychopharmacology: Official Publication of the American College of Neuropsychopharmacology, 42*(11), 2114–2127.

Limanaqi et al. (2018). Epigenetic effects induced by methamphetamine and methamphetamine-dependent oxidative stress. *Oxidative Medicine and Cellular Longevity, 2018,* 28. Article ID 4982453. https://doi.org/10.1155/2018/4982453.

Lindahl, J. S., Kjellsen, B. R., Tigert, J., & Miskimins, R. (2008). In utero PCP exposure alters oligodendrocyte differentiation and myelination in developing rat frontal cortex. *Brain Research, 1234,* 137–147.

Liu, F., Paule, M. G., Ali, S., & Wang, C. (2011). Ketamine-induced neurotoxicity and changes in gene expression in the developing rat brain. *Current Neuropharmacology, 9*(1), 256–261.

Malanga, C. J., & Kosofsky, B. E. (2003). Does drug abuse beget drug abuse? Behavioral analysis of addiction liability in animal models of prenatal drug exposure. *Brain Research Developmental Brain Research, 147,* 47–57.

Manitt, C., Labelle-Dumais, C., Eng, C., Grant, A., Mimee, A., Stroh, T., et al. (2010). Peri-pubertal emergence of UNC-5 homologue expression by dopamine neurons in rodents. *PLoS One, 5,* e11463.

Manitt, C., Mimee, A., Eng, C., Pokinko, M., Stroh, T., Cooper, H. M., et al. (2011). The netrin receptor DCC is required in the pubertal organization of mesocortical dopamine circuitry. *Journal of Neuroscience, 31,* 8381–8394.

Mann, K., Bladström, A., Torup, L., Gual, A., van den Brink, W. (2013). Extending the treatment options in alcohol dependence: A randomized controlled study of as-needed nalmefene. *Biological Psychiatry, 73*(8), 706.

Mansvelder, H. D., Mertz, M., & Role, L. W. (2009). Nicotinic modulation of synaptic transmission and plasticity in cortico-limbic circuits. *Seminars in Cell & Developmental Biology, 20*(4), 432–440.

Martins, S. S., & Ghandour, L. A. (2017). Nonmedical use of prescription drugs in adolescents and young adults: not just a Western phenomenon. *World Psychiatry: Official Journal of the World Psychiatric Association (WPA), 16*(1), 102–104.

Mason, B. J., et al. (2013). Gabapentin Treatment for alcohol dependence: A randomized clinical trial. *JAMA Internal Medicine*. Published online November 04, 2013.

Medina, K. L., Hanson, K., Schweinsburg, A. D., Cohen-Zion, M., Nagel, B. J., & Tapert, S. F. (2007a). Neuropsychological functioning in adolescent marijuana users: Subtle deficits detectable after 30 days of abstinence. *Journal of the International Neuropsychological Society, 13*(5), 207–220.

Medina, K. L., Hanson, K. L., Schweinsburg, A. D., Cohen-Zion, M., Nagel, B. J., & Tapert, S. F. (2007b). Neuropsychological functioning in adolescent marijuana users: Subtle deficits detectable after a month of abstinence. *Journal of the International Neuropsychological Society: JINS, 13*(5), 807–820.

McCabe, S. E., West, B. T., Veliz, P., McCabe, V. V., Stoddard, S. A., & Boyd, C. J. (2017). Trends in medical and nonmedical use of prescription opioids among US adolescents: 1976–2015. *Pediatrics, 139*(4), e20162387.

McCann, U. D., Eligulashvili, V., Mertl, M., et al. (1999). Altered neuroendocrine and behavioral responses to m-chlorophenylpiperazine in3,4-methylenedioxymethamphetamine (MDMA) users. *Psychopharmacology (Berl), 147*, 56–65.

McClung, C. A., & Nestler, E. J. (2003). Regulation of gene expression and cocaine reward by CREB and DeltaFosB. *Nature Neuroscience, 6,* 1208–1215.

McKenna, M. L., & Ho, B. T. (1980). The role of dopamine in the discriminative stimulus properties of cocaine. *Neuropharmacology, 19,* 297–303.

Meshi, D., Tamir, D. I., & Heekeren, H. R. (2015). The emerging neuroscience of social media. *Trends in Cognitive Sciences, 19,* 771–782. https://doi.org/10.1016/j.tics.2015.09.004.

Miura, H., Fujiki, M., Shibata, A., & Ishikawa, K. (2006). Prevalence and profile of methamphetamine users in adolescents at a juvenile classification home. *Psychiatry and Clinical Neurosciences, 60,* 352–357.

Molina, P. E., Amedee, A., LeCapitaine, N. J., Zabaleta, J., Mohan, M., Winsauer, P., et al. (2011). Cannabinoid neuroimmune modulation of SIV disease. *Journal of Neuroimmune Pharmacology: The Official Journal of the Society on NeuroImmune Pharmacology, 6,* 516–527.

Monitoring the Future Survey: High School and Youth Trends. (2017, December). Retrieved from https://www.drugabuse.gov/publications/drugfacts/monitoring-future-survey-high-school-youth-trends.

Mule, S. J., Jukofsky, D., Kogan, M., De Pace, A., & Verebey, K. (1977). Evaluation of the radioimmunoassay for benzoylecgonine (a cocaine metabolite) in human urine. *Clinical Chemistry, 23,* 796–801.

National Institute on Drug Abuse. (2016). Substances of Abuse. https://www.drugabuse.gov/.

National Institute on Alcohol Abuse and Alcoholism (NIAAA). *Alcohol Alert*, No. 67, "Underage Drinking," 2006. Available at: https://pubs.niaaa.nih.gov/publications/AA67/AA67.htm.

Nestler, E. J. (2014, January). Epigenetic mechanisms of drug addiction. *Neuropharmacology*, *76*(Pt B), 259–268. https://doi.org/10.1016/j.neuropharm.2013.04.004. Epub April 30, 2013.

Nielsen, D. A., Hamon, S., Yuferov, V, et al. (2010). Ethnic diversity of DNA methylation in the OPRM1 promoter region in lymphocytes of heroin addicts. *Human genetics, 127*(6), 639–649.

Nielsen, D. A., Utrankar, A., Reyes, J. A., Simons, D. D., & Kosten, T. R. (2012). Epigenetics of drug abuse: predisposition or response. *Pharmacogenomics, 13*(10), 1149–1160.

Novikova, S. I., He, F., Bai, J., Cutrufello, N. J., Lidow, M. S., & Undieh, A. S. (2008). Maternal cocaine administration in mice alters DNA methylation and gene expression in hippocampal neurons of neonatal and prepubertal offspring. *PLoS One, 3,* e1919.

Oei L. J., et al. Neonatal Abstinence Syndrome and High School Performance. *Pediatrics*. February 2017, VOLUME 139/ ISSUE 2.

Opioids. (2018, October). Retrieved from https://www.drugabuse.gov/drugs-abuse/opioids.

Ostby, Y., Tamnes, C. K., Fjell, A. M., Westlye, L. T., Due-Tonnessen, P., & Walhovd, K. B. (2009). Heterogeneity in subcortical brain development: a structural magnetic resonance imaging study of brain maturation from 8 to 30 years. *Journal of Neuroscience, 29,* 11772–11782.

Ozgur, K., Isikoglu, M., Seleker, M., & Donmez, L. (2005). Semen quality of smoking and non-smoking men in infertile couples in a Turkish population. *Archives of Gynecology and Obstetrics, 271,* 109–112.

Pani, P. P., et al. (2010, January). Disulfiram for the treatment of cocaine dependence. *Cochrane Database of Systematic Review*, *20*(1), CD007024.

Paradise, J. (2014). Electronic cigarettes: smoke-free laws, sale restrictions, and the public health. *American Journal of Public Health, 104,* e17–e18.

Pasqualotto, F. F., Sobreiro, B. P., Hallak, J., Pasqualotto, E. B., & Lucon, A. M. (2006). Cigarette smoking is related to a decrease in semen volume in a population of fertile men. *BJU International, 97,* 324–326.

Paus, T. (2010). Growth of white matter in the adolescent brain: Myelin or axon? *Brain and Cognition, 72,* 26–35.

Pétursson, H. (1994). The benzodiazepine withdrawal syndrome. *Addiction, 89*(11), 1455–1459.

Perry, E., Walker, M., Grace, J., & Perry, R. (1999). Acetylcholine in mind: a neurotransmitter correlate of consciousness?. *Trends in neurosciences, 22*(6), 273–280.

Pettinati, H. M., Anton, R. F., & Willenbring, M. L. (2006). The COMBINE study-: An overview of the largest pharmacotherapy study to date for treating alcohol dependence. *Psychiatry (Edgmont (Pa.: Township)), 3*(10), 36–39.

Pharmacologic mechanisms of crystal meth. (2008). *CMAJ: Canadian Medical Association journal = journal de l'Association medicale canadienne, 178*(13), 1679–1682.

Ponomarev, I. (2018). Epigenetic control of gene expression in the alcoholic brain. *Alcohol Research: Current Reviews, 35*(1). Retrieved November 17, 2018, from https://pubs.niaaa.nih.gov/publications/arcr351/69-76.htm.

Racial and Ethnic Minority Populations. Retrieved August 16, 2018, from https://www.samhsa.gov/specific-populations/racial-ethnic-minority.

Rawson, R. A., Gonzales, R., Obert, J. L., McCann, M. J., & Brethen, P. (2005). Methamphetamine use among treatment-seeking adolescents in Southern California: Participant characteristics and treatment response. *Journal of Substance Abuse Treatment, 29,* 67–74.

Reneman, L., Booij, J., Schmand, B., et al. (2000). Memory disturbances in "ecstasy" users are correlated with an altered brain serotoninneurotransmission. *Psychopharmacology (Berl), 148,* 322–324.

Ricuarte, G. A., McCann, U. D., Szabo, Z., & Scheffel, U. (2000). Toxicodynamics and long-term toxicity of the recreational drug, 3,4-methylenedioxymethamphetamine(MDMA, "ecstasy"). *Toxicology Letters, 113,* 143–146.

Rose, J. E., et al. (2013). Adapting smoking cessation treatment according to initial response to precessation nicotine patch. *American Journal of Psychiatry, 170,* 860–867.

Ruiz, P., Strain, E. C., & Lowinson, J. H. (2011). *Lowinson and Ruiz's substance abuse: A comprehensive textbook.* Philadelphia: Wolters Kluwer Health/Lippincott Williams & Wilkins.

Salo, R., Flower, K., Kielstein, A., Leamon, M. H., Nordahl, T. E., & Galloway, G. P. (2011). Psychiatric comorbidity in methamphetamine dependence. *Psychiatry Research, 186,* 356–361.

SBIRT: Screening, Brief Intervention, and Referral to Treatment. Retrieved November 20, 2018, from https://www.integration.samhsa.gov/clinical-practice/sbirt.

Schmid, Y., Enzler, F., Gasser, P., Grouzmann, E., Preller, K. H., Vollenweider, F. X., et al. (2015). Acute effects of lysergic acid diethylamide in healthy subjects. *Biological Psychiatry, 78,* 544–553.

Scott, J. C., Woods, S. P., Matt, G. E., Meyer, R. A., Heaton, R. K., Atkinson, J. H., et al. (2007). Neurocognitive effects of methamphetamine: A critical review and meta-analysis. *Neuropsychology Review, 17,* 275–297.

Slotkin, T. A., & Seidler, F. J. (2009). Nicotine exposure in adolescence alters the response of serotonin systems to nicotine administered subsequently in adulthood. *Developmental Neuroscience, 31,* 58–70.

Slotkin, T. A., Card, J., & Seidler, F. J. (2014). Nicotine administration in adolescence reprograms the subsequent response to nicotine treatment and withdrawal in adulthood: sex-selective effects on cerebrocortical serotonergic function. *Brain Research Bulletin, 102,* 1–8.

Sofikitis, N., Miyagawa, I., Dimitriadis, D., Zavos, P., Sikka, S., & Hellstrom, W. (1995). Effects of smoking on testicular function, semen quality and sperm fertilizing capacity. *Journal of Urology, 154,* 1030–1034.

Sowell, E. R., Delis, D., Stiles, J., & Jernigan, T. L. (2001). Improved memory functioning and frontal lobe maturation between childhood and adolescence: a structural MRI study. *Journal of the International Neuropsychological Society, 7,* 312–322.

Sowell, E. R., Thompson, P. M., Holmes, C. J., Batth, R., Jernigan, T. L., & Toga, A. W. (1999). Localizing age-related changes in brain structure between childhood and adolescence using statistical parametric mapping. *Neuroimage, 9,* 587–597.

Spear, L. P. (2000). The adolescent brain and age-related behavioral manifestations. *Neuroscience and Biobehavioral Reviews, 24*(4), 417–463.

Spear, L. P., & Varlinskaya EI. (2005). Adolescence. Alcohol sensitivity, tolerance, and intake. *Recent Dev Alcohol. 17,* 143–159.

Stewart, S. A. (2005). The effects of benzodiazepines on cognition. *The Journal of clinical psychiatry, 66*(Suppl 2), 9–13.

Strajhar, P., Schmid, Y., Liakoni, E., Dolder, P. C., Rentsch, K. M., Kratschmar, D. V., et al. (2016). Acute effects of lysergic acid diethylamide on circulating steroid levels in healthy subjects. *Journal of Neuroendocrinology, 28,* 12374.

Squeglia, L. M., Jacobus, J., & Tapert, S. F. (2009). The influence of substance use on adolescent brain development. *Clinical EEG and Neuroscience, 40*(1), 31–38.

Squeglia, L. M., Sorg, S. F., Schweinsburg, A. D., et al. (2011). Binge drinking differentially affects adolescent male and female brain morphometry. *Psychopharmacology (Berl), 220,* 529–539.

Squeglia, L. M., Jacobus, J., & Tapert, S. F. (2014). The effect of alcohol use on human adolescent brain structures and systems. *Handbook of Clinical Neurology, 125,* 501–510.

Szyf, M. (2013). The genome- and system-wide response of DNA methylation to early life adversity and its implication on mental health. *Canadian Journal of Psychiatry, 58,* 697–704.

Szyf, M. (2015). Nongenetic inheritance and transgenerational epigenetics. *Trends in Molecular Medicine, 21,* 134–144.

Szutorisz, H., & Hurd, Y. L. (2015). Epigenetic effects of cannabis exposure. *Biological Psychiatry, 79*(7), 586–594.

Teicher, M. H., et al. (1995). Evidence for dopamine receptor pruning between adolescence and adulthood in striatum but not nucleus accumbens. *Developmental Brain Research, 89,* 167–172. https://doi.org/10.1016/0165-3806(95)00109-Q.

Tomasiewicz, H. C., Jacobs, M. M., Wilkinson, M. B., Wilson, S. P., Nestler, E. J., & Hurd, Y. L. (2012). Proenkephalin mediates the enduring effects of adolescent cannabis exposure associated with adult opiate vulnerability. *Biological Psychiatry, 72,* 803–810.

U.S. (2016). Department of Health, and Human Services, Centers for Disease Control and Prevention, National Center for Chronic Disease, Prevention and Health Promotion, Office on Smoking and Health. *E-Cigarette Use Among Youth And Young Adults: A Report of the Surgeon General—Executive Summary*.

U.S. Department of Health and Human Services. (2014). *The Health Consequences of Smoking—50 Years of Progress: A Report of the Surgeon General*. Department of Health and Human Services, Centers for Disease Control and Prevention, National Center for Chronic Disease Prevention and Health Promotion, Office on Smoking and Health, Atlanta, GA, USA.

Van Batenburg-Eddes, T., Lee, N. C., Weeda, W. D., Krabbendam, L., & Huizinga, M. (2014). The potential adverse effect of energy drinks on executive functions in early adolescence. *Frontiers in Psychology, 5,* 457. https://doi.org/10.3389/fpsyg.2014.00457.

Vassoler, F. M., Byrnes, E. M., & Pierce, R. C. (2013). The impact of exposure to addictive drugs on future generations: Physiological and behavioral effects. *Neuropharmacology*, *76 Pt B*(0 0), 269–75.

Venners, S. A., Wang, X., Chen, C., Wang, L., Chen, D., Guang, W., et al. (2004). Paternal smoking and pregnancy loss: a prospective study using a biomarker of pregnancy. *American Journal of Epidemiology, 159,* 993–1001.

Volkow, N. D., et al. (2001). Association of Dopamine Transporter Reduction With Psychomotor Impairment in Methamphetamine Abusers. The American Journal of Psychiatry.

Walker, D. M., et al. (2017, November 8). Adolescence and reward: making sense of neural and behavioral changes amid the chaos. *The Journal of Neuroscience*, 37(45), 10855–10866.

Wachman, E. M., et al. (2013). Association of OPRM1 and COMT single-nucleotide polymorphisms with hospital length of stay and treatment of neonatal abstinence syndrome. *JAMA, 309*(17), 1821.

Wang, J., Zhou, M., Wang, X., Yang, X., Wang, M., Zhang, C., et al. (2014). Impact of ketamine on learning and memory function, neuronal apoptosis and its potential association with miR-214 and PTEN in adolescent rats. *PLoS One, 9*(6), e99855. https://doi.org/10.1371/journal.pone.0099855.

Whelan, P. J., et al. (2012 January–April). Buprenorphine versus methadone treatment A review of evidence in both developed and developing worlds. *Journal of Neurosciences in Rural Practice*, 3(1), 45–50.

Woolverton, W. L., & Trost, R. C. (1978). Cocaine as a discriminative stimulus for responding maintained by food in squirrel monkeys. *Pharmacology, Biochemistry and Behavior, 8*, 627–630.

Xu, Z., Seidler, F. J., Cousins, M. M., Slikker, W., Jr., & Slotkin, T. A. (2002). Adolescent nicotine administration alters serotonin receptors and cell signaling mediated through adenylyl cyclase. *Brain Research, 951*, 280–292.

Yang, X., Hegde, V. L., Rao, R., Zhang, J., Nagarkatti, P. S., & Nagarkatti, M. (2014). Histone modifications are associated with Delta9-tetrahydrocannabinol-mediated alterations in antigen-specific T cell responses. *The Journal of Biological Chemistry, 289*, 18707–18718.

Yazigi, R. A., Odem, R. R., & Polakoski, K. L. (1991). Demonstration of specific binding of cocaine to human spermatozoa. *JAMA, 266*, 1956–1959.

Yuan, M., Cross, S. J., Loughlin, S. E., & Leslie, F. M. (2015). Nicotine and the adolescent brain. *The Journal of Physiology, 593*(16), 3397–3412.

Zapata, L. B., Hillis, S. D., Marchbanks, P. A., Curtis, K. M., & Lowry, R. (2008). Methamphetamine use is independently associated with recent risky sexual behaviors and adolescent pregnancy. *Journal of School Health, 78*, 641–648.

Zou, X., Patterson, T. A., Sadovova, N., Twaddle, N. C., Doerge, D. R., Zhang, X., et al. (2009). Potential neurotoxicity of ketamine in the developing rat brain. *Toxicological Sciences: An Official Journal of the Society of Toxicology, 108*(1), 149–158.

Zweben, J. E., Cohen, J. B., Christian, D., Galloway, G. P., Salinardi, M., Parent, D., et al. (2004). Psychiatric symptoms in methamphetamine users. *The American Journal on Addictions 13*, 181–190.

Chapter 5
Cannabis

2017 data from Monitoring The Future (MTF) survey, a national study designed and conducted by research scientists at the University of Michigan's Institute for Social Research and funded by the National Institute on Drug Abuse that surveys students in grades 8th, 10th, and 12th revealed that cannabis use among adolescents and teens rose in 2017; however, the use of other illicit substances declined. Cannabis is the substance that is commonly used by teens. Approximately, 45,000 students in some 380 public and private secondary schools have been surveyed each year in this U.S. national study (Johnston et al. 2018).

This marked the first significant increase in 7 years. According to 2017 MTF data, past-year use of marijuana significantly increased from 1.3 to 24% in 2017 for 8th, 10th, and 12th graders combined. Broken down by group:

- 8th graders rose from 0.8 to 10.1%.
- 10th graders rose from 1.6 to 25.5%.
- 12th graders rose from 1.5 to 37.1%.
- When 8–12th grade increases in use were combined, it was deemed significant.

2017 MTF data also revealed a considerable increase in marijuana vaping. 10% of 12th graders indicated that they had vaped marijuana in the past years, 8% of 10th graders and 3% of 8th graders endorsed vaping marijuana as well. Johnston et al. study concluded the following about this trend in marijuana vaping: these annual levels are about the same as the levels for *lifetime* prevalence1 of vaping marijuana use, indicating that almost all marijuana vaping had occurred within 1 year of the survey (Johnston et al. 2018).

To date, there are ten states + Washington DC where both recreational and medical marijuanas are legal to include Washington, Oregon, California, Nevada, Alaska, Colorado, Michigan, Vermont, Massachusetts, and Maine.

To date, states that have legalized medical marijuana *only* include Montana, Utah, Arizona, New Mexico, North Dakota, Minnesota, Oklahoma, Missouri, Illinois, Arkansas, Louisiana, Florida, Ohio, West Virginia, Pennsylvania, Maryland, New York, New Jersey, Deleware, Rhode Island, and Connecticut.

A. Moreland-Capuia, *Training for Change*,
https://doi.org/10.1007/978-3-030-19208-2_5

States to include Colorado, Washington, and Oregon were among early legalizers. Preliminary studies on the impact of legalization have been done in these states.

A study by Paschall et al. investigated the association between medical marijuana patients and licensed growers per 1,000 population in 32 Oregon counties from 2006 to 2015, and marijuana use among youth over the same period. The study employed data from multiple sources which include registered medical marijuana patients and licensed growers from the Oregon Medical Marijuana Program with specific data focus on youth marijuana use; Oregon Healthy Teens survey with a focus on perceived parental disapproval and demographic characteristics. Through 32 Oregon counties, the mean rate of marijuana patients per 1,000 population increased from 2.9 in 2006 to 18.3 in 2015; grower rate increased from 3.8 to 11.9. The study suggests that there was significant positive associations between rates of marijuana patients and growers per 1,000 population and the prevalence of past 30-day marijuana use, controlling for youth demographic characteristics and further that a greater number of registered marijuana patients and growers per 1,000 population in Oregon counties was associated with a higher prevalence of marijuana use among youth from 2006 to 2015, and that this relationship was partially attributable to perceived norms favorable toward marijuana use (Paschall et al. 2017).

According to a report by Dr. Hagler entitled: Marijuana Use Detrimental to Youth, a report from the American College of Pediatricians; there is evidence legalization of marijuana limited to medical dispensaries and/or adult recreational use has led to increased unintended exposure to marijuana among young children as evidenced by increased rates of poison center calls for accidental pediatric marijuana ingestion. Accidental ingestion more than tripled in states that decriminalized marijuana before 2005. In states which passed legislation between 2005 and 2011, call rates increased nearly 11.5% per year. There was no similar increase in states that had not decriminalized marijuana as of December 31, 2011. Equally, in states where marijuana was legalized between 2005 and 2011, there was a notable spike in pediatric intensive care unit admission for moderate to severe symptoms related to marijuana exposure and use (Wang 2014; Hagler 2017). Marijuana use by adolescents has grown steadily as more states enact various decriminalization laws (Cerda et al. 2012).

According to a JAMA publication entitled "Problems With Medicalization of Marijuana," there is no clear optimal dose of marijuana for its various approved medical conditions (i.e., nausea, vomiting, migraines, etc.). The concentration of THC and other cannabinoids in each marijuana cigarette, the size of cigarettes, and the quantity of smoke inhaled by users can vary considerably (Wilkinson 2014). At current, there are still limited controlled clinical trial data on medical use of Marijuana, it is emerging, but there is still much unknown. Wilkinson et al. highlight the fact that because medical marijuana is approved for most chronic conditions that require long-term dosing, licensed medical providers must be aware of the development of tolerance and dependence (as evidenced by downregulation of the brain cannabinoid receptors), as well as withdrawal on discontinuation (Budney and Hughes 2006).

There is concern that the Monitoring The Future Survey data may not accurately reflect the profound impact of marijuana legalization in states like Colorado (which was among one of the first states to legalize marijuana medical and recreational).

Wang et al. conducted a retrospective review of marijuana-related adolescent emergency department visits at one of the Children's hospital in Colorado. ICD codes and urine drug screens were reviewed over a 10-year period (from 2005 to 2015) in persons 13–21 years of age. In their review, they found over 4,000 marijuana-related visits. Out of this pool of over 4,000, the following evaluations and assessments were done (Wang et al. 2018):

- 67% had behavioral health evaluations (accounted for close to 2,800 adolescents)—a psychiatric diagnosis was given in 71% of person who had a behavioral health evaluation.
- Alcohol use combined with heavy cannabis was observed in 21% of persons.
- Marijuana-related emergency room visits spiked considerably from 1.8 per 1,000 visits in 2009 to 4.9 per 1,000 visits in 2015—this spike is deemed significant (Wang et al. 2018).

The study demonstrated that marijuana legalization has correlated with an increase in detrimental and disproportionate negative impact on adolescents (Hopfer 2014). This phenomenon might not be adequately captured in the Monitoring The Future (MTF) Surveys (Wang et al. 2018).

In an article by Cerda et al. 2017, the impact of marijuana legalization in the state of Washington was highlighted. The study pointed out that in the state of Washington, the rate of perceived harmfulness of marijuana use decreased and the rate of past-month use increased among 8th and 10th graders following the passage of recreational marijuana laws (Cerda et al. 2017). I would contend that this is what makes marijuana use in the adolescent population so potentially dangerous—the mere fact that they don't see marijuana as harmful has been associated with increased use and experimentation, which undoubtedly increases the potential threat to brain development.

In a review, published in the New England Journal of Medicine, Volkow et al. summed up the strongest scientific literature on the short- and long-term impact of cannabis use in adolescents.

In high doses = increased incidence of paranoia and psychosis Short-term use and effects: Short-term memory impaired + consolidation of memory is compromised; motor skills slowed, increasing risk for inattention and motor vehicle accidents; limited judgment, increased risk of sexual behaviors, which increases risk of exposure to sexually transmitted diseases; in high dose, there is increased incidence of paranoia and psychosis
Long-term effects or heavy use included: Increased risk of addiction; change in brain development; an association between early exposure to marijuana use and dropout rates + other poor educational outcomes; cognitive impairment with lower IQ in frequent users during adolescence; poor quality of life; more lung infections; increased risk of psychosis in persons with a predisposition to psychosis (Volkow et al. 2014)

There appears to be an inversely proportional relationship to cannabis use among young people and legalization (in some states) versus increased medical use versus perceived harm of cannabis. There have been notable increases in recreational use and medical marijuana. The running conviction that cannabis is natural (because the brain has receptors for it and it is grown) has shaped attitudes and behaviors toward its use—the great misnomer is that cannabis (because it grows from the earth) is not harmful. Equally, it appears that some have interpreted legalization of cannabis and medical as "benign and without consequences." "Give the brain a fighting chance" is still an appropriate theme in the context of cannabis and its use while the brain is developing.

Disproportionately, justice-involved youth with a history of trauma are consuming cannabis at a higher rate than youth who aren't incarcerated and who don't have a history of trauma. Substance use, *a history of trauma and incarceration is trauma compounded* - acute on chronic trauma. Cannabis use must be placed in context. When we place it (cannabis use) in the context of the developing brain, we might draw different conclusions about youth having access to and consuming it.

According to Dougherty et al. 2013, early and sustained use of cannabis can affect memory, attention, and ability to think clearly, making it difficult to concentrate, learn new things, and make sound decisions.

Filbey et al. suggest that chronic marijuana use is associated with complex neuroadaptive processes and that onset and duration of use have unique effects on these processes. Specifically, they measured gray matter (GM) volume via structural MRI across the whole brain and observed orbitofrontal gray matter volume loss with chronic use.

While Filbey and team suggest more studies are needed to investigate this phenomenon further, one can conclude that Cannabis use is not benign when it comes to impact on the brain. This chapter is dedicated to understanding cannabis and its potential role in compromising cognition, judgement, and emotions in youth.

The purpose of this chapter is to present what we know and understand about cannabis thus far. You get to be the judge. I believe when we know better, we must do better.

By the end of this chapter, you should be able to

- Understand the basic neurobiology of endocannabinoids,
- Know cannabis intoxication,
- Understand cannabis withdrawal,
- Comprehend the impact of cannabis on the developing brain.
- Understand the threat of cannabis on cognition, and
- Know how to counsel youth on the deleterious effects of cannabis.

Neurobiology of endocannabinoids

The endocannabinoid system is made up of endocannabinoids, which are neurotransmitters that bind to cannabinoid receptors. Delta-9-tetrahydrocannabinol (THC) and cannabidiol (CBD) are cannabinoids that act at the cannabinoid receptors in the brain. Cannabinoids receptors are found throughout the entire brain to include the medulla, cerebellum, basal ganglia, cerebral cortex, hypothalamus, hippocampus, and spinal cord. Each of these brain structures has specific functions—see Fig. 5.1.

The endocannabinoid system is theorized to play an important regulatory role in the secretion of hormones related to reproductive functions and response to stress (Zou, Morena-Patel).

Distinguishing cannabinoids from endocannabinoids

Again, human beings have an endocannabinoids system that responds to cannabinoids (anandamides) produced naturally by human beings (Alger 2013). The endocannabinoid system is present at birth and plays a role in neuron development (Fernandez-Ruiz 1999). It also is theorized to play a role in the bodies stress response (Morena-Patel et al. 2015) and reproductive system (Zou and Kumar 2018).

Endogenous cannabinoids (e.g., anandamides)—made naturally in the human body and theorized to play a role in brain development, reproductive processes, and the stress response—activate the endocannabinoid system (Kendall and Yodowski 2017).

Exogenous cannabinoids—THC and CBD (cannabinoids produced outside the human body) when consumed—activate the endocannabinoid system but have a very different impact on the body compared to endogenous cannabinoids.

There are two main cannabinoid receptors, cannabinoid receptor 1 and 2 (CB1 and CB2 receptors).

CB_1 receptor is the most prominent, they are G protein-coupled receptors (GPCRs) in the central nervous system, and is found in particularly high levels in the neocortex, hippocampus, basal ganglia, cerebellum, and brain stem (Herkenham et al. 1991; Marsicano and Kuner 2008), outlined in Fig. 5.1.

According to an article by Kendall, D. A. et al., CB_2 receptor exhibits a more defined pattern of expression in the brain than CB_1 receptors and is found predominantly in cells and tissues of the immune system (Klein 2005; Mackie 2006). In the CNS, CB_2 receptor expression is associated with inflammation and it is primarily localized to microglia, resident macrophages of the CNS (Mackie 2008; Palazuelos et al. 2009). Additionally, several studies have discovered CB2 receptors in microglia (Walter et al. 2003), brain stem (Van Sickle et al. 2005), cerebellum, striatum, midbrain, and hippocampus (Cacciola et al. 2010; Onaivi 2006).

CB 1 receptors are found in these parts of the brain according to the following studies:	**Function**
Basal ganglia (Joy JE, 1999)	Movement
Cerebellum (Joy JE, 1999)	Movement
Cerebral cortex (Joy JE, 1999)	Cognition
Hippocampus (Joy JE, 1999)	Learning, Stress, Memory
Medulla (Grotenhermen, 2005; Navari et al., 2006)	Nausea, Vomiting (Guzman 2003)
Hypothalamus (Martin BR, 2004)	Appetite
Spinal Cord (Joy JE, 1999)	Peripheral Sensation, Pain

Fig. 5.1 Several studies investigating the use of cannabis in cancer treatment have revealed both the location and function of cannabinoid receptors in the brain (Joy 1999; Martin 2004; Grotenhermen 2005; Navari et al. 2006)

Neurobiological impact of cannabis

THC and CBD act on cannabinoid receptors. THC and CBD impact the brain's reward pathway similar to other drugs by stimulating neurons in the reward pathway to release high levels of dopamine, disturbing the hippocampus from functioning normally, which increases its salience and risk for dependence.

Several species:

- *Cannabis sativa*—THC predominant.
- *Cannabis indica*—CBD predominant.
- *Cannabis ruderalis—theorized to be less psychoactive.*
- Psychoactive components of the plant are thought to be produced to defend the plant from predators ***(in its natural environment, the very substance that humans use to get high, THC, holds the function of staving off predators. Let this sink in.)***.
- There are male, female, and hermaphrodite versions of each plant.
- Most concentrated in the flowers of the female plant.

Physiologic impact of cannabis—this is what happens with short-term use of cannabis

- Heart rate increases by 20–50% for 3 h.
- Blood pressure (a user can become orthostatic with use).
  - Increases when sitting.
  - Decreases when standing.
- Dilation of bronchioles in lungs.
- Conjunctival injection (red eyes from small blood vessels bursting).
- Hypothermia (body temperature falling below its normal functioning temperature can lead to death).
- Reaction time and motor skills are significantly reduced (Hall 2012).
- Mild euphoria (experiencing pleasure and high from dopamine surge in reward pathway).
- Relaxation.
- Perceptual alterations (neurons in the reward pathway increasing the release of dopamine can increase risk of paranoia and other forms of psychosis in the form of hallucinations, etc.).
- Time distortion.
- Intensification of normal experiences (everything is felt and experienced deeply).
- Increased sociability and laughter.
- Increase in appetite.
- ***Loss of short-term memory*** (can be profound).

A study by Crean et al. (2011) revealed clear evidence that during intoxication with cannabis contributes to impairment in short-term and working memory. This impairment persists beyond use and subjective effects. There is still controversy (mixed data) over cognitive decline in adult users, and cognitive impairment was strongly associated with continuous intoxication.

Several studies (Jager and Ramsey 2008; Meier 2012) demonstrate the impact of cannabis on the adolescent brain. For users who begin use prior to age 18, their developmental trajectory was significantly altered as evidenced by a persistent decrease of eight points in IQ and difficulty in learning new material.

Quick reminder on gray matter versus white matter in the brain
Gray Matter: Neuron cell bodies, glial cells, give nutrients and energy to neurons. Mostly unmyelinated.

White Matter: Myelinated bundles of axons and neurons that connect areas of gray matter to one another. Carries impulses.

I wish to highlight a very strong study by Filbey et al. 2014 that investigated long-term effects of marijuana use on the brain. The specifics of the study:

- Long-term and heavy use was defined as >4 days per week use of marijuana for 6 months or greater.
- UDS + for THC –COOH (secondary metabolite of THC, not psychoactive, but longer half-life and is theorized to be implicated for anti-inflammatory/anti-pain properties).

Controlled for sex, age, and the onset of use (IQ of marijuana users lower than controls)

- Average years of use ranged between 2 and 18 years.
- Ages ranged roughly between 22 and 36.
- Age of onset of use: ranged between 15 and 21 (why is this significant?).

Three groups

- 62 control (nonusers).
- 48 marijuana users (tobacco and alcohol confounding).
- 27 marijuana only users (group was added after post hoc analysis).

Three different imaging techniques employed

- High-resolution T1 weighted to measure gray matter volume.
- Resting state functional MRI to assess functional connectivity.
- Diffusion tensor scan to assess structural connective between brain regions via white matter tracts.

Of note: Voxel-based morphology—used for MRI analysis. Neuroimaging analysis that allows for further investigation of focal differences in brain anatomy. Sophisticated statistical analysis is employed.

Chronic marijuana users compared to control

- Decrease in volume bilaterally in the orbitofrontal cortex (OFC).
- Increased structural connectivity (connectivity in the OFC and in the tracts that innervate the OFC, i.e., forceps minor).
- Increased functional connectivity (statistical dependence of the signal from different areas).
- Suggests a neuroadaptive process.

- Marijuana Problem Survey (MPS) > marijuana users compared to controls.
- Should note that marijuana + alcohol + tobacco group demonstrated the same changes in OFC volume as Marijuana ONLY group—this could represent a compound effect.

Some challenges with the study

- The "n" in the study is low.
- Results are deemed "equivocal" although studies in animal models have demonstrated neurotoxicity (reduction in CB1 density, neuronal loss, etc.).
- Unclear of whether marijuana users are smoking only or using edibles, tinctures, oils, etc.—this may make a difference.
- Unclear if marijuana use is THC or CBD predominant.
- Endogenous cannabinoids play an important role in synaptic pruning, and 9-tetrahydrocannabinol (THC) might disrupt this process (predominantly in the OFC).

While there are some challenges in Filbey et al. study, I don't think the findings of volume decreases in the orbitofrontal gray matter cortex can be ignored. These findings should be placed in context of the developing brain and other studies confirming decrease in cognition with sustained use of cannabis, namely, THC.

A 35-year cohort study published on August 2012 in Proceedings of the National Academy of Sciences and funded partly by NIDA and other NIH institutes reported an association between long-term cannabis use and neuropsychological decline, even after controlling for education. The use of marijuana before age 18 was associated with lasting harm to a person's intelligence, attention, and memory, and was suggestive of neurological harm from cannabis. Quitting cannabis did not appear to reverse the loss. However, individuals who started cannabis use after the age of 18 did not show similar declines (Meier 2012).

Is CBD safe in adolescence?

Many of the studies highlight the deleterious impact of THC's activity at the cannabinoid 1 (CB1) receptor on brain development and function. Current literature suggest that CBD is neuroprotective, anti-inflammatory, and antipsychotic. It should be noted that most of these CBD studies have been done in animal models and not adequately studied in humans. Again, the issue of cannabis is highly controversial. While there aren't sufficient studies to adequately answer the question of whether CBD is safe in adolescence or not, from my clinical experience, I can confidently state that CBD should be avoided in the context of the developing brain. Clinically, I've witnessed increased anxiety and paranoia with pure CBD use.

Let's think about CBD for one moment and its origins. CBD is derived from the marijuana plant (which is cannabis sativa and/or indica), and theorized to have more THC content. CBD is also derived from the hemp plant (cannabis sativa primarily), and theorized to have less THC content. THC again is theorized to have greater capacity to contribute to psychosis because of the receptors that it acts on, where it acts in the brain and its proclivity for contributing to changes in dopamine and other neurochemicals. CBD is theorized to be less psychoactive because of the receptors it acts on, where it acts in the body and the way it impacts important neurochemicals in the body. CBD and THC come from the same plant. Metaphorically, I think of THC and CDB in terms of caffeinated versus de-caffeinated coffee, respectively. THC is caffeinated and CBD is the de-caffeinated version. It is well understood that de-caffeinated means low concentration of caffeine, and it does mean that there is no caffeine present. I see CBD as having a very low concentration of THC—in other words, I contend that CBD does have some psychoactive component, but it is relatively low compared to THC. This certainly pans out in terms of what I experience clinically with adolescents who are using CBD predominantly. There are clear impacts on cognition and mood. In my clinical opinion, both CBD and THC should be avoided while the brain is still developing. “Give the brain a fighting chance.”

Cannabis's epigenetics impact
Various studies reveal accumulating data in humans and animal models have begun to reveal irregular epigenetic modifications in brain and the periphery linked to cannabis exposure (Szutorisz and Hurd 2015).

DNA methylation marks at specific gene loci have been shown to even persist during the maturation of germ cells (egg and sperm) (Szyf 2013, 2015) and thus are interesting candidates for the propagation of the long-term effects of cannabis throughout multiple generations.

Histone lysine methylation is known to maintain stable gene expression alterations, and it is also the nucleosomal modification that has been associated with the long-term effects of marijuana and different cannabinoids in neurons and other cell types (Aguado et al. 2007; DiNieri 2013; Tomasiewicz et al. 2012; Yang et al. 2014).

Noncoding RNA's (ncRNAs) regulate gene expression at the transcriptional and posttranscriptional level. Changes in miRNA (one of three different noncoding RNA) profiles have been associated with cannabinoid exposure in the mammalian brain, peripheral blood cells, and the gut (Chandra et al. 2015; Hegde et al. 2013; Jackson et al. 2014; Molina et al. 2011).

Studies have demonstrated cannabis's ability to change genes and expression of specific proteins. As discussed at the beginning of this chapter, cannabis use has transgenerational implications.

Cannabis's reproductive impact
It is theorized that cannabinoids are involved in the regulation of reproductive functions; THC has been noted to inhibit the release of luteinizing hormone (LH) and prolactin and stimulates the release of stress hormones through corticotrophin (Murphy et al. 1999; Pagotto et al. 2006). Cannabinoids have been described as critical signals of the intricate network that control male and female reproduction, at multiple levels: locally and centrally, having as target both the hypothalamus and the pituitary (Schuel and Burkman 2005; Cacciola et al. 2010).

Gunderson et al. conducted a study on over 1,200 young Danish men aged 18–28. They were enrolled between 2008 and 2012 during the time that they participated in a required medical exam to determine fitness for military service. Each participant underwent physical exam, had blood drawn, and provided a semen sample. A questionnaire on marijuana and recreational drug use within the last 3 months was administered. Specific categories included no use; once per week or less, more than once per week.

The study revealed the following:

- Near half of the participants indicated that they had smoked marijuana within the last 3 months.
- A little under 1/3 of participants smoked more than once per week, regularly.
- After adjustment for cofounders, it was determined that 29% had lower sperm concentration and a lower total sperm count.
- Combined use of marijuana more than once per week and other recreational drugs reduced the sperm concentration by 52% (95% CI: –68, −27) and total sperm count by 55% (95% CI: –71, –31).
- Marijuana smokers had higher levels of testosterone within the same range as cigarette smokers (Gunderson et al. 2015; Santaella-Tenorio et al. 2017).

Cannabis's impact on driving

Inattention continues to be cited among the top cause of motor vehicle accidents in the country. The impact of cannabis on attention and reaction times has been of great interest in the public health world. A systematic review of nine case-control studies and culpability studies revealed that recent cannabis use almost doubled the odds of having a motor vehicle crash. The increased risk was marginally larger in better designed studies (2.21 *v* 1.78), in case control rather than culpability studies (2.79 *v* 1.65), and in studies that examined deaths rather than injuries (2.10 *v* 1.74). While confounding factors may exist, the results are consistent with experimental evidence that cannabis use leads to dose-related impairments in simulated driving, psychomotor skills, and on-road driving (Ramaekers et al. 2004; Grotenhermen et al. 2007).

When states like Colorado, Oregon, and Washington legalized cannabis, one of the primary concerns was whether or not cannabis intoxication would impair driving ability and even capacity to work. The studies on this subject matter are mixed. Some studies could not determine a significant impact of cannabis use in impaired driving compared to controls. A study by Jayson Aydelotte et al. concluded that 3 years after recreational marijuana legalization, changes in motor vehicle crash fatality rates for Washington and Colorado were not statistically different from those in similar states without recreational marijuana legalization (Jayson and Aydelotte 2017). Other studies noted minimum association between legalization of cannabis and increase in motor vehicle accidents secondary to cannabis intoxication (Drug facts NIDA 2012). A recent study conducted by the Insurance Institute of Highway Safety sought to review the effects of recreational marijuana sales on police-reported crashes in Colorado, Oregon, and Washington. The study concluded that cannabis-related motor vehicle collisions increased as high as 6% in Washington, Oregon, and Colorado when compared with neighboring states that haven't legalized recreational use of cannabis. This is one of the strongest studies thus far because of estimates of the frequency of collision claims per insured vehicle year, controlling for differences in other factors that could contribute to an accident, to include age, location, job status, and weather—increases were still appreciated (Monfort 2018; Salomonsen-Sautel et al. 2014).

Cannabis-induced mood disorders

Some users may experience an anxiety reaction to cannabis intoxication. Anxiety is more likely to occur in the following individuals:

- Inexperienced users.
- Large doses.
- Oral route of administration.

Anxiety can develop to panic, depersonalization, derealization, delusional thinking, and fear of "losing one's mind (Duperrouzel et al. 2018)."

A cohort study over a span of 6 years sets out to determine if cannabis use in adolescence predisposed to higher rates of depression and anxiety in adulthood. The study included 44 schools in Victoria, Australia. Over 1600 students between the ages of 14 and 15 were followed for 7 years total. Anxiety and depression were evaluated with scales and interviews. The study found (Patton et al. 2002)

- By age 20, two-thirds of participants had used cannabis.
- 7% were daily users.
- Daily use in young women was associated with a fivefold increase (compared to the general population) in reporting a state of depression and/or anxiety (after adjustments were made for potential use of other substances).
- Weekly or more frequent use in teenagers predicted a twofold increase (compared to the general population) in risk for later depression and anxiety after adjustment for other confounding factors.
- Of note, teenagers with depression and anxiety did not predict later cannabis use (weekly or daily use).
- The study concluded that frequent cannabis use in teenage girls predicated later depression and anxiety. Daily users had the highest risk (Patton et al. 2002).

A prospective study examined the association between anxiety symptoms and cannabis use and whether anxiety influenced cannabis use or if cannabis use contributed to higher incidences of anxiety. 250 adolescents who were identified as Hispanic between the ages of 14 and 17 with a history of exposure to drugs, alcohol, and/or cigarettes were included in this study. They completed three assessments over 1-year period. Sophisticated statistics and calculations were employed to determine associations between cannabis use and mood. The results revealed that during adolescence, early exposure to cannabis had a greater influence on prospective reports of anxiety. However, early anxiety did not appear to influence cannabis use. Adolescents with higher initial levels of cannabis use had more self-reported anxiety symptoms over time compared to their counterparts who were using less frequently (Deperrouzel 2017).

Cannabis and schizophrenia

For many years, the association of cannabis and psychotic disorder was known, but not well understood. Evidence now supports that cannabis precipitates psychosis in vulnerable individuals. It is not clear whether cannabis produces psychosis that would not have otherwise occurred. The amount of drug used, the age at first use, and genetic vulnerability can all influence this relationship. There is an increased risk of psychosis among adults who had used marijuana in adolescence *and* who also carried a specific variant of the gene for catechol-O-methyltransferase (COMT), an enzyme that degrades neurotransmitters such as dopamine and norepinephrine (D'Souza et al. 2009; Hall and Degenhardt 2008; Burns 2013).

A study by Caspi et al. examined the relationship between cannabis use in young people and risk for the development of psychotic symptoms in adulthood as evidenced by hallucinations and delusions (fixed false beliefs). Caspi pointed out that not every young person with early exposure to cannabis develops psychosis, which motivated the hypothesis that perhaps there is a genetic vulnerability to the harmful impacts of cannabis use. They conducted a longitudinal study of a representative cohort that was tracked to adulthood. The study revealed a functional polymorphism in the catechol-O-methyltransferase (COMT) gene. This change is theorized to influence the risk of the development of adult psychosis stemming from adolescent cannabis use. Carriers of the COMT valine158 allele were most likely to exhibit psychotic symptoms and to develop schizophreniform disorder if they used cannabis (Caspi et al. 2005). This, once again, highlights the epigenetic impact that substances can have on genes.

Study done by Gage et al. summarizes numerous studies that have indicated a relationship between cannabis use and psychosis. In brief, the study critically and thoughtfully outlines some confounding factors to include things like early access to trauma age of use and varying strains to name a few; the following is concluded: there are a number of facets of the evidence presented above that are consistent with a causal association between cannabis and psychosis. The longitudinal, case-control, and cross-sectional studies conducted to date have, for the most part, found consistent evidence of an association, even after adjustment for covariates (Gage et al. 2015).

Neurochemical disruption with cannabis and other substances

A review by Bloomfield et al. reviews the human and animal studies on cannabis's impact on the dopamine system. Bloomfield (along with other studies) highlights the working understanding that heavy cannabis use is associated with reductions in dopaminergic function (DiNieri et al. 2011). Further, it is noted that the THC's psychosis-producing capacity and reward/pleasure-producing response are heavily influenced by the dopaminergic system (Bloomfield et al. 2016).

It is not outside the realm of possibility that changes in one neurochemical may impact other neurochemicals. In other words, changes in dopamine are likely to contribute to changes in serotonin, norepinephrine, GABA, and glutamate as well. Shifts in neurochemicals increase the risk for mood components like anxiety, depression, and psychosis (broad categories). This is also why it is not outside of the realm of possibility that mood states like depression and anxiety happen in withdrawal and when an individual stops using a substance all together. Substance use contributes to neurochemical chaos, when the substance is stopped, it leaves the system to the task of recalibrating and attempting to restore.

Cannabis and increased emergency room visits
Zhu et al. investigated the impact of cannabis use on emergency room visits in the adolescent population. The study obtained data from the 2004–2011 Drug Abuse Warning Network and analyzed trends in cannabis-involved ED visits for persons aged ≥12 years and stratified by type of cannabis involvement (cannabis-only, cannabis-polydrug). They used logistic regressions to determine correlates of cannabis-involved hospitalization versus cannabis-involved ED visits only. The study found that ED visit rates increased from 51 to 73 visits per 100,000 population aged ≥12 years for cannabis-only use and from 63 to 100 for cannabis-polydrug use between 2004 and 2011. Adolescents aged 12–17 years showed the largest increase in the cannabis-only-involved ED visit rate. The most prevalent ED visits were noted among non-Hispanic blacks. Among cannabis-involved visits, the odds of hospitalization (versus ED visits only) increased with age strata compared with aged 12–17 years (Zhu et al. 2016).

There has been an increase in reported incidents of cannabis-related paranoia and psychosis and a phenomenon called cannabinoid hyperemesis syndrome.

Cannabinoid Hyperemesis Syndrome
According to a review by Galli et al., the increase in cannabis abuse tends to coincide with the recognition of a new clinical condition known as cannabinoid hyperemesis syndrome. Cannabinoid hyperemesis syndrome is branded by chronic cannabis use, cyclic episodes of nausea and vomiting, and frequent hot bathing. Symptoms usually last up to 48 h; treatment is mainly supportive with fluids and anti-nausea medication. While the mechanism is unknown, there are a few working theories. Despite the well-established antiemetic properties of marijuana, there is increasing evidence of its paradoxical effects on the gastrointestinal tract and central nervous system (Galli et al. 2011).

THC, as mentioned above, when consumed, can powerfully contribute to notable changes in psychomotor behavior, impairment in short-term memory, stimulation of appetite, and analgesia (Iverson, 2003).

CB1 receptors are found in the gastrointestinal tract and when activated can result in the following (Galli et al. 2011):

- Inhibition of gastric acid secretion, lower esophageal sphincter relaxation in dogs (Lehmann et al. 2002).
- Altered intestinal motility (Hinds et al. 2006; Esfandyari et al. 2007).
- Visceral pain and inflammation (Izzo and Camilleri 2008; Pertwee, 2001).
- Reduction in gastric motility and results in delayed gastric emptying in rat models (Krowicki et al. 1999; Izzo et al. 1999).
- In humans, THC given at doses used to prevent chemotherapy-induced nausea and vomiting causes a significant delay in gastric emptying (McCallum et al. 1999; Galli et al. 2011).

It is thought that changes in THC concentration (discussed earlier in this chapter) may be contributing to this hyperemesis phenomenon. THC concentrations have increased from as low as 3–30%. Major concerns are for severe dehydration leading to acute kidney injury.

Cannabis use and pregnancy/prenatal exposure
The 2017 American College of Pediatricians addressed the risk of using marijuana during pregnancy. The report asserts that prenatal marijuana exposure in infants and children result in higher incidence of neurobehavioral problems. Because THC and other compounds in marijuana are similar to the human brain's cannabinoid-like chemicals, prenatal marijuana exposure may alter the developing endocannabinoid system in the fetal brain—with consequences in attention deficit, difficulty with problem-solving, and poorer memory (Hagler 2017; Drug Facts, NIDA 2012).

There are data that point to an association between prenatal marijuana exposure and impaired executive functioning skills beyond the age of 3. The literature cites that children with a history of cannabis exposure are found to have an increased rate of impulsivity, attention deficits, and difficulty solving problems requiring the integration and manipulation of basic visuoperceptual skills (Fried 2001; Hagler 2017).

Cannabis

According to Burgdorf et al. (2011), typical THC content >10%, twice as high as 10 years ago. The major psychoactive ingredient is Δ9-tetrahydrocannabinol (THC). There are several other cannabinoids including cannabidiol (CBD), cannabinol (CBN), and tetrahydrocannabivarin (THCV). However, the main two cannabinoids are THC and CBD, which will be the focus of this chapter. The most important part of the THC molecule is its carbon-rich side chain, and the potency of THC is manipulated by adding more carbons on to it.

THC binds to *cannabinoid* receptors located on the surface of nerve cells. Again, a high concentration of cannabinoid receptors can be found in areas of the brain that modulate pleasure, memory, thinking, concentration, movement, coordination, and sensory and time perception.

When someone smokes marijuana, THC stimulates the cannabinoid receptors which blocks the function and activity of the naturally occurring endogenous cannabinoids (like anandamide), disrupting function of the natural, or endogenous, cannabinoids. The impact is notable. As time progresses, protracted stimulation of THC (a cannabinoid that is not naturally produced in the human brain and/or body) can effectively change the function of cannabinoid receptors and contribute to the following symptoms: distorted perception (paranoia), impaired coordination, difficulty with thinking and problems solving, and compromised learning and memory (Burgdorf et al.).

There are animal and human studies that demonstrate reduction in hippocampal volume with heavy and protracted THC use and suggest a protective benefit with CBD (Yücel et al. 2016) The cannabis literature is myriad and studies on its impact on youth and adults alike are mixed. As an addiction psychiatrist, I encourage everyone to review all literature with caution, meaning, I would consider the source. Who is funding the study? Cannabis is a multi-billion dollar industry. The healthy, safety, and well-being of America's youth should not be compromised for economic gain.

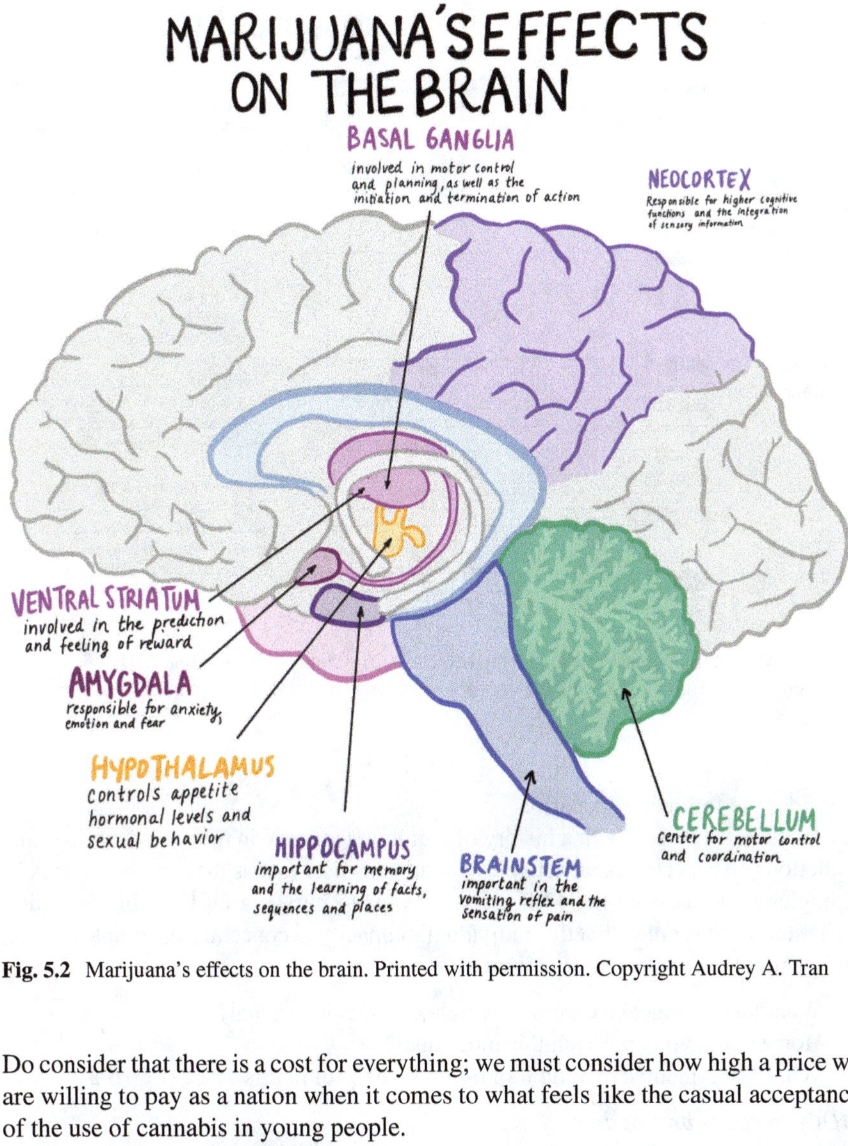

Fig. 5.2 Marijuana's effects on the brain. Printed with permission. Copyright Audrey A. Tran

Do consider that there is a cost for everything; we must consider how high a price we are willing to pay as a nation when it comes to what feels like the casual acceptance of the use of cannabis in young people.

See Fig. 5.2 which highlights marijuana's effects on the brain.

Practical application/Exercise 5.1
By way of reminder, the purpose of this chapter was to consider the current literature on cannabis. Ultimately, the future vitality, health, and strength of our youth are determined by what we deem acceptable and/or unacceptable. If the goal is healthy, sustained change over time, then strong consideration must be given to the things that could potentially detract from the goal. Current literature suggests that cannabis use may pose more negative risks than benefit to the developing brain.

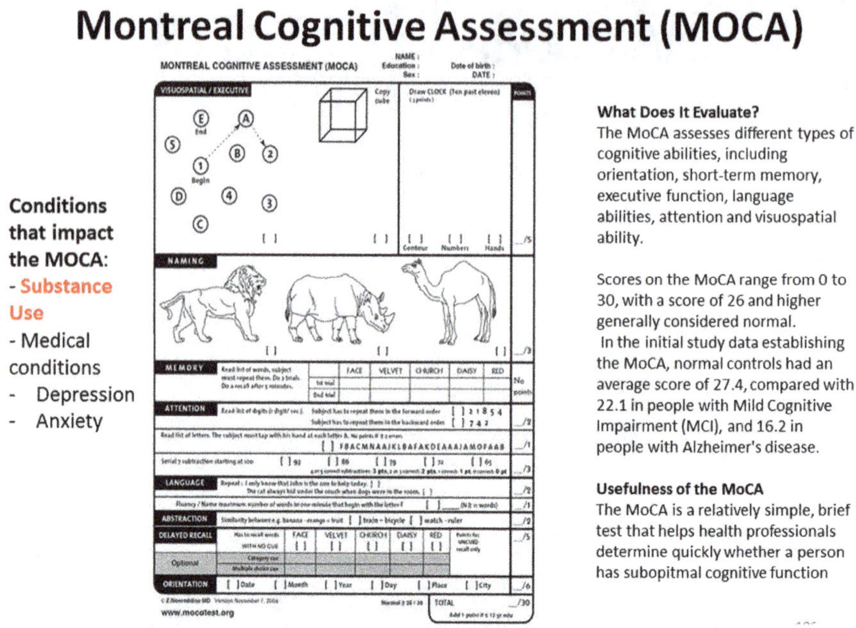

Fig. 5.3 Montreal Cognitive Assessment (MOCA). Copyright Z. Nasreddine MD. Reproduced with permission. Copies are available at www.mocatest.org. Printed with permission. Copyright Audrey A. Tran

Consider the following scenario:
An 18-year-old person with a history of childhood trauma, in recovery from cocaine addiction (4 years clean), an active daily cannabis user (states they use it to "relax"), struggles to get beyond the 11th grade, so opts to pursue a GED. While pursuing GED studies, it is noted that this individual's capacity to concentrate, complete tasks, and comprehend instructions is limited.

1. What factors must be carefully weighed in this individual?
2. How should you approach this individual?
3. What assessment/screening tool might be helpful in this case? (Fig. 5.3).

MOCA sections broken down

Visuospatial (ability to represent, analyze, and mentally deploy objects)/executive function (the ability to plan, organize, and complete tasks) = associated mainly with the prefrontal cortex.
Naming = also a measure of prefrontal cortex.
Memory = involves amygdala, hippocampus, cerebellum, and links to the prefrontal cortex.
Attention = prefrontal cortex.
Language = mainly cortex, frontal, parietal, occipital, and temporal lobes; and the cerebellum is involved in speaking and understanding language.

Abstraction = measure of mental flexibility is found, namely, in the prefrontal cortex.
Delayed recall = namely, the anterior cingulate cortex, which is part of the prefrontal cortex.

A significant portion of the MOCA relies heavily on top brain, cortical function.

Sometimes it is too hard to get through an entire MOCA with a young person. One way to quickly assess top brain function is to complete the "Clock Draw" component of the MOCA.

In the section circled, the "Clock Draw," you give the following instructions:

- Ask the individual to draw a circle.
- Ask individual to draw numbers in the circle as they would appear on a clock.
- Finally ask individual to make the clock read a quarter past eleven.

You are looking for whether or not the circle was drawn decently, whether the numbers were placed appropriately as they would appear on a clock, and finally whether or not they were able to distinguish between the long- and shorthand.

If there are any glaring shortcomings in this quick test, it should serve as an indication that the individual is not readily accessing the top (cortical) part of their brain. This should inspire a greater desire to understand why? A few potential reasons have been mentioned in this chapter and others. Things to consider are as follows:

- Are there learning challenges.
- Might substances be involved.
- Consideration for trauma.
- Mood component—fear versus anxiety versus depression.
- Lack of sleep.
- Medical concerns that could compromise memory.

You are not expected to an expert, only to be aware and to know when to refer appropriately and how to manage expectations at the moment.

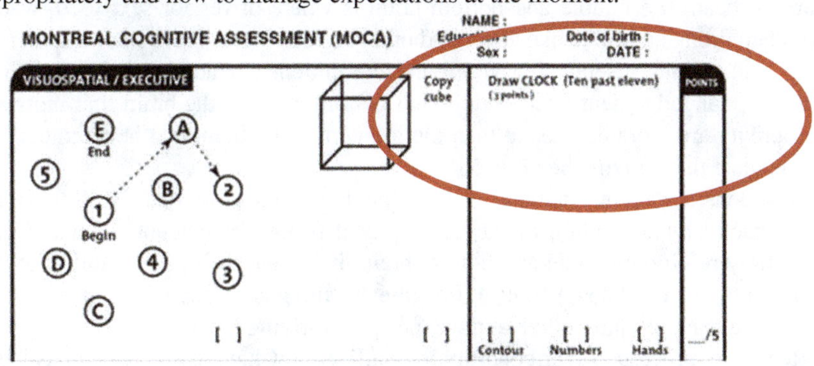

Making the connection—cannabis's impact on the developing brain and trauma
As stated in Chap. 4, when we are born, one could argue that the most developed part of our brain is the bottom and to a certain extent, the limbic (middle)—these are

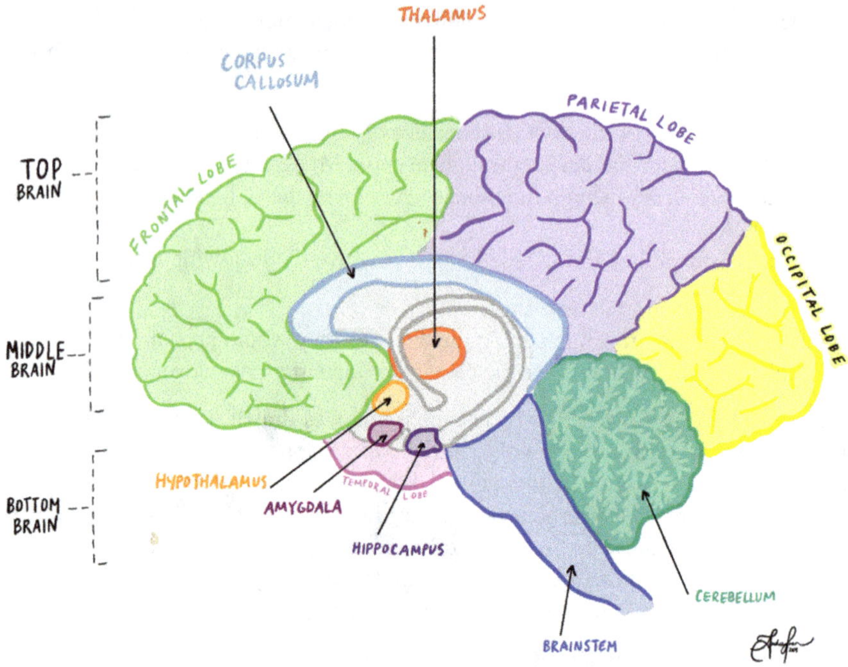

Fig. 5.4 Cannabis like other substances of abuse strengthen middle and bottom brain functioning at the expense of top brain development and functioning Printed with permission. Copyright Audrey A. Tran

parts of the brain that help us to "survive." We are born with the natural proclivity for survival as we respond to threat, seek safety, and allow us to breathe and our hearts to beat. The middle and bottom brain is where drives for sex, food, water, and other strong emotions like anger and other impulses live. From a developmental standpoint, it makes sense that youth are intermittently irrational, impulsive, and exercise poor judgement—the middle and bottom parts of the brain that motivate this activity are more developed than the top part of the brain that helps to control and regulate this activity. See Fig. 5.4.

Now consider adding cannabis and trauma in with the brain that is still forming. The capacity for disruption of the development process is evident. Cannabis can powerfully reinforce middle and bottom brain living and disrupts the ability of the top brain to exert top-down control. Imagine the amygdala gone wild.

Survival can, at times, come at the expense of thriving.

Recall the process of fear conditioning outlined in Chap. 3, also known as "fear that doesn't turn off," also known as neurobiological trauma impacts the same areas of the brain that substances of abuse do.

Getting back to the clinical case
An 18-year-old person with a history of childhood trauma, in recovery from cocaine addiction (4 years clean), an active daily cannabis user (states they use it to "relax") struggles to get beyond the 11th grade, so opts to pursue a GED. While pursuing GED studies, it is noted that this individual's capacity to concentrate, complete tasks, and comprehend instructions is limited.

Breaking down the case

Many of the systems that serve youth require them to engage in sophisticated cognitive ways. For example,

In juvenile justice community supervision models, youth are required to adhere to cognitive behavioral therapy models.

In education, youth are required to sit for long periods of time, access the top part of their brain to actively learn and retain information.

At some business and health offices, there is a working expectation that everyone can read and comprehend—forms are required to be filled out with limited inquiry about how individuals learn and/or process information.

If the goal is comprehension, which it should be as comprehension is a minimum requirement for change, then it would that considering a different approach might be beneficial.

What if systems considered the following concerning youth:

- Have they had sufficient sleep as poor sleep significantly impacts the ability to concentrate, focus, and be attentive.
- Have they eaten a meal and/or do they get proper nutrition as poor nutrition and hunger are drivers of irritability and also lower the ability to concentrate, focus, and be attentive.
- Might they be anxious and/or depressed? It is difficult to engage the top part of the brain, when the middle and bottom are predominating (this is a recurrent theme throughout this text).
- Is there a history of trauma?
- Are substances involved?

Historically, youth have been deemed non-adherent and/or noncompliant when they don't readily participate in cognitive-based models. The assumption that they are not trying hard enough and/or not following rules further exacerbates underlying trauma and distrust of the systems that were designed to support them. Taking a pause and considering these elements can powerfully change interactions and move systems closer to the goal of effectively and safely serving youth.

How to talk about the effects of Cannabis with youth

Psychiatrist, Dr. Kevin Hill has written extensively on cannabis. He wrote an article for the Carlat Report 2015: Addiction Treatment, providing practical information on how to talk with clients about marijuana. There were many useful tips that remain relevant to the conversation currently. In the report, the following was outlined (Hill 2015):

When talking with clients, typically two key issues emerge to include

- The possibility of negative effects of cannabis use; the impact of cannabis use when a client has a diagnosis of depression, anxiety, etc; the impact of cannabis use in specific populations, namely youth.
- Second, there are questions about how legitimate cannabis is in terms of its medical implications. Dr. Hill referred to an article he published in the Journal of Psychiatric Practice to further drive home this point.

Dr. Hill answers these questions by highlighting research and literature on the impact of cannabis on the developing brain and more importantly, it answers the question of whether or not marijuana use interferes with treatment of anxiety and/or depression. It was determined that cannabis and other substances are best avoided in the context of treating anxiety and/or depressive disorders.

Brief intervention(s)

- Introducing the issue.
- Give feedback.
  - Customized feedback on substance use patterns.
  - Discussion of where use fits in compared to population norms.
- Provide information.
  - Consequences of continued substance use.
  - Reasons to cut down or quit.
- Establish a goal.
  - Identification of future goals for health, activities, hobbies, relationships, and financial stability.
- Give advice on limits.
  - Setting a goal that is achievable.
- Summarizing and reaching closure.

Summary

- Cannabis use has increased in adolescence, and there appears to be a correlation between legalization/medicalization and dramatic shifts in attitude regarding cannabis's safety versus harm risk among young people.
- Cannabis use is a form of trauma to the developing brain.
- Cannabis has increased in potency over the years.
  This increase in potency, in the form of THC (the psychogenic component of cannabis), is theorized to be responsible for increases in paranoia and/or other forms of psychotic expression.
- THC (an exogenous cannabinoid that mimics endogenous cannabinoids) acts on cannabinoid receptors in the brain having a different impact of brain and body

function compared to naturally occurring, endogenous cannabinoids like anandamide. Cannabinoid receptors have multiple functional roles in reproduction and in neuron development.
- Elements of cannabis intoxication can last long after subjective intoxication, including memory and cognitive impairments.
- Short-term health consequences include anxiety reactions, risk for psychosis, and driving impairment.
- Cannabis-induced hyperemesis is a phenomenon.
- Long-term health consequences are still being explored.
- Cannabis is known to have significant impact on cognition—this should be explored with youth who are using.
- Education and counseling on the impact of cannabis (especially on the developing brain is critical).

Cannabis use remains a controversial topic. Some studies demonstrate severe cognitive, attentional, and behavioral impact and others don't. Individuals are divided into two powerful ways (Baker et al. 2003), those who do not believe cannabis has harmful impact in humans and those who do not believe it is benign. In the case of the youth and from my clinical experience as a double board certified addiction psychiatrist, I believe it is critical to consider the fact that brain is still developing and the brain must be given a fighting chance to develop to its full potential. I contend (and some may vehemently disagree) that many substances should be avoided until brain development is near complete (around the age of 26). The impact of cannabis on the developing is important enough to actively think about in terms of negative impacts on IQ, attention, cognition, etc. Again, this textbook is about transforming systems that serve youth, which also requires facilitating powerful transformation in and of youth. We can all agree that what we've been doing has not been effective. I encourage an open mind with a focus on solutions and healing moving forward. Youth with a history of trauma are at increased risk for and are using at higher rates compared to their counterparts without a complicated history of trauma.

Exercise 5.2
Questions and discussion

- What impact can cannabis have on cognition? The brain?
- Why might it be important to discourage cannabis use in individual younger than 26?
- What are some of the epigenetic impacts of cannabis?
- Might cannabis use increase and/or decrease symptoms of anxiety and/or depression?

References

Aguado, T., Carracedo, A., Julien, B., Velasco, G., Milman, G., Mechoulam, R., et al. (2007). Cannabinoids induce glioma stem-like cell differentiation and inhibit gliomagenesis. *The Journal of Biological Chemistry, 282,* 6854–6862.

Alger, B. E. (2013). Getting high on the endocannabinoid system. *Cerebrum: The Dana Forum on brain science, 2013*, 14.

Baker, D., Pryce, G., Giovannoni, G., & Thompson, A. J. (2003). The therapeutic potential of cannabis. *Lancet Neurology, 2*(5), 291–298.

Bloomfield, M. A., Ashok, A. H., Volkow, N. D., & Howes, O. D. (2016). The effects of Δ^9-tetrahydrocannabinol on the dopamine system. *Nature, 539*(7629), 369–377.

Budney, A. J., & Hughes, J. R. (2006). The cannabis withdrawal syndrome. *Current Opinion in Psychiatry, 19*(3), 233–238.

Burgdorf, J. R., Kilmer, B., & Pacula, R. L. (2011). Heterogeneity in the composition of marijuana seized in California. *Drug and Alcohol Dependence, 117*(1), 59–61.

Burns, J. K. (2013). Pathways from cannabis to psychosis: A review of the evidence. *Frontiers in Psychiatry, 4,* 128.

Cacciola, G., Chianese, R., Chioccarelli, T., Ciaramella, V., Fasano, S., Pierantoni, R., et al. (2010). Cannabinoids and reproduction: A lasting and intriguing history. *Pharmaceuticals, 3*(10), 3275–3323. https://doi.org/10.3390/ph3103275.

Caspi, A, Moffitt, T. E., Cannon, M. et al. (2005). Moderation of the effect of adolescent-onset cannabis use on adult psychosis by a functional polymorphism in the catechol-Omethyltransferase gene: Longitudinal evidence of a gene X environment interaction. *Biological Psychiatry*, *57*(10), 1117–1127. Retrieved from http://www.drugabuse.gov/publications/research-reports/marijuana/there-link-between-marijuana-use-mental-illness.

Cerdá, M., Wall, M., Feng, T., Keyes, K. M., Sarvet, A., Schulenberg, J., et al. (2017). Association of state recreational marijuana laws with adolescent marijuana use. *JAMA Pediatrics, 171*(2), 142–149.

Cerda, M., Wall, M., Keyes, K. M., Galea, S., & Hasin, D. (2012). Medical marijuana laws in 50 states: Investigating the relationship between state legalization of medical marijuana and marijuana use, abuse and dependence. *Drug and Alcohol Dependence, 120*(1–3), 22–27.

Chandra, L. C., Kumar, V., Torben, W., Vande Stouwe, C., Winsauer, P., Amedee, A., et al. (2015). Chronic administration of Delta9-tetrahydrocannabinol induces intestinal anti-inflammatory microRNA expression during acute simian immunodeficiency virus infection of rhesus macaques. *Journal of Virology, 89,* 1168–1181.

Crean, R. D., Crane, N. A., & Mason, B. J. (2011). An evidence based review of acute and long-term effects of cannabis use on executive cognitive functions. *Journal of Addiction Medicine, 5*(1), 1–8.

DiNieri, J. A., Wang, X., Szutorisz, H., Spano, S. M., Kaur, J., Casaccia, P., et al. (2011). Maternal cannabis use alters ventral striatal dopamine D2 gene regulation in the offspring. *Biological Psychiatry, 70,* 763–769.

Drug Facts. (2012). National Institute on Drug Abuse. Retrieved from www.drugabuse.gov/drugs-abuse/marijuana. Published December 2012.

Duperrouzel, J., et al. (2018). The association between adolescent cannabis use and anxiety: A parallel process analysis. *Addictive Behaviors, 78,* 107–113. https://doi.org/10.1016/j.addbeh.2017.11.005. Epub 2017 Nov 4.

Dougherty, D. M., Mathias, C. W., Dawes, M. A., et al. (2013). Impulsivity, attention, memory, and decision-making among adolescent marijuana users. *Psychopharmacology (Berl), 226*(2), 307–319.

D'Souza, D. C., Sewell, R. A., & Ranganathan, M. (2009). Cannabis and psychosis/schizophrenia: Human studies. *European Archives of Psychiatry and Clinical Neuroscience, 259*(7), 413–431.

Esfandyari, T., Camilleri, M., Busciglio, I., et al. (2007). Effects of a cannabinoid receptor agonist on colonic motor and sensory functions in humans: A randomized, placebo-controlled study. *American Journal of Physiology. Gastrointestinal and Liver Physiology, 293,* 137–145.

Fernandez-Ruiz, J. J. et al. (1999). Role of endocannabinoids in brain development. *Life Sciences, 65*(6–7), 725–736.

Filbey, et al. (2014). Long-term effects of marijuana use on the brain. *PNAS, 111*(47), 16913–16918.

Fried, P. A., & Smith, A. M. (2001). A literature review of the consequences of prenatal marijuana exposure. An emerging theme of a deficiency in aspects of executive function. *Neurotoxicology and Teratology, 23*(1), 1–11.

Gage, S. H., Hickman, M., & Zammit, S. (2015). Association between cannabis and psychosis: epidemiologic evidence. *Biological Psychiatry*. http://dx.doi.org/10.1016/j.biopsych.2015.08.001.

Galli, J. A., Sawaya, R. A., & Friedenberg, F. K. (2011). Cannabinoid hyperemesis syndrome. *Current Drug Abuse Reviews, 4*(4), 241–249.

Grotenhermen, F., Leson, G., Berghaus, G., Drummer, O. H., Kruger, H. P., Longo, M., et al. (2007). Developing limits for driving under cannabis. *Addiction, 102,* 1910–1917.

Grotenhermen, F. (2005). *Current Drug Targets: CNS and Neurological Disorders, 4*(5), 507–530.

Gunderson, T. D. (2015). Association between use of marijuana and male reproductive hormones and semen quality: A study among 1,215 healthy young men. *American Journal of Epidemiology, 182*(6), 473–481. https://doi.org/10.1093/aje/kwv135. Epub 2015 Aug 16.

Guzman, M. (2003). Cannabinoids: Potential anticancer agents. *Nature Reviews, 3,* 745–755.

Hagler, D. (2017). Marijuana use: Detrimental to youth. *American College of Pediatricians—April 2017.* Retrieved from https://www.acpeds.org/the-college-speaks/position-statements/effect-of-marijuana-legalization-on-risky-behavior/marijuana-use-detrimental-to-youth.

Hall, W., & Degenhardt, L. (2008). Cannabis use and the risk of developing a psychotic disorder. *World Psychiatry, 7*(2), 68–71.

Hall, W. (2012). Driving while under the influence of cannabis. *BMJ*, 344. Retrieved from https://doi.org/10.1136/bmj.e595 (Published 09 February 2012). Cite this as: BMJ 2012;344:e595.

Hegde, V. L., Tomar, S., Jackson, A., Rao, R., Yang, X., Singh, U. P., et al. (2013). Distinct microRNA expression profile and targeted biological pathways in functional myeloid-derived suppressor cells induced by Delta9-tetrahydrocannabinol in vivo: Regulation of CCAAT/enhancer-binding protein alpha by microRNA-690. *The Journal of Biological Chemistry, 288,* 36810–36826.

Herkenham, M., Lynn, A. B., Johnson, M. R., Melvin, L. S., de Costa, B. R., & Rice, K. C. (1991). Characterization and localization of cannabinoid receptors in rat brain: A quantitative in vitro autoradiographic study. *Journal of Neuroscience, 11,* 563–583.

Hill, K. P. (2015). Marijuana in 2015: What should we say to our patients?. Carlat Report 2015.

Hinds, N. M., Ullrich, K., & Smid, S. D. (2006). Cannabinoid 1 (CB1) receptors coupled to cholinergic motor neurones inhibit neurogenic circular muscle contractility in the human colon. *British Journal of Pharmacology, 148,* 191–199.

Hopfer, C. (2014). Implications of marijuana legalization for adolescent substance use. *Substance Abuse, 35*(4), 331–335.

Iverson, L. (2003). Cannabis and the brain. *Brain, 126,* 1252–1270.

Izzo, A. A., & Camilleri, M. (2008). Emerging role of cannabinoids in gastrointestinal and liver diseases: Basic and clinical aspects. *Gut, 57,* 1140–1155.

Izzo, A. A., Mascolo, N., Capasso, R., et al. (1999). Inhibitory effect of cannabinoid agonists on gastric emptying in the rat. *Naunyn Schmiedebergs Archives of Pharmacology, 360,* 221–223.

Jackson, A. R., Nagarkatti, P., & Nagarkatti, M. (2014). Anandamide attenuates Th-17 cell-mediated delayed-type hypersensitivity response by triggering IL-10 production and consequent microRNA induction. *PLoS One, 9,* e93954.

Jager, G., & Ramsey, N. F. (2008). Long-term consequences of adolescent cannabis exposure on the development of cognition, brain structure and function: An overview of animal and human research. *Current Drug Abuse Reviews, 1*(2), 114–123.

Jayson, D., Aydelotte, M. D. et al. (2017). Crash fatality rates after recreational marijuana legalization in Washington and Colorado. *American Journal of Public Health, 107*(8), 1329–1331.

Johnston, L. D., O'Malley, P. M., Miech, R. A., Bachman, J. G., & Schulenberg, J. E. (2018). *Monitoring the Future national results on adolescent drug use: Overview of key findings, 2017*. Ann Arbor, MI: Institute for Social Research, the University of Michigan.

Joy, J. E. et al. (eds.). (1999). In J. E. Joy, S. J. Watson Jr., & J. A. Benson Jr. (Eds.), *Marijuana and medicine: Assessing the science base*. Washington (DC): Institute of Medicine (US), National Academies Press (US).

Kendall, D. A., & Yudowski, G. A. (2017). Cannabinoid receptors in the central nervous system: Their signaling and roles in disease. *Frontiers in Cellular Neuroscience, 10,* 294.

Klein, T. W. (2005). Cannabinoid-based drugs as anti-inflammatory therapeutics. *Nature Reviews Immunology, 5,* 400–411.

Krowicki, Z. K., Moerschbaecher, J. M., Winsauer, P. J., et al. (1999). Delta9-tetrahydrocannabinol inhibits gastric motility in the rat through cannabinoid CB1 receptors. *European Journal of Pharmacology, 371,* 187–196.

Lehmann, A., Blackshaw, L. A., Brandon, L., et al. (2002). Cannabinoid receptor agonism inhibits transient lower esophageal sphincter relaxation and reflux in dogs. *Gastroenterology, 123,* 1129–1134.

Mackie, K. (2006). Mechanisms of CB_1 receptor signaling: Endocannabinoid modulation of synaptic strength. *International Journal of Obesity (London), 30,* S19–S23.

Mackie, K. (2008). Cannabinoid receptors: Where they are and what they do. *Journal of Neuroendocrinology, 20,* 10–14.

Marsicano, G., & Kuner, R. (2008). Anatomical distribution of receptors, ligands and enzymes in the brain and in the spinal cord: circuitries and neurochemistry. In A. Köfalvi (ed.) *Cannabinoids and the brain* (pp. 161–201). Boston, MA, USA: Springer.

Martin, B. R. et al. (2004). Mechanism of action of cannabinoids: how it may lead to treatment of cachexia, emesis, and pain. *Journal of Supportive Oncology, 2*(4):305–314; discussion 314–316.

McCallum, R. W., Soykan, I., Sridhar, K. R., et al. (1999). Delta-9-tetrahydrocannabinol delays the gastric emptying of solid food in humans: A double-blind, randomized study. *Alimentary Pharmacology and Therapeutics, 13,* 77–80.

Meier, M. H., et al. (2012). Persistent cannabis users show neuropsychological decline from childhood to midlife. *PNAS 109*(40), E2657, July 30, 2012.

Molina, P. E., Amedee, A., LeCapitaine, N. J., Zabaleta, J., Mohan, M., Winsauer, P., et al. (2011). Cannabinoid neuroimmune modulation of SIV disease. *Journal of Neuroimmune Pharmacology: The Official Journal of the Society on NeuroImmune Pharmacology., 6,* 516–527.

Monfort, S. (2018). Effect of recreational marijuana sales on police-reported crashes in Colorado, Oregon, and Washington. *Insurance Institute for Highway Safety*, October 2018.

Morena, M., Patel, S., Bains, J. S., & Hill, M. N. (2015). Neurobiological interactions between stress and the endocannabinoid system. *Neuropsychopharmacology: Official Publication of the American College of Neuropsychopharmacology, 41*(1), 80–102.

Murphy, L. L., Adrian, B. A., & Kohli, M. (1999). Inhibition of luteinizing hormone secretion by delta9-tetrahydrocannabinol in the ovariectomized rat: Effect of pretreatment with neurotransmitter or neuropeptide receptor antagonists. *Steroids, 64,* 664–671.

Navari, R. M. et al. (2006). Emerging drugs for chemotherapy-induced emesis. *Expert Opinion on Emerging Drugs, 11*(1), 137–151.

Onaivi, E. S. (2006). Neuropsychobiological evidence for the functional presence and expression of cannabinoid CB2 receptors in the brain. *Neuropsychobiology, 54,* 231–246.

Pagotto, U., Marsicano, G., Cota, D., Lutz, B., & Pasquali, R. (2006). The emerging role of the endocannabinoid system in endocrine regulation and energy balance. *Endocrinology Reviews, 27,* 73–100.

Palazuelos, J., Aguado, T., Pazos, M. R., Julien, B., Carrasco, C., Resel, E., et al. (2009). Microglial CB2 cannabinoid receptors are neuroprotective in Huntington's disease excitotoxicity. *Brain, 132,* 3152–3164.

Paschall, M. J., Grube, J. W., & Biglan, A. (2017). Medical marijuana legalization and marijuana use among youth in oregon. *The Journal of Primary Prevention, 38*(3), 329–341.

Patton, G. C., Coffey, C., Carlin, J. B., Degenhardt, L., Lynskey, M. & Hall, W. (2002). Cannabis use and mental health in young people: Cohort study. *British Medical Journal, 325*(7374), 1195–1198.

Pertwee, R. G. (2001). Cannabinoids and the gastrointestinal tract. *Gut, 48,* 859–867.

Ramaekers, J. G., Berghaus, G., van Laar, M., & Drummer, O. H. (2004). Dose related risk of motor vehicle crashes after cannabis use. *Drug and Alcohol Dependence, 73,* 109–119.

Salomonsen-Sautel, S., Min, S., Sakai, J. T., Thurstone, C., & Hopfer, C. (2014). Trends in fatal motor vehicle crashes before and after marijuana commercialization in Colorado. *Drug and Alcohol Dependence, 140,* 137–144.

Santaella-Tenorio, J., Mauro, C. M., Wall, M. M., Kim, J. H., Cerdá, M., Keyes, K. M., et al. (2017). US traffic fatalities, 1985–2014, and their relationship to medical marijuana laws. *American Journal of Public Health, 107*(2), 336–342.

Schuel, H., & Burkman, L. J. (2005). A tale of two cells: Endocannabinoid-signaling regulates functions of neurons and sperm. *Biology of Reproduction, 73,* 1078–1086.

Szutorisz, H., & Hurd, Y. L. (2015). Epigenetic effects of cannabis exposure. *Biological Psychiatry, 79*(7), 586–594.

Szyf, M. (2013). The genome- and system-wide response of DNA methylation to early life adversity and its implication on mental health. *Canadian Journal of Psychiatry, 58,* 697–704.

Szyf, M. (2015). Nongenetic inheritance and transgenerational epigenetics. *Trends in Molecular Medicine, 21,* 134–144.

Tomasiewicz, H. C., Jacobs, M. M., Wilkinson, M. B., Wilson, S. P., Nestler, E. J., & Hurd, Y. L. (2012). Proenkephalin mediates the enduring effects of adolescent cannabis exposure associated with adult opiate vulnerability. *Biological Psychiatry, 72,* 803–810.

Van Sickle, M. D., Duncan, M., Kingsley, P. J., Mouihate, A., Urbani, P., Mackie, K., et al. (2005). Identification and functional characterization of brainstem cannabinoid CB2 receptors. *Science, 310,* 329–332.

Volkow, N. D., Baler, R. D., Compton, W. M., & Weiss, S. R. B. (2014). Adverse health effects of marijuana use. *New England Journal of Medicine, 370*(23), 2219–2227.

Wang, G. S., et al. (2018). Impact of marijuana legalization in colorado on adolescent emergency and urgent care visits. *Journal of Adolescent Health, 63*(2), 239–241. https://doi.org/10.1016/j.jadohealth.2017.12.010. Epub 2018 Mar 30.

Wang, G. S., Roosevelt, G., Le Lait, M. C., Martinez, E. M., Bucher-Bartelson, B., Bronstein, A. C. et al. (2014). Association of unintentional pediatric exposures with decriminalization of marijuana in the United Sates. *Annals of Emergency Medicine*. Retrieved September 6, 2014 from http://www.annemergmed.com/article/S0196-0644(14)00079-1/abstract.

Walter, L., Franklin, A., Witting, A., Wade, C., Xie, Y., Kunos, G., et al. (2003). Nonpsychotropic cannabinoid receptors regulate microglial cell migration. *Journal of Neuroscience, 23,* 1398–1405.

Wilkinson, S. T. et al. (2014). Problems with the medicalization of marijuana. *JAMA, 311*(23), 2377–2378. https://doi.org/10.1001/jama.2014.6175.

Yang, X., Hegde, V. L., Rao, R., Zhang, J., Nagarkatti, P. S., & Nagarkatti, M. (2014). Histone modifications are associated with Delta9-tetrahydrocannabinol-mediated alterations in antigen-specific T cell responses. *The Journal of Biological Chemistry, 289,* 18707–18718.

Yücel, M., Lorenzetti, V., Suo, C., Zalesky, A., Fornito, A., Takagi, M. J., et al. (2016). Hippocampal harms, protection and recovery following regular cannabis use. *Translational Psychiatry, 6*(1), e710. https://doi.org/10.1038/tp.2015.201.

Zhu, H., & Wu, L. T. (2016). Trends and correlates of cannabis-involved emergency department visits: 2004 to 2011. *Journal of addiction Medicine, 10*(6), 429–436.

Zou, S., & Kumar, U. (2018). Cannabinoid receptors and the endocannabinoid system: Signaling and function in the central nervous system. *International Journal of Molecular Sciences, 19*(3), 833. https://doi.org/10.3390/ijms19030833.

Chapter 6
Mental Health and the Brain

This chapter explores the connection between mental health disorders and trauma and substance use as their respective impacts on/in the developing brain are similar. Equally, to achieve optimal healing for youth (and really anyone with a history of trauma), an integrated understanding and approach that considers trauma, substance use, and mental health must be employed. Earlier chapters addressed the Adverse Childhood Experiences study which demonstrated that early and prolonged exposure to toxic stress and trauma increases the risk for development of chronic physical and mental health conditions. Complete, genuine healing is difficult to achieve in the absence of addressing trauma. A focus on mental wellness for youth is critical and the possibility for healing is optimized when mental wellness is considered, honored.

This chapter will address the most common classes of mental health challenges and their respective impact on the brain to include

- Depression and the brain,
- Psychosis and the brain,
- ADHD and the brain, and
- Anxiety and the brain.

By the end of this chapter you should be able to

- Understand the following mental health conditions and their impact on the brain:
  - Depression,
  - Psychosis,
  - ADHD, and
  - Anxiety.
- Recognize and reconcile the potential mental health threats (and concomitant brain disruption) in youth/adolescence.

Quick review: The Developing brain, making the connections is important
Inside the Brain: Neurons and Neural Circuits

- Neurons are the cells (building blocks) of brain and nervous system. These cells are highly specialized to conduct messages.

A. Moreland-Capuia, *Training for Change*,
https://doi.org/10.1007/978-3-030-19208-2_6

A neuron has three basic parts (see Fig. 6.1):

- *Cell body* which includes the nucleus, cytoplasm, and cell organelles. The nucleus contains DNA and information that the cell needs for growth, metabolism, and repair. Cytoplasm is the substance that fills a cell, including all the chemicals and parts needed for the cell to work properly including small structures called cell organelles.
- Dendrites branch off from the cell body and act as a neuron's point of contact for receiving chemical and electrical signals called impulses from neighboring neurons.
- *Axon* which sends impulses and extends from cell bodies to meet and deliver impulses to another nerve cell. Axons can range in length from a fraction of an inch to several feet.

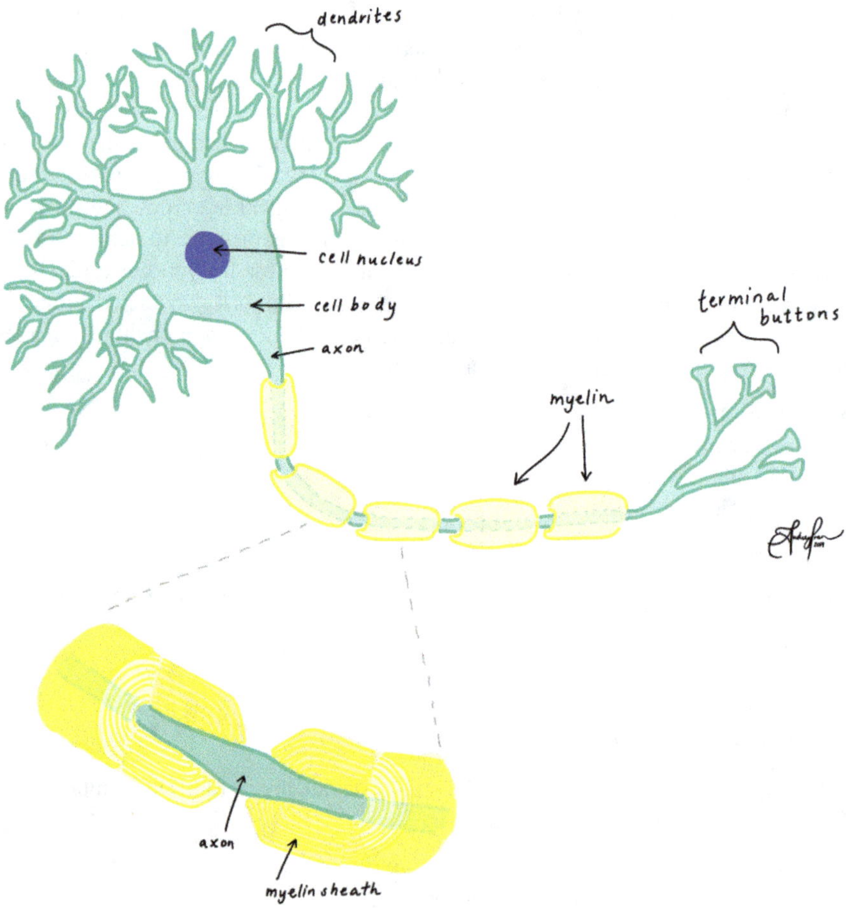

Fig. 6.1 The neuron (also known as cells of the brain). Printed with permission. Copyright Audrey A. Tran

Neurons are the building blocks of the brain. Chapter 1 was dedicated to demonstrating how the brain develops through the development of a neuron. The brain develops from the bottom-up and the inside-out. Neurons start out undifferentiated and immature, when they reach their final destination (i.e., the neurons in the hippocampus versus neurons in the amygdala), they mature through the process of axon elongation and eventually myelination. Disruption of neuronal development results in disruption in brain development. It is also understood that disruption in neuron development (epigenetic impacts, poor nutrition, and early exposure to trauma and substance use, poverty, etc.) increases the risk of the development of mental health conditions.

Quick review on the connection between fear, trauma, and substance use

- It is important to understand that fear is a natural response, protective even, until it's not.
- Every human being has experienced fear, anxiety, and stress at some point in their lives, but not everyone has experienced fear that never shuts off.
- Fear "on" all the time = fear conditioning = trauma.

Aspects of the brain involved in the fear response:

- Thalamus, the giant switchboard, directs information to other parts of the brain (represents the sensory aspect of fear).
- Hippocampus sensory cortex and amygdala give context to the situational and emotional aspects of fear (memory emotion aspect of fear).
- Frontal and temporal lobes, and higher cortical areas where the experience of dread happens. Dopamine is released and can cause panicked and irrational behavior (cognitive aspect of fear).
- Hypothalamus, fight-or-flight or freeze response is activated (physiologic aspect of fear).

Aspects of the brain involved in the fear conditioning response:

- Medial Prefrontal Cortex (MPFC), involved in decision-making and retrieval of remote long-term memory.
- Amygdala, responsible for processing of memory, decision-making, and emotional reactions, modulates memory consolidation (which happens over time), and has a role in aggression; amygdala activity at the time of encoding information correlates to the retention for that information.
- Anterior Cingulate Cortex (ACC) is responsible for autonomic function (i.e., blood pressure and heart rate), early learning, problem-solving, rational cognitive functions, reward anticipation, decision-making, empathy, impulse control, and emotion.

Aspects of the brain involved in the reward pathway involved in substance use processes:

- Prefrontal cortex (top brain responsible for exercising good judgement, emotion regulation, etc.).
- Nucleus accumbens (active in reward pathway).
- Striatum = caudate, putamen, and ventral striatum. Ventral striatum includes the nucleus accumbens.
- Ventral tegmental area (works with the nucleus accumbens to create feeling of pleasure).
- Amygdala, which imparts agreeable or disagreeable affective colorations to perceptions.
- Hippocampus facilitates memory of the pleasurable experience.
- Insula gets sensory input from the thalamus and sends signals to several structures found in the limbic system (amygdala and ventral striatum) and the orbitofrontal cortex. The insula is also part of the limbic system theorized to be essential in active pleasure seeking associated with substances and food.
- Substantia nigra, midbrain structure involved in reward and movement.
- Locus coeruleus (found on the pons of the brain stem) produces norepinephrine (NE) and is involved in the drive to seek pleasure again and again. *Also, involved in responses related to fear and anxiety*.
- Raphe nucleus (cluster of nuclei) in the brain stem produces serotonin (5HT) and sends to various parts of the brain.

Quick review summary: fear, trauma, and substance use impact the brain in similar ways. Now let's explore the impact of specific conditions that pose a threat to mental wellness and the respective impact on the brain. Might we appreciate a pattern?

Depression

Depression is often characterized by low mood, irritability, and difficulty finding joy. Depression is commonly diagnosed and can lead to significant impairment in function if not treated and/or managed. In youth, notable changes in behavior and/or attitudes should be explored.

According to the 2016 National Survey on Drug Use and Health, an estimated 2.2 million adolescents aged 12–17 in the United States had at least one major depressive episode with severe impairment, representing 9.0% of the U.S. population aged 12–17. Of note, the prevalence of major depressive episode was highest among adolescents reporting two or more races (13.8%). Of adolescents with major depressive episode, approximately 70% had severe impairment (Center for Behavioral Health Statistics and Quality 2017).

Types of Depression

Major depression

- Significant symptoms that interfere with work, sleep, appetite, and ability to enjoy life.

- Can occur once or several times in person's lifetime (distinction between a single episode and persistent).

Persistent depressive disorder

- Depressed mood > or equal to 2 years.
- Oscillates between notable depression and less severe depression (once known as dysthymia).

Psychotic depression

- Defined by depression with delusions (fixed false beliefs), hearing and/or seeing things (or any other type of perceptual disturbance).

Postpartum depression

- More serious than the "baby blues" that many women experience after giving birth, when hormonal and physical changes and the new responsibility of caring for a newborn can be overwhelming.
- It is estimated that 10–15% of women experience postpartum depression after giving birth (National Institute of Mental Health 2017).

Seasonal Affective Disorder (SAD)

- Prominent during winter months (less light is the trigger).
- Typically improves with spring.
- 50% get better with light therapy, the other 50% require light therapy and an antidepressant + psychotherapy (National Institute of Mental Health 2017).

Bipolar Disorder

- Characterized by "mania".
- Extreme low moods (depression).

Theories of neurotransmitters involved in depression

While serotonin (which regulates mood, appetite, and sleep and has some role in memory and learning) is the most commonly discussed neurotransmitter involved in depression, recent studies have highlighted the fact that there are other key players that must be considered.

Acetylcholine (implicated in learning and memory), dopamine (implicated in reward, psychosis), glutamate (implicated in memory, modulation of dopamine), GABA 9 (implicated in substance use, anxiety), and norepinephrine (involved in stress response, etc.) are all theorized to play a role in depression (Duman et al. 1997).

Acetylcholine and Depression

- A high-level study investigated acetylcholine (Ach) signaling in the hippocampus and its role in promoting behaviors related to anxiety and depression behaviors in mice. The following was also noted (Mineur et al. 2013).

- Changes in Ach levels in the hippocampus can lead to symptoms of depression in humans.
- Human imaging study has suggested that acetylcholine (ACh) levels are elevated in patients who are actively depressed, as measured by occupancy of nicotinic receptors throughout the brain, and remain high in patients who have a history of depression (Saricicek et al. 2012).
- Hindering cholinergic (both muscarinic and nicotinic) receptors can prompt antidepressant-like responses (Furey and Drevets 2006).
- While the mechanism is not well understood, it was observed that hyperactivity of brain cholinergic (Ach) systems can contribute to depression (Minuer et al. 2013).

Dopamine and Depression
One of the main criteria for major depression according to the DSM-5 is a phenomenon called anhedonia and/or limited pleasure in things that used to bring pleasure. According to a review article by Belujon et al., it is theorized that anhedonia is an expression of disrupted dopamine concentration and linked to disruption of the reward pathway of the brain (Der-Avakian and Markou 2012). More specifically, anhedonia is theorized to involve disruption of the anticipation, motivation, and decision-making processes involved in obtaining a reward (Treadway and Zald 2011). According to Belujon et al., anhedonia is intimately associated with a downregulation of the DA system (Belujon and Grace 2017). According to an article by Spear on neurobehavioral changes in adolescence, the dopamine system maturation is closely associated with adolescence. The adolescent period is marked by a surge in dopaminergic input to the prefrontal cortex and an increase in the density of dopaminergic fibers and transporters (Spear 2000a).

γ-aminobutyric acid (GABA) and Depression
A review article by Luscher et al. outline studies that suggest an association between Major Depressive Disorders (MDDs) and GABA insufficiencies is evidenced by

- Reduced brain concentrations of GABA and changes in the structure of GABA subunits in depressed patients.
- GABA playing a role in the brains modulation of stress.
- GABA playing a role in the development and maturation of hippocampal neurons.
- GABA deficits produced in mice models have behavioral, cognitive, and neuroanatomical manifestations (Luscher et al. 2010).

Glutamate and Depression
Glutamates exact role in depression is not well understood; however, it is known that glutamate is widely distributed in the brain.

Mathews et al. reviewed data supporting the involvement of the glutamate in depression and discussed the usefulness of glutamatergic agents as novel therapeutics. The article explores agents like Ketamine, *N*-methyl-D-aspartate (NMDA) antagonist in the treatment of depression. Ketamine does impact glutamate concentration and has been demonstrated to modulate mood. The article implicates glutamate in depression. There is still more to be understood, but it does appear to play a role (Mathews et al. 2012).

Norepinephrine and Depression
According to Moret et al., norepinephrine plays a determinant role in executive functioning regulating cognition, motivation, and intellect, which are fundamental in social relationships. Social dysfunction is possibly one of the most important factors affecting the quality of life in depressed patients (Moret and Briley 2011).

Epigenetics and depression
In an article by Lolak et al., it was pointed out that environmental changes in genes (transporters, neurotransmitters, etc.) could possibly both increase predisposition to and predict treatment outcomes for depression (Lolak et al. 2014).

According to a review article by Lohoff et al., there is documented evidence for a genetic component to mood disorders demonstrated in family, twin, and adoption studies. Twin studies suggest a heritability of 40–50%, and family studies indicate a twofold to threefold increase in lifetime risk of developing MDD among first-degree relatives (Lohoff 2010).

- There have been some inconsistent findings and no established genetic risk factor identified for depression yet linkage studies in MDD have revealed several regions in the genome that might harbor risk alleles (Lohoff 2010). Additionally, many candidate genes show promising preliminary results and are worth considering in the case of depression (Lohoff 2010).
- Various studies implicate the serotonin transporter gene (*SLC6A4*) in MDD (Caspi et al. 2010; Goldman et al. 2010; Uher and McGuffin 2010).
- Case-control association studies of the serotonin receptor gene *HTR2A* and major depression have yielded similar mixed results as for the serotonin transporter gene (Anguelova et al. 2003).
- *5-HTTLPR*, changes in this gene that codes for the serotonin transporter, has been implicated in depression.
- Brain-Derived Neurotrophic Factor (BDNF) helps with nerve growth, and may play an important role in affective disorder (Castren and Rantamaki 2010; Post 2007).
- New studies reveal that there might be a connection between tryptophan hydroxylase (rate-limiting enzyme in brain serotonin synthesis), serotonin, and depression (Walther and Bader 2003).

Depression and pregnancy
Depression affects about 20% of women during their lifetime, with pregnancy being a period of high vulnerability. Prevalence of depression during pregnancy ranges from 4 to 20% (Ajinkya et al. 2013). There have been myriad studies demonstrating the impact of stress, trauma, and mood states like depression on children after they are born. However, many have been concerned with the impact that stress and mood states like depression can have on the developing brain prenatally and in utero. A review by Kinsella et al. outlines the research aimed at identifying the in utero

effects of prenatal psychological stress in pregnant women. The review suggests that prenatal psychological distress has implications on fetal behavior, brain and child development. The review concludes that pregnant women's psychological health may have consequences for fetal neurobehavioral development, and consequently child outcomes (Kinsella and Monk 2009).

Impact of depression on the brain

The brain develops from the bottom-up and the inside-out. The prefrontal cortex is the last part of the brain to fully develop—it is responsible for planning, organizing, thinking, exercising good judgment, and emotion regulation. Adolescence marks a period of significant neuron volume changes through pruning and changes in connections between neurons. Brain development in the adolescent phase is sensitive to threats like depression and other mood states. As depression and other mood states are a form of trauma that can arrest, disrupt, and negatively impact normal brain development. A review article by **Weir et al.** (2012) reveals the following about depression and the impact on the developing brain:

- Risk for depression peaks during the transition from childhood to adolescence (Kessler et al. 2001).
- Neural change and maturation is at its peak during adolescence (Gogtay et al. 2004; Paus 2010).
- Normal developmental transitions in adolescence mark a sensitive period that by their very nature increase the risk for the activation of specific processes involved in the onset, persistence, and recurrence of depressive episodes (Andersen and Teicher 2008; Davey et al. 2008; Rudolph et al. 2006).
- Neurotransmitters are changing at a rapid rate during the transition from childhood to adolescence. Developmental studies have shown that neurotransmitter systems typically model a pattern of overproduction and pruning, such that changes in expression typically peak during late childhood/early adolescence and are then reduced to reach adult levels. According to several developmental studies, this outline of overproduction and reverting purging is believed to procure efficiency of the brain and also represents a state of vulnerability to environmental influences (Spear 2000b; Paus et al. 2008; Andersen 2003; Maughan et al. 2013).
- Both animal and human studies have focused on the hippocampus and its likely role in depression. The hippocampus has been noted to be highly sensitive to stress, namely, during development (MacQueen and Frodl 2011; Sapolsky 2003; Spinelli et al. 2009; McEwen 1999).
- Reduction in the hippocampal volume has been associated with depression in both the pediatric and adult populations (MacQueen and Frodl 2011; McKinnon et al. 2009).
- Inconstant changes in the amygdala have been associated with depression and outlined in various human adult studies (Hamilton et al. 2008; McEwen 2011).
- Changes in prefrontal cortical volume have been appreciated in adult with depression, according to various human studies. Volume reductions in the areas of the brain to include the anterior cingulate, orbitofrontal cortex, and the sub-genual region of the prefrontal cortex (Koolschijn et al. 2009; Lorenzetti et al. 2009).

- Striatal gray matter changes have been noted in depressed adults, namely, in the caudate nucleus. Several studies in depressed adults reported gray matter deficits in the striatum, especially in the caudate nucleus (Koolschijn et al. 2009; Kim et al. 2008).

Depression and other mood states have epigenetic impact (can change the functionality of specific genes that code for transporters in the brain, i.e., serotonin); in utero impact (impact neuron architecture, structure, growth, maturation, and function); and can change an individuals' cognition capacity and aspects of executive function over time (Fig. 6.2).

Psychosis
Psychosis is a general term used to characterize conditions that impact the mind typically described by loss of contact with reality. Symptoms of psychosis may include thought and perceptual disturbance, difficulty distinguishing between what is real versus what is not real; fixed false beliefs (delusions); hallucinations (auditory, visual, tactile, and/or olfactory); disorganized, non-sensical, and/or paucity of speech; thought blocking (sudden pause in speech mid-sentence); and signs of depression and anxiety may also be present as evidenced by disturbances in sleep, lack of

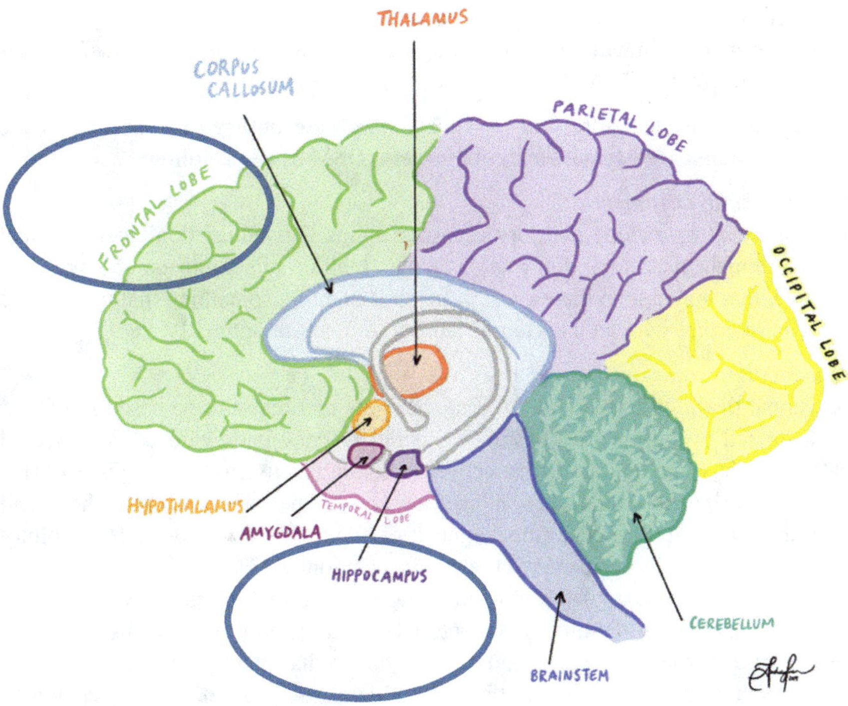

Fig. 6.2 Depression and the brain (**main areas impacted are circled**). Printed with permission. Copyright Audrey A. Tran

motivation, and reduction in ability to function. Schizophrenia is one of the most studied conditions defined by psychosis. According to a 2017 Lancet systematic review on the global burden of disease, schizophrenia is among the top 20 leading causes of disability, globally. While Schizophrenia's prevalence (the proportion of a population who have a specific characteristic in a given time period) is low, its structural impact is great (with profound impact on social, economic, and health conditions) (Global, regional, and national incidence, Lancet 2017).

Signs of psychosis

- Difficulties with communicating and changes in speech patterns.
- Changes in hygiene and/or self-care.
- Decline in grades and/or functionality in job performance.
- Notable changes in ability to concentrate and/or thinking.
- Emergence of new ideas that seem more paranoid, behavior that seems more suspicious.
- Changes in social interactions with others—markedly less interaction and/or more anxiety associated with interacting with others.
- Increase and/or emergence of isolative behaviors, spending more time alone, withdrawing from others that they would normally spend time with.
- Withdrawing socially, spending a lot more time alone than usual.
- Difficulty in distinguishing what is real and what is not real.
- Notable changes in feelings: Not feeling emotions versus feeling intensely versus feeling "different" (NIMH).

Primary and prevalent forms of psychosis which are outlined by the Diagnostic Statistical Manual of Mental Health Disorders (DSM 5) are as follows:

Brief Psychotic Disorder
Hallucinations to include auditory (hearing things that others don't hear), visual (seeing things that others don't see), tactile (feeling something on the skin, for example, that may not be there), and olfactory (smelling something that may not be real) can interfere with an individual's ability to function optimally.

Delusional disorder
Delusional disorder consists of fixed core beliefs that may not be based in reality, characterized by inflexibility to adjust a belief when sound evidence is presented that contradicts that belief. Just as beliefs are many, delusions, too, are many. This condition can be crippling. Delusions are a key clinical manifestation of psychosis and have particular significance for the diagnosis of schizophrenia (Kiran and Chaudhury 2009; Kapur 2003; American Psychiatric Association 2013).

Schizophrenia is one of the most debilitating conditions, especially in the case of early onset. Schizophrenia is characterized as a primary thought disorder with perceptual disturbances (seeing and hearing things that other people don't hear or see, tactile hallucinations, and/or olfactory hallucinations—smelling things that may not be real). There are multiple studies that suggest early assessment and treatment of psychosis can help heal the brain and result in better functional outcomes for young people (Compton et al. 2008).

Schizoaffective disorder

Schizoaffective disorder might be understood as a disorder that includes perceptual disturbances as seen in schizophrenia in addition to a changing mood component.

Several studies like Frazier et al. outline challenges in distinguishing between schizoaffective disorder and schizophrenia. Specifically, the study demonstrates that distinguishing between schizoaffective disorders in early-onset schizophrenia may prove difficult as the psychotic syndrome continues to evolve as the development of the youth progresses (Frazier et al. 2007).

These are some of the main forms of psychosis, it should be mentioned that DSM-V outlines various permutations and combinations of psychosis to include but not limited to substance-induced psychosis, and psychosis-related medical conditions, psychotic expression of bipolar disorder, major depression, postpartum, and PTSD. Knowing the DSM-V and making a diagnosis are not required; however, it is important to be familiar with common conditions that may impact youth to appropriately triage and refer for services.

Theories of neurotransmitters involved in psychosis

There is a very clear, consistent, and close relationship between dopamine and psychosis. Dopamine has a role in movement, aggression, motivation, pleasure, and cognition. A review article by Tost et al. beautifully summarizes studies confirming dopamine as the neurobiological basis for and main culprit in psychosis (of all forms as described above). In Tost et al. article, psychosis is described as a neurodevelopmental disease model. Early hypothesis by researchers like Weinberger suggested that psychosis arises from a prenatal disturbance of prefrontal–subcortical network formation (Weinberger 1987). Weinberger theorized a dysfunction in the prefrontal cortex (PFC) mediated in part by dopamine D_1 receptors is at the core of treatment-resistant cognitive deficits and negative symptoms. Laruelle and Abi Dargham described formation of hallucinations and delusions (forms of psychotic expression) in the following way: "Due to the deficient top-down control of phylogenetically older brain areas the subcortical D_2 receptor function is thought to become disinhibited, thereby raising 'the wind of the psychotic fire'" (Laruelle and Abi-Dargham 1999).

Dopamine D_1 receptors are found throughout the human brain with high levels of expression in the amygdala, putamen, caudate, hippocampus, and prefrontal cortex. D_2 receptors are ubiquitously present in the cortex and impact on a wide range of brain functional systems (Tost et al. 2009).

Again, while dopamine has been proven over and over again to be the main player in psychosis, there has been emerging studies implicating glutamate, GABA, and the hypofunction of the ionotropic glutamate N-methyl-D-Aspartate (NMDA) receptor as well. Seaman's et al. point out that dopaminergic and glutamatergic projections converge and interact on multiple levels of the brain. On the one hand, dopamine optimizes the signal-to-noise characteristics or "fine tuning" of neural networks in the prefrontal cortex and hippocampus by modulating the excitability of glutamate and γ-aminobutyric acid (GABA) neurons (Seamans et al. 1998). This phenomenon has been mostly appreciated in the context of increased use of the psychosis producing capacity of phencyclidine (PCP) and ketamine, which are non-competitive NMDA receptor antagonists.

Epigenetics and psychosis
Mill J, et. al. included samples of subjects who held a diagnosis of schizophrenia and bipolar disorder (two forms of psychosis) and was the first epigenome-wide study characterizing DNA methylation in major psychosis. In the study, 12,000 GC-rich regions were surveyed, including CpG islands, in the prefrontal cortex of the brain (Mill et al. 2008).

Specifically, Mills J, et al. study revealed hypomethylation of two glutamate receptor-related genes (*WDR18* and *GRIA2*) and of two genes related to GABA signaling (*MARLIN-1* encoding an RNA-binding protein involved in $GABA_B$-receptor production and *KCNJ6* encoding a G protein-coupled potassium channel (Mill et al. 2008; Ruzicka 2015).

Mill J, et al. study recognized various DNA sites with methylation alterations. Some changes were sex specific. When loci of the affected group (study group) were compared to that of controls—significant epigenetic differences were noted in genes involved in brain development and neurotransmitter pathways, previously associated with major psychosis (Mill et al. 2008; Labrie et al. 2012).

In the case of psychosis, the HLA complex group 9 gene (*HCG9*), which maps to chromosome 6p21.33 has exhibited an association with psychosis in genome-wide associated studies (Purcell et al. 2009).

DNA methylation patterns in *HCG9* were separately analyzed and identified in approximately 1400 DNA samples from major psychosis patients and controls (Kaminsky et al. 2011).

Patients with a history of bipolar disorder displayed a lower degree of *HCG9* methylation in several tissues, including the postmortem prefrontal cortex and sperm cells from living individuals (Kaminsky et al. 2011). An inheritance and/or acquired pattern is theorized: the DNA methylation change in *HCG9* across many tissues suggests the occurrence of an epimutation that is inherited or acquired before tissue differentiation in embryogenesis (Mill et al. 2008).

Psychosis and Pregnancy
Psychosis and depression are considered a form of prenatal stress in pregnant mothers. Brain development starts from the point of conception, the early stages of development from neurons growing, and traveling to the right spot and making the right connections all happens during the prenatal phase (Markham and Koenig 2010). This process, neuronal development as the foundation of brain development, is tenuous and is subject to myriad environmental threats. Pre- and perinatal (obstetric complications) trauma are known risk factors for the development of schizophrenia- and psychotic-related disorders (Fusar-Poli et al. 2017; Redman et al. 2017). These threats can change the trajectory of gene expression, brain function, behavior, and risks for development of specific behavioral health disorders.

Markham and colleagues outlined the following:

- Maternal infection during pregnancy has been consistently associated with an increased risk of schizophrenia in the offspring (Brown and Susser 2002; Markham and Koenig 2010).
- Immunological abnormalities, including, most notably, cytokine imbalances have also been characterized for individuals with schizophrenia themselves (Muller et al. 2009).
- Animal models have demonstrated that the heightened immunological/inflammatory process during pregnancy increased inflammatory factors in the fetal environment and brain, mostly (Ashdown et al. 2006; Gayle et al. 2004; Liverman et al. 2006; Urakubo et al. 2001).
- One of many conclusions drawn from Markham and colleagues article is that experimental evidence supports the notion that pathological changes in adult behaviors related to psychosis, cognition, and schizophrenia may arise as a result of stressful perturbations during the prenatal period (Markham and Koenig 2010).

Impact of Psychosis on the brain
A study comparing psychotic and non-psychotic expression in bipolar II patients versus controls highlighted structural brain changes through MRI (Carlo Altamura et al. 2018):

- Extensive gray matter volume decreases were appreciated in psychotic patients via MRI. Specific gray matter volume decreases were appreciated in the following brain areas:

  - Frontal cortex—part of the brain responsible for executive functions like planning, organizing, exercising good judgment, and emotion regulation.
  - Posterior cingulate cortex—highly connected and metabolically active brain region theorized to play an important role in cognition (Leech and Sharp 2013).
  - Postcentral and angular gyri in the left hemisphere—several studies suggest that the angular gyrus is involved in semantic processing, word reading and comprehension, number processing, default mode network, memory retrieval, attention and spatial cognition, reasoning, and social cognition (Seghier 2013).
  - Superior temporal cortex in the right hemisphere—has a role in processing auditory stimuli and language. Might also play a role in social cognition.

- Bipolar patients with psychotic and non-psychotic features had higher gray matter volume changes in the putamen compared to controls. The putamen is mostly responsible for movement. Gray matter traverses areas in the brain responsible emotion regulation and control (prefrontal cortex), emotions (amygdala), memory (hippocampus), and many other areas. Gray matter volume loss and/or damage can profoundly impact these functions. By way of reminder, gray matter is made up of mostly nerve cell bodies and branching dendrites, when gray matter (nerve cell bodies) is damaged, it is difficult for a neuron to survive.
- Age-related changes were noted in the context of gray matter shortages.
- More severe age effects were noted on gray matter volume in bipolar patients with psychotic expression compared to bipolar without psychotic expression and controls.

- Bipolar with psychotic expression showed stronger age-related gray matter volume changes in the thalamus (gray matter structure that has a role in sensory process and pain perception), putamen (responsible for movement), and amygdala (plays a role in aggression, emotion, drives, and memory) of the right hemisphere when compared to non-psychotic and control.
- Bipolar with psychotic expression also demonstrated significant age impacts in the inferior orbitofrontal cortex, inferior temporal cortex, supramarginal gyrus (somatosensory association cortex and the right hemisphere supramarginal gyrus are theorized to play a role in empathy) and calcarine cortex (visual cortex) of the left hemisphere, and in amygdala, precuneus (responsible for visuospatial imagery, episodic memory retrieval, and self-processing operations), mid-temporal cortex (hearing and auditory perception), and insula of the right hemisphere (pain perception, emotions, and empathy) (Carlo Altamura et al. 2018).

Numerous studies explain how untreated psychosis can cause cognitive problems and changes in the brain:

- In an early critical review assessing the correlation between the long-term impact of untreated psychosis and brain toxicity, it was revealed that some studies demonstrated the toxic impact of psychosis on the brain when not treated and some studies did not (Goldberg et al. 2009; Rund 2013; Wyatt 1991). More recent studies have more consistently demonstrated that untreated psychosis was shown to be biologically toxic to the brain, motivating the need for early and appropriate intervention (McGorry et al. 2008; Kane et al. 2015; Marshall and Rathbone 2011).
- Inability to regulate presynaptic dopamine release into the limbic system associated with structural neuronal changes and changes response to treatment for psychosis (Sheitman and Lieberman 1998).
- Psychosis is associated with increased release of stress-related hormones. When neurons are exposed to more stress hormones, they are more prone to damage (Wood et al. 2009).

Liddle and colleagues employed Positron Emission Tomography (PET) scans to assess changes in blood flow patterns in the brains of persons identified as having schizophrenia. The study employed the Stroop test, which is commonly used psychological assessment tool that measures a person's selective attention capacity and skills, as well as their processing speed ability. The study focused on cerebral blood patterns in three syndromes of schizophrenia and compared them to healthy controls:

- Psychomotor poverty syndrome characterized by limited ability to generate words was associated with decreased perfusion of the dorsolateral prefrontal cortex in persons who identified as having schizophrenia compared to control. Dorsolateral prefrontal cortex was activated normally in control subjects when they were generating words (Liddle et al. 1992).
- Disorganization syndrome characterized impaired suppression of inappropriate responses in the Stroop test, and was associated with increased perfusion of the right anterior cingulate gyrus in control subjects performing the Stroop test (Liddle et al. 1992).

- Reality distortion syndrome characterized by disordered internal monitoring activity was associated with increased perfusion in the medial temporal lobe at a locus activated in normal subjects during the internal monitoring of eye movements.

Karlsgodt and colleagues reviewed established and emerging literature on the impact of Schizophrenia on the brain structure and function. The article highlighted the following:

- In the case of Schizophrenia, structural and functional changes have been appreciated in several key brain structures, including prefrontal (working memory) and medial temporal lobe (declarative memory) regions as captured by functional neuroimaging techniques during critical points of brain development (Karlsgodt et al. 2010).
- Schizophrenia is now understood and characterized as a disorder of disrupted neural connectivity. Further disrupted neural connectivity is influenced by genetic and environmental risk factors that mediate brain development in the prenatal and adolescent period (Karlsgodt et al. 2010) (Fig. 6.3).

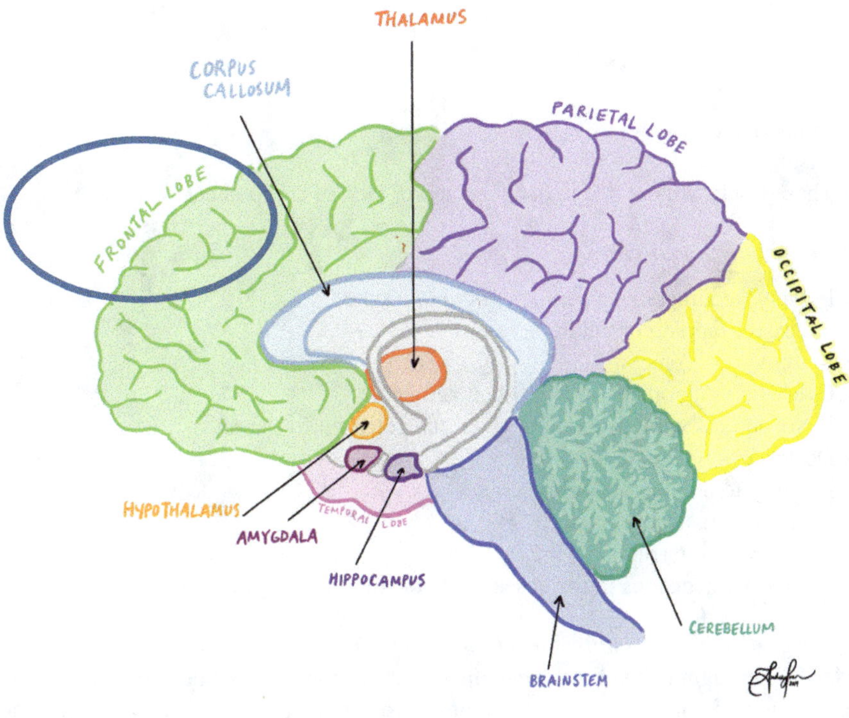

Fig. 6.3 Psychosis and the brain **(main area(s) impacted are circled)**. Printed with permission. Copyright Audrey A. Tran

Attention Deficit-Hyperactivity Disorder (ADHD)
According to the Centers for Disease Control Prevention Study, in 2016, an estimated 6.1 million U.S. children 2–17 years of age (9.4%) had ever received an ADHD diagnosis. Of these, 5.4 million currently had ADHD, which was 89.4% of children ever diagnosed with ADHD and 8.4% of all U.S. children 2–17 years of age (Prevalence of Parent-Report ADHD Diagnosis and Treatment 2016). Blum and colleagues confirm that twin studies indicate that 75–90% of ADHD is caused by genetic factors. If one person in a family is diagnosed with ADHD, there is a 25–35% probability that another family member also has ADHD, compared to a 4–6% probability for someone in the general population. Between 10 and 35% of children with ADHD have a first-degree relative with past or present ADHD. Approximately, one-half of parents who had ADHD have a child with the disorder. Non-genetic factors may increase risk as well to include but not limited to prenatal exposure to nicotine by mothers who smoked, anoxia in the neonatal period of infancy, and childhood exposure to high quantities of lead (Blum et al. 2008).

Attention Deficit-Hyperactivity Disorder (ADHD) is a neurodevelopmental brain disorder marked by an ongoing pattern of inattention and/or hyperactivity–impulsivity that gets in the way of functioning and/or development. The types of ADHD include predominantly inattentive, predominantly hyperactive/impulsive, and/or combined type (inattentive and hyperactive/impulsive).

Inattentive

- Easily gets off task.
- Lacks persistence.
- Limited ability to focus.
- Disorganized.
- These issues are not due to defiance and/or lack of comprehension.

Hyperactivity/Impulsivity

- Fidgety (in situations where it's not appropriate).
- Excessive tapping or talking.
- Extreme restlessness.
- Overwhelming others with constant activity.
- Hasty actions without thinking about the potential for harm.
- Desire for immediate reward.
- Inability to delay gratification.
- Socially intrusive.
- Excessively interrupts others.
- Makes key decisions in the absence of considering long-term consequences.

Theories of neurotransmitters involved in ADHD
ADHD is thought to involve three main neurotransmitters to include norepinephrine, serotonin, and dopamine. Several studies have alluded to deficits in norepinephrine and serotonin (with notable changes in transporter genes, respectively) as being more closely involved in the inattentive predominant type of ADHD (Blum et al. 2008).

The impulsive/inattentive predominant expression of ADHD is theorized to involve changes in the dopamine transporter gene (affecting dopamine levels in the brain) and pathways. More specifically, Blum and his colleagues highlight powerful similarities between a general umbrella disorder understood as the reward deficiency syndrome (RDS) and ADHD (Blum et al. 2008). ADHD is a heritable neuropsychiatric condition linked to pathogenesis of brain dopamine (Swanson et al. 2007; Volkow et al. 2007; Shaw et al. 2007).

As described in the review article by Blum et al., RDS emerges from dysfunction in the brain reward path. The reward path is made up of a series of complex interactions among brain neurotransmitters in the reward pathway. A direct link has been made between a defect in the DRD2 dopamine receptor gene and abnormal craving (Blum and Kozlowski 1990).

Abnormalities in the DRD2 dopamine receptor gene explain the neurobiological underpinning of RDS in the following way:

- Persons with DRD2 dopamine gene receptor abnormalities = limited number of dopamine receptors sites in the brain.
- Limited dopamine receptor sites in the brain = limited amount of dopamine in the reward center of the brain.
- Limited amount of dopamine in the reward center of the brain = reduction in the amount of dopamine produced. Dopamine concentrations are significantly reduced.
- The overall result is insufficient dopamine activity in the brain.
- Insufficient dopamine activity in the brain is theorized to inspire individuals to engage in activities that will increase brain dopamine function (i.e., drug use, impulsive behavior, etc.).

The RDS phenomenon described above is shaped by DRD2 dopamine gene abnormalities leading to dopamine insufficiency which drives certain behaviors. Mood is modulated through the interaction of dopamine with serotonin, norepinephrine, and other neurotransmitters (Blum et al. 2008).

Epigenetics of ADHD

According to Comings et al., ADHD is conceptualized as a polygenic disorder shaped by additive effects of genes affecting dopamine, norepinephrine, serotonin, GABA, and other neurotransmitters (Comings et al. 2000). Comings and colleagues highlight the following genes (Comings et al. 2000):

- Specific loci involved are dopamine genes DRD_1, DRD_2, DRD_4, DRD_5, dopamine–beta-hydroxylase, and the dopamine transporter;
- Norepinephrine and epinephrine genes ADRA2A, ADRA2C, PNMT, norepinephrine transporter, MAOA, and catechol-O-methyltransferase (COMT);
- Serotonin genes TDO2, HTR1A, HTR1DA, and serotonin transporter;
- GABA genes GABRB3;
- Androgen receptor and other genes (Comings et al. 2000; Blum et al. 2008);

- At least one genetic aberration in the dopamine D2 receptor has been identified that leads to an alteration in the reward pathways of the brain (Bowirrat and Oscar-Berman 2005).

ADHD's impact on the brain

In the case of ADHD, several brain imaging studies demonstrate that the brain develops in a normal pattern, but development is likely delayed by 3 to 4 years (Berger et al. 2013). The delay is most pronounced in thinking, paying attention, and planning with the cortex shows delayed maturation. There is evidence that the corpus callosum, the white structure matter that communicates between both halves of the brain is compromised in ADHD (Hynd et al. 1991; Luders et al. 2016; Gilliam et al. 2011).

Jacobson and colleagues did one of the first comprehensive examinations of cortical volume in preschool children with ADHD which provided proof that irregular brain structure in ADHD is apparent very early in development. With over 90 medication-naïve preschoolers (ages 4–5) with symptoms of ADHD, Jacobsen et al. used high-resolution anatomical images and cognitive behavior measures to assess the impact of ADHD. Neuroimaging results showed reductions in bilateral frontal, parietal, and temporal gray matter volumes in children with ADHD compared to their peers. The greatest impact was noted in the right frontal and left temporal lobes. The differences highlighted in neuroimaging results and comparisons were confirmed by and consistent with parent reports of preschooler ADHD symptomology (Jacobson et al. 2018).

What these brain findings indicate

- Bilateral frontal lobes are impacted in ADHD = has a role in motor function, problem-solving, memory, language, initiation, ability to be spontaneous, judgement, impulse control, and social and sexual behavior (Gehricke et al. 2017; Vaidya 2012);
- Bilateral parietal lobes are impacted in ADHD = processing sensory information regarding the location of parts of the body as well as interpreting visual information and processing language and mathematics (Hale et al. 2014);
- Bilateral temporal gray matter is impacted in ADHD = main auditory cortex (Lei et al. 2014).

Jacobson et al. study provided further evidence that ADHD is a neurodevelopmental process and revealed significant and robust structural changes as early as age 4 or 5 (Jacobson et al. 2018) (Fig. 6.4).

Anxiety

According to Krain AL, et al., the prevalence of anxiety disorders range from 4 to 20% (Krain et al. 2007). Anxiety in childhood and adolescence is normal until it is not. The process of recognizing, understanding, reconciling, and managing fear is very much a part of childhood and adolescence. Concerning anxiety is characterized by worry and fear that result in limited ability to function.

Just like many disorders, anxiety is best understood on a spectrum. Generalized Anxiety Disorder (GAD) is a common, primary disorder, many of its core symptoms

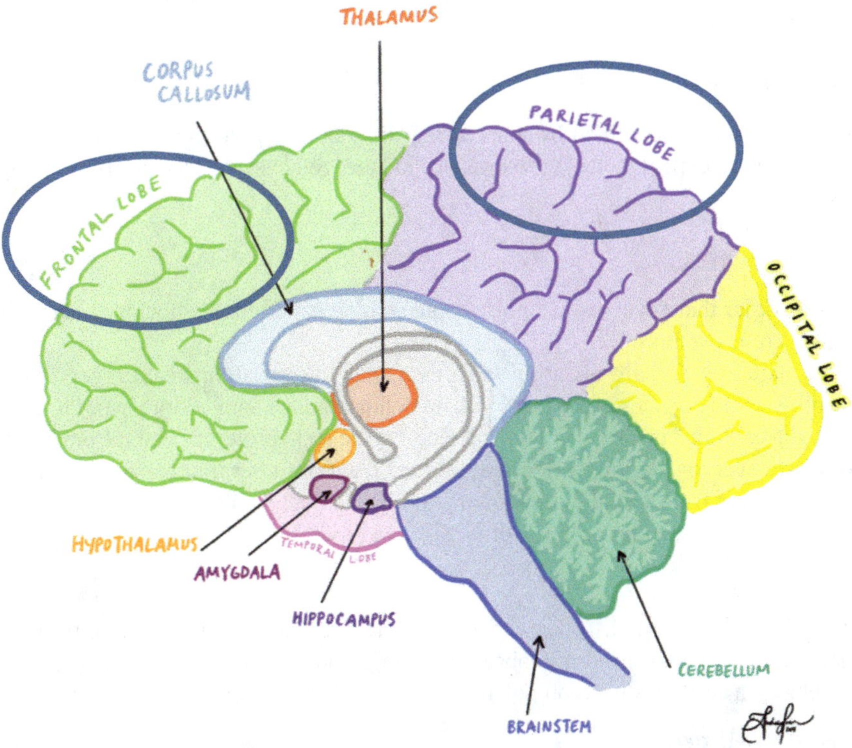

Fig. 6.4 ADHD and the brain (**main areas are circled**). Printed with permission. Copyright Audrey A. Tran

can be seen in other anxiety and anxiety-related disorders. According to Costello EJ and colleagues, some of the more common anxiety disorders among children are specific phobia, social phobia, generalized anxiety disorder, and separation anxiety disorder having mean prevalence rates between 2.2 and 3.6%. Agoraphobia (1.5%) and post-traumatic stress disorder (1.5%) are less prevalent, whereas panic and obsessive–compulsive disorders are relatively rare (i.e., below 1%) (Costello et al. 2011).

Anxiety-related disorders
Panic Disorder
Panic disorder is characterized by recurrent unexpected panic attacks, which are sudden periods of intense fear that may include

- Palpitations,
- Pounding heart,
- Accelerated heart rate,
- Sweating,
- Trembling or shaking,
- Sensations of shortness of breath smothering or choking, and

- Feeling of impending doom.

Social Anxiety

- Social anxiety is defined by marked fear of social or performance situations in which they expect to feel embarrassed, judged, rejected, or fearful of offending others.

PTSD

- A disorder that develops in some people who've experienced shocking, scary, or dangerous event(s).
- It is natural to feel afraid during and after a traumatic situation. Fear triggers many split-second changes in the body to help defend against danger or to avoid it. This "fight-or-flight" response is a typical reaction meant to protect a person from harm.
- Nearly everyone will experience a range of reactions after trauma, yet most people recover from initial symptoms naturally. Those who continue to experience problems may be diagnosed with PTSD.

OCD
is an anxiety-related disorder defined by the presence of recurring, unwanted thoughts, ideas, or sensations (obsessions) that compel them to do certain things or behave in certain ways (compulsions) in a repetitive fashion.

Separation Anxiety
Separation anxiety (fear and worry about being away from parental figures) is part of a normal developmental trajectory until about the age of 3 (Beesdo et al. 2009). It starts to transition into a disorder when the symptoms are intense and get in the way of a child's ability to function and to appropriately pursue independence outside of the home and the supervision of parental figures. Social anxiety disorder is marked by

- Anticipatory anxiety—just thinking about being away from the ones you love and/or home causes physical and mental distress.
- Persistent worry about losing a loved one to death, disaster, or illness.
- Recurrent and/or excessive distress of being away from home or the ones you love.
- Can have physical symptoms like stomach aches and/or headaches, disturbed sleep with nightmares.

Phobias
An excessive fear reaction that is mostly irrational.

Agoraphobia
Intense fear of two or more of the following situations:

- Using public transportation,
- Being in open spaces,
- Being in enclosed spaces,

- Standing in line or being in a crowd, and
- Being outside of the home alone.

According to Beesdo and colleagues, anxiety disorders are one of the most common psychiatric disorders in children and adolescents. Further, there is persuasive evidence from a range of studies that anxiety disorders are the most frequent mental disorders in children and adolescents, and thus seem to be the earliest of all forms of psychopathology. The *onset of anxiety disorders* (or symptoms/syndromes of anxiety) has been assessed in youth and adult samples, in cross-sectional and longitudinal surveys (Beesdo et al. 2009).

Prior chapters have addressed early exposure to trauma and other forms of toxic stress and the link to development of anxiety and depressive disorders, prominently highlighted in Felitti and Anda's Adverse Childhood Experiences study. The subject of fear has been discussed a number of times. Fear is described as having a very critical role in helping humans appropriately discriminate between threat and non-threat and to respond appropriately.

The way threat is perceived and experienced is determined by both environment and genetics. It turns out that a discussion on early attachment is essential when considering the role and impact of fear in human life. The brain develops from the point of conception to about the age of 26. When babies are born, the fear response is predominant and raw. It takes the love and connection of mother to child to help quiet the fear response. When a baby breastfeeds and bonds with mother, a hormone oxytocin is released through the hypothalamic–pituitary–adrenal axis (HPA axis). Oxytocin has been termed the attachment hormone as it helps to create a sense of closeness and connectedness required for human survival.

Psychologists John Bowlby and Mary Ainsworth did a lot of early work on attachment theory. Bowlby and Ainsworth described attachment as a deep and enduring emotional bond that connects one person to another across time and space (Ainsworth 1991; Bowlby 1969). Bowlby further defined attachment as "lasting psychological connectedness between human beings."

They further describe attachment as a sort of tempering measure for fear as children's natural proclivity is to move toward safety (which typically is represented as a secure parental figure) when they were emotionally dysregulated, afraid, and/or threatened. Secure attachments were developed when a fearful child sought safety and found it. Insecure attachments were developed when a fearful child sought safety and could not secure it.

The attachment theory has implications for later developmental phases. It helped to shape our collective understanding of how children with insecure attachments would be more prone to anxiety-related disorders and struggle with their own social/emotional relationships and behavior.

With this frame in mind, one could begin to understand why anxiety is a common condition in young people. Anxiety is a form of fear. Fear is a natural human proclivity for survival…until it is not. There is a relationship between early insecure attachment as a form of trauma and increased risk for anxiety.

Do take note that the basis of anxiety and anxiety-related conditions is fear.

Epigenetics of Anxiety
There are several animal and human studies on the epigenetics of anxiety. Human genes that have been studied in the epigenetics of anxiety include the following (Nieto et al. 2016):

- SLC6A2—involved in norepinephrine transmission.
- SLC6A4—involved in serotonin transmission.
- MOAA—involved in dopamine, serotonin, and norepinephrine processing. (*MAOA*) gene has been found to be altered in panic disorder (Ziegler et al. 2016).
- OXTR—oxytocin receptor.
- GAD1—expressed in the brain and is theorized to convert glutamate to GABA.
- COMT—epigenetic changes in COMT is associated with PTSD (a condition that falls along the anxiety spectrum) (van Rooij et al. 2016).

Various genes have been studied in animal models from the mu receptor gene to serotonin and stress hormone gene receptors.

Anxiety and pregnancy
A systematic review by Shahhosseini et al. (2015) and colleagues specifically investigated studies on the impact of anxiety during pregnancy. The article highlighted the following mental and behavioral impacts of anxiety during pregnancy on children:

- High association between maternal anxiety and mental disorders, emotional/concentration and hyperactivity disturbances in offspring (Glover 2014; Santos et al. 2014; Teyhan et al. 2014).
- Cognitive and developmental impairment in children (Glover 2014; Buitelaar et al. 2003).
- Changes in stress hormones like cortisol and sex hormones—these changes are theorized to contribute to anxiety and impact cognition, language development (Huizink et al. 2004; van den Huevel 2015).
- Sustained crying in the neonatal period has been witnessed in the offspring of mothers who had anxiety during pregnancy (Petzoldt et al. 2014).
- Notable irritability and restlessness (van den Heuvel et al. 2015a).
- Increased fear in dealing with life events (Braeken et al. 2013).
- Diminished interaction between mother and child (Webb and Ayers 2014).
- Nervous system development and growth is negatively impacted (van den Huevel et al. 2015b).
- Anxiety in pregnancy is associated with shorter gestation and has adverse implications for fetal neurodevelopment and child outcomes (Dunkel Schetter and Tanner 2012).

Anxiety's impact on the brain
According to Duval et al., fear and anxiety have considerable overlap with respect to subjective, behavioral, physiological, and neurological characteristics. However, some key differences separate the two. Fear is typically defined as a phasic and abrupt fight-or-flight response accompanied by intense arousal in response to an immediate and identifiable threat. Alternatively, anxiety is often defined by a more prolonged

state of tension, worry, and apprehension regarding uncertain, and potentially negative, future events (Barlow 2000; Duval et al. 2015). Duval's focused review also pointed out that many of the same regions making up the fear circuitry (discussed thoroughly in Chap. 3) also lie beneath anxiety (Duval et al. 2015).

The following brain structures are impacted in anxiety:

(a) *Auditory and visual stimuli*

Anxiety changes early sensory-perceptual processes in the auditory system (Cornwell et al. 2007; Vytal et al. 2013).

Anxiety changes early sensory-perceptual processes in the visual system (Lim et al. 2009; Shackman et al. 2011; Vytal et al. 2013).

These sensory-perceptual process changes are theorized to play a role in detecting/sensing threat and access the cognitive resources needed to respond to a threat, perceived, and/or real. As a result, performance on tasks that involve attention, maintenance of information, and rapid sensory perception may be impaired (Vytal et al. 2013).

(b) *Olfactory and tactile stimuli*

Krusemark et al. reviewed the role of olfactory sensory perception of threat in anxiety. Of particular interest was the relevance of potential olfactory biases to threat in anxiety, given that smells evoke powerful emotional responses in humans (Krusemark and Li 2012; Yeshurun and Sobel 2010; Bensafi et al. 2002; Schiffman 1974), and the olfactory system is intimately related to the limbic emotion system (Zald and Pardo 2000; Carmichael et al. 1994). The article highlighted the historical fact that non-humans keen ability to smell (through the olfactory system) aids in detecting, locating, and identifying predators in the environment. The ability to smell is functional and protective (Kats and Dill 1998). Krusemark and colleagues were intrigued by the role that the olfactory system plays in threat in animals and wanted to know how it translated to humans. In brief, it was determined that smell, as one of the human senses, does play a role in anxiety (Krusemark and Li 2012).

(c) *Bed Nucleus of the Stria Terminalis*

Involved in the stress response, protracted fear states, and social behavior. It is an extension of the limbic system (emotion center of the brain), located in the basal forebrain and is described as the center for integration of limbic information (Lebow and Chen 2016).

(d) *Thalamus*

Thalamus represents the sensory aspect of fear and anxiety in this case. The thalamus acts as a switchboard and plays the role of integrating sensory input from the primary sensory cortices and sends output to the amygdala (Duval et al. 2015).

(e) *Frontal Cortex*

The frontal cortex represents the higher brain and plays the role of modulating behavior and impulses. The frontal cortex regulates emotions and impulses by way of imposing top-down control on the limbic system. The frontal cortex has several subcomponents. As mentioned in prior chapters, emotions like anxiety and fear are functional in that they help humans appropriately seek safety. The question is what happens when anxiety and fear are always on, what impact does that have on the brain and behavior? Fear on all the time = trauma. Fear on all the time = the frontal cortex being limited in its role in controlling the middle-bottom part of the brain.

The frontal cortex is broken down in the following way (Martin et al. 2009):

- Prefrontal Frontal Cortex (PFC) = specifically responsible for executive functions such as planning, decision-making, predicting consequences for potential behaviors, and understanding and moderating social behavior.
- Orbitofrontal Cortex (OFC) codes information, controls impulses, and regulates mood.
- Ventromedial PFC = has a role in reward processing (Keedwell et al. 2005).
- Ventromedial PFC = plays a role in the visceral response to emotions (Drevets 2001; Martin et al. 2009).

(f) *Amygdala*

The amygdala, a part of the limbic system, plays a key role in fear and anxiety. In animal models, it has a clear role in fear conditioning and controlling emotional behaviors (LeDoux 2000; Steimer 2002).

In humans as evidenced by functional MRI studies, the cognitive representation of fear may preferentially involve the left amygdala (Phelps et al. 2002).

Activation of the amygdala by threatening stimuli then influences cognitive processes, perception, selective attention, and explicit memory (Steimer 2002).

(g) *Locus Ceruleus*

The locus coeruleus produces norepinephrine, activates the sympathetic nervous system in a fear/anxiety state ("fight-or-flight"), and communicates closely with the amygdala.

(h) *Hippocampus*

According to Cominski and colleagues, human studies suggest that a poorly functioning hippocampus may be a vulnerability factor for the development of Post-Traumatic Stress Disorder (an anxiety-related disorder). Further, limited functionality of the hippocampus has been associated with the development of persistent avoidance responding and, thus, may confer vulnerability to the development of anxiety disorders and PTSD (Cominski et al. 2014) (Fig. 6.5).

Summary

Understanding the intersection of certain mental health disorders, trauma, and substance use is critical in serving youth. The fact that the developing brain lends itself

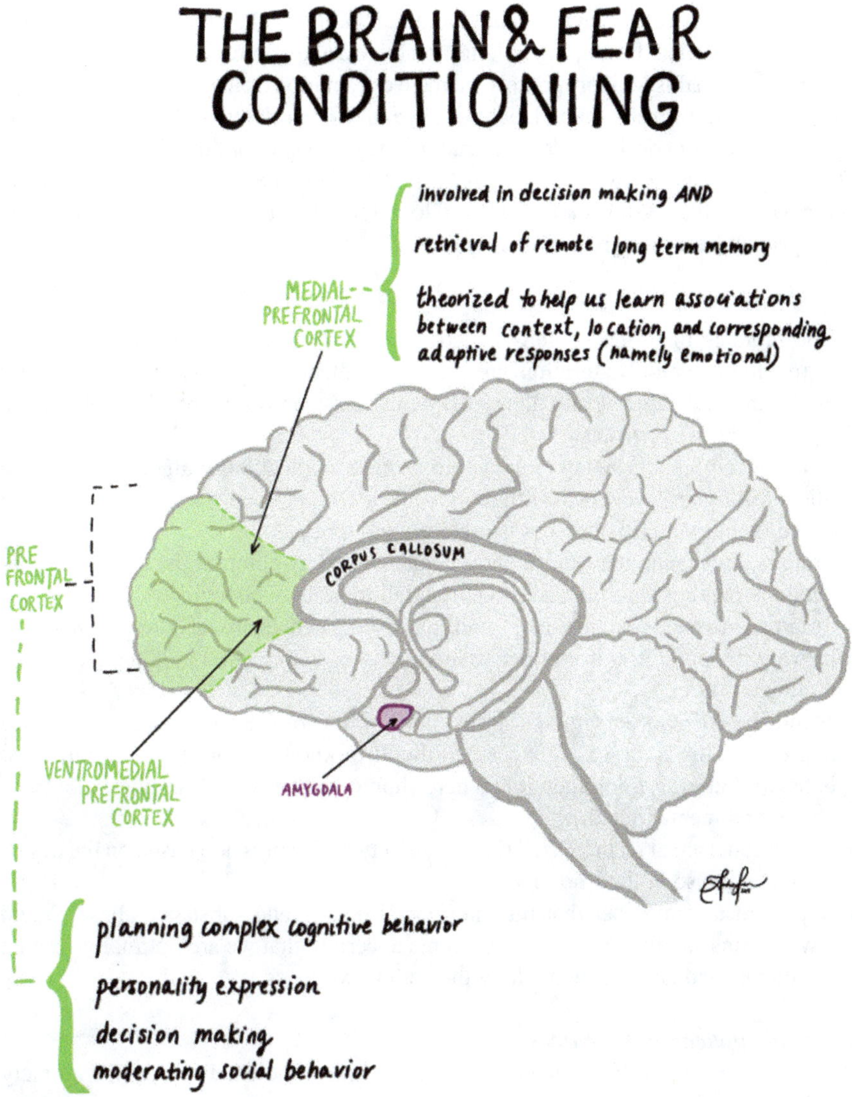

Fig. 6.5 The parts of the brain involved in fear conditioning are also involved in anxiety. Printed with permission. Copyright Audrey A. Tran

to impulsivity, novelty-seeking behavior, and is highly vulnerable to threats should be considered when developing policies, practices, and approaches in serving youth. The ultimate goal is to appropriately manage expectations, change systems to match the scientific and developmental realities of youth, and to effectively facilitate change.

This is all about designing and restructuring systems for optimal service to youth. This chapter was not written to suggest that systems be expert in mental health diagnosis, but that systems know what to look for, when to assess, and when/how to appropriately refer for greater intervention.

Key takeaways

- The brain is made up of cells called neurons. Neuronal formation, migration, segmentation, and maturation are heavily influenced by environment. Various environmental threats can change the genes that control neuronal development. Epigenetics is important.
- In the developing, growing brain, neurons make connections with one another and allow for higher level cortical functions like learning, memory consolidation, and mood regulation. This process is precious and tenuous.
- Trauma, substance use, and mental health disorders compromise neuronal connections making learning and mood regulation more challenging.
- Trauma-informed practices like mindfulness help heal neuronal connections—improving the possibility for effective learning, exercising good judgment, and regulating mood.
- Mental health disorders impact similar parts of the brain that trauma and substance abuse do. This sometimes makes it difficult to know the origins of a particular behavior but everything mentioned here should be considered (trauma, substance abuse, and mental health).
- Adolescents are at an increased risk for anxiety and depression based on the developmental phase of their brain.
- Important to remember that trauma, mental health, and substance abuse should always consistently be assessed for to make certain that we are optimally serving our clients and helping them along the path to wellness.

Practical application/Resources

Does your system routinely assess for common mental health disorders like anxiety and depression?

If so, how do you assess?

One quick screening tool for generalized anxiety

There are several tools to assess for anxiety. One quick, valid, and reliable tool for self-reported symptoms consistent with anxiety is the GAD-7. This tool assesses the level of worrying an individual does and considers the impact that such worry might have on ability to function optimally. Spitzer RL and colleagues constructed this tool and it can be accessed through SAMHSA website (Spitzer et al. 2006).

The GAD-7 screening results are usually interpreted in the following manner (Spitzer et al. 2006):

- A score below 10 = observe, monitor.
- A score above 10 = warrants further assessment, refer to a professional.
- A score of 15 and/or higher = warrants treatment, professional support.

One quick way to screen for depression
The Patient Health Questionnaire-9 (PHQ-9) is the most common questionnaire used to screen for mood and then refer out for any positive result. The PHQ-9 has been modified for adolescents as well. The PHQ-9 is a valid tool.

A copy of the modified PHQ-9 can be accessed on the SAMHSA-HRSA Center for Integrated Health Systems website under "Screening Tools" for depression.

References

Ainsworth, M. D. S. (1991). Attachments and other affectional bonds across the life cycle. In C. M. Parkes, J. Stevenson-Hinde, & P. Marris (Eds.), *Attachment across the life cycle* (pp. 33–51). London: Routledge.

Ajinkya, S., Jadhav, P. R., & Srivastava, N. N. (2013). Depression during pregnancy: Prevalence and obstetric risk factors among pregnant women attending a tertiary care hospital in Navi Mumbai. *Industrial Psychiatry Journal, 22*(1), 37–40.

American Psychiatric Association. (2013). *Diagnostic and statistical manual of mental disorders* (5th ed., (DSM-5)). Washington, DC: American Psychiatric Publishing.

Andersen, S. L. (2003, January–March). Trajectories of brain development: Point of vulnerability or window of opportunity? *Neuroscience and Biobehavioral Reviews, 27*(1–2), 3–18.

Andersen, S. L., & Teicher, M. H. (2008, April). Stress, sensitive periods and maturational events in adolescent depression. *Trends in Neurosciences, 31*(4):183–191.

Anguelova, M., Benkelfat, C., & Turecki, G. (2003). A systematic review of association studies investigating genes coding for serotonin receptors and the serotonin transporter: I. Affective disorders. *Molecular Psychiatry, 8,* 574–591.

Ashdown, H., Dumont, Y., Ng, M., Poole, S., Boksa, P., & Luheshi, G. N. (2006). The role of cytokines in mediating effects of prenatal infection on the fetus: Implications for schizophrenia. *Molecular Psychiatry, 11,* 47–55.

Barlow, D. H. (2000). Unraveling the mysteries of anxiety and its disorders from the perspective of emotion theory. *American Psychologist, 55*(11), 1247–1263.

Beesdo, K., Knappe, S., & Pine, D. S. (2009). Anxiety and anxiety disorders in children and adolescents: developmental issues and implications for DSM-V. *The Psychiatric clinics of North America, 32*(3), 483–524.

Belujon, P., & Grace, A. A. (2017). Dopamine system dysregulation in major depressive disorders. *The International Journal of Neuropsychopharmacology, 20*(12), 1036–1046.

Bensafi, M., Rouby, C., Farget, V., Bertrand, B., Vogouroux, M., & Holley, A. (2002). Psychophysiological correlates of affects in human olfaction. *Clinical Neurophysiology, 32,* 326–332.

Berger, I., Slobodin, O., Aboud, M., Melamed, J., & Cassuto, H. (2013). Maturational delay in ADHD: Evidence from CPT. *Frontiers in Human Neuroscience, 7,* 691. https://doi.org/10.3389/fnhum.2013.00691.

Blum, K., & Kozlowski, G. P. (1990). Ethanol and neuromodulator influences. A cascade model of reward. In H. Ollat, S. Parvez, & H. Parvez (Eds.), *Alcohol and behaviour: Basic and clinical aspects*. Utrecht, Netherlands: VSP.

Blum, K., Chen, A. L., Braverman, E. R., Comings, D. E., Chen, T. J., Arcuri, V., et al. (2008). Attention-deficit-hyperactivity disorder and reward deficiency syndrome. *Neuropsychiatric Disease and Treatment, 4*(5), 893–918.

Bowirrat, A., & Oscar-Berman, M. (2005). Relationship between dopaminergic neurotransmission, alcoholism, and reward deficiency syndrome. *American Journal of Medical Genetics Part B: Neuropsychiatric Genetics, 132,* 29–37.

Bowlby, J. (1969). *Attachment. Attachment and loss: Vol. 1. Loss*. New York: Basic Books.

Braeken, M. A. K. A., Kemp, A. H., Outhred, T., Otte, R. A., Monsieur, G. J., Jones, A., et al. (2013). Pregnant mothers with resolved anxiety disorders and their offspring have reduced heart rate variability: Implications for the health of children. *PLoS One, 8*(12), e83186.

Brown, A. S., & Susser, E. S. (2002). In utero infection and adult schizophrenia. *Mental Retardation and Developmental Disabilities Research Reviews, 8,* 51–57.

Buitelaar, J. K., Huizink, A. C., Mulder, E. J., de Medina, P. G., & Visser, G. H. (2003). Prenatal stress and cognitive development and temperament in infants. *Neurobiology of Aging, 24*(Suppl 1), S53–S60.

Carlo Altamura, A., Maggioni, E., et al. (2018, June). The impact of psychosis on brain anatomy in bipolar disorder: A structural MRI study. *Journal of Affective Disorders, 233,* 100–109.

Carmichael, S. T., Clugnet, M. C., & Price, J. L. (1994). Central olfactory connections in the Macaque monkey. *The Journal of Comparative Neurology, 346,* 403–434.

Caspi, A., Hariri, A. R., Holmes, A., et al. (2010). Genetic sensitivity to the environment: the case of the serotonin transporter gene and its implications for studying complex diseases and traits. *The American Journal of Psychiatry, 167,* 509–527.

Castren, E., & Rantamaki, T. (2010). The role of BDNF and its receptors in depression and antidepressant drug action: reactivation of developmental plasticity. *Developmental Neurobiology, 70,* 289–297.

Center for Behavioral Health Statistics and Quality. (2017). *2016 national survey on drug use and health: Methodological summary and definitions*. Rockville, MD: Substance Abuse and Mental Health Services Administration.

Comings, D. E., Gade-Andavolu, R., Gonzalez, N., et al. (2000). Multivariate analysis of associations of 42 genes in ADHD, ODD and conduct disorder. *Clinical Genetics, 58*(1), 31–40. https://doi.org/10.1034/j.1399-0004.2000.580106.x

Cominski, T. P., Jiao, X., Catuzzi, J. E., Stewart, A. L., & Pang, K. C. (2014). The role of the hippocampus in avoidance learning and anxiety vulnerability. *Frontiers in Behavioral Neuroscience, 8,* 273. https://doi.org/10.3389/fnbeh.2014.00273.

Compton, M. T., Goulding, S. M., Ramsay, C. E., Addington, J., Corcoran, C., & Walker, E. F. (2008). Early detection and intervention for psychosis: Perspectives from North America. *Clinical Neuropsychiatry, 5*(6), 263–272.

Cornwell, B. R., Baas, J. M., Johnson, L., Holroyd, T., Carver, F. W., Lissek, S., et al. (2007). Neural responses to auditory stimulus deviance under threat of electric shock revealed by spatially-filtered magnetoencephalography. *Neuroimage, 37,* 282–289. https://doi.org/10.1016/j.neuroimage.2007.04.055.

Costello, E. J., Copeland, W., & Angold, A. (2011). Trends in psychopathology across the adolescent years: What changes when children become adolescents, and when adolescents become adults? *Journal of Child Psychology and Psychiatry, 52,* 1015–1025.

Danielson, M. L., Bitsko, R. H., Ghandour, R. M., Holbrook, J. R., Kogan, M. D., & Blumberg, S. J. (2018). Prevalence of parent-reported ADHD diagnosis and associated treatment among U.S. children and adolescents, 2016. *Journal of Clinical Child and Adolescent Psychology* (Published online before print January 24, 2018).

Davey, C. G., Yucel, M., & Allen, N. B. (2008). The emergence of depression in adolescence: Development of the prefrontal cortex and the representation of reward. *Neuroscience and Biobehavioral Reviews, 32*(1), 1–19.

Der-Avakian, A., & Markou, A. (2012). The neurobiology of anhedonia and other reward-related deficits. *Trends in Neurosciences, 35,* 68–77.

Drevets, W. C. (2001). Neuroimaging and neuropathological studies of depression: implications for the cognitive-emotional features of mood disorders. *Current Opinion in Neurology, 11,* 240–249.

Duman, R. S., Heninger, G. R., & Nestler, E. J. (1997). A molecular and cellular theory of depression. *Archives of General Psychiatry, 54*(7), 597–606. https://doi.org/10.1001/archpsyc.1997.01830190015002.

Dunkel Schetter, C., & Tanner, L. (2012). Anxiety, depression and stress in pregnancy: Implications for mothers, children, research, and practice. *Current Opinion in Neurology, 25*(2), 141–148.

Duval, E. R., Javanbakht, A., & Liberzon, I. (2015). Neural circuits in anxiety and stress disorders: A focused review. *Therapeutics and Clinical Risk Management, 11,* 115–126. https://doi.org/10.2147/tcrm.s48528.

Frazier, J. A., et al. (2007). Treatment of early-onset schizophrenia spectrum disorders (TEOSS): Demographic and clinical characteristics. *Journal of the American Academy of Child and Adolescent Psychiatry, 46*(8), 979.

Furey, M. L., & Drevets, W. C. (2006). Antidepressant efficacy of the antimuscarinic drug scopolamine: A randomized, placebo-controlled clinical trial. *Archives of General Psychiatry, 63*(10), 1121–1129.

Fusar-Poli, P., Tantardini, M., De Simone, S., Ramella-Cravaro, V., Oliver, D., Kingdon, J., et al. (2017). Deconstructing vulnerability for psychosis: Meta-analysis of environmental risk factors for psychosis in subjects at ultra-high-risk. *European Psychiatry, 40,* 65–75.

Gayle, D. A., Beloosesky, R., Desai, M., Amidi, F., Nunez, S. E., & Ross, M. G. (2004). Maternal LPS induces cytokines in the amniotic fluid and corticotropin releasing hormone in the fetal rat brain. *American Journal of Physiology-Regulatory, Intergrative and Comparative Physiology, 286,* R1024–R1029.

Gehricke, J. G., Kruggel, F., Thampipop, T., Alejo, S. D., Tatos, E., Fallon, J., et al. (2017). The brain anatomy of attention-deficit/hyperactivity disorder in young adults—A magnetic resonance imaging study. *PLoS One, 12*(4), e0175433. https://doi.org/10.1371/journal.pone.0175433.

Gilliam, M., Stockman, M., Malek, M., Sharp, W., Greenstein, D., Lalonde, F., et al. (2011). Developmental trajectories of the corpus callosum in attention-deficit/hyperactivity disorder. *Biological Psychiatry, 69*(9), 839–46.

Global, regional, and national incidence, prevalence, and years lived with disability for 328 diseases and injuries for 195 countries, 1990–2016: a systematic analysis for the Global Burden of Disease Study 2016. (2017 September 16). *Lancet, 390*(10100), 1211–1259.

Glover, V. (2014). Maternal depression, anxiety and stress during pregnancy and child outcome; what needs to be done. *Best Practice & Research: Clinical Obstetrics & Gynaecology, 28*(1), 25–35.

Gogtay, N., Giedd, J. N., Lusk, L., et al. (2004, May 25) Dynamic mapping of human cortical development during childhood through early adulthood. *Proceedings of the National Academy of Sciences of the United States of America, 101*(21), 8174–8179.

Goldberg, T. E., Burdick, K. E., McCormack, J., et al. (2009). Lack of an inverse relationship between duration of untreated psychosis and cognitive function in first-episode schizophrenia. *Schizophrenia Research, 107,* 262–266.

Goldman, N., Glei, D. A., Lin, Y. H., et al. (2010). The serotonin transporter polymorphism (5-HTTLPR): allelic variation and links with depressive symptoms. *Depression and Anxiety, 27,* 260–269.

Hale, T. S., Kane, A. M., Tung, K. L., Kaminsky, O., McGough, J. J., Hanada, G., et al. (2014). Abnormal parietal brain function in ADHD: Replication and extension of previous EEG beta asymmetry findings. *Frontiers in Psychiatry, 5,* 87. https://doi.org/10.3389/fpsyt.2014.00087.

Hamilton, J. P, Siemer, M., & Gotlib, I. H. (2008, November). Amygdala volume in major depressive disorder: a meta-analysis of magnetic resonance imaging studies. *Molecular Psychiatry, 13*(11), 993–1000.

Huizink, A. C., Mulder, E. J., & Buitelaar, J. K. (2004). Prenatal stress and risk for psychopathology: Specific effects or induction of general susceptibility? *Psychological Bulletin, 130*(1), 115–142.

Hynd, G. W., et al. (1991, March). Corpus callosum morphology in attention deficit-hyperactivity disorder: Morphometric analysis of MRI. *Journal of Learning Disabilities, 24*(3), 141–146.

Jacobson, L. A., et al. (2018). Anomalous brain development is evident in preschoolers with attention deficit hyperactive disorder. *Journal of the International Neuropsychology Society*. https://doi.org/10.1017/s1355617718000103.

Kaminsky, Z., et al. (2011). A multi-tissue analysis identifies HLA complex group 9 gene methylation differences in bipolar disorder. *Molecular Psychiatry*.

Kane, J. M., et al. (2015, October 20) Comprehensive versus usual community care for first-episode psychosis: 2-year outcomes from the NIMH RAISE early treatment program. *The American Journal of Psychiatry*. https://doi.org/10.1176/appi.ajp.2015.15050632.

Kapur, S. (2003). Psychosis as a state of aberrant salience: A framework linking biology, phenomenology, and pharmacology in schizophrenia. *The American Journal of Psychiatry, 160,* 13–23.

Karlsgodt, K. H., Sun, D., & Cannon, T. D. (2010). Structural and functional brain abnormalities in schizophrenia. *Current Directions in Psychological Science, 19*(4), 226–231.

Kats, L. B., & Dill, L. M. (1998). The scent of death: Chemosensory assessment of predation risk by prey animals. *Ecoscience, 5,* 361–394.

Keedwell, P. A., Andrew, C., Williams, S. C., et al. (2005). The neural correlates of anhedonia in major depressive disorder. *Biological Psychiatry, 58,* 843–853.

Kessler, R. C., Avenevoli, S., & Ries Merikangas, K. (2001, June 15). Mood disorders in children and adolescents: an epidemiologic perspective. *Biological Psychiatry, 49*(12), 1002–1014.

Kim, M. J, Hamilton, J. P., & Gotlib, I. H. (2008, November 30). Reduced caudate gray matter volume in women with major depressive disorder. *Psychiatry Research, 164*(2), 114–122.

Kinsella, M. T., & Monk, C. (2009). Impact of maternal stress, depression and anxiety on fetal neurobehavioral development. *Clinical Obstetrics and Gynecology, 52*(3), 425–440.

Kiran, C., & Chaudhury, S. (2009). Understanding delusions. *Industrial Psychiatry Journal, 18*(1), 3–18.

Koolschijn, P. C, van Haren, N. E., Lensvelt-Mulders, G. J., Hulshoff Pol, H. E., Kahn, R. S. (2009, November). Brain volume abnormalities in major depressive disorder: A meta-analysis of magnetic resonance imaging studies. *Human Brain Mapping, 30*(11), 3719–3735.

Krain, A. L, Ghaffari, M., Freeman, J., Garcia, A., Leonard, H., & Pine, D. S. (2007). Anxiety disorders. In A. Martin & F. R. Volkmar (Eds.), *Lewis's child and adolescent psychiatry* (4th ed., pp. 538–48). Philadelphia: Lippincott Williams and Wilkins.

Krusemark, E. A., & Li, W. (2012). Enhanced olfactory sensory perception of threat in anxiety: An event-related fMRI study. *Chemosensory Perception, 5*(1), 37–45.

Labrie, V., Pai, S., & Petronis, A. (2012). Epigenetics of major psychosis: Progress, problems and perspectives. *Trends in Genetics: TIG, 28*(9), 427–435.

Laruelle, M., & Abi-Dargham, A. (1999). Dopamine as the wind of the psychotic fire: New evidence from brain imaging studies. *Journal of Psychopharmacology, 13,* 358–371.

Lebow, M. A., & Chen, A. (2016). Overshadowed by the amygdala: The bed nucleus of the stria terminalis emerges as key to psychiatric disorders. *Molecular Psychiatry, 21*(4), 450–463.

LeDoux, J. (2000). Emotion circuits in the brain. *Annual Review of Neuroscience, 23,* 155–184.

Leech, R., & Sharp, D. J. (2013). The role of the posterior cingulate cortex in cognition and disease. *Brain: A Journal of Neurology, 137*(Pt 1), 12–32.

Lei, D., Ma, J., Du, X., Shen, G., Jin, X., & Gong, Q. (2014). Microstructural abnormalities in the combined and inattentive subtypes of attention deficit hyperactivity disorder: A diffusion tensor imaging study. *Scientific Reports, 4,* 6875. https://doi.org/10.1038/srep06875.

Liddle, P. F., Friston, K. J., Frith, C. D., & Frackowiak, R. S. (1992). Cerebral blood flow and mental processes in schizophrenia. *Journal of the Royal Society of Medicine, 85*(4), 224–227.

Lim, S. L., Padmala, S., & Pessoa, L. (2009). Segregating the significant from the mundane on a moment-to-moment basis via direct and indirect amygdala contributions. *Proceedings of the National Academy of Sciences of the United States of America, 106,* 16841–16846. https://doi.org/10.1073/pnas.0904551106.

Liverman, C. S., Kaftan, H. A., Cui, L., Hersperger, S. G., Taboada, E., Klein, R. M., et al. (2006). Altered expression of pro-inflammatory and developmental genes in the fetal brain in a mouse model of maternal infection. *Neuroscience Letters, 399,* 220–225.

Lohoff, F. W. (2010). Overview of the genetics of major depressive disorder. *Current Psychiatry Reports, 12*(6), 539–546.

Lolak, S., et al. (2014). Epigenetics of depression. *Progress in Molecular Biology and Translational Science, 128,* 103–137. https://doi.org/10.1016/b978-0-12-800977-2.00005-x.

Lorenzetti, V., Allen, N. B., Fornito, A., & Yucel, M. (2009, September). Structural brain abnormalities in major depressive disorder: A selective review of recent MRI studies. *Journal of Affective Disorders, 117*(1–2), 1–17.

Luders, E., et al. (2016, October 30). Associations between corpus callosum size and ADHD symptoms in older adults: The PATH through life study. *Psychiatry Research: Neuroimaging, 256,* 8–14. https://doi.org/10.1016/j.pscychresns.2016.08.009. Epub 2016 August 26.

Luscher, B., Shen, Q., & Sahir, N. (2010). The GABAergic deficit hypothesis of major depressive disorder. *Molecular Psychiatry, 16*(4), 383–406.

MacQueen, G., & Frodl, T. (2011, March). The hippocampus in major depression: evidence for the convergence of the bench and bedside in psychiatric research? *Molecular Psychiatry, 16*(3), 252–264.

Markham, J. A., & Koenig, J. I. (2010). Prenatal stress: Role in psychotic and depressive diseases. *Psychopharmacology, 214*(1), 89–106.

Marshall, M., & Rathbone, J. (2011). Early intervention for psychosis. *Cochrane Database of Systematic Reviews* (6), CD004718.

Martin, E. I., Ressler, K. J., Binder, E., & Nemeroff, C. B. (2009). The neurobiology of anxiety disorders: brain imaging, genetics, and psychoneuroendocrinology. *The Psychiatric clinics of North America, 32*(3), 549–575.

Mathews, D. C., Henter, I. D., & Zarate, C. A. (2012). Targeting the glutamatergic system to treat major depressive disorder: rationale and progress to date. *Drugs, 72*(10), 1313–1333.

Maughan, B., Collishaw, S., & Stringaris, A. (2013). Depression in childhood and adolescence. *Journal of the Canadian Academy of Child and Adolescent Psychiatry* [Journal de l'Academie canadienne de psychiatrie de l'enfant et de l'adolescent], *22*(1), 35–40.

McEwen, B. S. (1999). Stress and hippocampal plasticity. *Annual Review of Neuroscience, 22,* 105–122.

McEwen, B. S. (2011). Effects of stress on the developing brain. *Cerebrum: The Dana Forum on Brain Science, 2011,* 14.

McGorry, P. D., Killackey, E., & Yung, A. (2008). Early intervention in psychosis: Concepts, evidence and future directions. *World Psychiatry: Official Journal of the World Psychiatric Association (WPA), 7*(3), 148–156.

McKinnon, M. C., Yucel, K., Nazarov, A., & MacQueen, G. M. (2009, January). A meta-analysis examining clinical predictors of hippocampal volume in patients with major depressive disorder. *Journal of Psychiatry & Neuroscience: JPN, 34*(1), 41–54.

Mill, J., et al. (2008). Epigenomic profiling reveals DNA-methylation changes associated with major psychosis. *American Journal of Human Genetics, 82*(3), 696–711. https://doi.org/10.1016/j.ajhg.2008.01.008

Mineur, Y. S., Obayemi, A., Wigestrand, M. B., Fote, G. M., Calarco, C. A., Li, A. M., et al. (2013). Cholinergic signaling in the hippocampus regulates social stress resilience and anxiety- and depression-like behavior. *Proceedings of the National Academy of Sciences of the United States of America, 110*(9), 3573–3578.

Moret, C., & Briley, M. (2011). The importance of norepinephrine in depression. *Neuropsychiatric Disease and Treatment, 7*(Suppl 1), 9–13.

Muller, N., Riedel, M., Gruber, R., Ackenheil, M., & Schwarz, M. J. (2009). The immune system and schizophrenia. An integrative view. *Annals of the New York Academy of Sciences, 917,* 456–467.

National Institute of Mental Health. (2017). *Mental Health Disorders*. https://www.nimh.nih.gov/health/topics/index.shtml.

Nieto, S. J., Patriquin, M. A., Nielsen, D. A., & Kosten, T. A. (2016). Don't worry; be informed about the epigenetics of anxiety. *Pharmacology, Biochemistry and Behavior, 146–147*, 60–72.

Paus, T. (2010, February). Growth of white matter in the adolescent brain: Myelin or axon? *Brain and Cognition, 72*(1), 26–35.

Paus, T., Keshavan, M., & Giedd, J. N. (2008, December). Why do many psychiatric disorders emerge during adolescence? *Nature reviews. Neuroscience, 9*(12), 947–957.

Petzoldt, J., Wittchen, H. U., Wittich, J., Einsle, F., Hofler, M., & Martini, J. (2014). Maternal anxiety disorders predict excessive infant crying: A prospective longitudinal study. *Archives of Disease in Childhood, 99*(9), 800–806.

Phelps, E. A., O'Connor, K. J., Gatenby, J. C., Gore, J. C., Grillon, C., & Davis, M. (2002). Activation of the left amygdala to a cognitive representation of fear. *Nature Neuroscience, 4*, 437–441.

Post, R. M. (2007). Role of BDNF in bipolar and unipolar disorder: Clinical and theoretical implications. *Journal of Psychiatric Research, 41*, 979–990.

Purcell, S. M., et al. (2009). Common polygenic variation contributes to risk of schizophrenia and bipolar disorder. *Nature, 460*, 748–752.

Redman, S. L., Corcoran, C. M., Kimhy, D., & Malaspina, D. (2017). Effects of early trauma on psychosis development in clinical high-risk individuals and stability of trauma assessment across studies: A review. *Archives of psychology, 1*(3), 28.

Rudolph, K. D., Hammen, C., & Daley, S. E. (2006). Mood disorders. In D. A. Wolfe & E. J. Mash (Eds.), *Behavioral and emotional disorders in adolescents: Nature, assessment, and treatment* (pp. 300–342). New York: Guilford Press.

Rund, B. R. (2013). Does active psychosis cause neurobiological pathology? A critical review of the neurotoxicity hypothesis. *Psychological Medicine*, 1–14. https://doi.org/10.1017/s0033291713002341.

Ruzicka, W. B. (2015). Epigenetic mechanisms in the pathophysiology of psychotic disorders. *Harvard Review of Psychiatry, 23*(3), 212–222.

Santos, I. S., Matijasevich, A., Barros, A. J., & Barros, F. C. (2014). Antenatal and postnatal maternal mood symptoms and psychiatric disorders in pre-school children from the 2004 Pelotas Birth Cohort. *Journal of Affective Disorders, 164*, 112–117.

Sapolsky, R. M. (2003, November). Stress and plasticity in the limbic system. *Neurochemical Research, 28*(11), 1735–1742.

Saricicek, A., et al. (2012). Persistent β2*-nicotinic acetylcholinergic receptor dysfunction in major depressive disorder. *The American Journal of Psychiatry, 169*(8), 851–859.

Schiffman, S. S. (1974). Physicochemical correlates of olfactory quality. *Science, 185*, 112–117.

Seamans, J. K., Floresco, S. B., & Phillips, A. G. (1998). D1 receptor modulation of hippocampal-prefrontal cortical circuits integrating spatial memory with executive functions in the rat. *The Journal of Neuroscience, 18*, 1613–1621.

Seghier, M. L. (2013). The angular gyrus: multiple functions and multiple subdivisions. *The Neuroscientist: A Review Journal Bringing Neurobiology, Neurology and Psychiatry, 19*(1), 43–61.

Shackman, A. J., Maxwell, J. S., McMenamin, B. W., Greischar, L. L., & Davidson, R. J. (2011). Stress potentiates early and attenuates late stages of visual processing. *The Journal of Neuroscience, 31*, 1156–1161 https://doi.org/10.1523/jneurosci.3384-10.2011.

Shahhosseini, Z., Pourasghar, M., Khalilian, A., & Salehi, F. (2015). A review of the effects of anxiety during pregnancy on children's health. *Materia Socio Medica, 27*(3), 200–202.

Shaw, P., Gornick, M., Lerch, J., et al. (2007). Polymorphisms of the dopamine d4 receptor, clinical outcome, and cortical structure in attention-deficit/ hyperactivity disorder. *Archives of General Psychiatry, 64*, 921–931.

Sheitman, B. B., & Lieberman, J. A. (1998). The natural history and pathophysiology of treatment resistant schizophrenia. *Journal of Psychiatric Research, 32*, 143–150.

Spear, L. (2000a). Neurobehavioral changes in adolescence. *Current Directions in Psychological Science, 9*(4), 111–114.

Spear, L., P. (2000b). The adolescent brain and age-related behavioral manifestations. *Neuroscience and Biobehavioral Reviews, 24*, 417–463.

Spinelli, S., Chefer, S., Suomi, S. J., Higley, J. D., Barr, C. S., & Stein, E. (2009, June). Early-life stress induces long-term morphologic changes in primate brain. *Archives of General Psychiatry, 66*(6), 658–665.

Spitzer, R. L., Kroenke, K., Williams, J. B. W., & Lowe, B. (2006). A brief measure for assessing generalized anxiety disorder. *Archives of Internal Medicine, 166,* 1092–1097.

Steimer, T. (2002). The biology of fear- and anxiety-related behaviors. *Dialogues in Clinical Neuroscience, 4*(3), 231–249.

Swanson, J. M., Kinsbourne, M., Nigg, J., et al. (2007). Etiologic subtypes of attention-deficit/hyperactivity disorder: brain imaging, molecular genetic and environmental factors and the dopamine hypothesis. *Neuropsychology Review, 17,* 39–59.

Teyhan, A., Galobardes, B., & Henderson, J. (2014). Child allergic symptoms and mental well-being: The role of maternal anxiety and depression. *The Journal of Pediatrics, 165*(3), 592–9. e5.

Tost, H., Alam, T., & Meyer-Lindenberg, A. (2009). Dopamine and psychosis: Theory, pathomechanisms and intermediate phenotypes. *Neuroscience and Biobehavioral Reviews, 34*(5), 689–700.

Treadway, M. T., & Zald, D. H. (2011). Reconsidering anhedonia in depression: lessons from translational neuroscience. *Neuroscience and Biobehavioral Reviews, 35,* 537–555.

Uher, R., & McGuffin, P. (2010). The moderation by the serotonin transporter gene of environmental adversity in the etiology of depression: 2009 update. *Molecular Psychiatry, 15,* 18–22.

Urakubo, A., Jarskog, L. F., Lieberman, J. A., & Gilmore, J. H. (2001). Prenatal exposure to maternal infection alters cytokine expression in the placenta, amniotic fluid, and fetal brain. *Schizophrenia Research, 47,* 27–36.

Vaidya, C. J. (2012). Neurodevelopmental abnormalities in ADHD. *Current Topics in Behavioral Neurosciences, 9,* 49–66.

van den Heuvel, M., Johannes, M., Henrichs, J., & Van den Bergh, B. (2015a). Maternal mindfulness during pregnancy and infant socio-emotional development and temperament: The mediating role of maternal anxiety. *Early Human Development, 91*(2), 103–108.

van den Heuvel, M. I., Donkers, F. C., Winkler, I., Otte, R. A., & Van den Bergh, B. R. (2015b). Maternal mindfulness and anxiety during pregnancy affect infants' neural responses to sounds. *Social Cognitive and Affective Neuroscience, 10*(3), 453–460.

van Rooij, S. J., Stevens, J. S., Ely, T. D., Fani, N., Smith, A. K., Kerley, K. A., et al. (2016). Childhood Trauma and COMT genotype interact to increase hippocampal activation in resilient individuals. *Frontiers in Psychiatry, 7,* 156. https://doi.org/10.3389/fpsyt.2016.00156.

Volkow, N. D., Wang, G. J., Newcorn, J., et al. (2007). Depressed dopamine activity in caudate and preliminary evidence of limbic involvement in adults with attention-deficit/hyperactivity disorder. *Archives of General Psychiatry, 64,* 932–940.

Vytal, K. E., Cornwell, B. R., Letkiewicz, A. M., Arkin, N. E., & Grillon, C. (2013). The complex interaction between anxiety and cognition: insight from spatial and verbal working memory. *Frontiers in Human Neuroscience, 7,* 93. https://doi.org/10.3389/fnhum.2013.00093.

Walther, D. J., & Bader, M. (2003). A unique central tryptophan hydroxylase isoform. *Biochemical Pharmacology, 66,* 1673–1680.

Webb, R., & Ayers, S. (2014). Cognitive biases in processing infant emotion by women with depression, anxiety and post-traumatic stress disorder in pregnancy or after birth: A systematic review. *Cognition and Emotion,* 1–17 (ahead-of-print).

Weinberger, D. R. (1987). Implications of normal brain development for the pathogenesis of schizophrenia. *Archives of General Psychiatry, 44,* 660–669.

Weir, J. M., Zakama, A., & Rao, U. (2012). Developmental risk I: Depression and the developing brain. *Child and adolescent psychiatric clinics of North America, 21*(2), 237–259, vii.

Wood, S. J., Pantelis, C., Yung, A. R., et al. (2009). Brain changes during the onset of schizophrenia: implications for neurodevelopmental theories. *The Medical Journal of Australia, 190,* 10–13.

Wyatt, R. J. (1991). Neuroleptics and the natural course of schizophrenia. *Schizophrenia Bulletin, 17*(2), 325–351.

Yeshurun, Y., & Sobel, N. (2010). An odor is not worth a thousand words: From multidimensional odors to unidimensional odor objects. *Annual Review of Psychology, 61,* 219–241.

Zald, D. H., & Pardo, J. V. (2000). Functional neuroimaging of the olfactory system in humans. *International Journal of Psychophysiology, 36,* 165–181.

Ziegler, C., Richter, J., Mahr, M., Gajewska, A., Schiele, M. A., Gehrmann, A., et al. (2016). MAOA gene hypomethylation in panic disorder-reversibility of an epigenetic risk pattern by psychotherapy. *Translational Psychiatry, 6*(4), e773. https://doi.org/10.1038/tp.2016.41.

Chapter 7
Labeling Theory, The Power of Words, and Implicit Bias

Growing up, kids used to say: “Sticks and stones may break my bones, but words will never hurt me.” I recall thinking that this idiom was not true because words did hurt, they hurt deeply.

A key element in facilitating change in people and/or systems requires paying close attention to the words we use. Several sociological studies powerfully demonstrate the connection between narrative and self-efficacy and construction of one’s identity. Positive words and reinforcement build confidence and confidence inspires change. Economists will tell you that the market does well when there is confidence in it. If this rationale holds true for markets, how much more so should it, can it be applied to people? The purpose of this textbook is to inspire change… in people and in systems.

Trauma-informed approaches compel us to focus on narrative and chose our words wisely. All human beings are impressionable, but youth are incredibly impressionable. We impact positive change when we build positive environments with positive narrative.

This chapter focuses on labeling theory (the impact of labels), the power of words, and implicit bias. Words shape perception and drive behavior/actions. Behavior and actions can be changed by changing our words. The objective is to raise awareness around the impact and power of words and to challenge individuals (attached to systems) to work toward changing their narrative for the better. At the end of the day, what we seek is change. As people and systems change, so goes the individual that people and systems seek to serve. Change and healing happen in parallel.

By the end of this chapter, you should be able to

- Define Labeling Theory,
- Define Reintegrative Shaming Theory,
- Recognize the impact of words and how they (words) impact client–parole officer interaction and subsequent behavior—WORDS matter, and
- Appreciate the role of implicit bias in interactions with clients and its potential impact/threat to positive outcomes.

A. Moreland-Capuia, *Training for Change*,
https://doi.org/10.1007/978-3-030-19208-2_7

Exercise 7.1 How narratives play out in the media and shape perception?

During the 2016 Olympic Games in Rio de Janeiro, Brazil, a group of Olympians made the news for something other than their participation in the games. Ryan Lochte (who was 31 during the games in 2016), Jimmy Feigen (who was 26 during the games in 2016), Jack Conger (who was 21 during the games in 2016), and Gunnar Bentz (who was 20 during the games in 2016) had alleged that they were robbed by gunpoint at a gas station in Rio. There was damage done to the gas station. When the media caught wind of this story, there was no question about its validity. Why?

Offering up two poignant views for your consideration:

- Ryan, Jimmy, Jack, and Gunnar were subconsciously referred to a long-standing narrative about Rio and its history of violence. The insurgence of violence has been written about extensively in the New York Times and other top media outlets. In a 2017 New York Times article, Ernesto London writes the following in his opening about Rio De Janeiro:
  "For teachers in this seaside megacity, Rio de Janeiro's surge in violence has meant making a life-or-death judgment call with unnerving frequency: deciding whether to cancel classes because of nearby shootouts." The author writes about Rio's economic woes and makes several references to "gang violence." Additionally, there are references made to the World Cup and Olympics serving as inspiration for Rio to build healthy, safe communities. The references made in this 2017 article are similar to prior articles written about Rio. I am not arguing whether they are factual or not. I am pointing out that persistent narrative shapes who individuals think the citizens of Rio are or aren't; what they are worthy of versus what they are not! (Ernesto London 2017).
- All four individuals happened to be White males, which comes with what some would deem unmerited trust. When the world saw these young men, it was easy to picture them as individuals who could potentially be subject to violence, but not perpetrators of it. Socialization is powerful. They were automatically believed, no questions asked.

The narrative initially leaned in the direction of confirmation bias. In this case, there was a pre-existing, predominant belief that Rio is violent; therefore, everything and anything that alludes to Rio and violence must in fact be true.

Evidence shifted the narrative
Then video surveillance was discovered and demonstrated what really happened. The video revealed four inebriated White males (who happened to be Olympic athletes), moderately belligerent, who created some damage to the gas station. To avoid having the police called, they paid the attendants. Witness accounts corroborated the surveillance video.

When the evidence was brought to the gentlemen, Ryan Lochte was a bit of spokesperson and was quoted as admitting that he "over-exaggerated" the story and attributed his actions to "immature behavior."

Even after getting the full story, in the arena of public opinion, the following phrases and words were attached to Ryan and his colleagues:

- "young boys having fun,"
- "innocent,"
- "fabricated,"
- "embellished,"
- "made a mistake," and
- "benefit of the doubt."

There was a heated exchange between NBC's Billy Bush and Al Roker. Billy Bush readily offered the benefit of the doubt stating that Lochte in particular just "embellished." A visibly affected Al Roker reframed it and said "no he didn't embellish, he lied." The word embellish versus liar invokes different behavioral responses.

Consider the impact of these words:

- Lied,
- Fabricated, and
- Embellished.
  - Do each of the words above (lie vs. fabricated vs. embellish) have the same impact?
  - What is the subtext here?
  - Is there a much bigger conversation about who is accepted as a victim and who is not?

Other points to consider in this exercise

- Lochte was 31 at the time, well beyond the definition of a young boy, he was a young man. However, the cognitive distraction is to call a White male "young" because it confers a level of acceptance and forgiveness.
- The narrative used to soften the blow of the real tragedy here, which was dishonesty and irresponsibility, serves to abdicate these four men from offering a sincere apology to citizens of Rio. They either purposely and/or subconsciously created a distraction by highlighting violence in Rio, which is an issue they knew the larger public would cling to.
- Narrative is powerful in its ability to reinforce and maintain social constructs.

Exercise 7.2 How labels change behavior in certain social context

Colin Kaepernick, a former NFL athlete, in protest of the influx of black and brown males being killed by the police, decided to take a knee during the national anthem as opposed to standing. His action caused a windstorm of criticism. A man of color, who sometimes wears an afro and/or cornrows, indicated to America that he was tired of (and affected by) people of color being killed. Kaepernick stated that he would no longer stand for a flag and/or anthem that has not held true to its promise as "the land of the free." It has not held true to its promise that "all men are created equal."

The following labels followed his action:

- The president of the United States called him "unpatriotic."
- Some individuals burned Kaepernick's jersey because they disagreed with his personal protest.
- Kaepernick was deemed "disrespectful to women and men who serve in the armed forces."
- He had a difficult time being hired by any NFL team after the incident and his athletic prowess was downplayed, the focus became about how he was "not that good anyway" to justify not keeping him at the NFL level.

Consider the impact of this word:

- Unpatriotic?
- What feelings, thoughts, does the word unpatriotic invoke?

Other points/questions to consider are as follows:
First amendment rights were constantly weighed against the powerful social construct of racism. Why?

Discussions propped up about the NFL and other sports teams profiting from athletes of color. What are the implications of this critique?

What do you make of the narrative around Colin Kaepernick?

Is their bias? Name it.

These two exercises were designed to burst wide open conversation about the impact of narrative and labels. Further, it is critical to consider words, labels, narrative, and the potential deeper underlying meaning.

Narrative and labels have many powerful impacts:

- Narrative has the capacity to shape other's perception and drive behavior.
- Narrative and labels also have the power to shape how an individual thinks of themselves. This is best understood in labeling theory.

Labeling theory
Labeling theory posits that people come to identify and behave in ways that reflect how others label them. In a critical review of labeling theory by Johannes Knutson, it is explained that labeling theory served as a framework for what was deemed "criminal and deviant behavior." The theory heavily shaped criminal and social policy around the world. Unfortunately, as was pointed out by Knutson in 1977, labeling theory and its impact has been detrimental and is a weak theory that lacks a firm empirical foundation. Knutson contends that if labeling theory was meant to resolve and/or reduce behaviors associated with individuals who were deemed "criminal" …it fails on every level (Knutson 1977).

Howard Becker came up with the labeling theory in 1963 as he held the conviction that people live up to/become/behaviors match what they are labeled (a combined understanding from the Tannenbaum, Cooley, and Mead's earlier theories). Further, Becker contended that individuals came to accept the labels as their personal identity. In the 1960s, sociologists were grappling with the question of what factors influenced what they called "criminal and/or deviant behavior." The labeling approach influenced important social policies related to how the judicial system was constructed, and it powerfully shaped the discussions about the behaviors in individuals who committed crimes (and how society viewed this population). The article highlights Frank Tannenbaum and the dramatization of "evil" (which emerged in the late 1930s) essentially posited that there is no separation from the person and their behavior. In other words, Tannenbaum held the core belief that "you are how you behave." Tannenbaum's early work on deviant behavior provided some foundational elements for what was deemed the labeling theory. Additionally, the article highlighted George Herbert Mead and Charles Horton Cooley's theory on symbolic interaction, which contends that the construction of "self" is a social product. Mead and Cooley outlined symbolic interaction and aspect of self-awareness asserting that self-awareness consists, namely, of "me" and "I". In this case, "me" = a powerful social construct, a person is who society says they are and how society defines them. The other aspect is "I" = an individual's integrated self; a person represents the integration of society's view about them—a preface to modern-day "stereotype threat." The "me" is predictable and the "I" is spontaneous in Mead and Cooley's formulation. As a consequence of the constancy and predictability of the "me" as defined by Mead and Cooley, it ("me" in the symbolic interaction theory) undergirds the labeling theory (Knutson 1977). Similar to Mead, Sociologist Herbert George Blumer stressed that "meaning" is derived from social interaction through communication, using language and symbols.

In a 1977 article, Joseph Scimecca agrees that labeling theory is rooted in social construction (Scimecca 1977).

The criminal justice system and other social systems co-opted this very powerful understanding that labeling something can robustly shape its function and behavior. This was used to negatively construct the system, where words like "criminal," "deviant," "offender," and "felon" are used. These labels have and do shape an individual's conception of "self."

Why is labeling theory so important to understand and in my clinical opinion, move away from?

Individuals who represent forces of law and order and those who enforce the boundaries of what is considered normal behavior, such as the police, court officials, experts, and school authorities, provide the main source of labeling (Crossman 2018).

In an article on labeling theory, Crossman highlights the disparities within labeling (Fig. 7.1).

How labeling theory plays out in education

Studies show disproportionate discipline in schools based on race and class (Townsend 2000; Kaeser 1979; Skiba et al. 2002).

Students of color are suspended, harshly disciplined, and expelled at a higher rate. The studies that explore this phenomenon are very gentle in their analysis and tiptoe around the matter. History shall serve as our best teacher in this case. Before the official concept of labeling theory emerged, its impact and grip could be appreciated. The United States of America constituted exclusion. From the nation's founding,

Concept: What is developmentally accepted, understood behavior for some individuals is not for others	*Question:* What changes when **class and the powerful social construct of race is** applied to what is seemingly "normal behavior"?
Scenario: All children participate in deviant behavior at some point in time to include skipping school, climbing into the neighbor's yard	*Outcomes:* Two different outcomes and responses based on race: ▪ In affluent neighborhoods – cops, parents and teachers see this behavior as normal and a part of growing up ▪ In more destitute neighborhoods, the same behavior is regarded as criminal and delinquent

Fig. 7.1 When race and class intersect with the labeling theory (Crossman 2018)

written in the declaration of independence it read: "we hold these truths to be self-evident that all men are created equal." One question that emerges is: who was not included in this key founding document? People of color, women, immigrants, and the list goes on and on. Then America was built on the backs of free slave labor, who happened to be people of color, namely, Africans who were brought to the country via the transatlantic slave trade. Slavery maintained the heart of the economy of the Southern states by tending to cotton and tobacco fields. Slavery was and is the traumatic persistent stain on the white cloth that is America. The Revolutionary War gave birth to America. Slavery and the fight to abolish it through the Civil War influenced the culture of America. There was recognition that the constitution was flawed in that laws allowed for people of color to be deemed less human and devalued while dominant culture was valued. Abolitionists like Abraham Lincoln fought to end slavery and change the constitution to move toward a more inclusive and human existence. We eventually get to the 13th amendment, flowing from the Civil war which ended in 1865. The 13th amendment ended one form of slavery and laid the foundation for another form of slavery now known as the prison industrial complex. The 13th amendment had a clause that (in paraphrasing) stated that slaves should be free except they be criminal. Ah, there is that word again…"criminal." It is indeed not a coincidence that the origins of criminology and labeling theory came in the early 1900s. Their theories built the construct that now holds and reinforces specific systems that disproportionately punish and discard people of color. Let's consider the timeline:

Constitutionally, slavery ended in 1865:

- Reconstruction era takes place between 1865 and 1877—Big names like Ford, JP Morgan, and Rockefeller amass huge amounts of wealth in this new frontier. This is a commentary on the distribution of wealth and who had access to it.
- During the reconstruction era, from 1877 to 1950, marked the rise of Jim Crowism, laws that supported segregation. Jim Crow laws violated equal protection under the law clause (the 14th amendment in the constitution).
- In the early 1920s, a silent film entitled "The Birth of Nation" was popularized as it demonstrated Black men in particular as a predator, dangerous, violent.
- Lynching of African-Americans in the South was pronounced from the time that slavery was abolished in 1865 up to the Civil Rights movement which started in the early 1960s.
- Brown v. Board of education was an important Supreme Court decision that overturned the Plessy v Ferguson separate but equal clause. Brown v. Board of Education integrated schools with the goal of increasing quality education to all students, no matter what color.
- While laws mandated equality, they didn't mandate a change in behavior and/or perception. Many states were slow to fully adopt federal civil rights legislation. States like Oregon didn't ratify their constitution until 1926 to lift the ban on Blacks residing in the State and the state did not ratify the 14th amendment until 1973 for example.

We can appreciate the power of the labeling theory as early as the founding of this country, even though it was not officially formalized as a theory until the 1960s. Going back to the 13th amendment and its loophole, many would contend that the path to maintaining economic and social infrastructure that racism built, some form of slavery had to exist. The only way that another human being can treat something with cruelty and disrespect is to see them as "other." Think about the rise of Jim Crow laws immediately after slavery was abolished. Think about the construction of specific images of people of color as dangerous, deviant criminals as outlined by films like "The Birth of a Nation" in the 1920s. It was intentional. Laws were disproportionately applied. It is no secret that people of color experience harsher discipline not only in schools but in the criminal justice system as well.

If you are seen as bad, undervalued as and less than human, it makes it easier to not invest in your success and/or your health and wellness. Townsend and many of his colleagues confirm that the bias, which drives behavior, is influenced by narratives, history, and labels. Every system, historically, was established to value certain populations over another. This truth and practice must be acknowledged in order to be effectively deconstructed, rethought, and rebuilt.

Ellen Batlinger examined differences in school punishment in adolescents of different social classes. Young people who identified as high and low income were interviewed about their perceptions of their own and their peers' level of discipline and consequences in school. The results were as follows (Batlinger 1991).

Young people who identified as being high income indicated fewer misbehaviors and behaviors that were deemed playful.

Young people who identified as low income indicated greater intensity of punishment that didn't match the behavior cited as offensive. They also felt more humiliation and anger.

The results of Batlinger study suggested notable inequitable school conditions for low-income students impacted their behavior (the perception of being treated unfairly shaped the behavior, they act like you label them and treat them). Further, the study highlighted that the disproportionate disciplinary practices motivated anger and contributed to alienation.

Low-income adolescents' acting-out or withdrawal behaviors are likely to be perceived by others as signs of emotional disturbance and not as legitimate responses to social class inequities in school and society (Batlinger 1991).

Gordon and his colleagues reported on the Expose Racism & Advance School Excellence (ERASE) initiative, which called on schools across the nation to collect and use data around racial inequity as a means of improving and ensuring quality education for students of color. The article reads: "if the public schools regular failed to serve students of color in a single aspect of their education that would be bad enough. What the research reveals is far more pernicious…"

In assessing schools climate for racial inequality, Gordon and his colleagues highlighted these key findings when comparing students of color to their White counterparts (Gordon et al. 2000; Imich 1994):

- Statistical evidence that demonstrated significant racial inequalities in areas of school dropout rates, access to advanced placement courses, and entrance into college.
- African-American (mainly), Latino, and Native American students are suspended or expelled at a higher, disproportionate rate.
- Students of color are more likely to drop out or be pushed out of school.
- Students of color are less likely to graduate.
- Students of color have less access to advanced classes or programs for gifted students. Oakes et al. investigated how math and science learning opportunities were distributed and executed in the nations elementary and secondary schools, specifically in terms of science and math education, what was being taught, how it was being taught, who was teaching, and under what conditions. The study demonstrated that low-income, minority, and inner-city students have fewer opportunities to learn science and mathematics, less access to science and mathematics knowledge at school, fewer material resources, less-engaging learning activities in their classrooms, and less-qualified teachers. Characteristics of the school and the classroom were associated with the inequalities highlighted (Oakes et al. 1990)
- Culturally specific teach is rare. In other words, the racial makeup of the teaching staff rarely matched that of the student body (Gordon et al. 2000).

A study by J. F. Gregory analyzed national data regarding racial differences in school discipline in African-American children. In Gregory's introduction, the country is urged to consider the findings of profound disproportionately in the direction of the African-American male. Gregory encourages the reader to "take pause."

There is a congressional mandate to monitor civil rights in schools nationwide. Gregory turned to the US. Department of Education Office of Civil Rights for data and surveyed over 4,600 public school districts and over 43,000 public schools. Over 25 million children were accounted for in the survey. Gregory analyzed the 1992 OCR Elementary and Secondary School Civil Rights Compliance report that contained a detailed questionnaire sent to schools nationwide.

Survey had data broken down by race, ethnicity, and gender. Further, there was data on Special Education programs, students who were receiving Bilingual and/or English-as-a-Second Language Services, Talented and Gifted Programs, students enrolled in Advanced Placement, suspension data, corporal punishment data, and graduation rates (Gregory 1997).

Gregory found the following:

- African-American males received higher rates of corporal punishment compared to African-American girls, other students of color, and their White counterparts.
- African-American males were more frequently and harshly punished in all forms.
- African-American males versus the other groups of being put into such programs for the Behaviorally Disordered across the 184,414 cases reported in Gregory's analysis (Gregory 1997).

In a 1987 article, McCarthy and colleagues pointed out that Black adolescents were more likely to be entangled with the criminal justice system compared to their White counterparts even when both groups self-reported similar rates of not adhering to the law (McCarthy and Hoge 1987). McCarthy and colleagues also noted that public schools were patterned after the disproportionately in punishment and consequence in the criminal justice system. The study looked at school data, longitudinally to evaluate and try to account for disparities. The study concluded that disproportionate punishment of Black adolescents was multifactorial to include the teachers' perception and interpretation of the behavior of Black students (it was more likely to be experienced as aggressive and violent compared to their White counterparts); disproportionately in punishment for Black adolescents also seemed to flow from the teacher's knowledge of student's past record of discipline (Black students past indiscretions marked and followed them through their educational career. They were less likely to be given the benefit of the doubt); Black adolescents had poorer grades and deemed less well behaved—this reputation was amplified and reinforced by teachers as students moved along the education system—it is what I call "the soft bigotry of low expectation" or what Steele and Aronson would call "stereotype threat" or what sociologist would call "confirmation bias." Ultimately, McCarthy et al. concluded that disparities in Black adolescents in education could be attributed to powerful social constructs (McCarthy and Hoge 1987).

A National Association of Secondary School Principals report in 2000 expressed concern that zero-tolerance policies were negatively impacting the education system and disproportionately impacting minorities and students with disabilities. The report stated the following: "In the aftermath of a number of high profile, extremely violent incidents at public schools, many state and local education entities have adopted the same harsh and mandatory: 'take-no-prisoners' approach to disciple currently being used in this country's criminal justice system" (National Association of Secondary School Principals 2000).

Zero-tolerance policy, developed in the 1980–1990s, was a response to increased violence in schools in the form of school shootings. The objective was to increase safety in schools. The policy called for suspending or expelling students for a wide range of conduct, such as

- Bringing any weapon to school, including seemingly innocent items like nail clippers and toy swords,
- Having any alcohol or drugs on campus, including tobacco and over-the-counter medications like aspirin or Midol,
- Fighting, including minor scuffles,
- Threatening other students or teachers, or saying anything that could be perceived as a threat,
- Insubordination, which could include talking back to a teacher or swearing in the principal's office, and
- Any behavior considered disruptive, like cutting in a lunch line.

The report shed light on the impact of the application of zero tolerance in education. In 1998, over 3 Million children were suspended and over 87,000 were expelled. Principals characterized the policy as an overzealous approach to promoting safety and were concerned about it being assimilated in schools across the nation. More poignantly, minority children and children with disabilities were disproportionately impacted by the policies implementation (National Association of Secondary School Principals 2000).

As the political milieu changes in our country, so has the effort to soften the blow of zero-tolerance legislation and policies. Even with some minor adjustments, the harsh reality of disproportionate punishment for children of color, namely, males of color, persists. It fuels the discussion and phenomenon of the school-to-prison pipeline and the prison industrial complex.

School-to-prison pipeline
There is a link between overrepresentation in school discipline, negative school outcomes, and overrepresentation in the criminal justice system. As the studies cited in this chapter demonstrate, children and adolescents of color are disproportionately disciplined in the education system which results in poor educational outcomes. In order to resolve the issue, systems must get beyond acknowledging the historical, legislative, political, social, and economic underpinnings of the phenomenon and move more judiciously toward changing the outcome. This requires changing policies and practices to account for the inherent, unjust disparities, and inequities that exist for children and adolescents of color.

Prison industrial complex
From the history provided on the inception of this country to the 13th amendment, there is a deeper understanding of the social, legislative, and economic forces that influenced the prison industrial complex.

Activists noted the pattern of rising prison construction and a persistent drive to fill these new structures with human bodies. Further, it was pointed out that the core motivation for building and filling prisons is ideologies of racism and the pursuit of profit (Davis 2003).

A 1998 article in the Atlantic by Eric Schlosser wrote about the prison industrial complex this way: "Correctional officials see danger in prison overcrowding. Others see opportunity. The nearly two million Americans behind bars—the majority of them nonviolent offenders—mean jobs for depressed regions and windfalls for profiteers." Schlosser gave greater context for the prison industrial complex as he explained that it was a conspiracy theory but a real, intentional phenomenon anchored in "a set of bureaucratic, political, and economic interests that encourage increased spending on imprisonment, regardless of the actual need." The Prison industrial complex is described as (Schlosser 1998)

- A confluence of special interests that has given prison construction in the United States;
- Supported by politicians, both liberal and conservative, who have used the fear of crime to gain votes;
- An economy boost for impoverished rural areas where prisons have become a cornerstone of economic development.

Labeling theory and policing in America

Again, labeling theory posits that people come to identify and behave in ways that reflect how others label them (Townsend 2000). As important as the labeled is the "the labeler." How individuals are labeled and who labels them is the main driver in perception. People of color have historically been labeled as "less than," "dangerous," "predatory," "lazy," and the list goes on and on. These labels carry a set of expectations and inspire specific emotions like "fear" (covered in prior chapters) but will be discussed in greater detail in Chap. 8 of this textbook. With this backdrop, it is better understood how and why police officers are more likely to perceive a person of color as a threat compared to their White counterparts—because they are socialized to do so.

A 2016 report sponsored by the Center for Policing Equity examined racial disparities in use of force across 12 departments that participate in the National Justice. The overarching goal was to provide national-level data and analyses on police behavior. They investigated racial disparities in the use of force benchmarking against demographics of local arrest rates.

Analysis of the 12 departments (which were geographically and demographically diverse) demonstrated the following (Goff 2016):

- Racial disparities in police use of force were present even when they controlled for racial distribution of local arrest rates.
- Multiple departments had racial disparities when force incidents were benchmarked exclusively against certain violent arrests (Black residents were more likely compared to Whites to be targeted for force).
- Racial disparities were poignant across several categories of force to include hand weapons, spray, tasers, etc.

They note that the estimates of bias were conservative (happening at higher rates, but not consistently reported and not captures in the data set) (Goff 2016).

In his book, Suspect race: Causes and consequences of racial profiling, Jack Glaser asserts that the disparities in profiling, excessive use of force, arrest, and policing in communities of color might be understood through the lens of implicit bias, stereotypes, and the persistence of powerful social constructs like racism (Glaser 2014).

A study by Gunnar et al. examined the impact of labeling young teens on behavior and subsequent delinquency. The study demonstrated that labeling did influence behavior and continued involvement with the criminal justice system. In the case of teens being labeled "delinquent," "offenders," and "criminal," they identified with the label and behaved accordingly (Bernburg et al. 2006).

If we superimpose the labeling theory on other systems like employment, housing, health care, the trend in disparities for people of color is highlighted. Labeling theory constructs powerful narratives, powerful narratives heavily influence thinking, thinking drives behavior, and manifests itself in actions, i.e., execution of laws, policies, etc.

Exercise 7.3 The consequence of mislabeling

What can be the potential hazard of mislabeling?

Write down two potential hazards for mislabeling the following:

Medication

1.

2.

Street signs

1.

2.

Food

1.

2.

The consequence of mislabeling can be dire and result in death. There is a reason we are mandated to properly label things like food and medication. How might (or should) this same concept apply to people?

What came up for you in doing this exercise?

How has reading this chapter shifted your perspective on labeling? If at all.

Making the connection

Social and economic systems are the hub—the spokes that reinforce the system include employment, health, community, housing, criminal justice, and education. In the case of system change, the core of the issue must be understood and thoughtfully deconstructed (Fig. 7.2).

Making the connections, we are exploring the power of narrative and how it shapes unconscious, automatic behavior (implicit bias). In Schein's model, unconscious, automatic behavior is represented by "norms and values" and "underlying assumptions" (elements that are not observable, but applied and felt). Schein contends that

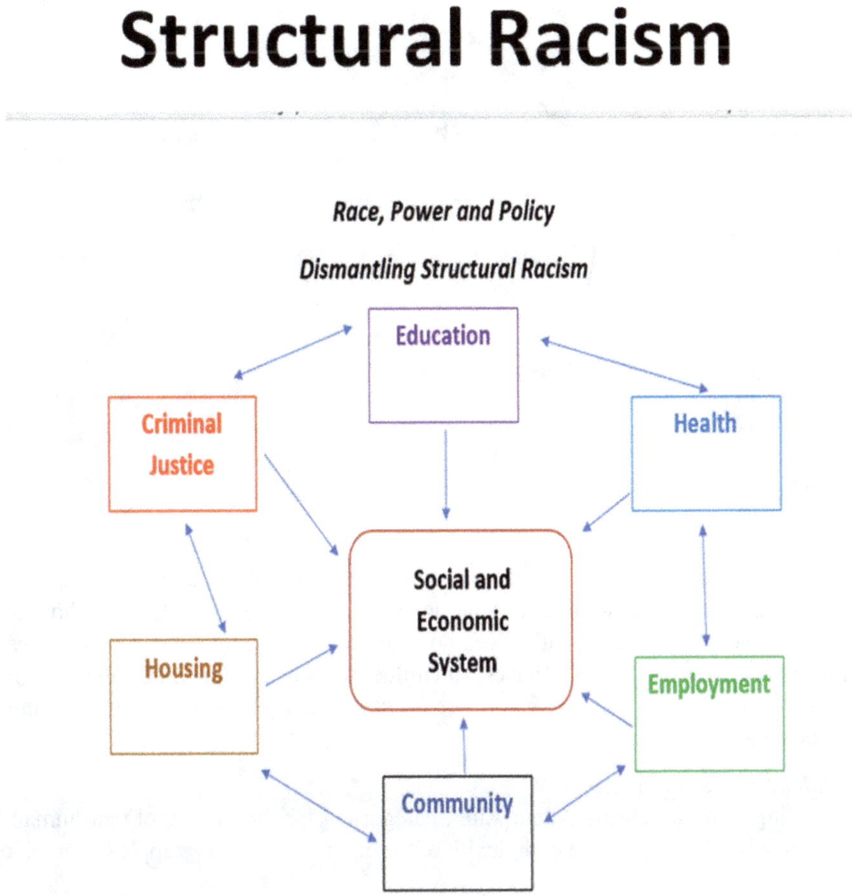

Fig. 7.2 Adapted with permission from Sandra Hinton

change is evaded if organizations/systems do not meaningfully and thoughtfully deal with their underlying assumptions (Fig. 7.3).

Personal construct theory

A psychologist by the name of George Kelly invented the personal construct theory. The theory is shaped by the following concepts:

- Individuals build mental structures that help them organize their beliefs about how the world works.
- These mental structures are referred to as constructs—the functionality of the construct is to help interpret and understand the things that individuals see and the things that happen.
- These constructs shape individual perception and reality.
- These constructs are influenced by what an individual sees and experiences.

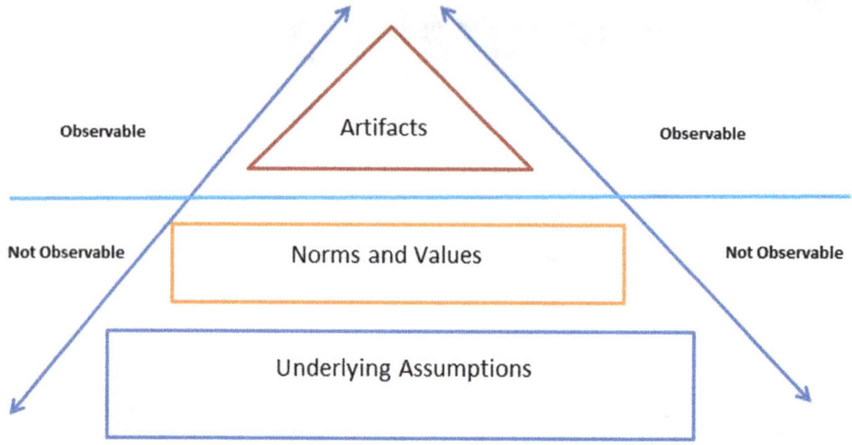

Fig. 7.3 Schein's organizational/culture model of change

Personal construct theory is heavily shaped by external environment and influences. Narrative, the things that an individual hears about themselves, influences how an individual sees themselves, influences how an individual thinks about themselves, influences how an individual behaves, and influences how an individual engages with the world around them. It is critical to see the connectivity between words, thinking, and behavior.

Why labeling is dangerous
According to an article by Adam Alter, categorical labeling is a tool that humans use to resolve the impossible complexity of the environments we grapple to perceive (Alter 2010).

We know why we label, but now we must understand the impact of labeling on youth. It is (and has been in various cases) a matter of life or death, surviving versus thriving.

Researchers began to study the cognitive effects of labeling in the 1930s, when linguist Benjamin Whorf proposed the linguistic relativity hypothesis (Carroll 1997). According to his hypothesis, the words we use to describe what we see aren't just idle placeholders—they actually determine what we see.

Alter demonstrates that labeling can limit possibilities. The article highlighted a study done by Rosenthal and Jacobson who demonstrated creating safe, positive learning environments free of preconceived notions and labels significantly increased student capacity greatness (Rosenthal and Jacobson 1992).

Reintegrative Shaming Theory = Restorative Justice
Many sociologists highlighted the fact that labeling theory as a foundational and fundamental ideology in criminology did not contribute greatly to the goals of recovery, healing, and rehabilitation (as indicated in the literature). The blind spots of the labeling theory were put on display and an effort to humanize it emerged. Theories like

Reintegrative Shaming Theory were established as an alternative to labeling theory. Reintegrative Shaming is appreciated as an integrated theory that combines elements of differential association and social bonds.

It was first created in 1989 by sociologist, John Braithwaite (1989)—the theory holds that punishments should focus on the offender's behavior rather than characteristics of the individual who becomes entangled with the law. Braithwaite contends that what flows from reintegrative shaming is a social process which builds consciences as well as informal social controls to stop future wrongdoing.

In a piece authored by Braithwaite (1989) on reintegrative shaming, he writes:

> Societies have lower crime rates if they communicate shame about crime effectively. They will have a lot of violence if violent behavior is not shameful…there are ways of communicating shamefulness of crime that increase crime, this is attached to stigma. Reintegrative shaming communicates shame to a wrongdoer in a way that encourages him or her to desist.

Braithwaite contends that societies that are forgiving and respectful while taking rime seriously have lower crime rates; societies that degrade and humiliate individuals who may have committed a crime have higher crime rates.

Reintegrative shaming is a move in a helpful direction, but it doesn't go far enough in terms of support of healing, restoration, and habilitation (not rehabilitation). The challenge is in the word "reintegrative shaming." Shame is powerful and can (and has) impede healing. Reintegrative shaming is also known as restorative justice.

My question: how restorative is "shame"?

What is shame? What role does shame play in supporting change, if any at all?

A common phrase used in society, mostly used in the context of disagreement and/or disapproval is "She and/or he should/or ought to be ashamed!" Shame is a powerful emotion and impacts behavior. The concept of shame as outlined by Nash and Kilday: "Shame is the primary social emotion…. If this line of thought is correct, shame would be the most frequent and possibly the most important of emotions, even though it is usually invisible" (Scheff 1988). Everywhere man blushes and conceals. Human life, under all conditions, seems to move within the frame of a fundamental pattern in which an attitude called shame may have a hidden place (Riezler 1943; Nash and Kilday 2010). Morrison (1984) points out that "shame is a central human effect that represents feelings of inferiority and failure of the self." Morrison contends that shame lies at the very center of the "self," with primary internal shaming (directed at the self's failures and inadequacies) permeating all aspects of an individual's life.

Michelle May writes the following about the dynamics of shame as formulated by several theorists (May 2017).

Shame is conceptualized as a social emotion, provoked by self-devaluing of one's action and is heavily impacted by others' view of the "self"—(Ellison 2005; Fullagar 2003).

Shame arises from one's own consciousness and is experienced in the presence of others with a focus on the self as bad (May 2017).

Braithwaite sums reintegrative shame up in the following way:

Reintegrative shame = shame + respect for individual + acceptance back into society.

Braithwaite endorses that opposite of reintegrative shaming is disintegrative shaming and sums it up in the following way:

Disintegrative shame = stigmatization + disrespect + isolation + degradation.

Shame is shame and it is known clinically that when "shame" is not appropriately managed and/or addressed, it can compromise healing.

Critical question

What happens when internal shame (an individual's internal view of themselves as a chronic failure) overwhelms external shame (society's subconscious and sometimes conscious labeling and treatment as "bad")? Is change possible?

Reintegrative shaming combines the concepts of differential association and social bonds.

Differential association

Differential association is a theory established by Edwin Sutherland asserting that individuals learn the values, attitudes, techniques, and motives for deviant behavior through interaction with others (Mongold and Edwards 2014).

Social bonds

According to Hirschi, an individual commits a delinquent act when their bonds to conventional society are broken (Mongold and Edwards 2014).

The words used in the original studies include words like

- Delinquent,
- Deviant, and
- Criminal.

The subtext for differential association and social bond theory is Freud, Heinz, Kohut's, and others' theory on "self-psychology," which might serve as more trauma-informed frame for considering the conditions that drive shame and that increase the likelihood that someone may act out of shame. In other words, hurt individuals act out of their hurt and hurt stems from some circumstances that an individual may have control over and some circumstances they do not.

Freud's work

- *Distinguishing "self" from "'other,"*
- *Dealing with the construction of self—a psychodynamic frame, and*
- *Idea that "self" is shaped by socio-historical context.*

Object relations

Margaret Mahler and Donald Winnicott*—Object Relations*

Basic premise: Humans have basic and profound need to be connected or attached to others (known as "objects").

- **Heinz Kohut**: Self-Psychology

Basic premise: Strong self-esteem ("healthy narcissism") develops through empathic responsiveness from others.

The power of words their influence on thinking and behavior
French philosopher, Rene Descartes, famously said: "I think, therefore I am." Many have interpreted this existential statement in various ways. One consistent analysis suggests that Descartes was questioning his very existence until he became consciously aware of the power of thought. To think something, indeed, makes it real for the person who is thinking it. This is a rather powerful sentiment because it is known that words shape thoughts.

In an article in Psychology Today, Benitez-Burraco (2017) makes the connection between language, thoughts, and culture. He contends that language is a filter, enhancer, or framer of perception and thought—a sentiment that neuroscientist, linguist, sociologist, and psychologists could likely get behind.

Consider multiple examples of individuals who have shared their stories about being told that they were failures and they believed it; told they were poor and they internalized it; told that they would amount to nothing and they lived like nothing, and the examples go on and on.

We do not have to look very far to appreciate the power of words and its impact on thinking and behavior.

If you (the reader) were asked to recall a time that you were told something about yourself or overheard someone say something about you and how it impacted your thinking/behavior?

Implicit bias (what we don't see, but feel)
The Implicit Association Test (IAT), established at Harvard, is a new sophisticated, computer evidence-based tool that measures bias associations (it relies on differences in response latency to demonstrate implicit bias) (Greenwald et al. 2009). More recent studies on implicit bias employ IAT in their methods. It has mostly been assumed that behavior is primarily driven by consciously controlled processes and could be judged or interpreted explicitly. We now understand the powerful impact of unconscious processes on behavior. As indicated in a prior chapter, bias is driven by underlying assumptions; underlying assumptions are shaped by environment, narratives, social constructs, and experiences. It is understood that most human beings learn by contextualizing. For example, when an individual moves to a new neighborhood and is learning the area, most individuals will secure a landmark as a point of reference, directionally. In an effort to learn, the human brain finds landmarks—these landmarks influence memory and shape behavior. Landmarking establishes a point of reference to increase capacity for recall. An individual may not be able to name a street, but they can find a location based on a landmark. This concept of learning by association is deemed associative learning. Associative learning is the one way human beings organize material for storage and future use. When we give context to something, it gives it greater meaning and increases the capacity to remember. There is benefit in clustering information—clustering, landmarking, and organizing things based on "sameness" are the brain's ways of consolidating/storing memory for later use. This principle is applied in implicit associations as well.

A working example in a question: What is the first thought that comes to mind when the word criminal is used?

- When you think of a doctor,
- When you think of a cop, and
- When you think of a nurse.

Whether you admit or not, there were immediate images that popped up, you may have course corrected, but the immediate thought and/or image is suggestive of underlying assumptions also known as implicit biases and associations. Unfortunately, it is the underlying, unconscious–automatic–implicit processes that do the most harm in systems and in society.

There are studies on the impact of unconscious–automatic–implicit processes/associations on individuals who interface with specific systems.

Implicit bias in health care

Fitzgerald and colleagues did a systematic review of implicit bias in healthcare professionals. Fitzgerald defined implicit bias as unconscious associations that lead to a negative evaluation of a person on the basis of irrelevant characteristics like race and/or gender. The review included peer-reviewed articles published over a 10-year period spanning 2003–2013 (Fitzgerald and Hurst 2017).

Exactly, 42 articles were included in the review:

- Seventeen studies employed the Implicit Association Test to measure the biases of healthcare professionals.
- Twenty-five studies involved the use of vignettes to assess the influence of patient characteristics on healthcare professionals' attitudes and medical decision-making.
- Twenty-seven studies investigated racial and ethnic bias.
- Thirty-five articles demonstrated evidence of active implicit bias in healthcare professionals.
- All studies in this review that examined correlations showed a significant positive relationship between the level of implicit bias and lower quality of care.

Overall, the findings highlighted the need for the healthcare profession to address the role of implicit biases in disparities in health care. Further, it was suggested that measures should be taken to raise awareness of the potential conflict between holding negative explicit attitudes toward some patient characteristics and provision of quality care and treatment (Fitzgerald and Hurst 2017).

A study by Blair et al. suggests that implicit bias may affect clinical judgment and decision-making (Blair et al. 2011).

- Implicit bias may also affect treatment through its effects on interpersonal communication. A number of studies have shown that people with more implicit ethnic/racial bias have poorer interpersonal interactions with minority individuals (Fazio et al. 1995; Greenwald 2009; Dovidio et al. 2002; Steele et al. 2002).
- The presence of implicit bias is generally consistent across the studies and suggests that clinicians have similar implicit biases to others in society (Blair 2011).
- Blair and colleagues conclude that implicit bias does impact clinical judgment and offer a number of solutions for healthcare providers to both assess and move away from implicit bias (Blair 2011).

Hall and colleagues did a systematic review of implicit racial/ethnic bias among healthcare professionals and its influence on healthcare outcomes. Hall and et al. had a section entitled the "plain language summary" which stated the following:

- Fifteen studies were considered "relevant" and included in the review.
- In the case of healthcare professionals, the review noted evidence of low to moderate levels of implicit racial/ethnic.
- Implicit bias scores are similar to those in the general population.
- Levels of implicit bias against Black, Hispanic/Latino/Latina, and dark-skinned people were relatively similar across these groups.
- A core conclusion from article of Hall et al. was that implicit bias was significantly related to patient–provider interactions, treatment decisions, treatment adherence, and patient health outcomes (Hall et al. 2015).

Most studies on implicit bias and attitudes in health care come to similar conclusions: implicit attitudes negative impact the provision of medical care, resulting in lower quality of care.

Criminal justice and implicit bias
In an article by Mark Bennett on implicit racial bias in sentencing, he contends that implicit racial bias is now the most pervasive problem affecting the criminal justice system. The article highlights the following (Bennet 2017):

- Implicit racial bias and other implicit biases exist even, and sometimes particularly, in egalitarian individuals.
- The effects of implicit biases in the courtroom are invisible to the naked eye.
- In a very busy court system, where all participants are feeling overwhelmed; high demands and limited resources create the conditions for "systemic implicit racial biases" to persist in courtroom proceedings.
- Some empirical studies suggest that in the case of inmate populations, implicit racial bias increases in the length of sentences based on offenders' darker skin tone and more pronounced Afrocentric features.
- Bennet makes mention of the only two studies on implicit bias in judges established, unnervingly, that judges (state judges in the first study and both state and federal in the second) have equal or greater implicit racial biases than members of the general public.
- Highlights the emerging discovery of implicit racial bias arising out of the relationship between skin tone, Afrocentric features, and sentencing (King and Johnson 2016).

In the Yale Law Journal, L. Song Richardson writes about "systemic triage" and implicit bias in the courtroom. L. Song Richardson writes: "Judges, prosecutors, and defense lawyers in many criminal courtrooms across the country are laboring under the weight of far too many cases to give each one individualized treatment. This has systemic consequences as these professionals struggle to quickly sort defendants into those who are deserving of time and attention and those who are not, a process I describe as systemic triage. As I will explain, racialized justice is a foreseeable consequence of systemic triage because of the influence of implicit, i.e., unconscious, racial biases on behaviors, perceptions, and judgments" (Richardson 2017).

Richardson explains the concept of "systemic triage" paraphrased as busy individuals (in a busy system) who are moving fast, forcing them to make quick judgments—these quick judgments are based on inherent implicit bias that disproportionately and negatively impacts people of color.

Hiring and Implicit Bias

Rooth (2010) executed one of the first studies that provided empirical evidence for automatically activated associations that influenced discriminatory behavior among recruiters in a real-life hiring situation. The study pointed out that discrimination in the hiring process (comparing Arab Men to Swedish men) could possibly be due to conscious and unconscious negative stereotypes of the minority applicants. To test explicit attitudes, recruiters were asked to address their explicit attitudes and stereotypes in three questions:

- Feeling thermometer toward Arab men versus Swedish men,
- Hiring preference, and
- Performance stereotype rating.

The IAT was performed to assess implicit biases.

The relevant results from Rooth study were as follows:

- Over half of recruiters explicitly stated that they preferred hiring Swedish men;
- Over half of recruiters had more positive feelings toward Swedish me > Arab men;
- Over three-fourths of recruiters had no productivity differences; and
- There were strong, negative implicit stereotypes toward Arab men > Swedish men.

Explicit bias (what we see and feel)

Explicit bias requires that a person is aware of his/her evaluation of a group, believes that evaluation to be correct in some manner, and has the time and motivation to act on it in the current situation. Explicit attitudes have long been assumed to be central factors influencing behavior (Blair and Banaji 1996; Devine 1989; Fazio et al. 1995).

In a study on automatic and controlled processes in stereotype priming, Blair and his colleagues set out to investigate the automatic processes that might be attached to stereotyping and to investigate the role of intention and cognitive resources in modulating the influence of the automatic processes. They distinguished stereotype activation from stereotype application (Blair and Banaji 1996; Devine 1989).

Stereotype activation = defined as categorization and an automatic process that turns in the presence of certain/specific social cue.

Stereotype application = defined as a process that is influenced by conscious control.

Further, the article points out that stereotype cannot be used in judgment if those stereotypes have not been previously activated by situational cues. In this way, stereotype activation is a required but not complete explanation in the case of stereotyping.

- The study included 73 Yale graduate students: 27 men and 46 women.
- They were asked to participate in a study on "judging words" for compensation (20 participants) and/or experimental credit (52 participants).

- Participants completed a series of trials on which they responded to a male and/or female target name that was immediately preceded by a stereotype, a counter-stereotype, or a gender-neutral prime attribute.
- A third of the primes were stereotypically masculine; one-third were stereotypically feminine, and one-third were gender neutral.
- Half the primes (feminine, masculine, gender neutral) were negative and half were positive; within the traits that were masculine and feminine primes half were traits and half were non-traits; all gender-neutral primes were non-traits.

Some of Blair and Banaji's key conclusions included (Blair and Banaji 1996)

- Evidence for gender stereotype priming under baseline conditions.
- Male and female stereotypes were shown to influence responses in a task that did not involve making conscious stereotypic associations.
- Consistent finding of stronger stereotype priming with non-trait stereotypes than trait stereotypes.
- Stereotypes may be primed and influence responses when cognitive constraints are severe and perceivers do not have a specific stereotype intention in place.

Connecting unconscious, automatic drives to "how an individual is made to feel."
Maya Angelou famously stated: "I've learned that people will forget what you said, people will forget what you did, but people will never forget how you made them feel."

It is often was not said, but felt that powerfully moves people in a good and/or not so good way.

Have you ever had someone tell that you were amazing, but they didn't treat you like you were? The gap between words and actions is "feelings." It turns out that this "feeling" space is commanding. How people are left to feel feeds into self-efficacy, self-image, and self-worth and influences one's capacity and motivation for change.

Put another way, if you tell a young person that they are brilliant but your actions and maybe other forms of communication (written, body language) doesn't demonstrate the statement of brilliance, it can quickly be interpreted as disingenuous and can compromise any change process. Deep down inside most human beings have a shared understanding that "how" people make you feel is an indicator of what they really believe and think about you. In this way, actions represent subconscious or unconscious beliefs. These unconscious beliefs when applied can be detrimental (Fig. 7.4).

Implicit biases impact and the brain
As human beings, we make quick judgments based on what we see (or think we see). With very limited information and exposure, we draw very quick conclusions—the speed with which we draw these conclusions is multifactorial, but socialization and conditioning are key factors in this process. Many in society have written about this phenomenon, in *Blink*: The power of thinking without thinking, Gladwell addresses the utility and harm of making quick judgements based on limited information. Further, he challenges the reader to consider the following question: should I trust my instinct and/or take pause and question them? (Gladwell 2005). This is a worthwhile

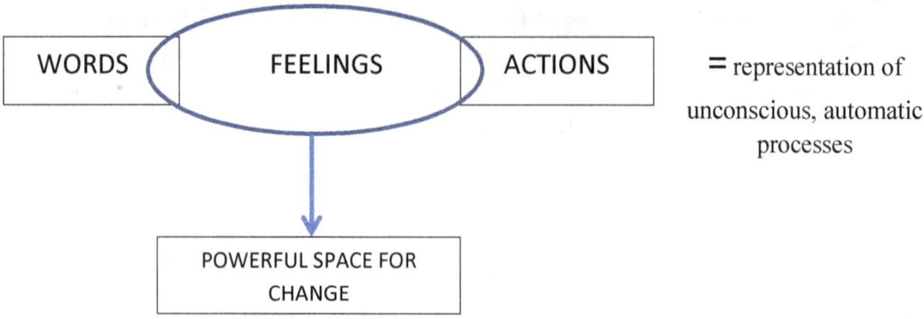

Fig. 7.4 The intersection of words, feelings, actions in implicit bias

question to ponder for sure. It is appropriate to assess whether or not a situation is safe or not. However, when snap judgments are an extension of socialization and underlying assumptions, there might be space to pause and re-assess.

Researchers have studied the brain and neural networks involved in making quick judgments. All judgements at base are not bad; the functional role of making a snap judgment is to move toward safety. In a study by Freeman et al., it was pointed out that similar areas of the brain that are involved in assessing threat are also involved in making snap judgments. This makes absolute sense. The article reads: "Consistent with the sensitivity of the amygdala to negative, threat-related stimuli, initial studies reported linear effects, with amygdala activation increasing for faces appearing less trustworthy (Winston et al. 2002; Engell et al. 2007). This effect held true regardless of task demands (Engell et al. 2007; Todorov and Engell 2008; Todorov et al. 2011), suggesting that the amygdala may code trustworthiness implicitly when a face is clearly visible." Studies prior to Freeman et al. demonstrated the amygdala's involvement in conscious detection of threat, safety, and trustworthiness, but this study suggests that the amygdala's starring role in unconscious, automatic processing of threat, and making judgement (Berry and Finch-Wero 1993).

Study design included two experiments, an average of 30 participants. With the application of functional MRI and sophisticated statistics and employment of a backward masking paradigm involving three levels of masked facial trustworthiness (low, average, high) in two experiments, responses facial stimuli were analyzed.

The research suggests that the brain's automatic response to a face's trustworthiness before it is even consciously perceived is consistent with other studies that have demonstrated that humans practice spontaneous (unconscious, automatic) judgment of others. The amygdala plays an important role in social and emotional behaviors and has been shown (in prior studies) to be involved in judging the trustworthiness of faces (LeDoux 2000; Todorov et al. 2005). Freeman and colleagues conclude that the amygdala is able to assess how trustworthy another person's face appears in the absence of conscious perception (Freeman et al. 2014).

Neural basis for prejudice and stereotyping
An article by David Amodio considers the neuroscience of prejudice and stereotyping. According to the article, the neural basis of prejudice has primarily focused on neural structures involved in emotion and motivation, such as the amygdala, insula, striatum, and regions of orbital and ventromedial frontal cortices (Amodio 2014).

The following brain structures are implicated in the process of stereotyping and prejudice:

- *Amygdala* = involved in the rapid processing of social category cues, including racial groups, in terms of potential threat or reward. Amygdala activity is frequently observed in individuals while they view members of racial outgroups, but it has also been found in response to viewing members of one's own group independently of race (Van Bavel et al. 2008).
- *Striatum* = approach-related instrumental responses are mediated by the striatum.
- *Insula* = supports visceral and subjective emotional responses toward social ingroups or outgroups. Insula is also implicated in pro-social emotions, such as empathy, toward liked individuals (Singer et al. 2004, 2006; Lamm et al. 2010).
- *Orbitofrontal cortex* = affect-driven judgements of social outgroup members rely on the Orbital Frontal Cortex (OFC). The social domain, the OFC, supports the monitoring of social cues and subsequent adjustment of one's behavior. OFC activity has been associated with subjects' deliberative judgements regarding the prospect of befriending Black, relative to White, individuals (Gilbert et al. 2012).
- *Medial prefrontal cortex (mPFC)* = involved in empathy and mentalizing. Medial prefrontal cortex activity has been primarily associated with the formation of impressions about other people.
- *Anterior cingulate cortex* = supports the detection of one's unwanted social biases and the engagement of cognitive control in order to avoid the expression of bias.

Making the connection—**the same areas of the brain involved in fear conditioning are implicated in stereotyping and prejudice** (Fig. 7.5).

Homophily
Homophily is defined as individual's proclivity for being attracted to others who are similar to them. A study by Smirnov et al. sought to determine whether homophily (the drive for sameness) was the result of a socialization process where individuals changed their traits according to the dominance of that trait in their local social networks, or if it results from a selection process, in which individuals reshape their social networks so that their traits match those in the new environment. They investigated homophily in academic achievements of high school and university students, analyzing the change in friendship networks of over 6,000 students over the course of 42 months. The study demonstrated that academic homophily was the result of selection, and students slowly but surely re-evaluated their social circles and re-organized based on individuals who were performing at their level. They didn't adapt to the group, and they secured individuals who were more like them over time (Smirnov and Thurner 2017).

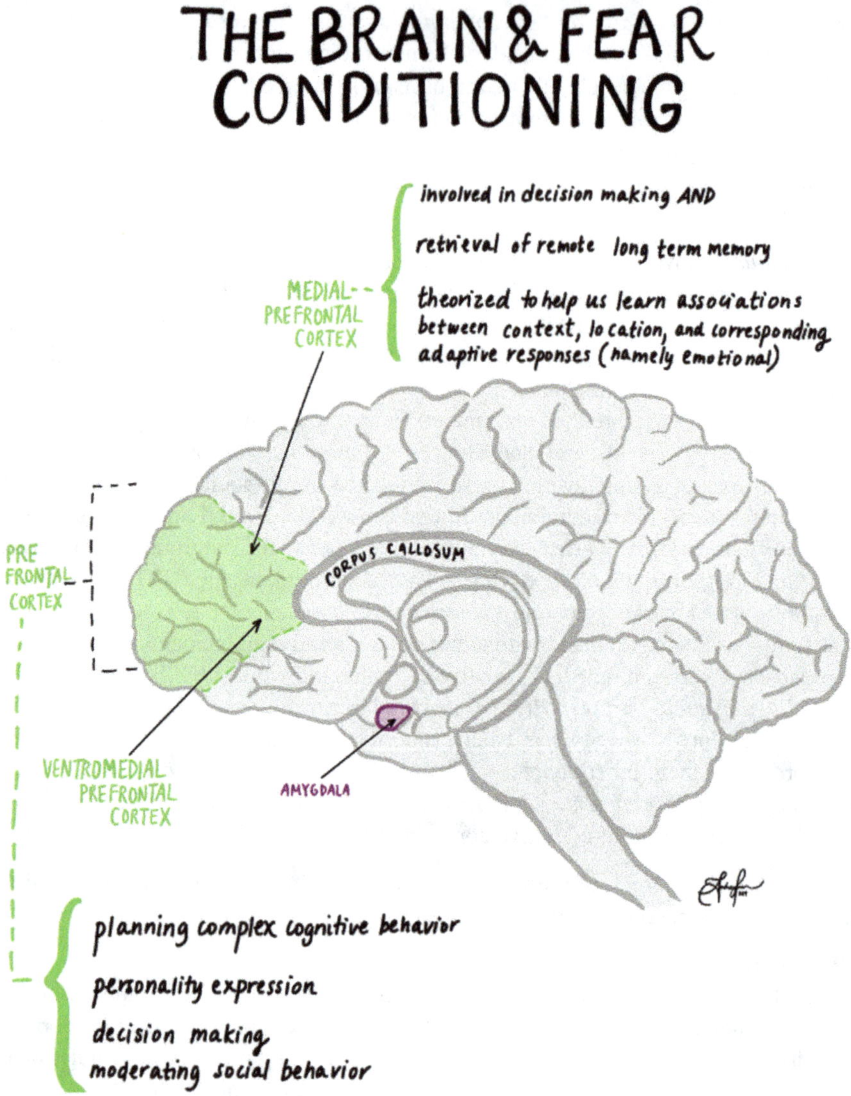

Fig. 7.5 Fear conditioning involves the medial prefrontal cortex, amygdala, and anterior cingulate cortex. What undergirds prejudice, racism, and stereotyping? FEAR

Homophily in race and ethnicity creates the strongest divides in our personal environments, with age, religion, education, occupation, and gender following in roughly that order (McPherson et al. 2001; Block and Grund 2014).

The drive for sameness leaves little room for appreciation of and respect for difference.

One of these things is not like the other

Core literature makes reference to implicit bias, which is the unconscious, automatic negative reaction to a person, place, or thing influenced by social conditioning. Explicit bias is a conscious, automatic negative, or unfavorable reaction to a person, place, or thing influenced by social conditioning. Implicit and explicit biases are palatable, less threatening terms when compared with racism. Bias is shaped by narrative.

Consider this: Many young children grew up watching Sesame Street. There is a very memorable episode where one of the Sesame Street characters puts up a series of shapes—three squares and one circle. The question that comes shortly thereafter is: which one of these things is not like the other?

In our education system as early as preschool, toddlers are asked to pick and match objects that are similar and to identify objects that are different. During our formative years, we are asked to recognize pattern and difference, but we are given very little context for why we are being asked to call out difference. Children who can readily call out difference with limited context transition to adults who readily appreciate difference with limited context. We are primed, socialized to note difference, but we do not, consistently, get to the next phase which is to teach that difference is strong, rich, powerful, and good and is what makes for industrious, vibrant, creative, and innovative communities. I firmly believe that if we start early in helping our children recognize the power and beauty of difference (as opposed to the fear of difference), we could appreciate a significant reduction in the negative impact of bias and move toward our collective path to healing, as a nation.

Summary

- Labeling theory is really the theory of self-fulfilling prophecy; youth will become what they are told they can become.
- Labeling can be dangerous.
- Words and narrative matter impact attitudes, beliefs, and behavior.
- Heightened awareness of the power of words and language will help improve policies and practices.
- Change in narrative can create positive conditions for change.
- The same areas of the brain that are involved in fear conditioning are also involved in prejudice and stereotype.

Understanding the intersection of certain mental health disorders, trauma, and substance use is critical in serving youth. The fact that the developing brain lends itself to impulsivity, novelty-seeking behavior, and is highly vulnerable to threats should be considered when developing policies, practices, and approaches in serving youth. The ultimate goal is to appropriately manage expectations, change systems to match the scientific, social, and developmental realities of youth, and to effectively facilitate change.

If we know from observation and research that individuals become what they are told they become; that individuals fall into the social constructs that are made for them, namely, through narrative—then logic would have it that if we change the narrative, we can encourage change in an individual. If we change narrative, we can change systems. Labeling theory is based on this premise—you are what they say you are.

Systems should place specific emphasis on the narrative. A few things to consider:

- Policies—does the narrative in your policies and daily practices reflect the change environment you seek?
- What kind of posters or artwork do you have on your walls? Does the physical environment support the change you seek?

Practical application(s)
Let us consider the cognitive behavioral therapy model in the process of changing individuals and systems.

Cognitive Behavioral Therapy (CBT) is an evidence-based structured practice that supports behavior change through skills building. The CBT frame focuses on the interplay between thoughts, feelings, and behavior. The basic premise is that increased awareness of thoughts can impact feelings and behavior or becoming aware of behavior can impact feelings and thoughts. There is fluidity in the model; the point is that there is keen recognition that our thoughts do in fact influence our behavior.

One of the main objectives of this textbook is to equip the reader (and the systems they are attached to) with tools for change as they facilitate change in youth. Change should happen in parallel. This is not just about an expectation for youth to change, but it is equally about systems that serve youth making change (Fig. 7.6).

Narrative therapy
Narrative therapy is based on the idea that all individuals have a running narrative or about themselves and that these narratives can be edited and/or adapted for improved functionality. The therapy was designed to effectively separate a person from the problem. When two therapists, David Epston and Michael White, established narrative therapy in the early 1980s, they sought to create conditions that would allow individuals to externalize issues (see themselves as good and capable of change) as opposed to internalize issue (not see themselves as good and incapable of change) (Freeman et al. 1997).

Narrative therapy employs the power of storytelling as a means of developing deeper understanding of "self," growth, development, and healing. Epston and White would provide an example similar to this: "You are a person who made a mistake versus seeing themselves as a mistake." The confidence to make change is in the narrative.

The foundational roots of narrative therapy are as follows:

- The therapy is respectful.
- The therapy is non-blaming—moves away from shame.

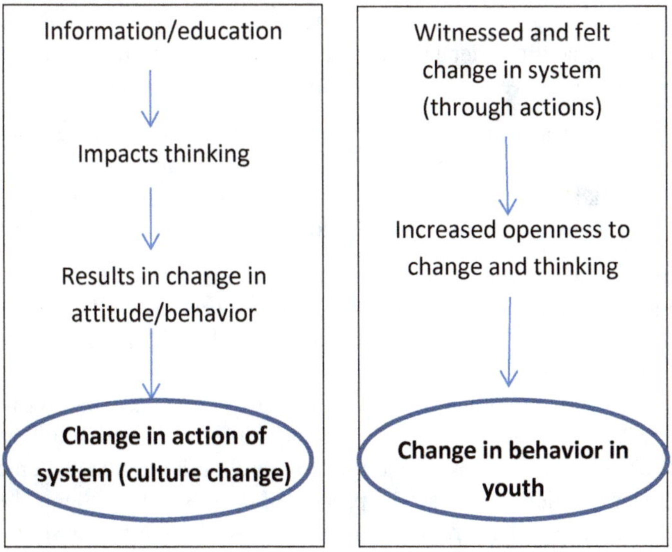

Fig. 7.6 Parallel change—as systems change, youth change

- The therapy allows the participant to be the expert.

Narrative therapy acknowledges external drivers of an individual's narrative:

- Environment shapes personal narrative, the things that are happening around an individual.
- Language (as we discovered in this chapter) shapes narrative.
- An individual's working narrative may serve as vehicle for understanding the world.
- Recognition that an individual's story may not be shared with others, but it doesn't render it any less valued and/or valuable.

Narrative therapy employs several techniques, but here are a few key ones (Epston and White 1995; Scott et al. 2013):

- Individual storytelling = allowing the individual to tell their respective story. When an individual can tell their story, they are more likely to find meaning and purpose too.
- Helping an individual effectively separates the problem or issue from themselves—"you are not the problem, the problem is the problem." This increases capacity for change.
- Taking problems down to their most common denominator—make the problems small and palatable. Tackle one element at a time, which allows for creating attainable goals that can be reached, which increases motivation for change.
- Open up the space and opportunity for individuals to create meaning from their own experiences and hold the reality that there is no absolute truth. This is termed

existentialism in the literature. This creates the condition for an individual to see the world as a new frontier providing a new opportunity to reconstruct a more positive and productive narrative of themselves.

Narrative therapy is a trauma-informed approach that employs the element of play and freedom to change that is required for accelerated change. This form of therapy or the framework at least can be used not just with youth, but in systems.

What is the narrative of your system? How can it be changed?

One way that a system can evaluate their implicit bias
The Implicit Association Test (IAT) is a free, online source that will allow for thoughtful assessment of implicit biases. You can access the IAT by searching for "the Harvard IAT."

I encourage every individual who works with a system to take the IAT if you have not done so. When you go the website, it provides a full explanation of what the IAT is, instructions on how to proceed and how to interpret the results that emerge.

Once biases are identified, start the process of deconstructing them.

Take the IAT after behavioral modification and see if your biases shift—use it as a means to measure shifts in behavior and biases.

References

Alter, A. (2010). Why its dangerous to label people: "Why labeling a person "black", "rich" or "smart" make it so. In *Psychology Today*.

Amodio, D. M. (2014). The neuroscience of prejudice and stereotyping. *Nature Reviews Neuroscience, 15,* 670–682.

Benitez-Burraco, A. (2017). How the language we speak affects the way we think. *Psychology Today*. Retrieved February 2017 from https://www.psychologytoday.com/us/blog/the-biolinguistic-turn/201702/how-the-language-we-speak-affects-the-way-we-think.

Bennett, M. W. (2017). The implicit racial bias in sentencing: The next frontier. *Yale LJF*, *126*, 381. www.yalelawjournal.com/forum/the-implicit-racial-bias-in-sentencing.

Bernburg, J. G., Krohn, M. D. & Rivera, C. J. (2006). Official labeling, criminal embeddedness, and subsequent delinquency: A longitudinal test of labeling theory. *Journal of Research In Crime & Delinquency*, *43*(1), 67–88 (Academic Search Premier). https://doi.org/10.1177/0022427805280068

Berry, D. S., & Finch-Wero, J. L. (1993). Accuracy in face perception: A view from ecological psychology. *Journal of Personality, 61,* 497–521.

Blair, I. V., & Banaji, M. R. (1996). Automatic and controlled processes in stereotype priming. *Journal of Personality and Social Psychology, 70*(6), 1142–1163.

Blair, I. V., Steiner, J. F., & Havranek, E. P. (2011). Unconscious (implicit) bias and health disparities: Where do we go from here? *The Permanente Journal, 15*(2), 71–78.

Block, P., & Grund, T. (2014). Multidimensional homophily in friendship networks. *Network Science, 2*(2), 189–212.

Braithwaite, J. (1989). *Crime, shame and reintegration*. Melbourne: Cambridge University Press.

Brantlinger, E. (1991). Social class distinctions in adolescents' reports of problems and punishment in school. *Behavioral Disorders, 17,* 36–46.

Carroll, J. B. (Ed.) (1997) [1956]. Language, thought, and reality: Selected writings of Benjamin Lee Whorf. Cambridge, Mass: Technology Press of Massachusetts Institute of Technology.

Crossman, A. (2018). An overview of labeling theory: Developed in the 1960s and still Widely relevant today. https://www.thoughtco.com/labeling-theory-3026627.

Davis, A. (2003). *Are prisons obsolete?* (p. 84). New York: Seven Stories Press.

Devine, P. G. (1989). Stereotypes and prejudice: Their automatic and controlled components. *Journal of Personality and Social Psychology, 56*(1), 5–18.

Dovidio, J. F., Kawakami, K., & Gaertner, S. L. (2002). Implicit and explicit prejudice and interracial interaction. *Journal of Personality and Social Psychology, 82*(1), 62–68.

Ellison, J. (2005). Definitions of, and distinctions between, shame and guilt: A facet analysis. *Dissertation Abstracts International*, *64*(03), 1537 (UMI No. 3085863).

Engell, A. D., et al. (2007). Implicit trustworthiness decisions: automatic coding of face properties in the human amygdala. *Journal of Cognitive Neuroscience, 19*:1508–1519. https://doi.org/10.1162/jocn.2007.19.9.1508, PMID: 17714012.

Epston, D., & White, M. (1995). Consulting your consultants: A means to the co-construction of alternative knowledges. In S. Friedman (Ed.), *The reflecting team in action: Collaborative practice in family therapy* (pp. 277–313). NewYork: Guilford Press.

Ernesto London. (2017). Rio de Janeiro, 'Complete Vulnerability' as violence surges. *The New York Times*. November 18, 2017.

Fazio, R. H., Jackson, J. R., Dunton, B. C., & Williams, C. J. (1995). Variability in automatic activation as an unobtrusive measure of racial attitudes: A bona fide pipeline? *Journal of Personality and Social Psychology, 69*(6), 1013–1027.

FitzGerald, C., & Hurst, S. (2017). Implicit bias in healthcare professionals: a systematic review. *BMC medical ethics, 18*(1), 19. https://doi.org/10.1186/s12910-017-0179-8.

Freeman, J., et al. (2014). Amygdala responsivity to high-level social information from unseen faces. *Journal of Neuroscience*, *34*(32), 10573–10581. https://doi.org/10.1523/JNEUROSCI.5063-13.2014.

Freeman, J. C., Epston, D., & Lobovits, D. (1997). *Playful approaches to serious problems: Narrative therapy with children and their families*. NewYork: W.W. Norton.

Fullagar, S. (2003). Wasted lives the social dynamics of shame and youth suicide. *Journal of Sociology, 39*(3), 291–307.

Gilbert, S. J., Swencionis, J. K., & Amodio, D. M. (2012). Evaluative versus trait representation in intergroup social judgments: Distinct roles of anterior temporal lobe and prefrontal cortex. *Neuropsychologia, 50,* 3600–3611.

Gladwell, Malcolm. (2005). *Blink: The power of thinking without thinking*. New York: Little, Brown And Co.

Glaser, J. (2014). *Suspect race*: *Causes and consequences of racial profiling*. Oxford, UK: Oxford University Press.

Goff, P. A. et al. (2016). *The science of justice*: *Race, arrests and police use of force.* Center for Policing Equity. Retrieved July 2016 from http://policingequity.org/wp-content/uploads/2016/07/CPE_SoJ_Race-Arrests-UoF_2016-07-08-1130.pdf.

Gordon, R., Della Piana, L., & Keleher, T. (2000). *Facing the consequences*: *An examination of racial discrimination in U.S. public schools*. Oakland, CA: Applied Research Center.

Greenwald, A. G., Poehlman, T. A., Uhlmann, E., Banaji, M. R. (2009). Understanding and using the implicit association test: III. Meta-analysis of predictive validity. *Journal of Personality and Social Psychology*, *97*(1), 17–41.

Gregory, J. F. (1997). Three strikes and they're out: African American boys and American schools'responses to misbehavior. *International Journal of Adolescence and Youth, 7*(1), 25–34.

Hall, W. J., et al. (2015). Implicit racial/ethnic bias among health care professionals and its influence on health care outcomes: a systematic review. *American Journal of Public Health, 105,* e60–e76.

Imich, A. J. (1994). Exclusions from school: Current trends and issues. *Educational Research*, (1), 3–11.

Kaeser, S. C. (1979). Suspensions in school discipline. *Education and Urban Society, 11,* 465–484.

King, R. D. & Johnson, B. D. (2016). A punishing look: Skin tone and afrocentric features in the halls of justice. *American journal of Chemical Society*, *122*, 90.

Knutson, J. (1977). *Labeling theory: A critical examination* (Rep. No. 3) Stockholm, Sweden: Scientific Group.

Lamm, C., Meltzoff, A. N., & Decety, J. (2010). How do we empathize with someone who is not like us? A functional magnetic resonance imaging study. *Journal of Cognitive Neuroscience, 22,* 362–376.

LeDoux, J. E. (2000). Emotion circuits in the brain. *Annual Review of Neuroscience, 23,* 155–184.

May, M. (2017). Shame! a system psychodynamic perspective. *Shame! the value of shame exploring a health resource in cultural contexts*, Chap. 2 (pp. 43–59). Springer.

McCarthy, J. D., & Hoge, D. R. (1987). The social construction of school punishment: Racial disadvantage out of universalistic process. *Social Forces, 65,* 1101–1120.

McPherson, M., et al. (2001). Birds of a feather: Homophily in social networks. *Annual Review of Sociology*, *27*, 415–444. https://doi.org/10.1146/annurev.soc.27.1.415.

Mongold, J., & Edwards, B. (2014). Reintegrative shaming: Theory into practice. *Journal of Theoretical and Philosophical Criminology*. *6*, 205–212.

Morrison, A. P. (1984). Working with shame in psychoanalytic treatment. *Journal of the American Psychoanalytic Association, 32*(3), 479–505.

Nash, D., & Kilday, A. M. (2010). The history and theory of shame—then and now. In *Cultures of Shame*. London: Palgrave Macmillan.

National Association of Secondary School Principals. (2000). *Statement on civil rights implications of zero tolerance programs*. Washington, DC: Testimony presented to the United States Commission on Civil Rights.

Oakes, J., Ormseth, T., Bell, R., & Camp, P. (1990). *Multiplying inequalities: The effects of race, social class, and tracking on opportunities to learn mathematics and science*. Washington, DC: Rand.

Richardson, L. S. (2017). Systemic triage: implicit racial bias in the criminal courtroom. *Yale LJ*, *126*, 862.

Riezler, K. (1943). Comment on the social psychology of shame. *The American Journal of Sociology, 48*(4), 457–465.

Rooth, D.-O. (2010). Automatic associations and discrimination in hiring: Real world evidence. *Labour Economics, 17,* 523–534.

Rosenthal, R., & Jacobson, L. (1992). *Pygmalion in the classroom* (Expanded ed.). New York: Irvington.

Scheff, T. J. (1988). Shame and conformity: The deference-emotion system. *American Sociological Review, 53*(3), 397–398.

Schlosser, E. (1998). The prison industrial complex. *The Atlantic*. Retrieved December 1998 from https://www.theatlantic.com/magazine/archive/1998/12/the-prison-industrial-complex/304669/.

Scimecca, J. A. (1977). Labeling theory and personal construct theory: Toward the measurement of individual variation. *Journal of Criminal Law & Criminology*, *68*, 652.

Scott, S. D., Brett-MacLean, P., Archibald, M., & Hartling, L. (2013). Protocol for a systematic review of the use of narrative storytelling and visual-arts-based approaches as knowledge translation tools in healthcare. *Systematic Reviews, 2,* 19. https://doi.org/10.1186/2046-4053-2-19.

Singer, T., et al. (2004). Empathy for pain involves the affective but not sensory components of pain. *Science, 303,* 1157–1162.

Singer, T., et al. (2006). Empathic neural responses are modulated by the perceived fairness of others. *Nature, 439,* 466–469.

Skiba, R. J., Michael, R. S., Nardo, A. C., et al. (2002). *The Urban Review, 34,* 317. https://doi.org/10.1023/A:1021320817372.

Smirnov, I., & Thurner, S. (2017). Formation of homophily in academic performance: Students change their friends rather than performance. *PLoS ONE, 12*(8), e0183473. https://doi.org/10.1371/journal.pone.0183473.

Steele, C., Spencer, S., & Aronson, J. (2002). Contending with group image: The psychology of stereotype and social identity threat. In M. Zanna (Ed.), *Advances in experimental social psychology* (pp. 379–440). New York: Academic Press.

Todorov, A., et al. (2011). Task-invariant brain responses to the social value of faces. *Journal of Cognitive Neuroscience*, *23*, 2766–2781. https://doi.org/10.1162/jocn.2011.21616, PMID: 21254805.
Todorov, A., & Engell, A. D. (2008). The role of the amygdala in implicit evaluation of emotionally neutral faces. *Social Cognitive and Affective Neuroscience*, *3*, 303–312, https://doi.org/10.1093/scan/nsn033, PMID: 19015082.
Todorov, A., Mandisodza, A. N., Goren, A., & Hall, C. C. (2005). *Science, 308,* 1623.
Townsend, B. L. (2000). The Disproportionate Discipline of African American Learners: Reducing School Suspensions and Expulsions. *Exceptional Children, 66*(3), 381–391. https://doi.org/10.1177/001440290006600308
Van Bavel, J. J., Packer, D. J., & Cunningham, W. A. (2008). The neural substrates of in-group bias: A functional magnetic resonance imaging investigation. *Psychological Science, 11,* 1131–1139.
Winston, J. S., et al. (2002). Automatic and intentional brain responses during evaluation of trustworthiness of faces. *Nature Neuroscience*, *5*, 277–283. https://doi.org/10.1038/nn816, PMID: 11850635.

Chapter 8
Digging Deeper into "Fear"

Fear is a natural primitive response for survival in all human beings. When there is a threat (perceived or real), the fear response kicks in and helps us to appropriately seek safety. In other words, fear is natural…until it is not. Fear is meant to be a time-limited response that should turn off (theoretically) once the threat is gone.

The reality is…some among us (i.e., youth with a history of trauma) live in a constant state of fear. Fear "on" all the time = trauma.

So many interactions are driven by fear:

Police–constituent,
Parent–child,
Teacher–student,
Youth–adult, and
White–Black.
We essentially have fear-on-fear interactions—which perpetuates trauma.

We must understand the role of fear in order to manage it and ultimately to be able to operate at the height of our moral beings. Racism and all the other "isms" won't go away until we acknowledge and eliminate the role of fear.

This chapter puts "fear" in greater context, familiarizing the reader with what it is, what it can do and then challenges all of us to acknowledge and manage it as a means of moving toward sustained systems change.

By the end of this chapter, you should be able to

- Understand the neurobiological basis of fear (quick review),
- Appreciate the **fear appeals theory**,
- Know the **drive theory**,
- Recognize the power of **fear** to impact behavior positively or negatively,
- Acknowledge **fear** as a primal and potentially dangerous drive,
- Appreciate the role fear has played in the construction and maintenance of systems, and
- Employ ways to eliminate **fear** from the work you are doing and further to remove fear from the change process (a huge requirement).

A. Moreland-Capuia, *Training for Change*,
https://doi.org/10.1007/978-3-030-19208-2_8

Setting the stage
In the early 1990s, a movie called *Boyz N The Hood* (this is the correct spelling, just in case you were wondering) came out. The film depicted the story of a young man named Tre (character was played by a young Cuba Gooding Jr.) who was sent to live with his father in South Central Los, Angeles. Tre had the structure, love, and support of family but had a group of friends who had limited exposure to the kinds of support he enjoyed. Tre, despite him being a relatively good kid, was subject to the harsh realities of being a young, Black male in South Central Los Angeles. Daily, Tre bore witness to relative injustices in the context of his friends and neighborhood; he saw hopelessness, watched friends die, police brutality, drug use, and chronic marginalization on the regular. Tre was a good kid, didn't cause trouble, and strived to live by the values that his father instilled him.

There were several impactful, discussion-worthy scenes in the movie; however, one of the most poignant scenes came when Tre was approached by the police. Tre hadn't done anything wrong other than be a Black man who fit an unfortunate stereotype of being a threat. In this scene, Tre and his friend were confronted by the police. Tre posed a question, which angered the officer, so as a show of power, the officer grabbed Tre by his jacket collar, pressed him up against the car and began telling him things like: "I can't stand little kids like you." He started with a line of assumptions to include that Tre was a gang member and/or a thug. When Tre tried to tell the office that he didn't do anything, the officer pulled out his Smith and Wesson gun, firmly pressed it against Tre's throat, and said: "you think you are tough? Who is tough now? I can blow your head off boy." As the officer continued with his narrative, tears began to stream down Tre's cheeks. Eventually, the officer recognized that his response may have been out of proportion to any perceived wrong—so he let Tre go.

From the scene and interaction, a few things were highlighted:

- The officers' assumption/narrative, which quickly evolved into threat and even perhaps a representation of the officers' past exposure to trauma on the job or elsewhere.
- The incredible fear that overtook Tre when the officers stopped him in the first place. Tre was very afraid.
- Power dynamics and what drives them.

When Tre was released from the grip of the officer, he made his way home, he was visibly shaken, but more than that he was angry. In the safety of his home, Tre threw down his jacket, started crying and air punching as he screamed: "I am tired of this sxxt!" The anger was so palpable.

What might we learn from the two scenes from the film *Boyz N The Hood* described here?

A. A fear-on-fear response is noted. The officer operating based on deep-seated underlying assumptions and narrative shaped by fear.
B. Tre conditioned by the environment and experiences to be afraid and mistrusting of police and the larger criminal judicial system.

Tre's story is the story of many youth in this country, disproportionately youth of color. Fear is functional until it is not. Fear is a robust emotion and driver of behavior. As a society, we do not talk about "fear" enough. To the extent that we recognize the role of "fear" in systems, interactions, and ways of living is the extent that we can effectively make changes.

As outlined in Chap. 7, the same areas of the brain that facilitate the brain's ability to make quick judgments (also the foundation for stereotype and prejudice) are the same areas of the brain that mediate the fear response. A coincidence? Not so much.

One of the overarching goals of this textbook is system change. Again, I hold the conviction that systems are intimately attached to people; systems don't change if people don't change and people don't change if they don't "feel" something. To this end, it is imperative to make a few connections. Understanding the pervasiveness of fear and the role it (historically and presently) plays in building and reinforcing systems is critical. We'll take a deductive approach, start out with the big picture (the system), and then get down to more specific elements (people who make up systems).

Let us focus on the founding of America in 1776. Some historians would argue that fear drove much of the decision-making of the framers of the constitution. The founders' greatest fear was that government if not constructed thoughtfully could oppress people as opposed to inspire and support individualism. They shared a core conviction that resolute power was lethal. To mitigate the feared lethality of resolute power, the Founders constructed the government via the constitution by doing the following:

- Three branches of government (legislative, judicial, and executive) were designed to balance one another.
- All branches were created to be a stopgap for the each other—each branch had power, but the power of each branch of government was designed to be checked and vetted by the power of the other established branches. This is what is deemed checks and balances.
- State power was maintained, and federal power was established as a check and balance to state power.
- Term limits were created for various government positions.
- There was a process created to remove individuals from government in the case of corruption.

"Fear" of power overtaking and overwhelming the country influenced the shaping of the country. "Fear" compelled our founders to establish laws that would limit and control the power of government. I am not making the argument that all "fear" is bad, but I am asking each reader to open their mind to understanding the role fear has played in powerful social, political, and economic constructs (also known as systems).

Staying on the theme of the use of "fear" in limiting and controlling.

Some historians would argue that the Civil War was about "fear" of losing honor and economic power. The southern states were benefitting richly from slave labor (tobacco and cotton fields predominant). The subtext was also about power, we've heard the cliché phrase that money is power—it is and historically has been. Over

600,000 people lost their lives in the Civil War—the price and burden of "fear" was heavy.

The Civil War abolished slavery…sort of. As mentioned in a prior chapter, many would contend that slavery took on a new form with the signing of the 13th amendment. There was a transition from slaves in the fields to slaves in prison. Disproportionately, communities of color were criminalized, imprisoned, and the subjects of free labor for major corporations—this was termed the prison industrial complex.

There was a focused effort to build an image of scary, inhumane, beastly individuals not worthy of love and/or care—this is the only way that enslaving individuals (in a field or in a prison system) was palatable; they had to be considered "other" and/or "not human." The othering was then supported by the stoking of fearing these "others" as dangerous threats to society. Are we able to appreciate the role of fear here?

Again, fear (as an emotional and neurobiological phenomenon) has a primitive, functional role in helping human beings appropriately seek safety in the face of threat. Fear, by itself, is not bad. What makes fear interesting is what I call socialized fear. In other words, it is who gets to construct threats. And how constructed threats function in how whole systems and communities behave.

When we talk about racism in America and abroad, we often talk about it from the reference point of power. However, I could contend that taking this approach has not resulted in notable change. What really undergirds racism (as a very powerful social construct) is fear.

Moving forward in history, we get to the Civil Rights movement. The Civil Rights movement was primarily about shifting the narrative. Activists were challenging individuals to get back to humanity, to move away from the powerful construction of "other" as a threat and as "dangerous" as "less than." The Civil Rights movement was really a movement in "addressing and eliminating fear."

What was feared? Fear that people of color would take something that artificially belonged to majority culture. Fear that the communities that had been built would be destroyed, ravaged, and overtaken. Fear that giving "others" access to wealth would somehow limit dominant cultures wealth. The fears were myriad and sundry. I could provide multiple examples in history, where fear was dominant and had a starring role in influencing policies, practices, laws, and systems.

Barry Glasner wrote *The Culture of Fear: Why Americans Are Afraid of the Wrong Things* and asserts that fear as communication tactic has been present every step of the way in the evolution of humanity, but specifically points to terrorism. He writes: "In the age of 9/11, the Iraq War, financial collapse, and Amber Alerts, our society is defined by fear." Glasner contends that given our collective history, it should come as no surprise that over 75% of Americans indicate that they are more fearful now than ever before (Glassner 1999). But are we living in exceptionally dangerous times?

The real question is: who gets to construct our current reality? Who gets to determine what is a threat or not? Might it be helpful for all systems that serve human beings, youth in particular, to consider the role of "fear" in their construction and operation? Further, consider if the current construction and operation are useful, effective.

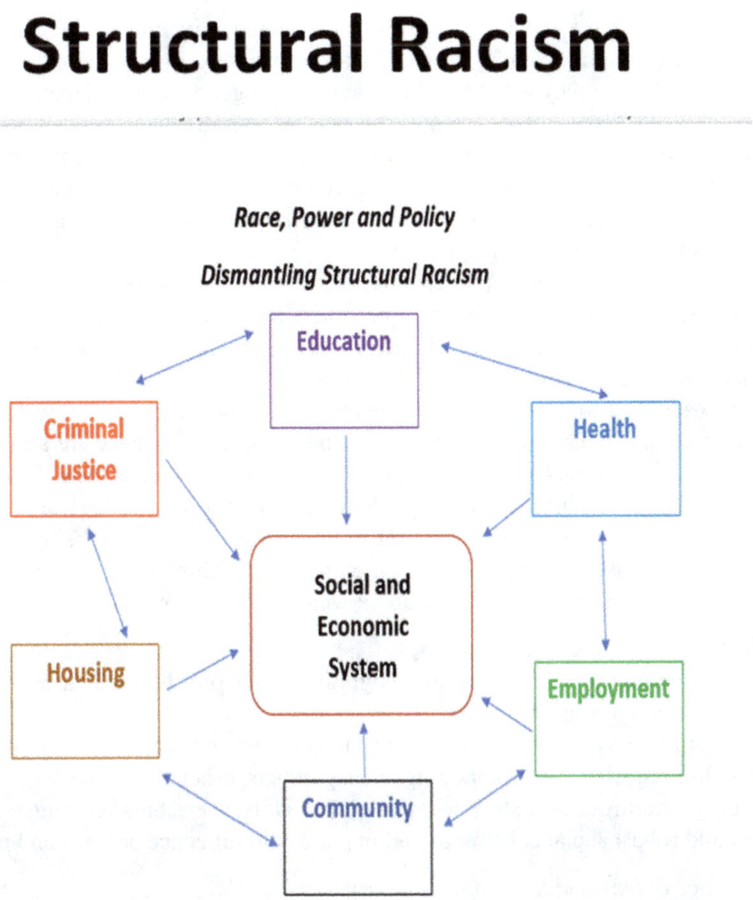

Fig. 8.1 Structural racism and systems that have historically supported it have been powerfully shaped by "fear" >>>>power

In Fig. 8.1, elements of structural racism have been shown in two prior chapters because it is a powerful image. In this context, however, I'd like the reader to think about each system represented and the role that "fear" has played in shaping the system. Further, how each of these fear-laden systems has undergirded social and economic structures.

Fear, quick review

- Fear is a natural response (protective even), until it is not. The fear response was designed to help human beings appropriately assess threat and seek safety accordingly.
- Every human being has experienced fear, anxiety, and stress at some point in their lives, but not everyone experiences fear that never shuts off.
- Fear "on" all the time = fear conditioning = trauma.

In prior chapters, I gave the example of a traditional scary movie where the character is running from a potential threat. Character has keys in hand, attempting to seek safety, but when they get to the door, they cannot get coordinated enough to get the key in the lock and end up dropping the keys. Most individuals can picture this scene and appreciate the phenomenon in "other" but often struggle to see it in themselves. The bottom line is that if you are alive, you have been afraid at some point in your life. If you are alive, you've had moments where you were so afraid that you couldn't think straight and/or "get it together."

It turns out that the "fear" response is mostly a "bottom brain" function. Fear is about survival and the brain, too, goes into survival mode. Areas of the brain that become most active include the amygdala, the limbic area (where emotions live), thalamus, and areas of the brain stem. Sound familiar? Yes, the medial prefrontal cortex and anterior cingulate cortex are involved in the fear process as well. However, all the studies point to the prominence of the amygdala when we are afraid.

If am a surviving (bottom brain predominant), it can come at the risk of not being able to thrive and think (top brain predominant). If this neurobiological phenomenon is understood, then it makes it easier to understand why human beings in a "fear" state often make poor decisions and aren't rational. Think survival mode. You have been in survival mode too. Think about what it felt like for you.

Making the connection

Fear is an emotion. If placed in a cognitive behavioral frame, fear as an emotion impacts thoughts and behavior.

In our society, "fear" has become an intentional tactic to motivate behavior—it has been used consistently in marketing to sell products, in health care to encourage or discourage healthy or unhealthy behavior, respectively, in teaching/rearing/socialization to build robust social constructs, and in politics to influence policies and practices.

The face of fear and fear appeals theory

- Charles Darwin thought that the ability of humans to display and perceive emotional states on a face evolved to convey nonverbal signals rapidly. Darwin's 1872 publication on Expressions is said to have been foundational in establishing the study of emotion and behavior, now known as psychology. Darwin focused on the biology of emotion, noted what he could about the physiology of emotion, and (where in his time much more was known) the anatomy of facial expressions. He was quoted as saying that he "notices things which easily escape attention, and observe them carefully" (Ekman 2009).
- An example of emotional states of the face driving nonverbal signals: If an individual's expression could communicate a potential threat, for example, his neighbors would be able to respond quickly and direct their attention to the source of the danger.
- Thus, a common view is that the **perception of fear** might guide appropriate visual motor behavior.

Work by Adolphs et al. provided additional perspective on fear and facial expressions and suggests that discerning fear in faces may depend on how one scrutinizes them in the first place. Adolph and colleagues include the element of perception a bit more robustly. Darwin, in his 1872 work, did allude to the fact that while there is universality in emotion, there might be cultural variation in how those facial expressions are interpreted (Ohman 1986; Adolphs et al. 2005). Adolph and colleagues point to the amygdala's role in fear recognition and perception of emotion. Further, the processing of eyes in emotion perception was illuminated in study of Adolph et al.

Other studies highlighted bilateral brain lesions in the amygdala, a region of the medial temporal lobe known to be critical for the perception of fear (Vuilleumier 2005).

Vuilleumier and colleagues had 26 participants with known lesions in the amygdala and hippocampus. Study design (Vuilleumier et al. 2004):

- There were 13 healthy controls matched for sex, age, etc.
- Both treatment group and controls were given pictures of fearful or neutral faces in a display (faces were shown in the context of task-relevant versus task-irrelevant). Task-relevant stimuli were things related to the study, and task-irrelevant stimuli were simply another term for distraction and not necessarily related to the task at hand.

Results include the following: Functional MRI revealed increased fusiform cortex activation for both treatment group and controls when the faces were in task-relevant position.

- When shown fearful faces, healthy controls, and individuals with hippocampal damage demonstrated increased activation in the fusiform (a part of the brain that plays a role in recognition, perception) and occipital cortex (visual cortex).
- When participants with amygdala damage were shown fearful faces, there was not robust activation of the fusiform and occipital cortex.

Study of Vuilleumier et al. demonstrated the connection between the visual cortex and the amygdala in the perception/interpretation of the emotion fear. A human beings ability to sense threat comes from our senses, for example,

- If you smell natural gas—this evokes a response.
- If you feel the ground beneath you moving—this evokes a response.
- If you see a big spider on the wall—this evokes a response and so on and so forth.

Vuilleumier and colleagues provide evidence from functional MRI to explain the connection between what a human can see (visually) and impact it has on emotions like fear. The amygdala and the visual cortex are connected (Vuilleumier et al. 2004).

Multiple studies have demonstrated and implicated the amygdala in early and even unconscious recognition of "fear" in faces (Troiani and Schultz 2013).

Back to the fear appeals theory.

In the literature, the fear appeals theory defines a strategy for motivating people to take a particular action, endorse a particular policy, or buy a particular product, by arousing fear.

The fear appeal is constructed as a cogent message that seeks to provoke fear as a means of modulating/influencing behavior and diverting behavior through the threat of impending danger or harm (De Hoog et al. 2005).

A fear appeal has the following components:

- Presents a risk,
- Presents the vulnerability to the risk, and
- May or may not provide a way to mitigate the risk.

De Hoog and colleagues investigated the use of fear in communications to educate and eventually support the changing of individual's behavior with regard to severe health risk. In specific, the study wanted to test the impact of the following components on severe health risk and impacting change in behavior through fear communication:

- Vulnerability to the severe health risk (communicating to persons with highest health risks),
- Quality of the argument supporting a recommendation to alleviate the risk (are the arguments sound),
- The source of the recommendation (the legitimacy of the knowledge and education around the health risk), and
- Processing and acceptance of recommendations being made to alleviate the risk.

Results were as follows:

- The quality of the argument heavily impacted attitudes toward the recommendation but did not impact intention to act on the recommendations (attitudes affected but action not so much).
- Vulnerability to the health risks did impact drive to act but no so much attitude (the study points out that this effect was heavily influenced by perceived threat and positive reactions to the recommendations).

Individuals are more open to change when something directly impacts them and/or is perceived as a threat and inspire the drive to seek safety.

Maddux, 1983 on Fear appeals theory
Fear appeals are persuasive messages that attempt to arouse fear by emphasizing the potential danger and harm that will befall individuals if they do not adopt the messages' recommendations (Dillard et al. 1996; Maddux and Rogers 1983).

The effects of fear appeals on persuasion were investigated in a study designed to examine a combined model of protection motivation theory and self-efficacy theory.

The study revealed that the probability of a threat's occurrence and the effectiveness of a coping response had positive impact on intentions (desire to act or respond to recommendations and/or a message) and to change behavior.

The study also highlighted the following concepts to include self-efficacy and its impact on intention, protection motivation theory, and two decision-making strategies that individuals employ in the presence of a fear appeal to include a precaution strategy and a hyper-defensiveness strategy.

The interaction effect was interpreted in terms of two new decision-making strategies that people use when confronted with a fear appeal: a *precaution* strategy and a *hyper-defensiveness* strategy.

The combination of protection motivation theory and self-efficacy (individuals' confidence in their ability to make change) is thought to be robust drivers for attitude change (Maddux and Rogers 1983).

Tannenbaum and colleagues conducted a comprehensive meta-analysis investigating fear appeals' effectiveness for influencing attitudes, intentions, and behaviors. The study concluded the following: "fear appeals are particularly effective when the communication depicts relatively high amounts of fear, includes an efficacy message, stresses severity and susceptibility, recommends one-time only behaviors, and targets audiences that include a larger percentage of female message recipients" (Tannenbaum et al. 2015).

Some would contend that the only reason we use fear to impact behavior is because it is the only thing we've been taught. Is there another way?

The Drive theory

The word drive is both a verb and a noun.

Webster's definition of "drive" the verb = propel or carry along by force in a specified direction

The noun (and psychological definition) for drive = an innate, biologically determined urge to attain a goal or satisfy a need. Other psychological definitions for drive include increased arousal and internal motivation to reach a specific goal.

In our culture, the word "driven" has mostly been formulated to speak to someone's level of motivation. The drive theory combines motivation, learning, conditioning, and the process of forming habits as a means of understanding and framing human behavior.

Traditionally, social scientists distinguish between a primary (primitive) drive and a secondary (acquired, influenced by culture and environment) drive. In the literature, primary drives are intimately attached to getting basic needs met like access to air, water, and food—all things needed for human survival. Secondary drives are things that humans take in and learn from their external environment; they consider forces that dictate cultural relevance like what is socially acceptable or popular. The drive theory suggests that all human beings are motivated by primary and/or secondary drives and the chief objective is secure means of quelling the drive. Quelling the drive inspires behavior. If a human being is thirsty or lonely (primary drives), they will do what they must to quell the thirst and/or the loneliness. In other words, the drive dictates the behavior.

Do take note of the importance of environment, conditioning, and socialization in the case of secondary drives.

In the book, Principles of Behavior, Clark L. Hull asserts that the process human beings pursue to decrease and quell a drive is critical in the process of learning. In this way, Hull made famous the drive reduction theory and highlighted its role in both learning and motivation (Hull 1943). Hull's work is consistent with the neurobiological understanding of fear acquisition as a conditioning process.

Cottrell and colleagues investigated the impact that an audience (active spectators) versus "the mere presence of others (passive spectators) had on dominant responses (also known as habits)." The original study consisted of 45 University students who were asked to perform a pseudo-recognition task. They were broken into the following three groups (Cottrell et al. 1968):

- 15 performed alone,
- 15 performed in front of an audience, and
- 15 performed in the presence of two people were not spectators.

The results included

- Those with an audience had heightened expression of habits. They defaulted to habits (which was not always favorable). If the habit was to mess up and forget words, this was the habit on display.
- The mere presence of people (no audience) did not result in heightened expression of habits (dominant responses).

The study concluded that the presence of an audience affects individual performance/behavior. Human beings default to what they've been taught (Zajonc 1965; Cottrell et al. 1968). A 2001 study by Platania and colleagues retested and confirmed the theory of social facilitation, the mere presence of others, and their respective influence on human's defaulting to learned behavior (Platania and Moran 2001).

Point: If humans default to what they've been taught in certain social context, so do systems.

Humans experience arousal (drive) to achieve a particular goal; habits (or dominant responses) dictate the means for reaching that goal.

Key aspects of the drive theory are as follows:

- Theory is shaped by the concept of "tension."
- Theory suggests that a threat (fear appeal) that portrays negative consequences of noncompliance to a recommended behavior is expected to create fear (broken down: there will be trouble, if you don't do it).
- Compulsion or the drive to relieve the built-up tension (emotional, physical, and mental) inspires behavior (acting out) with the goal of reducing the tension from primary and/or secondary drive.
- In terms of fear-based communication, the greater the fear, the greater the compliance to message recommendations (whether they be positive or negative).

Protection Motivation Theory

- This theory is originally applied in the health setting (behavior changes that may or may not result in improved health). The theory has implications socially as well…(Boer and Seydel 1996).
- Protection motivation theory describes adaptive and maladaptive coping with a health threat as a result of two appraisal processes. A process of threat appraisal and a process of coping appraisal, in which the behavioral options to diminish the threat, are evaluated (Boer and Seydel 1996; Lazarus 1966; Leventhal 1970; Milne et al. 2000).

- The appraisal of the health threat and the appraisal of the coping responses result in the intention to perform adaptive responses (protection motivation) or may lead to maladaptive responses.
- Maladaptive responses are those that place an individual at health risk (Boer and Seydel 1996).

The protection motivation theory proposes that the intention to protect oneself depends upon four factors (Boer and Seydel 1996; Chu 1966):

- Perception of the *severity* of a threatened event,
- Perception of the likelihood of the occurrence, or *vulnerability,*
- The strength of the efficacy of the recommended preventive behavior, and
- Individuals' perception of our confidence in their ability to make change—also known as self-efficacy in the literature.

Reaction to fear appeals: Precaution strategy

- Precaution (noun): a measure taken in advance to avert possible evil or to secure good results.
- Who gets to construct the message and shape the narrative?

Stirling, in a 2007 article, demonstrated the relationship between precaution as a strategy and risk assessment. Further, the article delineates the intersection of risk (appraisal and management), ambiguity, uncertainty, and ignorance. Stirling concludes: "precaution offers a way to be more measured and rational about uncertainty, ambiguity, and ignorance." Hence, its role in the fear appeals spectrum (Stirling 2007).

One other reaction to fear appeals: Hyper-defensiveness strategy. According to Maddux and Rogers, if individuals feel heightened threat and possess the confidence and capacity to change the behavior, they are more likely to change behavior (even in the absence of appreciating the benefits of the behavior change). The behavior change is theorized to be driven more so driven by human desire to relieve anxiety than avoidance of danger—this phenomenon is termed hyper-defensiveness in the literature and as one antidote to the fear appeals theory (Maddux and Rogers 1983).

A meta-analysis by de Hoog and colleagues investigated fear arousal as a staged model that (de Hoog et al. 2007)

- Delineate the cognitive processes underlying persuasion through fear-arousing communications.
- Demonstrate that threat-induced defensive processing does not interfere with the effectiveness of fear-arousing communications but actually contributes to it.
- Show that vulnerability and severity manipulations have differential effects on measures of attitude as compared with intention and behavior.

Fear-arousing communication employed in health education campaigns typically emphasizes the negative consequence of certain behaviors as a means of motivating behavior change. This meta-analysis has an intentional focus on the effectiveness of fear messaging on the following:

- Differentiating fear manipulations severity of consequence, personal vulnerabilities and
- Differentiating between the types of fear messaging.

The study concluded the following (de Hoog et al. 2007):

- Severity (not vulnerability) robustly impacted intention to change and behavior.
- Vulnerability played an active role in processing biases.
- Extremely "fear-arousing" messages were no more effective than messages that stated the negative consequences of a certain behavior.

From literature, it is understood and demonstrated that fear as a tactic has been employed to modulate human behavior, build, and maintain systems. What is communicated is just as powerful as how and by whom it is communicated.

Vicarious (indirect, observational) transmission of fear
As described in prior chapters, fear has a primitive, protective role, and it can also become a conditioned response. Fear is meant to be time-limited—to serve its purpose in helping humans to protect themselves from immediate real and/or perceived threat. Once the threat is gone, the fear should theoretically dissipate. However, robust studies on fear illustrate that fear can become a conditioned (learned) response over time. Fear conditioning = fear that doesn't turn off = trauma. Fear conditioning, at this time, had been described as the result of an individual being directly subject to a fear-provoking event. In a 1977 review, Rachman rendered a thoughtful inquiry on the theory of fear acquisition as a form of conditioning. The article highlighted the following (Bandura 1969; Bandura 1971; Rachman 1977; Bandura et al. 1969):

- Made the connection between observational learning and modeling and fear conditioning.
- Highlighted that human behavior and emotional responses are a product of what is deemed "vicarious learning experiences."
- At the time that Rachman penned this piece, the concept of vicarious fear/trauma was not as well studied; it was a proposal—the thinking at the time (now confirmed with current studies) that "fear could be acquired" with indirect and/or direct scary experiences.

Rachman proposed that there were three important pathways to fear acquisition and further postulated that the fear conditioning process was both direct (a consequence of an individual directly experiencing a fear-provoking event) and indirect (an individual indirectly experiencing a fear-provoking event via observing, witnessing, memories being triggered) (Rachman 1968, 1977):

- Repeated exposure to scary things and subsequent conditioning. Learned fear. Direct.
- Two indirect methods to include
- Fear acquired, vicariously and
- Fear through information and/or instruction—fear stoked by information.

More recent studies by Bruchey and colleagues and Olson and colleagues confirm fear conditioning by proxy or the indirect acquisition of fear. Bruchey et al. showed that the retrieval of a fear memory can influence fear conditioning. Further, the study pointed out that establishing and retrieving memories related to fear producing events is critical in the fear conditioning process and to human survival. Once threat has been experienced, the body and the mind keep the score so that any cue or reminder of the event allows for quick response and avoidance of what feels like danger (Bruchey et al. 2010).

Olsson et al. demonstrated indirect acquisition of fear through social observation of a troubling event—they demonstrated that a person witnessing a troubling event triggered the amygdala and the fear conditioning process similar to an individual who had directly been subject to threat/trouble (Olsson et al. 2007).

As we consider the fear appeals theory, might we appreciate the connection between it and fear conditioning through vicarious transmission?

Exercises on identifying "fear" in various systems
I contend that systems haven't had the space, place, and/or opportunity to take pause and consider how they are constructed and what holds them together. The next set of exercises might be difficult for a few reasons, first when systems are asked to "consider" anything, it automatically feels like it (the system) is being blamed and second, it is difficult to get hearts and minds to open up in the presence of defensiveness. The objective of the next series of exercises is to help the reader think about systems (and individuals attached to them) in nonthreatening, nonjudgmental way by simply asking "have we considered and might we consider?" If the overarching goals are to move toward positive, inclusive change, then this set of exercises might be one way to forge the path to change.

In the next set of exercises, you will be given a system and asked to consider attitudes, behaviors, and conditions that might contribute to the current construction of the system. Then you will be asked to consider what role fear might play in the system (given everything you have learned thus far). You will use Fig. 8.1 as a reference point for system construction.

Fear in schools/education system
In the case of schools and education, previous chapters addressed the school-to-prison pipeline, but didn't get to the heart of it.

As of late, there has been an uptick in gun violence in schools. There are legitimate reasons to be concerned with and for the safety of our youth. The focus should be on perpetuators of the violence (what conditions have made it more likely that a young person would act violently) and the school environment (what are the conditions?). *Review Fig. 8.1 and consider the following:*

Attitude/behavior/situation	Consider the conditions, external (social, political, economic), internal (personal struggle)	Identify the fear (might you appreciate the role of fear in individuals who make up the system and the system itself)
Attitudes of teachers toward students of color and students in general		
The achievement gap, what would you attribute it to?		
The current construction of the education system. What is the goal?		
Increased violence, namely, gun violence in schools		

Fear in health care

Racial and ethnic disparities in health care have been studied and noted in adolescents and adults (who were once adolescents). Systematic reviews by Elster et al., Narayan et al., Peek et al., and Davis et al. demonstrate the depth and width of such disparities (Elster et al. 2003; Narayan and Scafide 2017; Peek et al. 2007; Davis et al. 2007).

Health care is an important system that plays a starring role in keeping communities and families healthy. In America and abroad, access and quality of care have been fleeting. Health is far greater than wealth. Some would argue that health is wealth. Healthy people build healthy economies. This truth has been well understood and has driven decisions about whom society deem worthy enough to be well, to be healthy. *Review Fig. 8.1 and consider the following:*

Attitude/behavior/situation	Consider the conditions, external (social, political, economic), internal (personal struggle)	Identify the fear (might you appreciate the role of fear in individuals who make up the system and the system itself)
Attitudes/behaviors of providers in healthcare systems		
Healthcare disparities		
Healthcare outcomes		

Fear in parenting and families

Parenting, family is a powerful. Love, belonging, and connection have kept whole generations alive and thriving. When family, as a system, is disrupted, communities, generations, and societies are disrupted.

There is much history provided about the construction of the Child Protective Services (CPS) also known as Child Welfare Services (CWS). There was early recognition (in the early 1800s) that children had the potential to be subject to harm; however, there were no formal governmental structures established to support his belief. There were socially formed groups and individuals that took it upon themselves to do the work. In the 1900s, nongovernmental groups were constructed to support the work of protecting children. Around the time of the Great Depression and under the leadership of Franklin Delano Roosevelt, governmental involvement in the protection of children became prominent with his New Deal Legislation, and federal financial resources were dedicated through the Social Security Act to taking care of chronically vulnerable populations to include the poor and children. It wasn't until the late 1970s that a formal construction of what we now know and understand as CPS was established.

The system was established to keep children safe and reduce harm. Our children both need and deserve protection. CPS is a system designed in such a way that it requires certified individuals (called mandatory reporters) to report when they suspect harm is being done to a child and/or children. Mandatory reports include but are not limited to healthcare providers, teachers, social workers, etc.—all persons who are intimately attached to other systems (education, health care).

CPS has become a system; unfortunately, it is perceived as a system that shames parents and destroys families. Even more unfortunate is the recognition that CPS as a system has negatively and disproportionately impacted communities and youth of color (Font et al. 2012; Ards et al. 2003; Chibnall et al. 2003; Child Welfare Information Gateway 2011).

There are data that demonstrate that mandatory reporters are more likely to assess a child and/or children as being in greater danger when they are persons of color. The consequences of CPS involvement are direr in the case of people of color as there are greater instances of termination of parental rights as an outcome (Child Welfare Information Gateway 2011).

There have been real efforts to remedy this disparity. Some questions that have emerged from the recognition of disparities include the following:

Is there a perception of greater danger when it comes to CPS and families, parents of color?

What role do socialization, racism, and history play in the disparities in CPS reporting?

Review Fig. 8.1 and consider the following:

Attitude/behavior/situation	Consider the conditions, external (social, political, economic), internal (personal struggle)	Identify the fear (might you appreciate the role of fear in individuals who make up the system and the system itself)
Attitudes/behaviors in CPS systems		
Disparities in reporting		
Disparities in termination of parental rights		
Perception of harm >>>> when it involves children/families of color		

Fear in housing

Housing is a basic need (and I would contend a basic right) and is currently in crisis in many states in America at the current. Housing increases the risk of stability, safety, improved wellness, and longevity (Ortiz and Zimmerman 2013).

Housing/home ownership

From the inception of America, developed and developing nations, property ownership has been the cornerstone of wealth generation. Owning property provides opportunity to build equity and pass wealth down through generations. Owning property is also understood as a form of power (Searle et al. 2009).

Home ownership has been fleeting for persons of color. There have been a number of barriers that have prevented and reduced the possibility of home ownership—these matters go as far upstream as poor education which impacts employment (which kind of job an individual qualifies for and what kind of money an individual can make) and this impacts ability to meet basic needs (will the concept of basic needs in subsequent chapters) which leads to deeper social consequences and the ripple impact goes on, and so forth.

There is also the element of which homes are sold to and in what neighborhood.

Banking system and access to home loans

Various studies highlight the practice of banks' and loans' officers being less inclined to offer appropriate loans (subprime housing loan crisis) and/or offer loans at all to persons of color. Limited access to loans = limited access to the possibility of homeownership = limited capacity to build wealth across generations (Beeman et al. 2011; Herbert and Belsky 2006; Dreier et al. 2006).

Renting

Affordable and low-income housing is also a challenge in America right now and it, too, stems from the upstream trickledown impact of social (and historical challenges) of our time.

Rent prices are high, and minimum wage income has not kept pace with cost of living—the percentage of individuals working poor is prominent (Silverman and Patterson 2011). Combine the financial strain with bias—prejudice, preconceived notions, and racism have impacted who landlords will rent to.

Review Fig. 8.1 and consider the following:

Attitude/behavior/situation	Consider the conditions, external (social, political, economic), internal (personal struggle)	Identify the fear (might you appreciate the role of fear in individuals who make up the system and the system itself)
Attitudes/behaviors regarding housing, homeownership, and renting		
Disparities access to appropriate loans for people of color, chronically marginalized populations		
Limited housing affordability		
Challenges in homeownership in communities of color		

Fear in employment

Chapter 7 addressed implicit bias in employment. The national unemployment rate remains under four percent at this time. However, the unemployment rate in communities of color rests higher than the national average. One significant challenge is that there are jobs, but not enough skilled individuals to do the jobs.

A few components to consider are as follows:

(1) The unemployment rate in communities of color is higher than the national average. Some of the data around hiring practices and preferences were demonstrated in Chap. 7. Implicit and explicit biases are real phenomena's and impact an individual's ability to earn a living and participate in the larger global economy. This has trickled down effects. Ability to work = ability to meet basic needs = improved overall wellness (Tsui 2010; Subramanian and Kawachi 2000).
(2) Education and skills training: limited exposure to and education on the possibilities of work and career paths (Berget et al. 2010). **This** starts at the level of school career coaches and counselors as early as High School.
(3) Income inequality—working a job with limited opportunities for advancement and opportunities.

Attitude/behavior/situation	Consider the conditions, external (social, political, economic), internal (personal struggle)	Identify the fear (might you appreciate the role of fear in individuals who make up the system and the system itself)
Attitudes/behaviors in employment, hiring practices		
Disparities in income		
Disparities in vocational training and education on career possibilities		

Fear in politics

The concept of fear appeals theory is fundamental learning in any Politics 101 course. We don't have to search far to appreciate the impact that fear has had on policies and laws.

In 2018, let's consider one current issue (which are age old by the way), immigration.

Some would content that the narrative constructed around immigration has very much been about "othering" and "us versus them." Things like

- They are taking our jobs
- They are dangerous....

We know from drive theory and others before it that human beings will work to quell a threat when it is present. The desire to move toward safety from a perceived threat will make humans do almost anything, to include forgetting about what humanity is all about. The current geopolitical environment has stoked the strongest, most primitive emotion to the point of people forgetting about humanity.

Children were separated from their families at the border and even worse, and individuals were allowed to die.

Think about other current politic issues, *review Fig. 8.1, and consider the following:*

- Health care,
- Social security,
- SNAP benefits, and
- The economy.

Attitude/behavior/situation	Consider the conditions, external (social, political, economic), internal (personal struggle)	Identify the fear (might you appreciate the role of fear in individuals who make up the system and the system itself)
Attitudes/behaviors in Politics		
Policy disparities		
Law disparities		
Practices and outcomes		

Fear in the media

Individuals and system who are in the position of shaping narrative(s) that result in building reinforcing social constructs is powerful (Moussaïd et al. 2013; Hovland et al. 1953). The power of images and words combined, make for very robust narratives = elicits robust emotional response = robust impact on behavior.

Let's consider the media and its role in constructing narratives around criminality, for example:

Criminality—when the word criminal comes up, it provokes a visceral response and it is attached to an image. In both print and on television, more often than not the word "criminal" was associated with people of color. There have been more instances than one would like to count where a crime was committed (and it may not have been by a person of color), but the stock photo used in print to talk about the crime was the face or image of a person of color. Many would argue that this was not a coincidence.

Other examples of how the media powerfully constructs narratives and impacts human behavior:

- Who and what is deemed a threat.
- Natural disasters.

Attitude/behavior/situation	Consider the conditions, external (social, political, economic), internal (personal struggle)	Identify the fear (might you appreciate the role of fear in individuals who make up the system and the system itself)
Attitudes in the media		
Behavior impact		

In reviewing systems as demonstrated in the Structural Racism diagram below, what might you conclude about fear and its role within and without structures?

Going back to the Boyz N The Hood Case

I made mention of what I call the "fear"-on-"fear" response with main character Tre and the police (the judicial system). I've asked you to consider where "fear" may be operating, upholding, and reinforcing systems.

Now I'd like us to consider how "fear" in systems impact individuals who are subject to them.

What is mean by the "fear" on "fear" response?

In the case of Tre in Boyz N The Hood:

- Tre was socialized to fear the police because he bore witness to a system constructed to protect, not optimally adhere to its mission when it came to people of color. In this way, Tre's experience shaped his emotional and behavioral response to the police. Tre did not feel safe in their presence.
- The police officer in Boyz N The Hood should mention that the character who played the cop who shoved a gun in Tre's face was a Black cop. The reason that this is important is because it speaks more deeply to the system that shapes its members. The cop's running narrative was that Tre, as a young Black man, was a non-caring, apathetic thug.

Tre was operating from a place of fear, and the police officer was operating from a system of fear. In the end, the fear in both directions left both parties changed for the worse—fear was perpetuated and trauma conditions worsened.

If fear didn't have such a predominant role in these two characters view of each other, how might the interaction have gone different?

The story of Tre is the story of many youth and police across this country. The more we consider the root cause of the unproductive interactions, the more judiciously we can move toward healing for all parties involved.

Fear has been woven into policies, practices, laws, and systems. There is indeed a culture of fear by way of reminder; fear has a functional role until it doesn't. It has been challenging to determine where and how fear should persist in the culture.

- Franklin D. Roosevelt on fear: "The only thing we have to fear is fear itself."
- Napoleon on fear: "Men are moved by two levers only: fear and self-interest."
- Ralph Waldo Emerson on fear: "Fear defeats more people than any other thing in the world."
- Bertrand Russell on fear: "Fear….is one of the main sources of cruelty. To conquer fear is the beginning of wisdom."
- Edmund Burke on fear: "No passion so effectually robs the mind of all its powers of acting and reasoning as fear."
- Franz Kafka on fear: "My fear…is my substance, and probably the best part of me."
- John Dryden on fear: "He has not learned the first of life who does not every day surmount a fear."

While poets, politicians, sociologists, and philosophers from as early as the 1800s to current can speak and write eloquently and mostly accurate about pros and cons of fear, understanding alone hasn't yet lessened the impact of fear.

What role should fear play in our world moving forward?

Key points/Summary

- Fear appeals have been employed in various systems as a means of impacting behavior.
- Fear has functional role to help human beings appropriately seeks safety in the face of threat.
- Fear can become dysfunctional as dominant learned response, also known as fear conditioning, also known as the neurobiological definition of trauma (fear on all the time).
- Fear conditioning can result from direct and/or indirect exposure to a fear-invoking event.
- From a brain perspective, the amygdala plays an important role in fear recognition and response.
- Drive theory consists of primary and secondary drives. Primary drives are intimately attached to getting basic needs met like access to air, water, and food—all things needed for human survival. Secondary drives are things that humans take in and learn from their external environment and subsequently determine that they need for survival.
- Another way to understand "fear-on-fear" interactions is "primary on secondary drives."
- Cottrell contends that human beings default to dominant responses (shaped by secondary drives) when in social settings.

Questions and reflections

- What role has fear played in shaping this country?
- What role does fear play in systems?
- What role does fear play in the work you do?
- How might we start the process of deconstructing fear-based systems and practices?

Practical application(s)

As a means of managing fear and reducing its grip on system, slowing down its impact on shaping narrative, policies, and practices, would suggest the following:

(A) Take pause.
(B) Consider whether or not the fear (or threat) is real and if it is imminent.
(C) Take stock of who is constructing the narrative.
(D) Consider why the narrative is being constructed.
(E) Ask "where is the fear?" "what is the fear."
(F) Determine what action should be taken, if any.

There are implications for what has been taught—Cottrell and colleagues pointed to the fact that in social settings, individuals default to what they've been taught. They default to conditioned responses. This conditioned response impacts behavior.

Can systems be reconditioned?

Making the connections

Recognizing and managing fear

- Acknowledge the role that fear might play in your interactions with youth.
- Be aware of "fear" that undergirds systems, the fear that systems instill in people (including you), and how "fear" (a very primal drive) impacts behavior and practices (Fig. 8.2).

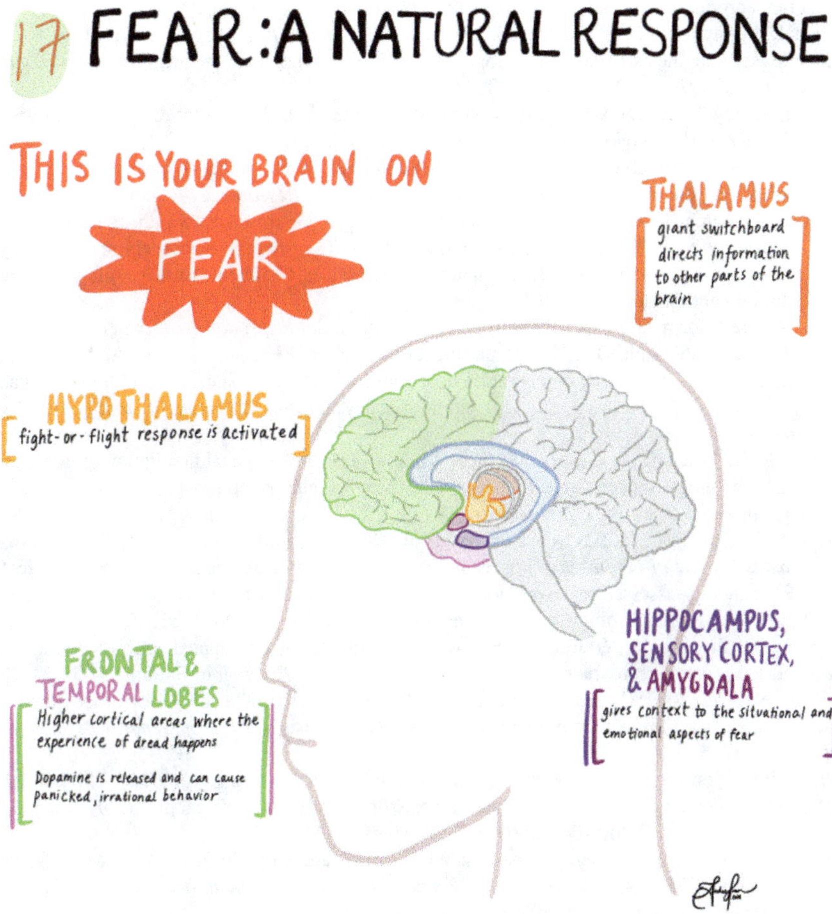

Fig. 8.2 Consider aspects of the brain involved in fear as a means of understanding behavior (fear acted out). Recall that fear has multiple components to include sensory aspect mediated by thalamus, emotional/memory aspect mediated by the hippocampus and amygdala, physiologic aspect mediated by the hypothalamus, cognitive aspect mediated by the frontal and temporal lobes—all aspects contribute to the "overall" behavior of fear. Printed with permission. Copyright Audrey A. Tran

References

Adolphs, R., et al. (2005, January 6). A mechanism for impaired fear recognition after amygdala damage. *Nature, 433*(7021), 68–72.

Ards, S. D., Myers, S. L., Malkis, A., Sugrue, E., & Zhou, L. (2003). Racial disproportionality in reported and substantiated child abuse and neglect: An examination of systematic bias. *Children and Youth Services Review, 25*(5–6), 375–392.

Bandura, A. (1969). *The principles of behavior modification*. New York: Holt, Rinehart & Winston.

Bandura, A. (Ed.). (1971). *Psychological modeling*. Chicago: Atherton Press.

Bandura, A., et al. (1969). The relative efficacy of desensitization and modeling approaches for inducing behavioural, effective and attitudinal changes. *Journal of Personality and Social Psychology, 13,* 173–199.

Beeman, A., Silfen Glasberg, D., & Casey, C. (2011). Whiteness as property: Predatory lending and the reproduction of racialized inequality. *Critical Sociology, 37*(1), 27.

Berget, R. J., Reynolds, C. F., Ricci, E. M., Quinn, S. C., Mawson, A. R., Payton, M., et al. (2010). A plan to facilitate the early career development of minority scholars in the health sciences. *Social Work in Public Health, 25*(6), 572–590.

Boer, H., & Seydel, E. R. (1996). Protection motivation theory. In M. Connor & P. Norman (Eds.), *Predicting health behavior*. Buckingham: Open University Press.

Bruchey, A. K., Jones, C. E., & Monfils, M. H. (2010). Fear conditioning by-proxy: Social transmission of fear during memory retrieval. *Behavioural Brain Research, 214*(1), 80–84.

Chibnall, S., Dutch Nicole, M., Jones-Harden, B., Brown, A., Gourdine, R., Smith, J., et al. (2003). *Children of color in the child welfare system. Perspectives from the child welfare community.* Washington, DC: Department of Health and Human Services, Children's Bureau, Administration for Children and Families.

Child Welfare Information Gateway. (2011). *Addressing racial disproportionality in child welfare* (pp. 1–28). Washington, DC: U.S. Department of Health and Human Services, Administration for Children and Families, Administration on Children, Youth, and Families, Children's Bureau.

Chu, G. C. (1966). Fear arousal, efficacy, and imminency. *Journal of Personality and Social Psychology, 4,* 517–524.

Cottrell, N. B., Wack, D. L., Sekerak, G. J., & Rittle, R. H. (1968). Social facilitation of dominant responses by the presence of an audience and the mere presence of others. *Journal of Personality and Social Psychology, 9*(3), 245–250.

Davis, A. M., Vinci, L. M., Okwuosa, T. M., et al. (2007). *Cardiovascular health disparities: A systematic review of health care interventions.* In Database of abstracts of reviews of effects (DARE): Quality-assessed reviews [Internet]. York (UK): Centre for Reviews and Dissemination (UK); 1995. Available from: https://www.ncbi.nlm.nih.gov/books/NBK74261/.

de Hoog, N., Stroebe, W., & John, B. F. (2005). The impact of fear appeals on processing and acceptance of action recommendations. *Personality and Social Psychology Bulletin, 31*(1), 24–33.

de Hoog, N., et al. (2007). The impact of vulnerability to and severity of health risk on processing and acceptance of fear-arousing communications: A meta-analysis. *Review of General Psychology, 11*(3), 258–285.

Dillard, J. P., Plotnick, C. A., Godbold, L. C., Freimuth, V. S., & Edgar, T. (1996). The multiple affective outcomes of AIDS PSAs: Fear appeals do more than scare people. *Communication Research, 23,* 44–72. https://doi.org/10.1177/009365096023001002.

Dreier, P. (2006). Federal housing subsidies: Who benefits and why? In R. G. Bratt, M. E. Stone, & C. Hartman (Eds.), *A right to housing: Foundations for a new social agenda* (pp. 105–138). Philadelphia: Temple University Press.

Ekman, P. (2009). Darwin's contributions to our understanding of emotional expressions. *Philosophical transactions of the Royal Society of London. Series B, Biological Sciences, 364*(1535), 3449–3451.

Elster, A., Jarosik, J., VanGeest, J., & Fleming, M. (2003). Racial and ethnic disparities in health care for adolescents: A systematic review of the literature. *Archives of Pediatrics and Adolescent Medicine, 157*(9), 867–874. https://doi.org/10.1001/archpedi.157.9.867.

Font, S. A., Berger, L. M., & Slack, K. S. (2012). Examining racial disproportionality in child protective services case decisions. *Children and Youth Services Review, 34*(11), 2188–2200.

Glassner, B. (1999). *The culture of fear: Why Americans are afraid of the wrong things*. New York, NY: Basic Books (Print).

Herbert, C. E., & Belsky, E. S. (2006). *The homeownership experience of low-income and minority borrowers and neighborhoods*. Washington, DC: US Department of Housing and Urban Development, Office of Policy Development and Research.

Hovland, C. I., Janis, I. L., & Kelley, H. H. (1953). *Communication and persuasion: Psychological studies of opinion change*. New Haven, CT: Yale University Press.

Hull, C. L. (1943). *Principles of behavior*. New York: Appleton-Century-Crofts.

Lazarus, R. S. (1966). *Psychological stress and the coping process*. New York: McGraw-Hill.

Leventhal, H. (1970). Findings and theory in the study of fear communications. In L. Berkowitz (Ed.), *Advances in experimental social psychology* (Vol. 5, pp. 119–186). New York: Academic Press.

Maddux, J. E., & Rogers, R. W. (1983). Protection motivation and self-efficacy: A revised theory of fear appeals and attitude change. *Journal of Experimental Social Psychology, 19*(5), 469–479.

Milne, S., Sheeran, P., & Orbell, S. (2000). Prediction and intervention in health-related behavior: A meta-analytic review of protection motivation theory. *Journal of Applied Social Psychology, 30*(1), 106–143.

Moussaïd, M., Kämmer, J. E., Analytis, P. P., & Neth, H. (2013). Social influence and the collective dynamics of opinion formation. *PLoS One, 8*(11), e78433. https://doi.org/10.1371/journal.pone.0078433.

Narayan, M. C., & Scafide, K. N. (2017). Systematic review of racial/ethnic outcome disparities in home health care. *Journal of Transcultural Nursing, 28*(6), 598–607.

Ohman, A. (1986). Face the beast and fear the face: Animal and social fears as prototypes for evolutionary analyses of emotion. *Psychophysiology, 23*(2), 123–145. https://doi.org/10.1111/j.1469-8986.1986.tb00608.x

Olsson, A., Nearing, K. I., & Phelps, E. A. (2007). Learning fears by observing others: The neural systems of social fear transmission. *Social Cognitive and Affective Neuroscience, 2*(1), 3–11.

Ortiz, S. E., & Zimmerman, F. J. (2013). Race/ethnicity and the relationship between homeownership and health. *American Journal of Public Health, 103*(4), e122–e129.

Peek, M. E., Cargill, A., & Huang, E. S. (2007). Diabetes health disparities: A systematic review of health care interventions. *Medical Care Research and Review: MCRR, 64*(5 Suppl), 101S–156S.

Platania, J., & Moran, G. P. (2001). Social facilitation as a function of mere presence of others. *Journal of Social Psychology, 141,* 190–197.

Rachman, S. (1968). *Phobias: Their nature and control*. Springfield: Thomas.

Rachman, S. (1977). The conditioning theory of fear-acquisition: A critical examination. *Behaviour Research and Therapy, 15,* 375–387 (Printed in Great Britain).

Searle, B. A., Smith, S. J., & Cook, N. (2009). From housing wealth to well-being? *Sociology of Health and Illness, 31*(1), 112–127.

Silverman, R., & Patterson, K. L. (2011). The four horsemen of the fair housing apocalypse: A critique of fair housing policy in the USA. *Critical Sociology, 38*(1), 123–140.

Stirling, A. (2007). Risk, precaution and science: Towards a more constructive policy debate. Talking point on the precautionary principle. *EMBO Reports, 8*(4), 309–315.

Subramanian, S. V., & Kawachi, I. (2000) Being well and doing well; Morris, J. N., Donkin, A. J., Wonderling, D., Wilkinson, P., & Dowler, E. A. A Minimum income for healthy living. *Journal of Epidemiology and Community Health, 54*(12), 885–889.

Tannenbaum, M. B., Hepler, J., Zimmerman, R. S., Saul, L., Jacobs, S., Wilson, K., et al. (2015). Appealing to fear: A meta-analysis of fear appeal effectiveness and theories. *Psychological Bulletin, 141*(6), 1178–1204.

Troiani, V., & Schultz, R. T. (2013). Amygdala, pulvinar, and inferior parietal cortex contribute to early processing of faces without awareness. *Frontiers in Human Neuroscience, 7,* 241. https://doi.org/10.3389/fnhum.2013.00241.

Tsui, E. K. (2010). Sectoral job training as an intervention to improve health equity. *American journal of public health, 100*(Suppl 1), S88–S94.

Vuilleumier, P. (2005, January 6). Cognitive science: Staring fear in the face. *Nature, 433,* 22–23 (Published online 5 January 2005).

Vuilleumier, P., Richardson, M., Armony, J., Driver, J., & Dolan, R. J. (2004). *Nature Neuroscience, 7,* 1271–1278.

Zajonc, R. B. (1965). Social facilitation. *Science, 149,* 269–274.

Chapter 9
Relationships, Restorative Justice, Reintegration, and Recidivism

The criminal justice system (a relatively large, pervasive system) represents the culmination of some futile systems, rendering it a prime system to examine. In some cases, before youth becomes entangled with the law, there are usually struggles in school, at home, in the community, and deviation from mental wellness.

All human beings desire and require two things in order to thrive: (1) to be understood and (2) to be connected. Relationships are all about connection and survival. Maslow's hierarchy of needs illustrates the critical nature of connectedness by equating food, water, and safety to love/belongingness as a basic physiologic needs that must be met on the journey to self-actualization. The power of relationships and connectedness cannot be underestimated in influencing change in youth. This chapter addresses imprisonment and its impact on families/relationships, explores the intersection between relationships, restorative justice, and recidivism, and considers criminal justice system, policies, and practices that may intentionally/unintentionally exclude/compromise important relationships and capacity to heal. We will dig deeper into significance of relationships, which by definition means "the state of being connected."

Please note that many of the studies I reference in this chapter use words like "offender" and "criminal." Because I believe in the impact of words and narrative, I've replaced these terms with words like "justice-involved individual" or "justice-involved youth" or "a youth who committed an act" as opposed to "crime."

By the end of this chapter, you should be able to

- Define relationships,
- Be familiar the impact of imprisonment on families/relationships,
- Habilitation >>>> rehabilitation,
- Understand shame versus toxic shame,

Electronic supplementary material The online version of this chapter (https://doi.org/10.1007/978-3-030-19208-2_9) contains supplementary material, which is available to authorized users.

A. Moreland-Capuia, *Training for Change*,
https://doi.org/10.1007/978-3-030-19208-2_9

- Understand the intersection between relationships, restorative justice, and recidivism,
- Identify the "real" and "perceived" mechanisms that perpetuate dysfunctional relationships,
- Consider systems, policies, and practices that may intentionally/unintentionally exclude/compromise important relationships and brain development, and
- Ponder why juvenile and criminal justice reform is needed.

Environment, relationships (early attachment and beyond), and brain development
Prior chapters discussed the developing brain and potential threats to the development process before conception (epigenetics), in utero (pre- and intra-natal), and post-natal (after birth). The one consistent and common threat to each of the developmental stages mentioned above is environment. Environmental influences on brain development cannot be ignored. As a matter of fact, changes in environment can help to heal the brain.

One specific environmental factor I'd like to focus on is relationships. Relationships are a form of human connectedness and connectedness is important for optimal brain development. Tierney and Nelson wrote an article on the brain development and role of experience from birth to 3 years of age. Birth to age 3 marks a critical period of brain development. The article referred to the importance of relationships in the brain development process in this way (Tierney and Nelson 2009):

- Mentioned a longitudinal study called the Bucharest Early Intervention Project (BIEP) based in Bucharest, Romania. The study has followed (a) an institutionalized group (group of children who've been in a group home like setting all their lives); (b) a group of children in foster care; and (c) children who've never been institutionalized and/or in foster care, but live with their biological families (Zeanah et al. 2003). Zeanah and colleagues have demonstrated that experience (defined by children's interaction with their environment) impacts brain structure.
- Healthy environments to include environments where basic needs were met, and love and relationships were intact had a positive impact on brain development. In cases where environments were deficient in love and positive relationships, brain development was negatively impacted, down to the wiring and functioning of the brain. Institutionalized and foster care children had notable negative brain changes compared to children who'd never been institutionalized (Tierney and Nelson 2009; Zeanah et al. 2003).

The study of Zeanah et al. and Tierney et al. can be viewed from lens of Erik Erickson's stages of psychosocial development. Erikson's matches age with what he termed the "psychosocial crisis":

The Trust versus mistrust, Autonomy versus Shame, and doubt phases of Erikson's model point to the clout of environment, specifically early attachments and relationships, in shaping brain development and behavioral consequences. Zeanah and colleagues, through their longitudinal study, have demonstrated the neurobiological impact of restricted/limited/deficient environments on optimal development (Fig. 9.1).

Fig. 9.1 Erik Erikson's stages of development (of becoming). Erikson and his colleagues theorized that human beings' conception of themselves and others is constantly changing and this process is influenced by environment (relationships and experiences)

Age	Psychosocial crisis
Infant – 18 months	Trust versus mistrust
18 months – 3 years	Autonomy vs. shame & doubt
3-5 years	Initiative vs. guilt
5-13 years	Industry vs. inferiority
13-21 years	Identity vs. role confusion
21-39 years	Intimacy vs. isolation
40-65 years	Generativity vs. stagnation
65 and older	Ego integrity vs. despair

Trust versus Mistrust: The first stages of life are centered on safety and getting basic needs met through the connection of infant and caregiver. When basic needs are met and there is safety, trust is more likely. In the absence of safety and basic needs getting met, there is mistrust.

Autonomy versus shame and doubt: This describes the interaction between child and its environment. This is the stage where children become more active, moving, touching, exploring, and working toward independence. If exploration, room for error, and independence are appropriately supported, independence can be optimally achieved. The absence of support of exploration, room for error, and independence creates the conditions for shame and doubt, low self-esteem, and confidence.

Initiative versus guilt: Children get to know themselves better through their interactions with those around them. This is a stage where interpersonal effectiveness can be learned.

Industry versus inferiority: This is the stage where children begin to outsource their sense of esteem and self-worth to their peers. The influence of what their peers think is predominant and can overwhelm the influence of the child's caregiver.

Identity versus role confusion: Re-evaluation of "self" and who "self" has become versus who "self" wants to be is critical in this phase.

Intimacy versus isolation: This stage is marked by adult's capacity to consider and give to others. In many ways, ability to be intimate is attached to self-esteem, worth, and attachment styles. One can appreciate the fluidity of Erikson's developmental stages in this way.

Generativity versus stagnation: At this stage, individuals have a strong desire to mentor and give to others. Individuals possess a desire to leave and/or create a legacy.

Ego integrity versus despair: At this stage, individuals take stock in accomplishments, assess relationships, and determine if what they've achieved in life was sufficient. It is normal to oscillate between having your ego reinforced and destabilized in this process.

The importance of the use of senses (Erikson's autonomy versus shame and doubt stage, Piaget's sensorimotor phase) in the developmental process. The ability for a child to touch, feel, hear, see, and taste as a means of interacting with the environment provides the brain with the cues it mandates for development. For example, Harry Harlow 1973 study on social deprivation in monkeys demonstrated that touch contact was a more robust determinant of attachment to a surrogate mother than feeding and that touch/connection deprivation (not as much so with visual and/or auditory) was a critical determinant of the autistic-like behavioral syndrome that resulted from early social deprivation (Harlow and Harlow 1973; Carlson and Earls 1997). Recent studies on social deprivation now include an understanding of how important the hypothalamic–pituitary–adrenal axis (HPA axis) is in regulating stress hormones in the body. As mentioned, increased stress hormones have a negative impact on brain development. Oxytocin, a hormone produced when safe connections are made, is implicated in helping to reduce stress and improve the quality of attachment in infants with caregivers (Carlson and Earls 1997; Main 1996; Hostinar et al. 2014).

We know from Bowlby's work on attachment theory that the early relationship between caregiver and infant is critical for overall development (Sroufe et al. 2005). The hope is for secure connections where infant connects with caregiver; infant has basic needs for survival (food) and safety, love, connection met; and the risk for normal brain development is optimized. The conditions that neurons require to properly develop are solidified in the context of safe and secure attachment.

Sullivan and colleagues highlight the impact of insecure, unsafe attachment (between infant and caregiver) on brain development. Article of Sullivan et al. provides evidence from various animal researches that have revealed aspects of the attachment circuitry within the brain. Attachment circuitry in animal brains (rat pups were referred to in Sullivan's work) is similar to the attachment circuitry in the human brain. The article contends that during the critical period of development, the developing brain attaches despite the environment. In the case of traumatic environments, gene expression changes, and neural circuits are connected under traumatic conditions—these changes under pressure have lasting effects that likely increase the risk of behavioral and physical compromise later in life (Sullivan 2012).

We've covered the literature on toxic stress and trauma on brain development. However, it is a worthwhile endeavor to make the connection between secure, early attachment (caregiver–infant relationships) and optimal brain development. Attachment involves ensuring safety for children which translates (neurobiologically) to modulating the amygdala and stress hormones in children. Secure and safe the attachment = the less prominent the amygdala and the lower the stress hormones. Insecure attachments (more trauma, unsafe environments, basic needs not met) = more prominent amygdala and higher stress hormones.

A prospective, longitudinal study by Moutsiana and colleagues investigated the long-term effects of early insecure attachments on amygdala volume (Moutsiana et al. 2014).

- The study had 59 participants who were mothers affected by depression, had normal deliveries, and were 2 months out from giving birth.
- The study looked specifically at infant attachment status: 24 infants were deemed as secure attachments and 35 infants were deemed as insecure attachments as observed at 18 months of age.
- The cohort was followed over time; by the age of 22, MRIs were completed on each participant.
- Participants who were deemed as insecure attachments had larger amygdala volumes in adulthood compared with their counterparts who were deemed as secure attachments (Moutsiana et al. 2014).

The impact of touch in context

Ardiel et al. wrote an article on the importance of touch in development and growth. The article highlighted human, animal, and organism studies that demonstrated the positive effects of supplemental mechanosensory stimulation in growth and development. The article concluded that organisms need sensory stimulation for normal development (Ardiel and Rankin 2010). Ellingsen and colleagues investigated the psychological and neurobiological mechanisms responsible for the integration of tactile "bottom-up" stimuli and "top-down" information into affective touch experiences. The study explained that touch must be placed in context as it depends on who is doing the touching and why. Touch can communicate love, concern, comfort, and pleasure, and it also can communicate disgust, displeasure, and fear. Universally, touch impacts human emotion. Ellingsen and colleagues point out that μ-opioids and oxytocin systems are said to be involved in affective touch processing—both systems involved in the reward pathways of the brain and in reducing anxiety- and stress-related effects and hormones (Ellingsen et al. 2016). A review by Sroufe et al. speaks about the emerging evidence that social support influences physical and mental health through stifling physiological stress responses, a phenomenon termed as the *social buffering of stress* (Hostinar and Gunnar 2015). There are studies that

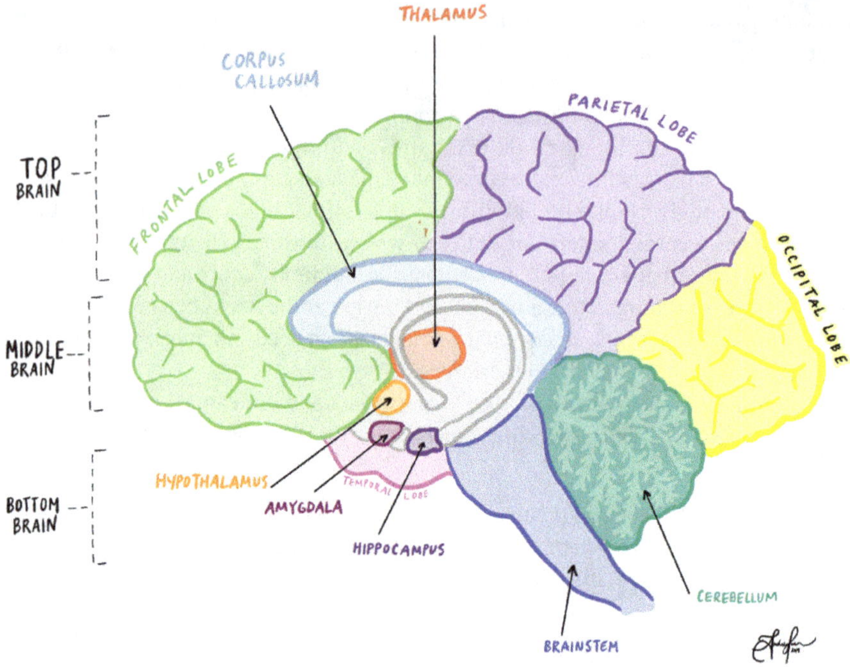

Fig. 9.2 In the case of insecure attachments, sensory deprivation (lack of touch), unmet basic needs, lack of safety, and the bottom and midbrain become more predominant compared to the top brain. This level of brain impact is seen in substance use, trauma, and mental health disorders. Environment matters: positive early attachment, positive relationships, safe living conditions, and access to basic needs are important in positive brain development. Printed with permission. Copyright Audrey A. Tran

speak to how touch (again, in context, appropriate touch) can lead to overall wellness (Walker and McGlone 2013). Inappropriate touch can trigger the fear and stress pathway negatively, while appropriate touch can heal through quelling the amygdala and reducing stress (Fig. 9.2).

Making the connection

It is not a stretch to consider the impact of a loveless, touchless, and isolated existence on human brain development and behavior. Institutionalization is a form of isolation and impacts brain development. The Bucharest Early Intervention Project which studies institutionalized youth has and continues to demonstrate this. Insecure attachments (at birth) impact brain development and behavior. As mentioned insecure attachments are intimately connected to getting basic needs met (like access to food, water, safe conditions, love, and belonging). We also know that access that not every human being has been fortunate enough to have all their basic needs met in life. There is a social component that accompanies the misfortune. I contend that the juvenile justice system as an extension of the criminal justice system represents the culmination of a series of systems that did not optimally serve youth. By the time they make it to prison, they have slipped through the seams of various systems that were designed to help and prevent. We know the value of relationships, but what happens when there are chronic and persistence of unsuccessful relationships that are passed down from one generation to the next? What impact does institutionalization (through imprisonment) have on relationship and the basic need for connectedness, love, and belonging?

Gabriela Bulisova, a documentary photographer and multimedia artist based in Washington, DC whose work focuses on underreported and overlooked stories affecting marginalized populations around the world and in the United States, posted a video clip of a series entitled: "Locked Apart: Impact of Incarceration on Family". The eight-minute and six-second clip highlights the disruptive nature of imprisonment on families and relationships, and further demonstrates the short- and long-term social/emotional/economic consequences of imprisonment.

Exercise 9.1—"The Koger-Harris Family," from the series "Locked Apart: The Impact of Incarceration on Families".

Many families are negatively impacted by incarceration. The ripple effect is profound when parents are incarcerated.

Gabriela Bulisova and Mark Isaac produced a profoundly provocative documentary entitled "Locked Apart: The Impact of Incarceration on Families" where they bring to life the real stories and show the faces, hearts, and minds that are impacted. The documentary allows the viewer a window into the harsh reality of incarceration and its ripple effect.

In this exercise, consider the impact:

- The psyche of the children of incarcerated parents;
- Developmental trajectory of children;
- Mental and physical health of children;
- Society—what does the world stand to lose?
- Systems—what systems and institutions must engage with children in the absence of parents?
- Long-term trajectory of children of incarcerated parents—does the risk of intergenerational incarceration increase or not?
- What should and can we do to mitigate the impact of incarceration on youth and families?

The eight-minute and six-second clip of "Locked Apart" is available in the online version of this textbook as Supplementary Material. Gabriela Bulisova and Mark Isaac, the producers of this important documentary, have granted me permission to share this clip—in an effort to encourage robust reflection on incarceration and the profound human impact.

Restorative Justice

The concept of reintegrative shaming theory, also known as restorative justice, was addressed in Chap. 7 of this textbook. It is important to revisit the concept in this chapter as we consider the impact of the culture of systems (the theoretical and philosophical underpinnings) on youth and relationships.

Restorative justice sounds much better than Reintegrative Shaming Theory. However, reintegrative shaming theory does undergird restorative justice. According to review by the Office of Juvenile Justice and Delinquency Prevention (OJJDP), restorative justice differs from former juvenile justice practices in that it seeks to repair harm from behavior versus punishing youth. Restorative justice aims to separate the youth from their behavior. Restorative justice changes the way that questions are posed with an intentional move away from focusing on the laws broken and/or indiscretions committed to "what is the nature of the harm resulting from an act and what must be done to repair it." The process highlights rehabilitation through collaboration with family, community, and individuals who are subject to the act (Development Services group OJJDP 2010).

OJJDP states that the restorative justice process helps youth who've been entangled with the law reconnect with community "*[b]y bringing together victims, offenders, families, and other key stakeholders in a variety of settings, restorative justice helps offenders understand the implications of their actions.*" (Development Services group OJJDP 2010).

Restorative justice is on the right track and does possess some trauma-informed elements with its intended purpose of separating youth from the unfortunate behavior that they may have demonstrated, but it is not complete. In reviewing the quote taken directly from the OJJDP review, the use of words like "offender" does seem to detract from the objective of separating the youth from their behavior.

We are talking about the power of relationship, connectedness, and belonging. When youth cannot see themselves separate from a behavior and/or act, it reduces the risk for positive change and healing. Restorative justice calls for the involvement of youth, the subject of the youth's act, and family to participate in a mediated process where youth is expected to apologize and accept responsibility for the impact of their behavior through a process referred to as family group conferences. The family group conference is a direct extension of the reintegrative shaming theory with anticipated outcome that the power of "shame" is robust enough to prevent or deter youth from participating in future negative behaviors. The data on the effectiveness of this approach are mixed. There is also the emergence of victim impact panels, designed to have persons who were subject to an act to educate the perpetrator of the act on the impact of their behavior/act. The studies on the effectiveness of this practice are also mixed.

Restorative justice might be optimally "restorative" if there was a more robust focus on the quality of the following relationships and narrative:

Caregiver and youth

- What was the youth's early exposure to getting needs met? Did they have ready access to food, water, and shelter?
- Did youth live in safe conditions?
- Was there a consistent caregiver presence in the youth's life?
- Attempting to understand these questions provide a window into attachment styles in youth and can help the system adjust their approach in serving and facilitating change.

Relationship between youth and parole/prison officer

- Is there a focus on ensuring basic needs of youth is met?
- Has the history of early trauma, psychosocial stressors (poverty, intermittent housing, and racism) been assessed and considered when engaging youth?

Youth and judge
Is close attention being paid to the narrative—use of words like "offender," "delinquent," and "criminal" versus "justice-involved youth."

Family and judge/parole officer

- Are families supported in their effort to help their youth heal and do and be better moving forward?
- Do they feel shame, blame, and embarrassment in the judicial process?

Better understanding these relationships do not excuse behavior, but it certainly increases understanding and provides greater context for the type of conditions that undesirable behavior may grow and thrive in. Understanding early and existing relationships might certainly impact and change the approach of the system as it relates to youth.

The criminal justice system is a relatively large, pervasive system that has touched and/or is touching large contingent of society. Youth of color are disproportionately involved in the system.

According to Glaze and Herberman (2013) (Glaze and Herberman 2013; Glaze and Maruschak 2010):

- Over the last 30 years in the U.S., the number of individuals entangled with the criminal justice system has increased exponentially.
- Approximately 1.6 million people are currently in prison and 4 million are on probation.
- 65 million have a record.
- Approximately 735, 601 of individuals with charges are confined to local jails.
- Substantial portions of the nations incarcerated are parents—52% incarcerated are state and 63% incarcerated are federal.
- The Bureau of Justice estimates for 2007 indicate that the nation's incarcerated report having an estimated **1,706,600** minor children, accounting for **2.3%** of the U.S. population under age 18.

Do note the impact of incarceration on families and children—both ways (parents incarcerated and/or children incarcerated).

Racial disparities noted by Glaze and Herberman (2013) (Glaze and Herberman 2013) (Glaze and Maruschak 2010):

- In 2007, the population of minor children of incarcerated parents consisted of approximately 484,100 White non-Hispanic children (one in 110 White children).
- 767,400 Black, non-Hispanic children (one in 15 Black children).
- 362,800 Hispanic children (one in 41 Hispanic children).
- About half of these children were age 9 or younger.

- Thirty-two percent were between the ages of 10 and 14.
- 16 percent were between the ages of 15 and 17.
- **Black (54%) and Hispanic (57%) men in state prison were more likely than White men (45%) to be parents.**

Prison's impact on families is real and profound.
Once youth are involved in the criminal justice system, there is an expectation that can willingly and thoughtfully participate in the treatment modalities placed before them. If the main objective is supporting youth in getting and doing better, then the current approaches and practices would benefit from re-evaluation.

Rehabilitation versus habilitation
The juvenile justice literature refers to rehabilitation as a form of supporting youth in changing behavior.

Anytime the prefix "re" is applied, it indicates that something is happening again. In order for something to happen again, it assumes that something happened before it. Dictionary definition of the prefix "re" is "again" and/or "again and again" (speaking to a process of repetition) and also holds the meaning "back" or "backward." Let's consider the word "rehabilitation"—the objective is to help youth move forward, learn, and not turn back. The contradictory component of the word "rehabilitation" is the prefix "re" as it assumes that youth had a set of skills, resources, etc. to begin with. I would contend that when youth become entangled with the law, it is a result of not having had the privilege of gaining a set of skills on how to navigate the world and life. So, a system cannot re-teach something that was never taught. Hence, I contend that the juvenile justice system should focus on habilitation. A publication by Doris MacKenzie asserts that the following practices and approaches have demonstrated their capacity to be "rehabilitative" (MacKenzie 2006) (Figs. 9.3 and 9.4).

CBT, MRT, and reasoning and rehabilitation are deemed rehabilitative modalities—optimal participation and benefit from these forms of treatment depends on youth's ability to tap into the cognitive (top part) of their brain. Much of this book has been about the brain development process and how just pure development itself lends itself to increased proclivity for impulsivity, lack of good decision-making, and increased novelty-seeking behavior in youth. If we superimpose early exposure to trauma, protracted exposure to trauma, insecure attachments, and extended periods of not getting basic needs met, on top of an already tenuous and susceptible developing brain, it is not hard to imagine limited capacity for actively engaging the top part of the brain.

Before effective and impactful treatment can take hold, safety must first be created. This concept will be illustrated further in subsequent chapters.

Getting back to concept of rehabilitation and how by nature of the use of the "re", it presupposes that young people have a set of skills. History, science, and experience demonstrate that "rehabilitation" may not be the best word and/or approach, but habilitation may have more traction.

MacKenzie and others deem the following approach "rehabilitative"	**Have you considered?**
Cognitive restructuring is a part of a cognitive behavioral therapeutic approach. It is the process of helping an individual challenge unproductive thoughts and reframe **Cognitive Behavioral Therapeutic (CBT)** modalities that require intentional use of the top part of the brain	History of youth If substances are involved? If youth is anxious, depressed? What part of the brain is youth in? Can we get them to the top, cognitive aspect of their brain?
Multisystemic Therapy (MST) is an intensive, family- and community-based intervention for youth and their families. Therapist provides weekly visits and therapy to youth and families for an average of four months.	Cultural factors that might come in to play by providing services in home? Whether or not home is a potential trigger for trauma and anxiety?
Reasoning and Rehabilitation is a cognitive behavioral therapeutic treatment that focuses on skill building	History of youth If substances are involved? If youth is anxious, depressed? What part of the brain is youth in? Can we get them to the top, cognitive aspect of their brain?
Moral Recognition Therapy (MRT) – Cognitive behavioral therapeutic model that focuses on confrontation of beliefs, attitudes, and behaviors; assessment of current relationships; reinforcement of positive behavior and habits; positive identity formation; enhancement of self-concept; decrease in hedonism and development of frustration tolerance; and development of higher stages of moral reasoning	Heavy on the cognitive, top brain function

Fig. 9.3 Rehabilitation services heavy on the cognitive behavioral therapeutic side and assumes that youth (in the context of anxiety, fear, not feeling safe) are in a position to optimally benefit from the approaches

Current practices that lean more toward habilitation
Providing and increasing access to substance use treatment services in jails, prisons, and in the community
Effective use of drug and community courts
Vocational and educational training

Fig. 9.4 Practices and approaches that remove assumption and focus on establishing safety (minimizing trauma triggers, recognizing anxiety and fear and addressing it) before developing skills tend to represent the spirit of habilitation

Habilitation
Habilitation focuses on helping an individual learn a set of skills. If I come from a space of teaching a set of skills that have never been learned versus someone who I think should know better and already, the approach changes based on the level of assumption.

I anticipate the criticism that habilitation is a deficit-based approach because it assumes that youth don't have skills. Not quite. I assert the contrary; habilitation is strengths based in that it assumes that youth have the capacity for greatness when given the opportunity to learn new and different skills that keep them on a continual path to improvement. This is a process that everyone can appreciate, the process of continual self-improvement.

To this end, Darryl Turpin developed Habilitation Empowerment and Accountability Therapy (H.E.A.T) which considers the impact of trauma from systemic and structural inequities on young males of color in particular. With structural and systemic considerations, HEAT incorporates spirituality, self, family, orientation, and community into the treatment of young African-American males who have been disproportionately impacted by the criminal justice system. HEAT is deemed an empirically based practice with great promise. An article by Marlowe and colleagues investigated the effectiveness of the HEAT model in the context of treatment for African-American men involved in drug courts. The study highlighted the results from two pilot studies where the HEAT curriculum was employed as a prominent modality of treatment in drug courts. Findings revealed (Marlowe et al. 2018) the following:

- Participants with serious charges and substance use histories were willing and able to complete the 9-month curriculum.
- Participants felt that HEAT was a satisfactory intervention.
- Participants in the HEAT curriculum graduated from drug court at substantially higher rates than are commonly observed among their peers with similar charges who did not participate in HEAT.

The numbers in the two pilot studies are small, but the results are promising and have implications for treatment moving forward for specialized populations. Darryl Turpin has adapted the HEAT curriculum for youth.

Challenges in Reintegration and Re-entry
The challenges of reintegration and re-entry of previously incarcerated individuals are challenging for various reasons. The communities that they anticipate will welcome them back are stymied by and with structural and systemic processes that compromise recovery and healing.

A few key challenges for persons emerging from incarceration:

- Capacity to earn a living wage and support themselves and respective families is limited after having a record (Geller et al. 2011). As mentioned prior, there are more jobs available than skilled individuals who can work them. There are some systems that provide vocational training while incarcerated so that individuals emerge with an actual trade (electrician, welder, construction, etc.). This is not a consistent practice, however.

- Housing is limited as there are certain places that won't rent to persons with a record. Housing is also cost prohibitive for an individual who cannot get a living wage job.
- Health care—most states have expanded their Medicaid population and offer services to women and children at the very least. However, when persons are incarcerated, healthcare coverage is usually suspended. Once out, they can sign up for continued coverage; without some type of navigator support services, signing up for healthcare coverage can be a barrier. There are some systems that assist with the process of re-activating healthcare coverage in anticipation of a release date.

A review of Morenoff et al. focuses on two complementary questions regarding incarceration, incarcerated individual's re-entry, and communities (Morenoff and Harding 2014):

- Whether and how mass incarceration has affected the social and economic structure of American communities? and
- How residential neighborhoods affect the social and economic reintegrations of returning from incarceration?

These two questions can be seen as part of a dynamic process involving a pernicious "feedback" loop, in which mass incarceration undercuts the structural and social organizations of some communities, thus creating more criminogenic environments for returning individuals with a history of imprisonment and further diminishing their prospects for successful re-entry and reintegration (Morenoff and Harding 2014).

The disruption of ties within families and primary groups can weaken *private controls* exercised within families or primary networks:

- Demonstrates how mass incarceration destroys communities and families; and
- Illustrates how *re-entry without strong infrastructure further contributes to the degradation of communities.*

Morenoff highlights the depth of the phenomenon of the "vicious cycle" and why it is more likely for persons once incarcerated to return and/or to continue with maladaptive behaviors that increase the risk of remaining entangled with the law. There are certain conditions that drive those that have been incarcerated back into dysfunctional relationships to include (Morenoff and Harding 2014) the following:

- Difficulty securing employment (some systemic to include having a felony, some personal to include limited education and skills training).
- Feelings of shame—shame is backed into foundational theories for the criminal justice system. A system that theorizes shame as a powerful motivator for sustained change…not so…shame (at the center) counters efforts to build self-efficacy and to effectively move toward healing.
- Lack of social capital—limited "people "resources in terms of who can help them get to the next level of functioning within community. The peer mentorship movement is that individuals with prior experience with incarceration who successfully

navigated and avoided the system are uniquely positioned individuals coming out of the system.

- Limited options in terms of environment and natural supports.

Markham explains the functional role of shame to include the fact that shame (or embarrassment) typically helps individuals modulate behavior in social settings. Shame helps individuals to effectively gauge what is socially acceptable in a specific environment and what is not socially acceptable (Markham 2016). In the developing child with the developing brain, shame triggers the prefrontal cortex (or should). Do recall that the prefrontal cortex is the area of the brain that develops until about the age of 26 and is responsible for impulse control, emotion regulation, organizing, planning, personality expression, exercising good judgment, and overall cognition. We learn to manage and modulate our behavior based on practice, reassurance, and support. How do I know not to yell in a library? Well, I remember my own youth; one day I found myself singing loudly in the library. The caring librarian came to me and kindly and appropriately redirected me by telling me that my voice was lovely and explaining that the library was probably not the best place to sing loudly because people were trying to study and concentrate. When the librarian corrected my behavior, I did feel a little embarrassed, but it quickly resolved when she complimented me and then offered me an alternative and more appropriate way to exercise my passion for singing. The shame made the issue salient, but the kindness, reassurance, and redirection made the shame or embarrassment useful. I was changed by the librarian's feedback, not crushed by it.

Psychologist and behaviorist who study shame contend that shame is attached to the capacity for self-control and self-regulation. Further that shame = voice of the conscience (Markham 2016).

Shame envelopes the feeling that a behavior doesn't match the environment so that a child is safe enough to self-correct. To avoid toxic shame, reassurance, redirection, and education must take precedence over punishment. Children learn appropriate behavior based on context and environment.

If we consider the developmental phase that most youth are in from birth to age 3 which marks the critical period for shaping a child's response to and perception of shame. From birth to age 3, the bottom survival part of the brain is more developed (but still subject to impact from the outside environment) than the top part of the brain. The top part of the brain includes mostly the cortex, to include the prefrontal cortex, a part of the brain responsible for regulating behavior and impulses.

Adolescence marks another critical developmental phase from a structural and functional brain perspective. Adolescents are primed to be mildly more impulsive, less inclined to consistently regulate behavior—this is a period in development where environment, narrative, and relationships (caring adult figures that model and teach regulation) matter in healthy brain development.

Unacceptable, unproductive behavior matched with punishment = toxic shame.

Unacceptable, unproductive behavior matched with reassurance, redirection, education = functional shame.

Shame has also been described as a means of conscious awareness raising—to teach valuable lesions (Au 2015). Some consider shame and shaming an aversive technique—to baseball bat (inappropriate tool and excessive) that is used to strike out unwanted behaviors. The question of persistent and open shaming has been raised. In recent years, the shaming of children and teens has been more visible with social media. Examples of parents making an example out of their children for not listening in school and/or not adhering to rules have become and do become viral. The consequences of such open and public shaming have been dire—some children and adolescents experience the shaming as too intense, too public, too embarrassing to overcome, and have taken drastic measures like ending their own lives. There is a warning against public shaming as it has the tendency to become toxic and insurmountable and feel irreversible. Equally important to consider is the role of hormones during adolescence and the capacity for intensified emotional responses in lieu of an ever-changing hormonal milieu. We've discussed the role of hormones on behavior and mood in prior chapters, but it is important to mention here as well. Public shame feels like persistent and unrelenting shame, and the consequences can be dire.

Other descriptors of shame include the following:

- Development of self-concept impacts experiences and expressions of shame and guilt (Barrett et al. 1993, 1998; Lewis 2000).
- Development of self-concept starts to emerge at age 2 and becomes more stable around age 3 (Eisenberg 2000; Kochanska et al. 2002; Thompson et al. 2006; Barrett et al. 1993; Zahn-Waxler et al. 1990).
- Shame and guilt are described as self-conscious emotions (Muris et al. 2015).
  Shame = deals with "self."
  Guilt = deals with "others."

Parisette-Sparks and colleagues investigated parental predictors of shame and concluded the following:

Parental factors that shape children expression of shame and guilt include parenting style: the psychological temperament of the parent and marital satisfaction. Early childhood is an informative developmental phase that provides a window to the emergence of shame and guilt and the factors associated with how they are expressed and experienced (Parisette-Sparks et al. 2015).

There is a functional and appropriate role for shame as it theoretically supports self-reflection and correction of unproductive behaviors. However, toxic shame can paralyze youth and can get in the way of change.

Replace shame with an opportunity to learn a more productive, functional behavior. Shame can be reduced when a skill is taught and appropriate behavior is modeled. Getting to the bottom of shame is critical in work with youth (and adults too).

Recidivism

Recidivism is defined as an individual with a history of incarceration continuing to demonstrate unhealthy behaviors that increase the risk of future and sustained involvement with the criminal justice system (arrest, charges, and/or repeat incarceration). Risk factors for recidivism have been studied.

Factors that have been demonstrated to reduce recidivism

- Education,
- Drug and alcohol treatment,
- Mental health treatment, and
- Family involvement.

Drug and alcohol treatment programs (Inciardi et al. 1997)

- Rates of unlawful acts are higher in individuals who consume substances.
- Drug and alcohol treatment has proven to reduce recidivism.
- 75% of individuals incarcerated who participated in prison drug and alcohol and an aftercare work release program were less likely to return to the system.

Education (Lewin 2001)

- The Correctional Education Association did a study comparing the recidivism rates of over 3000 justice-involved individuals in Maryland, Minnesota, and Ohio.
- They found that justice-involved individuals who had taken classes while incarcerated are less likely to repeat unlawful acts (recidivate).
- They also found that for every dollar spent on education for justice-involved individuals, the government saves two dollars in re-incarceration costs.

Family (Austin et al. 2004)

- Individuals entangled with the law are less likely to repeat an unlawful act (recidivate) if they live with their spouses after returning home from prison.
- Recidivism rates associated with the amount of contact they receive from their families while in prison. More contact while incarcerated = less likely to recidivate.

Is the prison system set up to support family involvement?

States like Pennsylvania have included family programs into the corrections system. Programs are designed to help incarcerated individuals maintain and improve their family relations.

Pennsylvania State's prisons for women include the following programs (Couturier 1995):

- Parenting classes,
- Child development classes,
- Counseling to assist in them in coping with the challenging task of parenting while incarcerated,
- Playrooms that allow children to interact with their mothers in a more natural environment,
- Mother–child retreats, and
- Offer housing for children and relatives who travel long distances so they can visit for multiple days.

Williams et al. did a study on "incarcerated individuals" childhood and family background.

The study (Williams et al. 2012):

- Examined incarcerated persons childhood and family background, their current family relationships, and associations between background/family characteristics and going back into the system, and/or falling back into old behaviors.
- Report was based on Wave 1 of a longitudinal cohort study (Surveying Prisoner Crime Reduction—SPCR), which tracked the progress of newly sentenced incarcerated persons in England and Wales.
- The study included a total of 3,849 incarcerated individuals.
- Consisted of two groups to include, group 1 = 1,435 incarcerated individuals sentenced from 1 month to 4 years.
- Group 2 = 2,414 incarcerated individuals sentenced to between 18 months and 4 years.

Many incarcerated persons in this study had challenging, traumatic backgrounds with the following characteristics (Williams et al. 2012):

- Had been in foster care at some point during their childhood.
- Of the individuals who indicated that they'd been in foster care—they were younger when they were first arrested and were more likely to reconvicted 1-year post-release compared to those who had never been in care.
- Was subject to abuse in all forms.
- Observed violence in the home as a child (this was more prevalent in persons who stated that they had a family member with an alcohol and/or drug issue).
- Early, protracted, and prolonged exposure to violence—persons who indicated a history of violence exposure in this study were more likely to continue in maladaptive patterns that resulted in re-engagement with the judicial system 1-year post-release.
- Had family members who'd been convicted of a crime.
- Had a history of being in the juvenile justice system in their youth.
- Incarcerated individuals with a convicted family member were more likely to be reconvicted in the year after release from custody than those WITHOUT a convicted family member.
- Endorsed a history of truancy, suspension, and/or being expelled from school—the school-to-prison pipeline.

In the study ofWilliams et al., over three-fourths of incarcerated persons indicated that they were close to their families and children. They expressed the significance of their families' emotional support while being incarcerated and cited their families and children as motivation for getting out and staying out of the system (Williams et al. 2012).

The characteristics (adverse childhood experiences) of persons incarcerated in this study is similar to the characteristics of incarcerated persons around the world. Early and protracted exposure to trauma is a significant risk factor for adopting maladaptive behaviors that may lead to an individual becoming entangled with the law (Williams et al. 2012).

A few points to amplify:

- Important to consider childhood exposures and experiences in youth (and adults too)—this should change approach. Again, no excuses for the behavior, but gives greater context to who the incarcerated individual has gone through and how that impacts behavior. This understanding should shape the approach for mitigating risks in the future.
- Family as one way to mitigate risk for ongoing engagement in the criminal judicial system.
- Appreciating how disruptive imprisonment is to families and communities.
- How can systems work to heal families as a means of healing a person and an entire community? Traditionally, the focus has been on providing services for the individual who'd been incarcerated. However, one effective approach (as indicated) involves providing services to the family unit (viewing the family as system) to heal the unit.

Laws, policies, and practices
The 1997 Federal Adoption and Safe Families Act requires states to file a petition to terminate parental rights on behalf of any child who has been abandoned or who has been in foster care for 15 consecutive months or more. States federal funding for child welfare services is contingent upon the execution of the Adoption and Safe Families Act.

The law provides exceptions to this requirement in the following cases:

- At the option of the state, the child is being cared for by a relative.
- The state has documented a compelling reason for determining that termination of parental rights would not be in the child's best interest.
- The state has not provided the child's family with services that support a child's safe return home.

Some would contend that the Adoption and Safe Families Act incentivizes adoption and removing children from their families over helping families heal. When the act was modified to establish a new timeline and conditions for when and how States should file for termination of parental rights (TPR)—there was little consideration given to understanding the conditions that increased the risk of incarcerated parents being incarcerated in the first place. The law now requires that states must file a petition to terminate parental rights and simultaneously identify, recruit, process, and approve a qualified adoptive family on behalf of any child, regardless of age, that has been in foster care for 15 out of the most recent 22 months. Perhaps unintentionally but inherently the system puts a lot of blame on parents and shames them into thinking that just because they exercised poor judgment and made unfortunate decisions that they are not capable of making better decisions in the future. The argument here is really a moral one—who gets to decide when or if someone is capable of change? Who gets to decide who is worthy of investment, time, and energy?

While there are legitimate cases where children might not be best served in the homes of their incarcerated and/or formerly incarcerated parents, there is also a legitimate case to be made for incarcerated and/or formerly incarcerated parents who need a little time, care, support, and love to heal. They can be phenomenal parents in their healed state.

Several studies have been done on the impact of the Adoption and Safe Families Act and conclude that under the Act children are adopted or removed from their parents at a higher rate than they are reunified (Phillips and Mann 2013; Rockhill et al. 2007).

The system has recognized that adopted and foster children's well-being is attached to maintaining some connection to a biological parent. Visitation and frequency of visitation have been outlined, but standardization of this process is immature (McWey et al. 2010). Is this a sufficient means of supporting child–parent connections? The results on the impact of biological parent connection to their adopted and/or foster children are mixed and gendered. In boys, there appeared to be a reduction in depressive symptoms, but not in girls (McWey et al. 2010). These matters are complicated, complex, and multifactorial. The gender differences demonstrate that there is an impact, which we must pay attention to.

The Oregon Story

- In 2001, Oregon established (by legislation) a planning and advisory committee to make recommendations on how to increase family bonding for children of incarcerated parents (Oregon Department of Corrections 2018).
- The legislation required representation by the corrections department, the state youth authority, the state court administrator, the state Commission on Children and Families, the Department of Education, the Department of Human Services, and several local boards and councils.
- The committee issued a report to the legislature in 2002, and in 2005, the legislature extended the committee through the 2005–2007 biennium.
- As one of the first states to address this issue at a high level, Oregon is now considered a national model for interagency collaboration and innovation.
- Oregon's effort began in 2000 with a Children's Project workgroup consisting of over 20 organizations.
- Parenting classes are skills based.
- ***The workgroup focused on changes in the prison system to include parent education classes, a therapeutic child-centered facility to serve children of women incarcerated, and improved policies regarding contact and visitation.***

Oregon is a leader in transforming the conditions for incarcerated persons and families. In 2017, The Washington Corrections Center for Women adopted a parenting program similar to Oregon's. The trend is catching on; the realization that supported healed parents can support and facilitate healing of their children is powerful.

The Power of Peer Mentorship

Mentorship is recognized benefit in almost every profession, at every stage in life and for every reason. In general, it is deemed helpful to have someone guiding, supporting, correcting, and encouraging you at various developmental stages (birth to adulthood). Many human beings can point to one or two people who've formally and/or informally mentored them and say that it made a difference. Eby and colleagues examined the effectiveness of mentorship via analyzing mentorship studies across three specific disciplines (work, academic, and youth) (Eby et al. 2008). The study compared individuals who had a mentor to individuals who did not. Results for individuals who were mentored were more favorable compared to individuals who were not mentored. Specific areas examined (and more favorable for individuals who were mentored) included behavioral (less likely to be suspended from school), attitudes (overall more positive), health-related (less likely to use substances), relational (possessed skills for developing positive relationships), motivational (commitment to setting and adhering to goals), and career (successful in the workplace from interpersonal effectiveness to competence) (Eby et al. 2008).

Mentorship for persons who were formerly incarcerated is a growing and effective trend.

Lebel examined the impact of formerly incarcerated persons helping incarcerated individuals re-integrating back into the community. Lebel's study employs the work of Frank Reissman and his "helper theory" (Lebel 2007). The helper theory approach involves the use of persons with a particular struggle to help other people with similar struggles in a more severe form (Reissman 1965). Reismman contends that the helper theory is about "self-persuasion through persuading others." (Reissman 1965). Lebel's study sampled and analyzed the impact of helping in over 200 former incarcerated persons in re-entry programs. The results confirmed Reissman's theory as the "helper orientation" in the formerly incarcerated persons who participated in this study demonstrated a positive relationship with higher self-esteem and greater satisfaction with life, and a negative relationship, less dysfunctional thinking and attitude, and the less re-arrest. In this case, helping not only benefits the helpee but the helper as well (Lebel 2007). The mutual benefits of mentorship for incarcerated individuals are significant (Lebel 2007; Lebel et al. 2015).

There are multiple forms of mentorship to include

- Peer recovery mentors/coaches—in support of a recovery-oriented system of care in substance use disorders.
- Alcoholic anonymous sponsors—mentorship and support for remaining clean and sober.
- Peer wellness specialist—in support of persons desiring to maintain mental and physical wellness.
- Parenting mentors—to support parents in developing skills to stay on the trajectory of positive, healthy parenting.
- Academic mentors/coaches—to support academic achievement and motivation to learn and overcome unavoidable obstacles.
- Career mentors/coaches—to support maintaining healthy and meaningful careers.

This is not an exhaustive list, but a demonstration that the utility of mentorship traverses several disciplines.

Hot off the press Bipartisan passing of the Criminal Justice Bill December 2018—Sentencing reform.

The First Step Act (149-page document) cites its purpose as follows: "to provide programs to help reduce the risks that prisoners will recidivate upon release from prison and for other purposes." These are the exact words verbatim from the bill. Of note is the terminology used throughout the bill—while the terminology employed in the bill is not very trauma-informed, the practical aspects of the policy have been constructed to reduce harm and trauma. I wish the terminology/narrative/words used to shape this bill matched its intent—which is to reduce harm and trauma. This gets at the heart of what it means to be trauma informed.

Key reforms as outlined by the First Step Act legislation:

- Increased opportunities for individuals with lesser chargers to shorten their sentences and/or enter into pre-release programs.
- Changing how incarcerated pregnant women are treated—prohibition of shackling.
- Significant reduction of solitary confinement for incarcerated youth given its known deleterious impact on mental wellness.
- Improving the possibility of incarcerated persons' engagement with family by making certain (when possible) that they are in facilities closer to where they live. This chapter addressed important role family can play in healing and recovery of incarcerated persons and youth.
- Sentencing changes at the Federal level (to name a few)
  - Reducing mandatory sentences for incarcerated persons with nonviolent charges,
  - Reduce and cap the mandatory sentence penalty to 25 years (as opposed to a life sentence), and
  - Provides judges with more judicial discretion in some cases involving mandatory minimums.
- Addresses disparities in drug sentencing—re-evaluate cases of crack versus cocaine.

The First Step Act is certainly a step in the right direction. Laws are important and they do help to guide behavior, but they haven't always changed it. Let's hope that a deeper understanding about the conditions that increase the likelihood that an individual becomes entangled with the law is considered.

Exercise 9.2

A case: Moral imperative to take good care of the most vulnerable among us

There was an individual who was detoxing from opioids while incarcerated. Opioid withdrawal is uncomfortable and can result in excessive vomiting and diarrhea, among others. Excessive fluid loss from vomiting and diarrhea (in the absence of being replete with fluids) can result in dehydration, electrolyte imbalances with impact to kidneys, heart, and the brain. This individual was severely dehydrated and weak from opioid withdrawal and in the absence of getting an IV fluid ended up dying in custody. This is an incredibly sad story that highlights the urgent need for reform. Many themes emerge from this case:

- Attitudes about substance use and who is worthy of help and care. Are there implications for standardizing detox protocols in jail and prison?
- Humanity—moving from apathy to empathy.
- What and who do we value as a society?
- Sentencing reform is important, but reform of the human heart and understanding must parallel it.

Can you think of other themes?

Exercise 9.3
Making the connection
The incarcerated tend to come from intense histories of cumulative disadvantage characterized by multiple risks such as family histories of victimization, mental health difficulties, substance misuse and addiction, and intergenerational incarceration (Arditti 2012).
Impact of imprisonment on families
Imprisonment also catalyzes a series of adversities, or "collateral costs" among the families of offenders such as unemployment, loss of income, homelessness, and the need for public assistance (Hagan and Dinovitzer 1999).

- What do you think is meant by Arditi's use of the term "cumulative disadvantage"?
- Hagan and Dinovitzer refer to the "collateral costs" of imprisonment to families, what might those costs be?
- When we consider the impact of prison on families and communities from the front end (family history, vicarious trauma, etc.) and on the backend (difficulty securing employment and/or a change of environment), what can the parole/probation officers, judges, and officials of the court do differently to more effectively engage young clients and their families?
- In the case of youth, what role might family relationships have in their recovery and subsequent healing?

Practical application(s)
Will refer to them as follows:

- **7 R's**
  Revisiting developmental phases,
  Restoring and Re-integrating families,
  Reducing toxic shame,
  Reiterating Habilitation,
  Reinforcing attachment,
  Reframing issues through reframing narratives
  , and Re-discovering and re-defining capacity for greatness in youth.
- **3 C's**
  Creating Conditions for Change.
- **2 H's**
  Helping youth heal through.
  Helping families heal.

Revisiting developmental phases

Reviewing and revisiting the developmental phases as outlined by Piaget and Erikson as a means of understanding where you might find youth who are entangled with the system. This is one way to get to the "what happened?"

Consider if youth ever transitioned out of one stage to the next. If not, why?

The answer should impact a systems approach with youth.

Restoring and Re-integrating families

Relationships and emotional support matter and, according to some epigenomic studies, can mitigate the physical and emotional impacts of trauma. A study by Shields et al. (2016) investigated the epigenetic impact of the safety, connectivity, and attachment strengthening value of relationships in the lives of African-American women with a history of childhood abuse. It was one of the first studies of its kind to examine a glucocorticoid receptor gene NR3C1 (involved in the inflammatory and stress response), a gene known to be methylated (and therefore changed in terms of expression) in cases of trauma. Shields, Wise, Ruiz-Narvaez, and colleagues postulated that women with a history of trauma would have higher rates of methylated NR3C1 compared to women without a history of trauma = this hypothesis held firm. Second hypothesis was that women with a history of trauma who indicated that received strong emotional support in the form of caring and loving relationships would demonstrate less severe methylation at the NR3C1 gene = this hypothesis held firm. The study concluded that relationships are powerful and serve to mitigate the risk of persistent harm from trauma (Shields et al. 2016).

Bottom line relationships matter and they can help youth along the path to healing (Shields et al. 2016).

Reducing toxic shame

Reducing toxic shame by replacing it with reassurance and skills building.

Systems should work hard to avoid reinforcing and/or reproducing shame.

We've reviewed some of the literature on institutionalization and impact on the developing brain and behavior. Institutionalization affects attachment and connection. Institutionalization is experienced as a form of perpetual, public shame. While there is a functional role for shame in helping to self-regulate behavior and strengthen capacity for sympathy and empathy, there is such a thing as toxic shame. Persistent, public shame is toxic shame that contributes to internalized embarrassment, which compromises the ability for change. Shame is most useful, functional in the presence of reassurance, redirection, and education.

Limited attachment and connection lead to negative outcomes in terms of healthy brain development. If the goal is healing and habilitation, then the conditions must be set to accomplish these goals.

Mushrooms are about one of the only things that can grow effectively in the dark and the light. However, a mushroom does not rely on energy from the sun to grow. They are considered fungi. They get everything they need for growth from a combination of organic decomposing vegetation. When you consider the conditions for growth for the mushroom, it seems contradictory and confusing.

- They can grow in light, but don't require light.

- The conditions for their growth include both living and decaying things.

Growth and change can be confusing and contradictory. I use the mushroom as a metaphor for some youth because mushrooms like some youth grow in difficult spaces, in the absence of light and in the presence of decaying things. The positive aspect of this metaphor is that even in the least ideal conditions, there is growth. The hope for youth that systems seek to serve is that they can also thrive in the presence of light and living things. The point is: systems working with youth must consider the conditions from which they emerge and work diligently to create conditions for life and light in support of sustained, healthy growth.

Reiterating Habilitation
Rehabilitation assumes that youth have gained a set of skills that they've moved through the psychosocial developmental phases as outlined by Erikson.

Communication skills are a key for survival and for ability to optimally function. *Consider the following*:
You are in kindergarten at recess and a group of your peers are playing kickball. Before the game starts, team captains are selected and are given the task of picking teams. The team captains start the process of selecting and you do not get picked for either of the teams.

How do you feel?

What are some of your possible reactions to not being picked?

- Some children might internalize a feeling of rejection and think they were not good enough to be selected. Think about the conditions that would make this response more likely at this age.
- Some children would get visibly upset and begin to call their colleagues names like "stupid head." The real emotion is hurt but is expressed as anger. Think about the conditions (home environment) that would make this response more likely at this age.
- Some children would get physical and start hitting. They cannot find words, so they start hitting instead.

These are real responses and scenarios.

The ability to learn to effectively communicate what you are feeling is modeled. More often than not, frustrated children who are learning to use their words often have to be reminded to use their words and not their hands. There is a natural frustration and tendency to communicate in whatever modality you know. In cases of safely attached, securely connected children, they learn to communicate discomfort and feelings. They are able to move away from hitting to communicate. What I am asking us to consider are the children who do not have the privilege of learning how to communicate without hitting. They grow into adults who didn't have the privilege and/or exposure as children to learn to effectively communicate.

Habilitation as a practice considers this scenario.

Reinforcing attachment
Erikson's model of psychosocial development demonstrates that every human being continues to develop over time. Each developmental phase as outlined in the model

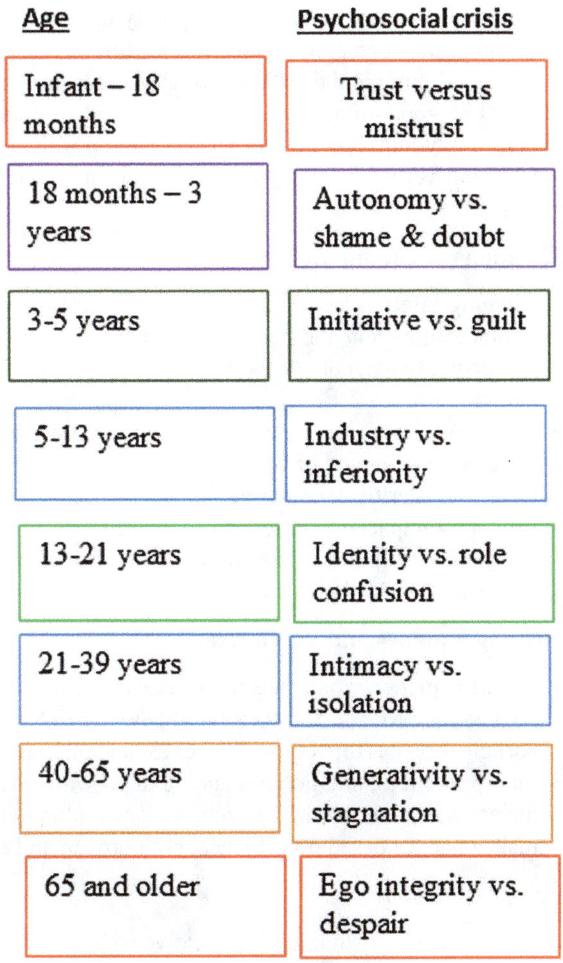

Fig. 9.5 Erik Erikson's stages of psychosocial development

below mandates some level of relationship, connectedness, and attachment. At every human developmental phase, attachment is important for survival and to thrive. Systems should closely consider these developmental phases in serving youth.
Example: Peer mentorship as a form of positive attachment (Fig. 9.5).

Reframing issues through reframing narratives
Consider the role of narrative and its impact on behavior.
From a system perspective:

Do policies consist of a narrative that lends itself to healing and change?
Do practices lend themselves to healing and change?
Words matter. How we use words, matters.
How we make people feel, matters.

Re-discovering and re-defining capacity for greatness in youth
Remember the "one good thing" rule. Everyone is waiting for someone to take note of one good thing in them. When young people are reminded of what they are good at, that one good thing can be used as a foundation for greatness. When confidence is placed in youth, it builds self-efficacy and positively impacts self-worth. It seems simple, but yet profound to reiterate this idea of speaking life into youth and they will live.

Creating the conditions for change

- Creating safety is key, what environment must be constructed that allows optimal brain development and healing for youth? This is the key question.
- Understand and reconcile the negative impact of institutionalization on brain development.
- Appreciate and reconcile the fact that connection and attachment matter and should be considered in any habilitation and healing process with youth.
- Narrative is critical; changing the narrative can powerfully shape conditions and positively impact outcomes.
- Peer mentorship is a demonstrated practice that can aid in helping youth improve in the area of relationships.

Helping Families and Youth Heal

- Families matter. Youth are more likely to heal when their families are also in the healing process. Termination of parental rights and limiting biological parent participation has dire consequences as demonstrated by the studies in this chapter.
- Laws, practices, and policies should align with current literature and research in the areas of neuroscience, psychosocial development, and trauma. Systems must make changes based on evidence, both proven and emerging.

Recommendations

- Make it a priority to know and involve persons, whom youth identify as family in the healing process as early and as often as possible and as appropriate.
- Consider the narrative of and in a system and assess whether or not if it lends itself toward creating the conditions for safety and optimal healing for youth.
- Consider the role of shame versus toxic shame.
- Consider the developmental phases and where youth and their families may fall along the spectrum.
- Consider early attachments and its role in creating safety; were early attachments secure and/or insecure?
- Consider the conditions that youth may have been exposed to. Again this is not a deficit-based approach, but an approach that considers structural, social, and economic components that may have curved a young person's developmental trajectory.
  For instance:
  For some children, hiding under a table in a game of hide and seek with a loving figure is representative of the wonder, freedom, and safety of play.

For some children, hiding under the table represents seeking safety from harm and perceived danger.

- Habilitation over rehabilitation.
  What skills do youth need? Were they ever taught how to use their words and not their hands?
- Advocate for familial involvement in others systems that youth may be involved in.
- Consider parent education as a critical element of support.

References

Ardiel, E. L., & Rankin, C. H. (2010). The importance of touch in development. *Paediatrics & Child Health, 15*(3), 153–156.

Arditti, J. A. (2012). *Parental incarceration and the family: Psychological and social effects of imprisonment on children, parents, and care-givers*. New York, NY: New York University Press.

Au, S. (2015, June 23). The psychological effects of shaming children. *Psychology Today*.

Austin, J., et al. (2004). The risks and needs of the returning prisoner population. *The Review of Policy Research, 21*(1), 13–29.

Barrett, K. C. (1998). The origins of guilt in early childhood. In J. Bybee (Ed.), *Guilt and children* (pp. 75–90). San Diego, CA: Academic Press.

Barrett, K. C., Zahn-Waxler, C., & Cole, P. M. (1993). Avoiders vs. amenders: Implications for the investigation of guilt and shame during toddlerhood? *Cognition and Emotion, 7*(6), 481–505. http://dx.doi.org/10.1080/02699939308409201

Carlson, M., & Earls, F. (1997). Psychological and neuroendocrinological sequelae of early social deprivation in institutionalized children in Romania. *Annals of the New York Academy of Sciences, 807,* 419–428.

Couturier, L. C. (1995). Inmates benefit from family service programs. *Corrections Today, 57,* 100.

Development Services Group, Inc. (2010). *Restorative justice*. Literature review. Washington, D.C.: Office of Juvenile Justice and Delinquency Prevention. https://www.ojjdp.gov/mpg/litreviews/Restorative_Justice.pdf.

Eby, L. T., Allen, T. D., Evans, S. C., Ng, T., & Dubois, D. (2008). Does mentoring matter? A multidisciplinary meta-analysis comparing mentored and non-mentored individuals. *Journal of Vocational Behavior, 72*(2), 254–267.

Eisenberg, N. (2000). Emotion, regulation, and moral development. *Annual Review of Psychology, 51,* 665–697.

Ellingsen, D. M., Leknes, S., Løseth, G., Wessberg, J., & Olausson, H. (2016). The neurobiology shaping affective touch: Expectation, motivation, and meaning in the multisensory context. *Frontiers in psychology, 6,* 1986. https://doi.org/10.3389/fpsyg.2015.01986.

Geller, A., Garfinkel, I., & Western, B. (2011). Paternal incarceration and support for children in fragile families. *Demography, 48*(1), 25–47.

Glaze, L. E., & Herberman, E. J. (2013). *Correctional populations in the United States, 2012*. Bureau of Justice Statistics Bulletin (NCJ 243936). Washington, DC: U.S. Department of Justice. Retrieved from http://www.bjs.gov/content/pub/pdf/cpus12.pdf.

Glaze, L. E., & Maruschak, L. M. (2010). *Parents in prison and their minor children: Special report*. Washington, DC: Bureau of Justice Statistics, U.S. Department of Justice Office of Justice Programs. Retrieved from http://www.bjs.gov/content/pub/pdf/pptmc.pdf.

Hagan, J., & Dinovitzer, R. (1999). Collateral consequences of imprisonment for children, communities, and prisoners. *Crime and Justice, 26,* 121–142.

Harlow, H. F., & Harlow, M. K. (1973). Social deprivation in monkeys. In *Readings from the scientific American: The nature and nurture of behavior* (pp. 108–116). San Francisco: W. H. Freeman Co.

Hostinar, C. E., & Gunnar, M. R. (2015). Social support can buffer against stress and shape brain activity. *AJOB Neuroscience, 6*(3), 34–42.

Hostinar, C. E., Sullivan, R. M., & Gunnar, M. R. (2014). Psychobiological mechanisms underlying the social buffering of the hypothalamic-pituitary-adrenocortical axis: A review of animal models and human studies across development. *Psychological Bulletin, 140*(1), 256–282. https://doi.org/10.1037/a0032671.

Inciardi, J. A., Martin, S. S., & Butzin, C. A. (1997). An effective model for prison-based treatment of drug involved offenders. *Journal of Drug Issues, 27,* 261–278.

Kochanska, G., Gross, J. N., Lin, M. H., & Nichols, K. E. (2002). Guilt in young children: Development, determinants, and relations with a broader system of standards. *Child Development, 73,* 461–482.

Lebel, T. P., et al. (2015, January). Helping others as a response to reconcile a criminal past: The role of the wounded healer in prisoner reentry programs. *Criminal Justice and Behavior, 42*(1), 108–120.

Lebel, T. P. (2007). An examination of the impact of formerly incarcerated persons helping others. *Journal of Offender Rehabilitation, 46*(1–2).

Lewin, T. (2001, November 16). Inmate education is found to lower risk of new arrests. *The New York Times*. Retrieved September 15, 2017.

Lewis, M. (2000). Self-conscious emotions: Embarrassment, pride, shame, and guilt. In M. Lewis & J. M. Haviland-Jones (Eds.), *Handbook of emotions* (2nd ed., pp. 623–636). New York, NY, US: Guilford.

MacKenzie, D. L. (2006). *What works in corrections: Reducing the criminal activities of offenders and delinquents* (p. 331). Cambridge University Press.

Main, M. (1996). Introduction to the special section on attachment and psychopathology: 2. Overview of the field of attachment. *Journal of Counseling and Clinical Psychology, 64,* 237–243.

Markham, L. (2016, April). How children develop toxic shame. *Psychology Today*.

Marlowe, D. B., et al. (2018). Developing a culturally proficient intervention for young African American men in drug court: Examining feasibility and estimating an effect size for Habilitation Empowerment Accountability Therapy (HEAT). *Journal of Advancing Justice*. Retrieved December 28, 2018, from https://scholarworks.iupui.edu/bitstream/handle/1805/15018/HEAT-Manuscript-PrePrint.pdf?sequence=1&isAllowed=y.

McWey, L. M., Acock, A., & Porter, B. (2010). The impact of continued contact with biological parents upon the mental health of children in foster care. *Children and Youth Services Review, 32*(10), 1338–1345.

Morenoff, J. D., & Harding, D. J. (2014). Incarceration, prisoner reentry, and communities. *Annual Review of Sociology, 40,* 411–429.

Moutsiana, C., Johnstone, T., Murray, L., Fearon, P., Cooper, P. J., Pliatsikas, C., et al. (2014). Insecure attachment during infancy predicts greater amygdala volumes in early adulthood. *Journal of Child Psychology and Psychiatry and Allied Disciplines, 56*(5), 540–548.

Muris, P., Meesters, C., Heijmans, J., van Hulten, S., Kaanen, L., Oerlemans, B., et al. (2015). Lack of guilt, guilt, and shame: A multi-informant study on the relations between self-conscious emotions and psychopathology in clinically referred children and adolescents. *European Child & Adolescent Psychiatry, 25*(4), 383–396.

Oregon Department of Corrections. (2018). *Children of incarcerated parents project*. Retrieved December 29, 2018, from https://www.oregon.gov/doc/OC/pages/oam_booklet.aspx.

Parisette-Sparks, A., Bufferd, S. J., & Klein, D. N. (2015). Parental predictors of children's shame and guilt at age 6 in a multimethod, longitudinal study. *Journal of Clinical Child and Adolescent Psychology: The Official Journal for the Society of Clinical Child and Adolescent Psychology, American Psychological Association, Division 53, 46*(5), 721–731.

Phillips, C. M., & Mann, A. (2013). Historical analysis of the adoption and safe families act of 1997. *Journal of Human Behavior in the Social Environment, 23*(7), 862–868. https://doi.org/10.1080/10911359.2013.809290.

Reissman, F. (1965, April). The "helper" therapy principle. *Social Work, 10*(2), 27–32.

Rockhill, A., Green, B. L., & Furrer, C. (2007). Is the adoption and safe families act influencing child welfare outcomes for families with substance abuse issues? *Child Maltreatment, 12*(1), 7–19.

Shields, A. E., Wise, L. A., Ruiz-Narvaez, E. A. et al. (2016). Childhood abuse, promoter methylation of leukocyte NR3C1 and the potential modifying effect of emotional support. *Epigenomics, 8*(11), 1507–1517.

Sroufe, L. A., Egeland, B., Carlson, E. A., & Collins, W. A. (2005). *The development of the person: The Minnesota study of risk and adaptation from birth to adulthood*. New York, NY: Guilford Press.

Sullivan, R. M. (2012). The neurobiology of attachment to nurturing and abusive caregivers. *The Hastings Law Journal, 63*(6), 1553–1570.

Tierney, A. L., & Nelson, C. A. (2009). Brain development and the role of experience in the early years. *Zero to Three, 30*(2), 9–13.

Thompson, R. A., Goodvin, R., & Meyer, S. (2006). Social development: Psychological understanding, self-understanding, and relationships. In J. L. Luby (Ed.), *Handbook of preschool mental health: Development, disorders, and treatment* (pp. 3–22). New York, NY US: Guilford Press.

Walker S. C., & McGlone, F. P. (2013). The social brain: Neurobiological basis of affiliative behaviours and psychological well-being. *Neuropeptides, 47*, 379–393. https://doi.org/10.1016/j.npep.2013.10.008.

Williams, K., et al. (2012, March). *Prisoners' childhood and family backgrounds: Results from the Surveying Prisoner Crime Reduction (SPCR) longitudinal cohort study of prisoners*. Ministry of Justice Research Series 4/12.

Zahn-Waxler, C., Kochanska, G., Krupnick, J., & McKnew, D. (1990). Patterns of guilt in children of depressed and well mothers. *Developmental Psychology, 26*, 51–59.

Zeanah, C. H., Nelson, C. A., Fox, N. A., Smyke, A. T., Marshall, P., Parker, S. W., et al. (2003). Designing research to study the effects of institutionalization on brain and behavioral development: The Bucharest Early Intervention Project. *Development and Psychopathology, 15*, 885–907.

Chapter 10
Self-care: Strong at the Broken Places

Self-care is important. You cannot pour from an empty cup. Supporting and facilitating change can be an all-consuming endeavor. Self-preservation and care are mandatory to strengthen one's capacity to care for and serve others, genuinely. Hurt systems are in need of healing. Hurt systems are made up of hurt people who've not had the privilege of pursuing their own healing. This chapter focuses on providers in a given system. A trauma-informed framework considers the individual a system seeks to serve and the individual who works/serves within a system. Healing "self" makes it more likely that one can assist in healing individuals and systems. This is especially critical in systems that seek to optimally serve youth.

Maslow's hierarchy of need summarizes universal human need. Meeting basic needs is a key element in wellness and self-care. Relaxation, exercise, good nutrition, and mindfulness are among some of the top recommendations for taking care of "self." Systems don't heal (change) if the people who work in the system don't heal (change). My core conviction regarding systems and system change is worthy of repeating here: systems don't change if people don't change and people don't change if they don't feel something. Taking care of oneself (or individuals who work in a system) creates the conditions needed for sustained, meaningful change within any given system.

At the end of this chapter, you should be able to

- Appreciate Maslow's Hierarchy of Needs (a needs assessment of systems and the individuals that work in them).
- Understand the concept of "Wellness."
- Comprehend the eight dimensions of wellness.
- Know how to use relaxation tools/methods.

A. Moreland-Capuia, *Training for Change*,
https://doi.org/10.1007/978-3-030-19208-2_10

Fig. 10.1 Maslow's hierarchy of needs—outlines basic needs versus psychological needs versus self-fulfillment needs

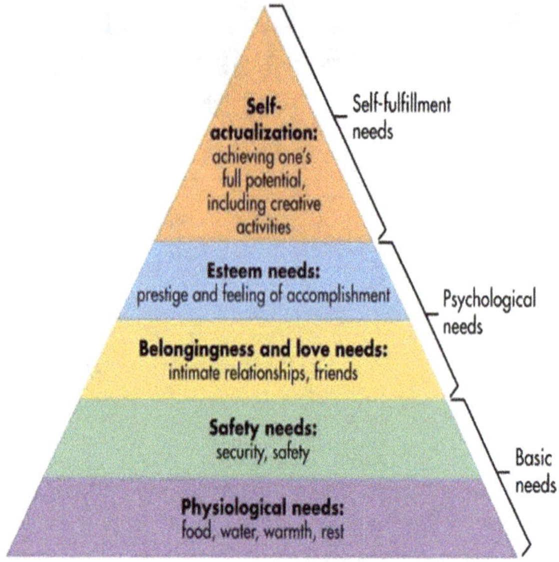

Up to now, we've focused primarily on the individuals who are served by a system, but there hasn't been a focus on the individuals that work within a given system. This textbook is about impacting systems for change. As quoted by Dr. Maya Angelou: when we know better, we can do better. A system doesn't change if the people who work within the system don't change. To this end, persons who work within systems require support, healing, and wellness (all around).

We've spent time talking about the basic needs of youth. The reality is that all human beings must have their basic needs met in order to survive. We've spent time talking about developmental phases as outlined by Erik Erikson, and these developmental phases apply to adults too. The question that I would like to deeply explore is what depth of change is possible within a system when the individuals who work within a system are well and their basic needs are met too (Fig. 10.1)?

Maslow (1943) stated that people are motivated to achieve certain needs and that some needs take precedence over others. Our most basic need is for physical survival, and this will be the first thing that motivates our behavior. Once that level is fulfilled, the next level up is what motivates us and so on (Fig. 10.2).

Maslow would contend that a human being must have basic-level needs fulfilled (satisfied) to achieve the next level and most folks often oscillate between levels (Henwood et al. 2015).

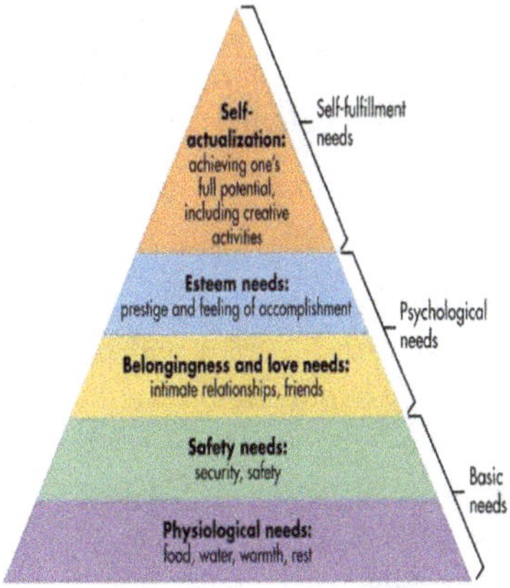

Conditions required for living and surviving:

Biological and Physiological needs = breathing, water, food, housing

↓ ↑

Safety needs = physical, financial, structural

↓ ↑

Love and belongingness needs = friendship, intimacy, trust and acceptance, belonging, connectedness

↓ ↑

Esteem needs = capacity to achieve, mastery, independence, status, dominance, prestige, self-respect, respect from others

↓ ↑

Self-Actualization needs = realizing personal potential, self-fulfillment, seeking personal growth and uttermost experiences

Fig. 10.2 Maslow's needs and conditions required for living and surviving

Physiologic Needs

- The physiological needs such as breathing, food, drink, sleep, intimacy, and housing (Kenrick et al. 2010).
- Every human being requires proper nutrition and housing to survive.
- When this most basic need is not fulfilled, people become preoccupied with filling those needs above all else and will do just about anything to attempt to fulfill it.

Safety Needs

- In Maslow's hierarchy, the safety needs come after the physiological needs.
- Maslow used the word "safety" to mean more than just physical safety.
- It included economic, social, vocational, and psychological security all of which fall underneath this second tier of human need.
- While safety needs are less immediate or demanding than the physiological needs, when one loses one's job, family, home, life savings, health insurance, etc., one is likely to feel "insecure and unsafe."

Belongingness and Love Needs

- We are social beings.
- Relationships (family, friendships, and intimate connections) MATTER!
- Numerous studies have shown that the healthiest, happiest people tend to be more involved in their communities, connected to and in relationship with others (Mineo

2017).

- Lack of interactions, human relationships, and the sense of belonging may result in depression or loneliness, while an abundance of love and community often sustain people through difficult times.

Esteem Needs

- There is a clear distinction between love and respect or esteem.
- Adhere to the core conviction that the ability to feel self-esteem and personal uniqueness emerges from being loved and embraced by families and communities.
- As human beings, we inherently wish to excel or be exceptional, to be noticed for our unique talents and capabilities. Even just to be seen by others. Once one has some measure of self-esteem and confidence, one gains the psychological freedom to be creative, to grow, and to be more generous to others.

Self-actualization
Maslow refers to peak experiences (the top of the hierarchy) as the experience of happiness. He notes that self-actualized people tend to experience a steadier, grounded sense of well-being, and satisfaction with life. According to Maslow, self-actualizing people

- Perceive reality accurately.
- Have a sense of awe, wonder, and gratitude about life.
- Not self-centered.
- Tend to be more problem-centered and focus on how to improve and are not deficiency-centered.
- Are independent thinkers.
- Are not overly influenced by general culture.
- Be life-affirming.
- Hold a deeply felt sense of kinship with the human race.

How does a system become self-actualized?

Answer: Through self-actualized individuals. The goal of any system seeking change is to create the conditions for individuals who work within the system to become self-actualized individuals. This can happen by making certain that basic needs are tended to.

Self-actualized

Safety achieved in the essential areas in one's life

Esteem is built

Loved and can demonstrate love towards others

Friendships are rich

Attached to something greater than oneself

Cared for by others and cares for others

Taps into resources around you

Unencumbered by life because basic needs are met

Anchored in a sense of self and purpose

Limitless in desire to serve others

Idealism about the world and others is preserved

Zeal for life is palpable

Empathetic

Dedicated to self-improvement and care

Exercise 10.1—Drilling down the "need"

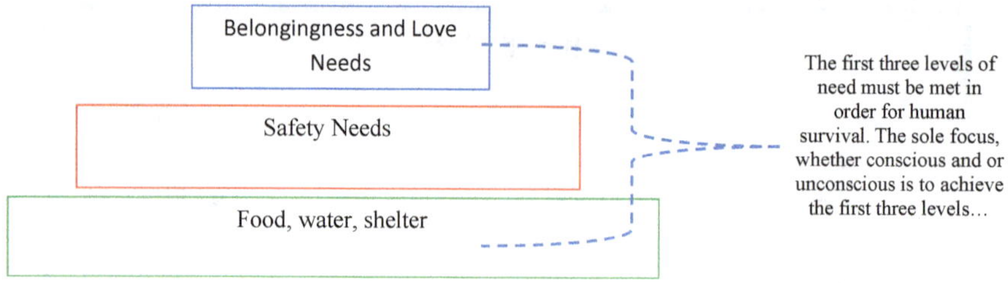

- What happens when basic physiologic needs aren't met? (Water, food, air, and shelter)
- What happens when safety needs aren't met?
- What happens when human live a disconnected life?

Exercise 10.2—Reaching the peak of Maslow's hierarchy gives humans an opportunity to get beyond surviving.

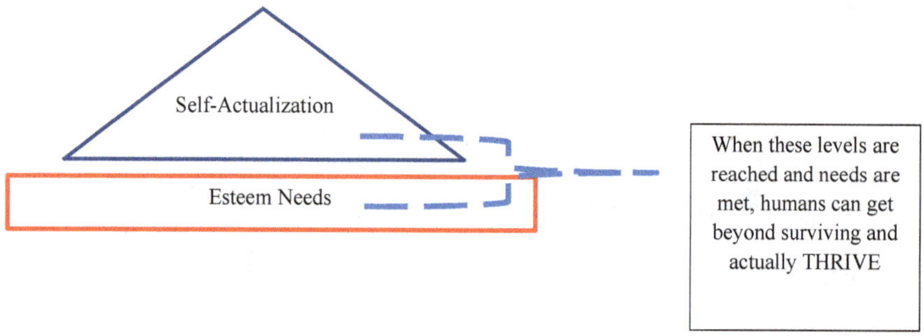

What is the importance of esteem?

How can a system prioritize meeting esteem needs for the persons that work within them?

When individuals feel good about themselves and the work they are doing, they are more likely to become self-actualized and display the qualities that Maslow highlighted almost six decades ago: Perceive reality accurately; have a sense of awe, wonder, and gratitude about life; not self-centered; tend to be more problem-centered and focus on how to improve and are not deficiency-centered; are independent thinkers; are not overly influenced by general culture; life-affirming; and hold a deeply felt sense of kinship with the human race.

We want more self-actualized human beings which can translate into self-actualized systems.

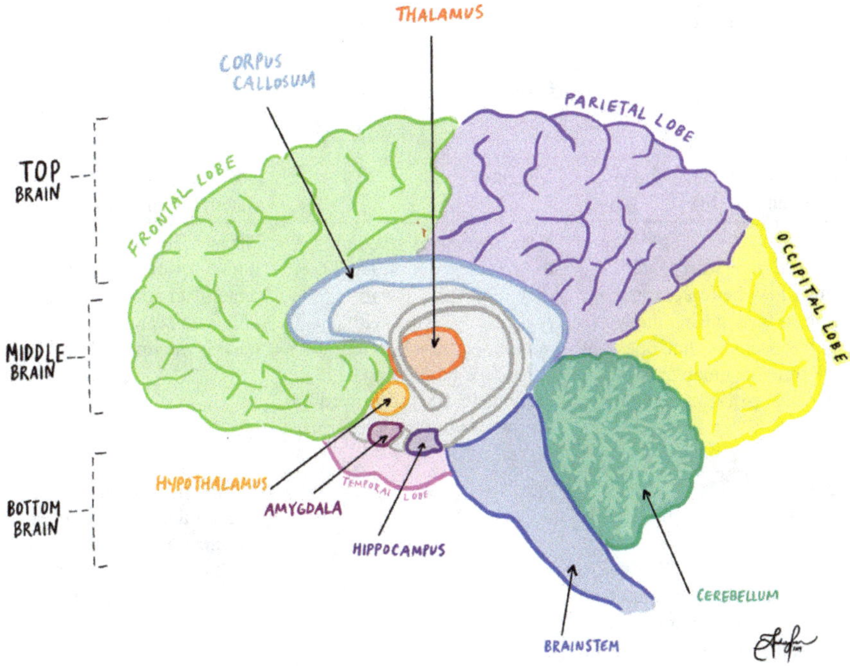

Fig. 10.3 Bottom brain is the most developed part of the brain when we are born. It is the "survival, primitive brain" Printed with permission. Copyright Audrey A. Tran

Making the connection.

Maslow's theory is consistent with brain development.

As mentioned in Chap. 1 of this textbook, the brain develops from the bottom-up and the inside-out. The most developed part of the brain for human beings when we are born is the bottom part of the brain. The bottom part of the brain includes the brain stem. The brain stem's main function is to help human's survive. How, our hearts wouldn't beat, nor would we breathe or have the capacity for consciousness without it. The brain stem also plays a role in the fear response. The brain stem is deemed the primitive brain (Fig. 10.3).

Takeaways:

- All human beings are born with the proclivity for survival.
- All human beings have basic needs for survival that must be met.
- Drive theory is applicable—where there are thirst and hunger, there is also a powerful drive to relieve quench the thirst and hunger. This holds true for every human being.
- Every human being requires love, connection, and safety to survive.

Consider the following: Have you ever been so hungry that you couldn't think straight and/or concentrate? So hungry that you were aggravated?

Have you ever been so tired that you couldn't focus or concentrate? So tired that you had no energy?
Exercise 10.3—Can you imagine?

System (individuals who work in a given system)	Imagine	Individuals served by a given system (youth, families, etc.)
Hunger/food In a system or workplace, hunger may be represented as being so busy during the work day that an individual does not have time for lunch or meals. A basic need is not being met	Now, if you can imagine these three examples and how they might play out in persons who work within a system, perhaps you might appreciate how it impacts individuals who are served by a system (youth, adolescents, and families)	Chronic Hunger (24-7 not knowing where a meal will come from and/or dealing with food scarcity) What is the impact?
Sleep In a system or workplace, lack of sleep may be represented by working long hours. Studies on poor sleep demonstrate concomitant changes in mood to include greater risk of irritability, anxiety, poor concentration, and manifest as higher levels of stress. Not getting enough sleep is a basic need not being met		Chronic poor sleep (intermittent housing or houseless and constantly on watch to the point of not sleeping to stay safe) What is the impact?
Safety In a system or workplace, not feeling safe may translate in exhibiting behaviors that are driven by fear (irrational, survival-based behavior)		Chronic, daily concerns of safety What is the impact?

Being hungry and tired impact behavior and performance.

If individuals within a system can recognize and acknowledge their own need, then it becomes a little easier to appreciate/recognize the needs in and of others.

Before there were Adverse Childhood Experiences (ACEs) there was Maslow and drive theory. It is well known that if basic needs are met the risks for various things are decreased.

Let's take trauma for instance: as indicated in prior chapters, studies show that when babies are securely connected and attached to their caregivers, good nutrition is provided, safety is established, and basic needs are met—their developmental trajectory (brain and behavior) is healthy (Cusick and Georgieff 2016; Rosales et al. 2009). The brain's amygdala is not as predominant, and survival and fear are quiet and only deployed in appropriate situations. The brain is free to develop independent of significant threat.

In the case of adults, emerging studies have demonstrated the importance of connection, love, and belonging in mitigating factors related to trauma.

I contend that when basic needs are met, the risk for violence can be significantly decreased. Careful analysis of the bottom of Maslow's hierarchy outlines the most basic of needs like food, water, shelter, air, and warmth—termed physiological needs. Just above physiologic needs, there is safety to include physical and financial safety—termed security needs. The level above security is belonging, connectedness, family, and love—termed social needs. The level above security is self-worth and accomplishment—termed esteem needs. At the peak of the hierarchy is self-awareness and personal growth—termed self-actualizing needs. Is the proclivity for violence connected to the most basic of needs not being met?

There are individuals experiencing poverty, racism, discrimination, trauma massive food, and housing insecurity in this country, which compromises a personal sense of safety. It is understood that when basic needs are not met, the human drive for survival turns on and the motivation to get needs met by any means necessary becomes prominent and can include exercising violent means, higher rates of substance use, and deep emotional pain.

All human beings have two fundamental desires—to be understood and to be connected. My working theory, supported by Maslow, is that aggressive behavior and drives are strongly influenced by "unmet need" which includes lack of connectedness (shaped by being understood), self-worth, and belonging (Alisha 2018).

Making sure that individuals within a system are healthy increases the risk of a given system being healthy.

Healthy (self-actualized, needs met) people = healthy (self-actualized, needs met) system = increased capacity to facilitate meaningful change.

> A fulfilled system translates into fulfilled people
>
> Fulfilled people translates into a fulfilled system

A fulfilled system, a self-actualized system, is a system that supports its members in pursuing wellness.

What is Wellness?

There are many working definitions of wellness, to include

- Good physical and mental health.
- Wellness is not the absence of illness or stress.
- One can still strive for wellness even if you are experiencing challenges in your life.
- Health is a state of complete physical, mental, and social well-being and not merely the absence of disease—***World Health Organization.***
- Wellness is an **active process** of becoming aware of and making choices toward a more successful existence—***National Wellness Existence***.

SAMHSA's Eight Dimensions of Wellness

- *Emotional*— Finding ways to manage the ups and downs of life and establishing nourishing relationships.
- *Environmental*— Occupying healthy, pleasant, and life-giving environments that support well-being.
- *Financial*— Current and future stability combined with opportunity to be upwardly mobile.
- *Intellectual*—Recognizing creative abilities and finding ways to expand knowledge and skills.
- *Occupational*—Personal satisfaction and enrichment from one's work.
- *Physical*—Appreciating the need for physical activity, healthy foods, and sleep.
- *Social*—Establishing a sense of connection, belonging, and a well-developed support system.
- *Spiritual*—Intensifying a sense of purpose and securing meaning in life.

If systems (workplaces) are spaces where meaningful connections happen, people are affirmed, esteem is built, opportunities for upward mobility are prominent, and there is safety—wellness is promoted.

A healthy system translates into healthy people

Healthy people translates into a healthy system

I pre-emptively propose a parallel change model in Chap. 7 of this textbook to prime readers for yet another parallel to change (Fig. 10.4).

Additional parallel change—in terms of systems is required
To achieve trauma-informed systems—then we must have trauma-informed people.

To achieve a healthy system—then we must have healthy individuals who work in the system.

To achieve systems change—then we must have individuals who work in the system appreciate the benefit of change. This can happen when they are connected to their own struggles, feelings, and needs. This connection increases the risk of them appreciating the struggles, feelings, and needs of those they seek to serve (Fig. 10.5).

Practical application(s)
Being aware of the levels of wellness of members within any given system is important. I use (and recommend use of) the "Strong at the Broken Places: Addressing Secondary Stress Self-Care Inventory by Saakvitne, Pearlman & Staff TSI/CAAP" as a wellness assessment.

Using this type of inventory to measure self-care efforts can inspire individual improvement and healing—resulting in improvement and healing in any given system.

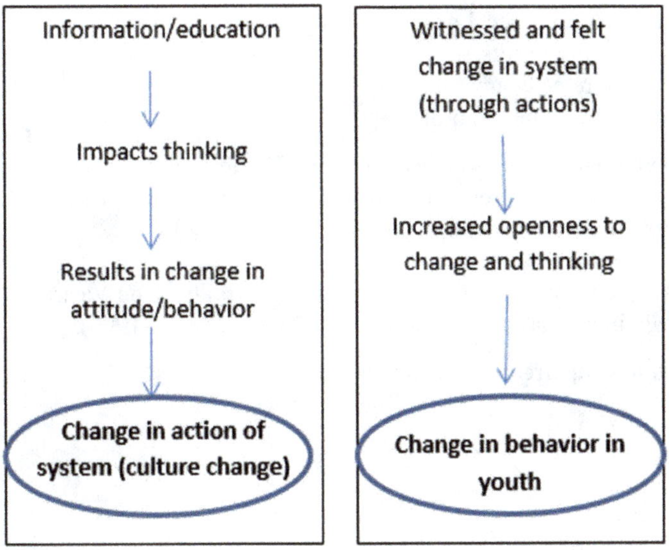

Fig. 10.4 Parallel change model

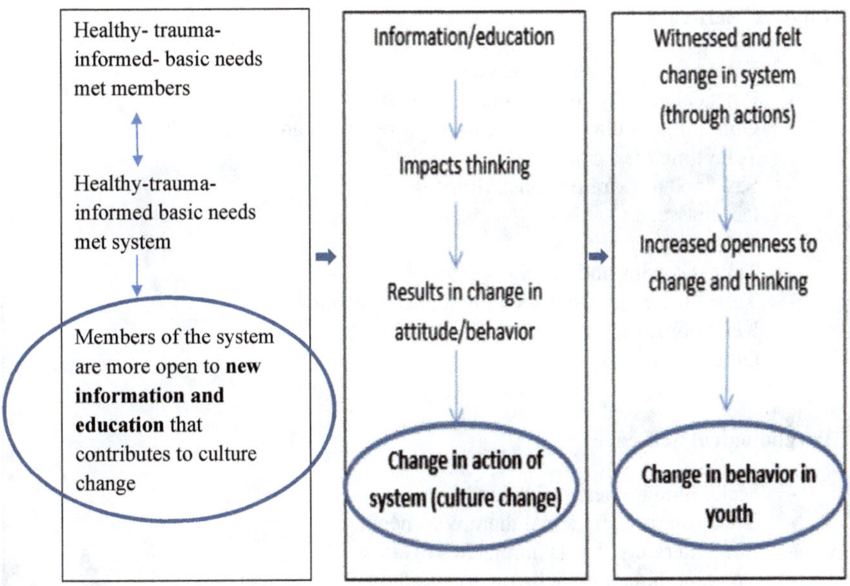

Fig. 10.5 If the system takes care of its members, members will take care of the system. Then the system will take better care of the individuals they seek to serve

- Take the inventory—**see 3 page inventory.**
- Review inventory results.
- Then work to remedy areas that require it.
- Watch overall wellness improve.

The intentional focus on wellness is critical. The version of the Self-Care Inventory that I am re-creating was revised by Wayne Scott, MA, LCSW 10/28/2013.

See the survey in the next three pages

Self-care Inventory

Source: Adapted from Transforming the Pain: A Workbook on Vicarious Traumatization. Saakvitne, Pearlman & Staff of TSI/CAAP (Norton, 1996).

Rate the following areas in frequency:

5 = Frequently,
4 = Occasionally,
3 = Rarely,
2 = Never, and
1 = It never occurred to me!

Physical Self-care

- Eating with regularity and healthily
- Physical activity for fitness and fun
- Obtaining regular medical care for prevention and when sick
- Take time off work
- Say “no” to extra responsibilities
- Get massages
- Get enough sleep
- Take day trips and or mini-vacations
- Take time away from social media and technology
- Keep home organized, clean, and safe
- Other

Psychological Self-care

- Make time for self-reflection
- Seek your own personal therapy as needed
- Read literature that is unrelated to your work
- Do something at which you are not the expert or in charge
- Engage your intelligence in a new area (e.g., go to an art museum, history exhibit, performance)
- Spend time with children
- Check vehicle for safety and maintenance
- Other

Revised by Wayne Scott, MA, LCSW 10/28/2013. Page 1 of 3

Self-care Inventory
Source: Adapted from Transforming the Pain: A Workbook on Vicarious Traumatization. Saakvitne, Pearlman & Staff of TSI/CAAP (Norton, 1996).
Rate the following areas in frequency:

5 = Frequently,
4 = Occasionally,
3 = Rarely,
2 = Never, and
1 = It never occurred to me!

Emotional Self-care

- Spend time with people you enjoy and limit time with those that drain you
- Stay in contact with important people in your life
- Identify comforting activities, objects, people, and places and seek them out
- Find things that make you laugh as often as possible
- Allow yourself to cry
- Connect with your neighbors
- Do family activities
- Express your opinion (e.g., letter to editor, marches, contribute in community)
- Other

Spiritual Self-care

- Make time for self-reflection
- Find a spiritual connection and or community
- Write in a journal, pray, meditate, sing, or dance
- Spend time in nature
- Be open to not knowing (getting comfortable with saying: "I don't know")
- Practice receiving kind words and actions from others
- Be aware of the non-material aspects of life
- Try not to be in charge or the expert at all times
- Other

Revised by Wayne Scott, MA, LCSW 10/28/2013. Page 2 of 3

Self-care Inventory
Source: Adapted from Transforming the Pain: A Workbook on Vicarious Traumatization. Saakvitne, Pearlman & Staff of TSI/CAAP (Norton, 1996).
Rate the following areas in frequency:

5 = Frequently,
4 = Occasionally,

3 = Rarely,
2 = Never, and
1 = It never occurred to me!

Workplace or Professional Self-care

- Give yourself affirmations – list accomplishments that make you proud
- Be curious and ask questions
- Take a break during the workday
- Arrange your workspace so that it is comfortable
- Find balance in your workload
- Identify and seek out work that is exciting and feels rewarding
- Set appropriate limits with colleagues and clients
- Get regular supervision, peer feedback, group, individual, and from manager
- Proactively work on developing a career path and professional network with others
- Set goals for accomplishment that are not directly related to your work
- Other

Revised by Wayne Scott, MA, LCSW 10/28/2013. Page 3 of 3

Managing Stress: Mindfulness Matters

The evidence for mindfulness was presented in prior chapters. Mindfulness helps to improve the immune system, it reduces the physiological and neurobiological impact of stress, and it can literally heal the brain. The daily practice of mindfulness supports sustained wellness.

Research has demonstrated that a shift in thought patterns can lead to decreased metabolism, rate of breathing and heart rate, and slower brain waves. This response was coined the "relaxation response" by Dr. Herbert Benson, "Founder of the Benson-Henry Institute."

How do you elicit the relaxation response?

There are two essential steps:

- Repeat one word, sound, phrase, or muscular activity.
- Passively disregard everyday thought that inevitably comes to mind and then return to your repetition.
- Practice for 10–20 min daily.

This is one of many mindfulness exercises that one can do. I strongly encourage members of any given system to practice mindfulness in their pursuit of wellness.

Other important considerations to remember in pursuing wellness:

- Physical health—reducing the use of substances (binge and/or excess).

- Increasing physical activity.
- Proper nutrition.
- Getting good sleep.
- Feeling safe (environment, home, and workplace).

Recommendations

- Every system should ensure that the basic needs of its members are being met. Maslow argues that inability meets the lowest level of need (food, water, and warmth) that prevents you from successfully moving up the pyramid to eventually reaching self-actualization.
- Give ample opportunity for members of any given system to tend to their personal wellness. There are eight aspects of wellness include social, occupational, financial, environmental, physical, intellectual, spiritual, and emotional. To the extent that the members of any given system can tend to the areas is the extent to which they contribute to and behave in the system.
- Use the self-care inventory with each member of your system. Assess wellness areas, if there are weaknesses identified, and work with members of your system to strengthen that area.
- Shift the system toward mindfulness by establishing, supporting, teaching, and making the practice of mindfulness accessible within your system. Relaxation response is a way to physically relieve stress and can be practiced 10 min per day.
- Recall the parallel change process and appreciate how it might apply to your system.
- Connecting with your own need helps to appreciate the need in others.

Remember:

Fulfilled, self-actualized, well members translate into a fulfilled, self-actualized, well system

These are the conditions under which change can happen!

References

Alisha, M. (2018). Applying a different lens to understand and reduce trauma, prevent. *International Journal of Public Health and Safety, 3*, 148.

Cusick, S. E., & Georgieff, M. K. (2016). the role of nutrition in brain development: The golden opportunity of the “first 1000 days”. *The Journal of Pediatrics, 175*, 16–21.

Henwood, B. F., Derejko, K. S., Couture, J., & Padgett, D. K. (2015). Maslow and mental health recovery: A comparative study of homeless programs for adults with serious mental illness. *Administration and Policy in Mental Health, 42*(2), 220–228.

Kenrick, D. T., Griskevicius, V., Neuberg, S. L., & Schaller, M. (2010). Renovating the pyramid of needs: Contemporary extensions built upon ancient foundations. *Perspectives on Psychological Science: A Journal of the Association for Psychological Science, 5*(3), 292–314.

Maslow, A. (1943). A theory of human motivation. *Psychological Review, 50,* 370–396.

Mineo, L. (2017, April 11). Good genes are nice, but Joy is better. The Harvard Gazette.

Rosales, F. J., Reznick, J. S., & Zeisel, S. H. (2009). Understanding the role of nutrition in the brain and behavioral development of toddlers and preschool children: identifying and addressing methodological barriers. *Nutritional Neuroscience, 12*(5), 190–202.

SAMSHA. Eight Dimensions of Wellness. (2017). https://www.samhsa.gov/wellness-initiative/eight-dimensions-wellness.

Self-care Inventory Adapted from Transforming the Pain: A Workbook on Vicarious Traumatization. Saakvitne, Pearlman & Staff of TSI/CAAP (Norton, 1996). Revised by Wayne Scott, MA, LCSW 10/28/2013.

Chapter 11
Quick Review

By the end of this chapter, you should be able to

- Recall how the brain develops and potential threats to healthy brain development;
- Identify areas of the brain associated with fear, trauma, and substance use;
- Understand racism and prejudice as a form of trauma from a neurobiological (brain perspective);
- Understand how substances impact the developing brain;
- Appreciate the role that mindfulness plays in healing the brain;
- Epigenetics;
- Recall structural racism and its role in toxic stress;
- Know stereotype threat;
- Know Maslow's hierarchy of needs;
- Be familiar with Reintegrative shaming;
- Appreciate theories on organizational change; and
- Apply your knowledge of the brain and its development to the system in which you work.

Review Questions

Chapter 1: The Developing Brain and Trauma

1. The brain develops in the following order:
    a. Inside-out, bottom-up
    b. Outside-in, downward
    c. Bottom-up, inside-out
    d. None of the above
    e. All of the above
2. Midbrain structures include
    a. Nucleus accumbens
    b. Ventral tegmental area
    c. Hippocampus

A. Moreland-Capuia, *Training for Change*,
https://doi.org/10.1007/978-3-030-19208-2_11

   d. None of the above
   e. All of the above

3. The prefrontal cortex plays a role in

   a. Personality expression
   b. Executive function
   c. Emotion regulation
   d. None of the above
   e. All of the above

4. Brain development starts at

   a. 3-month gestation
   b. 2-week gestation
   c. In utero
   d. At the point of conception
   e. None of the above

5. Folic acid supports the folding of neural tube, which becomes the blueprint for the development of the brain and spinal cord.

   a. True
   b. False

6. The neural plate folds to become the neural tube at

   a. 1-week gestation
   b. 2-week gestation
   c. 3–4-week gestation
   d. None of the above
   e. All of the above

7. Timeline and stages of brain development in the following order:

   a. Neurulation/Neuronal proliferation/Neuronal migration/Apoptosis/Synaptogenesis/Myelination
   b. Neuronal proliferation/Neurulation/Neuronal migration/Synaptogenesis/Apoptosis/Myelination
   c. Myelination/Apoptosis/Neuronal migration/Synaptogenesis/Neuronal Proliferation/Neurulation
   d. Apoptosis/Neuronal proliferation/Neurulation/Synaptogenesis/Myelination/Neuronal migration
   e. None of the above

8. The brain develops

   a. From birth to age 18 years old
   b. From 3 months to 20 years old

c. From 1 month to 22 years old
d. From conception—around 26 years of age
e. None of the above

9. Segmentation begins at

a. Week 1 of gestation
b. Week 2 of gestation
c. Week 3–4 of gestation
d. Week 5 of gestation
e. None of the above

10. The forebrain is the largest part of the brain and includes the following structures:

a. Cerebrum
b. Thalamus
c. Hypothalamus
d. Limbic system
e. All of the above

11. Hindbrain structures include

a. Medulla
b. Pons
c. Cerebellum
d. Spinal cord
e. All of the above

12. At 7 weeks of gestation, neurons and synapses form in the spinal cord.

a. True
b. False

13. Fetal movements happen as early as 7 weeks of gestation. The movements provide the brain with the sensory input that helps to support its development.

a. True
b. False

14. During neurogenesis (between 8–10 weeks of gestation), neurons experience a period of rapid growth at 200,000 neurons per minute.

a. True
b. False

15. Match the cell with its function:

a. Oligodendrocyte	i. Star-shaped glial cell found in the brain and spinal cord, cleans up debri within the brain
b. Astrocyte	
c. Neurons	ii. Glial cells involved in myelin production
	iii. Specialized cell that transmits nerve impulses

16. According to (Imada et al. 2006), language circuits in the frontal and temporal lobes are consolidated in the first year of life.

    a. True
    b. False

17. The brain doubles in size in the first year of life.

    a. True
    b. False

18. According to (Gilman et al., 2007; Nowakowski, 2006), by the age of 3, the brain reaches about 80% of adult brain volume.

    a. True
    b. False

19. Match structure with function

a. Occipital lobe	i. Spatial awareness/somatosensory
b. Temporal lobe	ii. Visual
c. Anterior/Posterior parietal lobe	iii. Hearing
	iv. Cognitive
d. Frontal lobe	

Chapter 1 Answers
Review Answers (in bold)

Chapter 1: The Developing Brain and Trauma

1. The brain develops in the following order:

    a. Inside-out, bottom-up

b. Outside-in, downward
c. **Bottom-up, inside-out**
d. None of the above
e. All of the above

2. Midbrain structures include

a. Nucleus accumbens
b. Ventral tegmental area
c. Hippocampus
d. None of the above
e. **All of the above**

3. The prefrontal cortex plays a role in

a. Personality expression
b. Executive function
c. Emotion regulation
d. None of the above
e. **All of the above**

4. Brain development starts at

a. 3-month gestation
b. 2-week gestation
c. In utero
d. **At the point of conception**
e. None of the above

5. Folic acid supports the folding of neural tube, which becomes the blueprint for the development of the brain and spinal cord.

a. **True**
b. False

6. The neural plate folds to become the neural tube at

a. 1-week gestation
b. 2-week gestation
c. **3–4-week gestation**
d. None of the above
e. All of the above

7. Timeline and stages of brain development in the following order:

a. **Neurulation/Neuronal proliferation/Neuronal migration/Apoptosis/Synaptogenesis/Myelination**
b. Neuronal proliferation/Neurulation/Neuronal migration/Synaptogenesis/Apoptosis/Myelination

c. Myelination/Apoptosis/Neuronal migration/Synaptogenesis/Neuronal Proliferation/Neurulation
d. Apoptosis/Neuronal proliferation/Neurulation/Synaptogenesis/Myelination/Neuronal migration
e. None of the above

8. The brain develops

a. From birth to age 18 years old
b. From 3 months to 20 years old
c. From 1 month to 22 years old
d. **From conception—around 26 years of age**
e. None of the above

9. Segmentation begins at

a. Week 1 of gestation
b. Week 2 of gestation
c. Week 3–4 of gestation
d. **Week 5 of gestation**
e. None of the above

10. The Forebrain is the largest part of the brain and includes the following structures:

a. Cerebrum
b. Thalamus
c. Hypothalamus
d. Limbic system
e. **All of the above**

11. Hindbrain structures include

a. Medulla
b. Pons
c. Cerebellum
d. Spinal cord
e. **All of the above**

12. At 7 weeks of gestation, neurons and synapses form in the spinal cord.

a. **True**
b. False

13. Fetal movements happen as early as 7 weeks of gestation. The movements provide the brain with the sensory input that helps to support its development.

a. **True**
b. False

14. During neurogenesis (between 8–10 weeks of gestation), neurons experience a period of rapid growth at 200,000 neurons per minute.

    a. **True**
    b. False

15. Match the cell with its function:

    a. Oligodendrocyte
    b. Astrocyte
    c. Neurons

    i. Star-shaped glial cell found in the brain and spinal cord, cleans up debri within the brain
    ii. Glial cells involved in myelin production
    iii. Specialized cell that transmits nerve impulses

16. According to (Imada et al. 2006), language circuits in the frontal and temporal lobes are consolidated in the first year of life.

    a. **True**
    b. False

17. The brain doubles in size the first year of life.

    a. **True**
    b. False

18. According to (Gilman et al., 2007; Nowakowski, 2006), by the age of 3, the brain reaches about 80% of adult brain volume.

    a. **True**
    b. False

19. Match structure with function

    a. Occipital lobe
    b. Temporal lobe
    c. Anterior/Posterior parietal lobe
    d. Frontal lobe

    i. Spatial awareness/somatosensory
    ii. Visual
    iii. Hearing
    iv. Cognitive

Review Questions

Chapter 2: Cultural Responsivity

1. Schein's organizational model of change includes the following elements:

    a. Artifacts (what is observed)
    b. Norms and values (not observed)
    c. Underlying assumptions (not observed)
    d. None of the above
    e. All of the above

2. Stereotype threat according to Steele and Aronson is

    a. A situational predicament in which people feel themselves to be at risk of confirming the stereotypes about their social group.
    b. Not a real phenomenon
    c. Doesn't impact self-esteem and/or self-worth
    d. All of the above
    e. None of the above

3. Intersectionality:

    a. Considers the impact interlocking systems of power on marginalized individuals
    b. Recognizes the interplay between multiple identities (i.e., gender, race)
    c. Is a concept established by law scholar Kimberlee Williams Crenshaw in the 1980s as a commentary on Black feminism
    d. All of the above
    e. None of the above

Review Answers (in bold)

Chapter 2: Cultural Responsivity

1. Schein's organizational model of change includes the following elements:

    a. Artifacts (what is observed)
    b. Norms and values (not observed)
    c. Underlying assumptions (not observed)
    d. None of the above
    e. **All of the above**

2. Stereotype threat according to Steele and Aronson is

    a. **A situational predicament in which people feel themselves to be at risk of confirming the stereotypes about their social group.**
    b. Not a real phenomenon
    c. Doesn't impact self-esteem and/or self-worth
    d. All of the above

e. None of the above

3. Intersectionality:

   a. Considers the impact interlocking systems of power on marginalized individuals
   b. Recognizes the interplay between multiple identities (i.e., gender, race)
   c. Is a concept established by law scholar Kimberlee Williams Crenshaw in the 1980s as a commentary on Black feminism
   d. **All of the above**
   e. None of the above

Review Questions

Chapter 3: Trauma-Informed—The intersection of Fear, Trauma, Aggression, and the Path to Healing

1. Fear is

   a. A natural human response
   b. Plays a functional role in human's capacity to seek safety
   c. Has a role in human survival
   d. All of the above
   e. None of the above

2. The brain stem has a role in

   a. Blood pressure regulation
   b. Heart rate regulation
   c. Digestion
   d. Respiration
   e. All of the above

3. The fear response involves multiple parts of the brain. Match the brain structure with its role in the fear response:

a. Thalamus	i. Emotional/Memory aspect of fear
b. Hippocampus/Amygdala	ii. Sensory aspect of fear
c. Hypothalamus	iii. Cognitive aspect of fear
d. Frontal/Temporal Lobe	iv. Physiologic aspect of fear

4. The fear response is meant to be time-limited, turns on in response to a perceived and/or real threat, and slows down when the threat is gone.

   a. True
   b. False

5. The "fight–flight–freeze" response is <u>primarily</u> mediated what brain structure:
    a. Thalamus
    b. Amygdala
    c. Hippocampus
    d. Hypothalamus
    e. None of the above
6. The fear conditioning response involves the following parts of the brain:
    a. Medial prefrontal cortex
    b. Amygdala
    c. Anterior cingulate cortex
    d. All of the above
    e. None of the above
7. The prefrontal cortex is involved in
    a. Planning
    b. Organizing
    c. Decision-making
    d. Moderating social behavior
    e. All of the above
8. The amygdala is involved in
    a. Processing of memory, decision-making, emotional reactions
    b. Memory consolidation
    c. Aggression
    d. None of the above
    e. All of the above
9. According to Larry Siever's work on the neurobiology of violence, a trauma history increases susceptibility to aggression.
    a. True
    b. False
10. According to a 1997 study by Bruce Perry, extreme neglect in childhood negatively impacts brain development by reducing cortical volume.
    a. True
    b. False
11. Felitti and Anda demonstrated that adverse childhood experiences increase the risk of adoption of health risk behaviors, and chronic physical and mental health challenges.
    a. True

b. False

12. Mindfulness is a trauma-informed practice that impacts the brain in the following ways when practiced consistently:

    a. Increases cortical volume
    b. Increases hippocampal volume
    c. Decreases the volume of the amygdala
    d. None of the above
    e. All of the above

Review Answers (in bold)

Chapter 3: Trauma-Informed—The intersection of Fear, Trauma, Aggression, and the Path to Healing

1. Fear is

    a. A natural human response
    b. Plays a functional role in human's capacity to seek safety
    c. Has a role in human survival
    d. **All of the above**
    e. None of the above

2. The brain stem has a role in

    a. Blood pressure regulation
    b. Heart rate regulation
    c. Digestion
    d. Respiration
    e. **All of the above**

3. The fear response involves multiple parts of the brain. Match the brain structure with its role in the fear response:

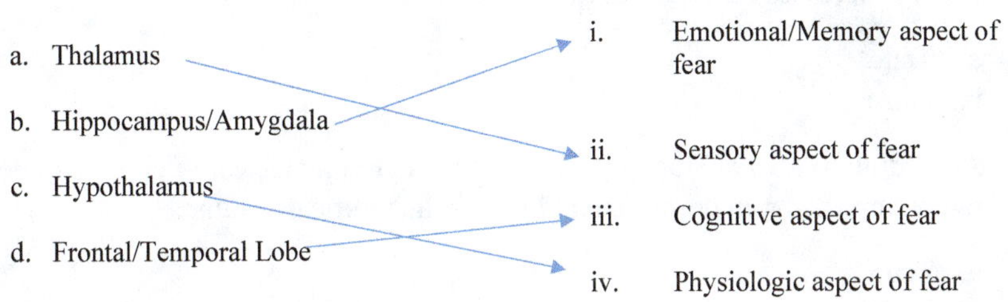

4. The fear response is meant to be time-limited, turns on in response to a perceived and/or real threat, and slows down when the threat is gone.

    a. **True**
    b. False

5. The "fight–flight–freeze" response is primarily mediated what brain structure:

   a. Thalamus
   b. Amygdala
   c. Hippocampus
   d. **Hypothalamus**
   e. None of the above

6. The fear conditioning response involves the following parts of the brain:

   a. Medial prefrontal cortex
   b. Amygdala
   c. Anterior cingulate cortex
   d. **All of the above**
   e. None of the above

7. The prefrontal cortex is involved in

   a. Planning
   b. Organizing
   c. Decision-making
   d. Moderating social behavior
   e. **All of the above**

8. The amygdala is involved in

   a. Processing of memory, decision-making, emotional reactions
   b. Memory consolidation
   c. Aggression
   d. None of the above
   e. **All of the above**

9. According to Larry Siever's work on the neurobiology of violence, a trauma history increases susceptibility to aggression.

   a. **True**
   b. False

10. According to a 1997 study by Bruce Perry, extreme neglect in childhood negatively impacts brain development by reducing cortical volume.

    a. **True**
    b. False

11. Felitti and Anda demonstrated that adverse childhood experiences increase the risk of adoption of health risk behaviors, and chronic physical and mental health challenges.

    a. True

b. False

12. Mindfulness is a trauma-informed practice that impacts the brain in the following ways when practiced consistently:

    a. Increases cortical volume
    b. Increases hippocampal volume
    c. Decreases the volume of the amygdala
    d. None of the above
    e. **All of the above**

Review Questions

Chapter 4: Substances of Abuse and the Brain

1. Montreal Cognitive Assessment (MoCA) assesses

    a. Attention
    b. Cognition
    c. Orientation
    d. Delayed recall
    e. All of the above

2. The reward pathway includes

    a. Ventral tegmental area
    b. Nucleus accumbens
    c. Hippocampus
    d. Prefrontal Cortex
    e. All of the above

3. The 3 C's of addiction stand for

    a. Cravings, loss of Control, continued use despite consequences
    b. Compulsion, control, culture
    c. Cost, cravings, compulsion
    d. None of the above
    e. All of the above

4. Addiction represents a loss of top-down control—the prefrontal cortex is less (salient), and the amygdala and ventral tegmental area are more (salient).

    a. True
    b. False

5. Cocaine's mechanism of action involves significant increase in the neurotransmitter dopamine.

    a. True
    b. False

6. Epinephrine increases blood pressure, heart rate, and respiration.

    a. True
    b. False

7. Once nicotine hits the bloodstream, it stimulates the adrenal glands which releases the hormone epinephrine.

    a. True
    b. False

8. Dopamine is a key neurotransmitter in the reward pathway.

    a. True
    b. False

9. Marijuana can negatively impact cognition, especially in the developing brain.

    a. True
    b. False

10. Cannabis use impacts the following:

    a. Judgment
    b. Reward
    c. Movement/coordination
    d. Memory/cognition
    e. All of the above

11. Substances of abuse impact certain areas of the brain that are similarly impacted in trauma:

    a. True
    b. False

Review Answers (in bold)

Chapter 4: Substances of Abuse and the Brain

1. Montreal Cognitive Assessment (MoCA) assesses

    a. Attention
    b. Cognition
    c. Orientation
    d. Delayed recall
    e. **All of the above**

2. The reward pathway includes

    a. Ventral tegmental area
    b. Nucleus accumbens

c. Hippocampus
d. Prefrontal Cortex
e. **All of the above**

3. The 3 C's of addiction stand for

a. **Cravings, loss of Control, continued use despite consequences**
b. Compulsion, control, culture
c. Cost, cravings, compulsion
d. None of the above
e. All of the above

4. Addiction represents a loss of top-down control—the prefrontal cortex is less (salient), and the amygdala and ventral tegmental area are more (salient).

a. **True**
b. False

5. Cocaine's mechanism of action involves a significant increase in the neurotransmitter dopamine.

a. **True**
b. False

6. Epinephrine increases blood pressure, heart rate, and respiration.

a. True
b. False

7. Once nicotine hits the bloodstream, it stimulates the adrenal glands which releases the hormone epinephrine.

a. **True**
b. False

8. Dopamine is a key neurotransmitter in the reward pathway.

a. **True**
b. False

9. Marijuana can negatively impact cognition, especially in the developing brain.

a. **True**
b. False

10. Cannabis use impacts the following:

a. Judgment
b. Reward
c. Movement/coordination

d. Memory/cognition
e. **All of the above**

11. Substances of abuse impact certain areas of the brain that are similarly impacted in trauma:

a. **True**
b. False

Review Questions

Chapter 5: Cannabis

1. Delta-9-tetrahydrocannabinol (THC) can contribute to paranoia and psychosis.

a. True
b. False

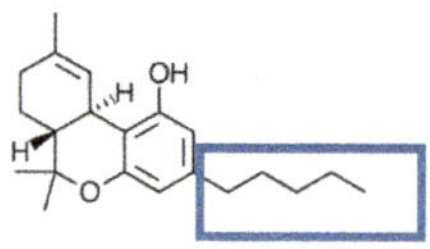

2. THC's (chemical structure is shown above) potency is determined by the length of its carbon side chain.

a. True
b. False

3. According to (Baker et al., 2003), Cannabinoid (CB1) receptors are found in the following brain areas:

a. Basal ganglia
b. Hippocampus
c. Amygdala
d. Caudate Nucleus
e. All of the above

4. Cannabinoid receptors have the highest concentration in parts of the brain that impact pleasure, memory, thinking, concentration, perception, coordination, and movement.

a. True
b. False

5. According to (Guzman, 2003), cannabis increases the release of dopamine in the reward center of the brain and interferes with hippocampal function.

a. True
b. False

6. In the first 3 h after cannabis use, an individual can experience the following physical symptoms:

   a. Changes in blood pressure—postural hypotension (changes in blood pressure when sitting versus standing)
   b. Red eyes (conjunctival injection)
   c. Decrease in body temperature (hypothermia)
   d. Decreased motor skills and reaction time
   e. All of the above

7. According to (Jager et al., 2008; Meier et al., 2012), individuals who use cannabis before the age of 18, the following can happen

   a. Change in the developmental course of the brain
   b. Decrease in IQ points as much as by eight points
   c. Difficulty learning new material
   d. None of the above
   e. All of the above

8. (D'Souza et al., 2009) & (Hall et al., 2008) studies demonstrated an increased risk of psychosis in adults who used marijuana in adolescence and who also carried a variant in the gene Catechol-O-methyltransferase (COMT).

   a. True
   b. False

9. Study by Filbey et al., 2014 demonstrated MRI findings of reduced orbitofrontal gray matter volume, bilaterally, with heavy cannabis use.

   c. True
   d. False

Review Answers (in bold)

Chapter 5: Cannabis

1. Delta-9-tetrahydrocannabinol (THC) can contribute to paranoia and psychosis.

   a. **True**
   b. False

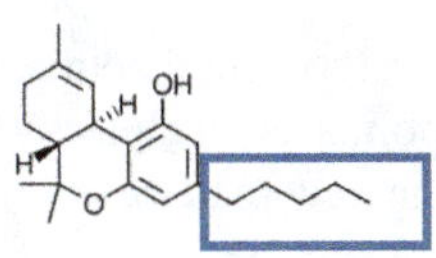

2. THC's (chemical structure shown above) potency is determined by the length of its carbon side chain.

   a. **True**
   b. False

3. According to (Baker et al., 2003), Cannabinoid (CB1) receptors are found in the following brain areas:

   a. Basal ganglia
   b. Hippocampus
   c. Amygdala
   d. Caudate Nucleus
   e. **All of the above**

4. Cannabinoid receptors have the highest concentration in parts of the brain that impact pleasure, memory, thinking, concentration, perception, coordination, and movement.

   a. **True**
   b. False

5. According to (Guzman, 2003), cannabis increases the release of dopamine in the reward center of the brain and interferes with hippocampal function.

   a. **True**
   b. False

6. In the first 3 h after cannabis use, an individual can experience the following physical symptoms:

   a. Changes in blood pressure—postural hypotension (changes in blood pressure when sitting versus standing)
   b. Red eyes (conjunctival injection)
   c. Decrease in body temperature (hypothermia)
   d. Decreased motor skills and reaction time
   e. **All of the above**

7. According to (Jager et al., 2008) & (Meier et al., 2012), individuals who use cannabis before the age of 18, the following can happen:

   a. Change in the developmental course of the brain
   b. Decrease in IQ points as much as by eight points
   c. Difficulty learning new material
   d. None of the above
   e. **All of the above**

8. (D'Souza et al., 2009) & (Hall et al., 2008) studies demonstrated an increased risk of psychosis in adults who used marijuana in adolescence and who also carried a variant in the gene Catechol-O-methyltransferase (COMT).

   a. **True**
   b. False

9. Study by Filbey et al., 2014 demonstrated MRI findings of reduced orbitofrontal gray matter volume, bilaterally, with heavy cannabis use.

   a. **True**
   b. False

Review Questions

Chapter 6: Mental Health and the Brain

1. Adverse childhood experiences increase the risk of mental health disorders in adulthood.

   a. True
   b. False

2. Depression involves disruption in the neurochemical serotonin.

   a. True
   b. False

3. Serotonin (5HT) presence is mostly found in the following areas:

   a. Intestinal tract
   b. Blood platelets
   c. Central nervous system (CNS)
   d. None of the above
   e. All of the above

4. Serotonin regulates

   a. Mood
   b. Appetite
   c. Sleep
   d. Memory/learning
   e. All of the above

5. Parts of the brain that are impacted by depression include

   a. Hippocampus
   b. Amygdala
   c. Prefrontal cortex
   d. None of the above
   e. All of the above

6. Prolonged exposure to cortisol (produced in times of stress) can reduce new neuronal growth and reduce hippocampal neurons.

   a. True
   b. False

7. The amygdala is theorized to increase or decrease in volume with prolonged stress and increased cortisol levels.

   a. Increase
   b. Decrease
   c. Neither

8. Psychosis and/or perceptual disturbances involve changes in the neurotransmitter dopamine.

   a. True
   b. False

9. Dopamine plays a role in

   a. Movement
   b. Cognition
   c. Pleasure/motivation
   d. Aggression
   e. All of the above

10. Risk factors for ADHD include smoking, alcohol use during pregnancy, genes, exposure to environmental toxins (i.e., lead), and low birth weight and brain injury.

    a. True
    b. False

Review Answers (in bold)

Chapter 6: Mental Health and the Brain

1. Adverse childhood experiences increase the risk of mental health disorders in adulthood.

   a. **True**
   b. False

2. Depression involves disruption in the neurochemical serotonin.

   a. **True**
   b. False

3. Serotonin (5HT) presence is mostly found in the following areas:

   a. Intestinal tract
   b. Blood platelets
   c. Central nervous system (CNS)
   d. None of the above
   e. **All of the above**

4. Serotonin regulates

   a. Mood
   b. Appetite
   c. Sleep
   d. Memory/learning
   e. **All of the above**

5. Parts of the brain that are impacted by depression include

   a. Hippocampus
   b. Amygdala
   c. Prefrontal cortex
   d. None of the above
   e. **All of the above**

6. Prolonged exposure to cortisol (produced in times of stress) can reduce new neuronal growth and reduce hippocampal neurons.

   a. **True**
   b. False

7. The amygdala is theorized to <u>increase</u> or <u>decrease</u> in volume with prolonged stress and increased cortisol levels.

   a. **Increase**
   b. Decrease
   c. Neither

8. Psychosis and/or perceptual disturbances involve changes in the neurotransmitter dopamine.

   a. **True**
   b. False

9. Dopamine plays a role in

   a. Movement
   b. Cognition
   c. Pleasure/motivation

d. Aggression
e. **All of the above**

10. Risk factors for ADHD include smoking, alcohol use during pregnancy, genes, exposure to environmental toxins (i.e., lead), and low birth weight and brain injury.

    a. **True**
    b. False

Review Questions

Chapter 7: Labeling Theory, The Power of Words, and Implicit Bias

1. Labeling theory asserts that people come to identify and behave in ways that reflect how others label them.

   a. True
   b. False

2. In 1977, Scimecca contended that race and gender are powerful social constructs; constructs driven by "labels."

   a. True
   b. False

3. Study by (Townsend, 2000) demonstrated disproportionate discipline in schools based on race and class.

   a. True
   b. False

4. According to an article by (Atler, 2000), categorical labeling is a tool that humans use to resolve the impossible complexity of the environments we struggle to perceive.

   a. True
   b. False

5. Reintegrative shaming is also known as restorative justice.

   a. True
   b. False

Review Answers (in bold)

Chapter 7: Labeling Theory, The Power of Words, and Implicit Bias

1. Labeling theory asserts that people come to identify and behave in ways that reflect how others label them.

   a. **True**
   b. False

2. In 1977, Scimecca contended that race and gender are powerful social constructs; constructs driven by "labels."

   a. **True**
   b. False

3. Study by (Townsend, 2000) demonstrated disproportionate discipline in schools based on race and class.

   a. **True**
   b. False

4. According to an article by (Atler, 2000), categorical labeling is a tool that humans use to resolve the impossible complexity of the environments we struggle to perceive.

   a. **True**
   b. False

5. Reintegrative shaming is also known as restorative justice.

   a. **True**
   b. False

Review Questions

Chapter 8: Digging Deeper into "Fear"

1. (Vuilleumier, 2005) suggests that the amygdala plays a role in fear recognition and perception.

   a. True
   b. False

2. According to (De Hoog et al., 2005), fear appeals theory involves the following components:

   a. Describes a strategy for motivating people to take a particular action by endorsing a particular policy or a particular product by arousing fear
   b. A persuasive message that diverts behavior through fear
   c. Presents a risk, presents the vulnerability to the risk
   d. May or may not suggest a form of protection
   e. All of the above

3. Fear appeals theory is applied in the following settings:

   a. Politics
   b. Marketing
   c. Public health
   d. None of the above
   e. All of the above

4. Drive theory is represented in the following pairs:

   a. Hunger—eat to relieve the hunger
   b. Thirsty—drink to quench the thirst
   c. Afraid—seek safety
   d. None of the above
   e. All of the above

5. Reintegrative shaming theory involves

   a. Differential association
   b. Social bonds
   c. Labeling theory
   d. None of the above
   e. All of the above

Review Answers (in bold)

Chapter 8: Digging Deeper into "Fear"

1. (Vuilleumier, 2005) suggests that the amygdala plays a role in fear recognition and perception.

   a. **True**
   b. False

2. According to (De Hoog et al., 2005), fear appeals theory involves the following components:

   a. Describes a strategy for motivating people to take a particular action by endorsing a particular policy or a particular product by arousing fear
   b. A persuasive message that diverts behavior through fear
   c. Presents a risk, presents the vulnerability to the risk
   d. May or may not suggest a form of protection
   e. **All of the above**

3. Fear appeals theory is applied in the following settings:

   a. Politics
   b. Marketing
   c. Public health
   d. None of the above
   e. **All of the above**

4. Drive theory is represented in the following pairs:

   a. Hunger—eat to relieve the hunger
   b. Thirsty—drink to quench the thirst
   c. Afraid—seek safety

d. None of the above
e. **All of the above**

5. Reintegrative shaming theory involves

a. Differential association
b. Social bonds
c. Labeling theory
d. None of the above
e. **All of the above**

Review Questions

Chapter 9: Relationships, Restorative justice, Reintegration, Recidivism

1. Relationships (at its core) means

a. The state of being connected
b. Family
c. Parents
d. None of the above
e. All of the above

2. Risk factors for individuals who become entangled with the law include but not limited to

a. History of childhood trauma
b. Substance use
c. Limited education
d. Family history of incarceration
e. All of the above

3. According to (Austin et al., 2004), formerly incarcerated individuals are <u>less</u> likely to recidivate when

a. If they stayed connected with family or loved ones while they were incarcerated
b. If they live with their spouses after returning home from being incarcerated
c. If contact and visits with loved ones was frequent and consistent when they were incarcerated
d. None of the above
e. All of the above

4. The 1997 Federal Adoption and Safe Families Act requires states to file a petition to terminate parental rights on behalf of any child who has been abandoned or who has been in foster care for 15 consecutive months or more.

a. True
b. False

5. According to (William, 2012), incarcerated individuals wanted their families involved in their lives, overwhelmingly so.

   a. True
   b. False

6. According to (Arditti, 2012), incarcerated individuals tend to emerge from histories of "cumulative disadvantage" characterized by multiple risks factors:

   a. Family history of victimization
   b. Mental health difficulties
   c. Substance misuse and addiction
   d. Intergenerational criminality
   e. All of the above

Review Answers (in bold)

Chapter 9: Relationships, Restorative justice, Reintegration, Recidivism

1. Relationships (at its core) means

   a. **The state of being connected**
   b. Family
   c. Parents
   d. None of the above
   e. All of the above

2. Risk factors for individuals who become entangled with the law include but not limited to

   a. History of childhood trauma
   b. Substance use
   c. Limited education
   d. Family history of incarceration
   e. **All of the above**

3. According to (Austin et al., 2004, formerly incarcerated individuals are <u>less</u> likely to recidivate when

   a. If they stayed connected with family or loved ones while they were incarcerated
   b. If they live with their spouses after returning home from being incarcerated
   c. If contact and visits with loved ones were frequent and consistent when they were incarcerated
   d. None of the above
   e. **All of the above**

4. The 1997 Federal Adoption and Safe Families Act requires states to file a petition to terminate parental rights on behalf of any child who has been abandoned or who has been in foster care for 15 consecutive months or more.

   a. **True**
   b. False

5. According to (William, 2012), incarcerated individuals wanted their families involved in their lives, overwhelmingly so.

   a. **True**
   b. False

6. According to (Arditti, 2012), incarcerated individuals tend to emerge from histories of "cumulative disadvantage" characterized by multiple risks factors:

   a. Family history of victimization
   b. Mental health difficulties
   c. Substance misuse and addiction
   d. Intergenerational criminality
   e. **All of the above**

Review Questions

Chapter 10: Self-Care: Strong in the Broken Places

1. Maslow's hierarchy of needs involves the following component(s):

   a. Love and belonging
   b. Safety (financial, emotional, physical)
   c. Self-actualization
   d. Physiologic (food, water)
   e. Esteem
   f. All of the above

2. Maslow contended that humans are "motivated" to achieve basic needs, to have and get basic needs met.

   a. True
   b. False

3. Mindfulness, when employed with consistency, supports brain healing, recovering, and overall wellness.

   a. True
   b. False

4. Systems are more likely to be well and open to change when individuals who work within the system are well and changed.

   a. True
   b. False

Review Answers (in bold)

Chapter 10: Self-Care: Strong in the Broken Places

1. Maslow's hierarchy of needs involves the following component(s):

    a. Love and belonging
    b. Safety (financial, emotional, physical)
    c. Self-actualization
    d. Physiologic (food, water)
    e. Esteem
    f. **All of the above**

2. Maslow contended that humans are "motivated" to achieve basic needs, to have and get basic needs met.

    a. **True**
    b. False

3. Mindfulness, when employed with consistency, supports brain healing, recovering, and overall wellness.

    a. **True**
    b. False

4. Systems are more likely to be well and open to change when individuals who work within the system are well and changed.

    a. **True**
    b. False

Chapter 12
The Challenge and Hope of System Change

This textbook is intentionally titled "Training for Change". I want to focus on the concept, practice, and process of change. Repeated in various chapters is my thought about how change happens within the context of a system. I have said that systems don't change if people don't change and people don't change if they don't feel something. The basic subtext of this textbook can be summarized by two Maya Angelo quotes to include "when we know better, we can do better" and "when you learn, teach, when you get, give." Nothing in history has ever changed among comfort or convenience nor has change occurred in the absence of some type of "feeling." My main objective was to cover the science and the stories as a means of tapping into that feeling space. My aim was to impact people to impact systems—this is a recurring theme throughout the text. I've presented E. Schein's model on organizational change which highlights a given system checking their underlying assumptions as a means of influencing a cultural shift. Change is the most resisted unavoidable phenomenon in human development.

The great question is how do we help systems effectively take "fear" out of the change process?

My formulation on how change happens differs from the traditional working models because of its emphasis on people and tapping into the feeling space.

There are several working theories on how change happens.

In the 1940s, Kurt Lewin established a three-stage change management model that includes the following phases (Devos):

- Unfreezing—it is a disruptive period that opens up a system to the idea of change; challenges old practices, beliefs, and behaviors; and accommodate resistance (appreciate the resistance as grist for the mill).
- Change (transition)—it involves taking everything unearthed and learned in the unfreezing phase and shaping it into meaningful change within a system.
- Freezing—this phase involves making certain that the conditions for sustaining adjustments made in the change phase are solid.

The McKinsey 7-S model was established in the 1980s by Tom Peters and Robert Watermen (both employed as consultants that the McKinsey and Company consulting

A. Moreland-Capuia, *Training for Change*,
https://doi.org/10.1007/978-3-030-19208-2_12

firm). Peters and Waterman created a framework for change that considered the following elements (Ravanfar 2015):

- *Strategy*—viewing change through lens of helping a system (business) stay on the cutting, competitive edge;
- *Structure*—reevaluating how decisions are made and by whom and whether it was still a relevant way to operate;
- *Systems* (internal operations)—assessing whether or not these systems were judicious and supported individuals in the system to remain competitive;
- *Shared values*—assessing the narrative and core beliefs of a system;
- Style—assessing how individuals within the system treat each other, how they communicate;
- *Staff*—do current individuals within the system have the tools they need to remain relevant, competitive, and poised for change?
- *Skills*—similar to staff is an assessment of whether or not individuals within the system have the tools and/or are capable of obtaining the tools required to remain competitive.

John Kotter introduced eight stages for change to include (Kotter 2000):

- Create a sense of urgency—make the case for why change is both urgent and imminent;
- Build a guiding coalition—another way of saying identify champions for change within an organization;
- Form a strategic vision and initiatives;
- Enlist a volunteer army;
- Enable action by removing barriers;
- Generate short-term wins;
- Sustain acceleration; and
- Institute change.

There is the Nudge theory which suggests that small, indirect changes eventually lead to meaningful, larger scale change. The theory employs positive reinforcement and indirect proposals are the vehicle for shaping the behavior and decisions of groups or individuals. It could be reformulated as the "baby steps" theory (Kosters and der Heijden 2015).

The ADKAR does consider a parallel change process as the model suggests that the organization and the employee must change at the same time. The organization is people and the employees are people too. Change must occur in "people" (Mulder 2013).

ADKAR was developed in 2003 by Jeff Hiatt and introduced as a tool that could be employed for organizational change by a change management consulting firm named Prosci.

ADKAR stands for

- Awareness—all parties must appreciate the desire for change;
- Desire—employees must have the desire to participate in and support the change;

- Knowledge—educate about the change process;
- Ability—assessing whether or not the organization and/or employees possess and/or can learn new skills to more smoothly adapt in the change process; and
- Reinforcement—creating the conditions that will codify the change sought.

Bridges' transition model is a model that focuses on transition as opposed to change. Transition seems more fluid (continuous) and less disruptive.

William Bridges established the Bridges transition model in the early 1990s, with the stages reminiscent of that of grief. Bridges contend that change involves three stages attached to various emotional/feeling states (Shy and Mills 2010):

- Ending, losing, and letting go;
- Neutral zone; and
- The New Beginning.

Bridges' model acknowledges the "feeling" space as critical in the transition/change process.

Kübler-Ross' change curve and Elisabeth Kubler-Ross are known for their work around death and dying. She asserts that loss is change and change can feel like loss. The stages of change according to Kubler-Ross are as follows (Shoolin 2010):

- Denial;
- Anger;
- Bargaining;
- Depression; and
- Acceptance.

Family therapist Virginia Satir developed the Satir change management model. In her five-stage model, each phase describes the effects and each stage has on feelings, thinking, performance, and physiology (Satir 1991).

- Late status quo—every member impacted by the change knows what to expect and how to react and behave;
- Resistance—will be present, but must be managed;
- Chaos—a period of seeming instability and uncertainty;
- Integration—puts the resistance and chaos to good use, moving the change agenda forward; and
- New status quo—safety has been established in the change process, and acclimation to the change is occurring.

All these change theories provide important frameworks for how to engage and inspire people to change. Each theory builds on one another and the complex nature of change is demonstrated. As has been my experience in working the arena of impacting systems for change, systems change when people change and people change when they feel something.

When we talk about changing a system, the most immediate, visceral response comes from individuals attached to the system—people interpret change as something they did not do correctly or a result of a mistake they made. This dynamic is what renders systems change challenging and promising. There is an opportunity to reframe the systems change process as a means of tending to, strengthening, and supporting people attached to systems because (a) they deserve it and (b) everyone benefits in the end. People work is systems work.

Sanchez asserts that "how" information is communicated to individuals subject to the change is more important than "what" is being communicated. Further, Sanchez contends lack of understanding that the change process is hard and failed to relay that understanding empathetically can compromise the change process. The article highlights the following critical considerations in facilitating change (Sanchez 2018):

- The needs and wants of individuals subject to the change will shift throughout—frequent check-ins and revaluation of the process are warranted;
- Considerate, thoughtful listening is a must in the change process;
- Asking permission and giving individuals a preemptive heads up is key in any change process; and
- Widening the bench to include as many people at every level to participate in facilitating change is critical.

Itzchakov and Kluger write about the importance of listening in the context of change.

Feedback is distinguished from listening. Feedback is described as telling folks that they need to change, whereas listening and asking questions might increase the likelihood that would want to change (Itzchakov and Kluger 2018).

Change can be scary and literally experienced as scary as pointed out by an article by Walter McFarland in the Harvard Business Review. The limbic system (emotion, fear center of the brain) can be triggered at the thought of a change process. Fear must be addressed and managed in any change process (McFarland 2012).

Theories are only as good as they are useful. The real question is how to employ these theories of organizational systems change in changing the system you might be in?

In 2016, I was invited by the Multnomah County Department of Community Justice (DCJ) to assess their juvenile and adult community supervision programs. In 2011, Multnomah County adopted a University of Cincinnati Corrections Institute model entitled Effective Practices in Community Supervision (EPICS). EPICS, a proven supervision model, demonstrated its effectiveness in reducing rearrest and sustained entanglement with the law in individuals with a history of incarceration and/or at risk of incarceration. EPICS was designed to provide tools to parole and probation officers to more judiciously engage youth and adults with a history of incarceration; prevent reincarceration; facilitate change; and support sustained change over time. EPICS combined coaching, cognitive behavioral therapeutic principles, principles of effective intervention, and core correctional practices—all of which will be addressed later in this chapter. Parole and probation are alternatives to incarceration and differ in the following ways:

- Parole is early release from being incarcerated.
- Probation happens before and often in the place of being incarcerated.

When Multnomah County adopted EPICS, a reduction in rearrests in specific populations was expected (as had been demonstrated in other settings that had adopted the EPICS model). Five years into the model, Multnomah County DCJ noted that the change they sought wasn't the change they had anticipated. DCJ's initial aim was change in the individuals they serve, but what was appreciated instead was a mild culture shift in the parole and probation officers who were being trained in the EPICS model. Probation and parole officers were more open to the use of evidence-based practices and their drive to learn new things peaked. This is a good change, no doubt. The question still remained, what about reducing rearrests in specific populations? How might this goal be achieved? In a desire to take the change further and move toward the initial intended goal, DCJ did an internal audit of the model and came back with the resolve that more was needed in the model. As a result, DCJ applied for a federal SMART Grant with the objective of reinforcing/amplifying/strengthening the EPCIS model to integrate culturally responsivity, neurogenetics and brain development, and trauma-informed practices and approaches. The SMART Grant targeted and focused on young males of color between the ages of 15 and 25, a group disproportionately represented in the judicial systems and historically ineffectively served in community supervision settings.

Given my expertise in working with youth, families, and understanding the complexity and trauma, I was asked to participate as a subject matter expert on the SMART grant. The quick and short summary is that by partnering with a team of eager, open-minded parole and probation officers within Multnomah County's DCJ, I was able to impact a system for good. A subculture was changed, and narratives, beliefs, and practices were changed. The end result is that youth and adults formerly incarcerated are better served and the goals of reducing rearrest are realized.

I am going to take the next half of this chapter to share with you "how" the change happened and is happening. Perhaps, you can draw on some of the information as you seek to impact your own system for change.

Case Study: Multnomah County Department of Community Justice, changing a system to support meaningful change in justice-involved youth.

The criminal justice system is colossal and complex. Youth entanglement with the criminal justice system represents the culmination of several systems prior that have let them down. My logic holds that if the criminal justice system (a large, complicated system) can change, then any system can change. We've discussed in the recent passage of new criminal justice legislation called *The First Step Act*, which attempts to mitigate the harms of institutionalization with a focus on releasing persons with nonviolent chargers to the community, increasing community supervision via parole and probation coupled with vocational, educational, and housing support. There is also a special focus on changing the way that juveniles are treated when they are institutionalized with a recommendation to end solitary confinement secondary to its detrimental impact on the psyche. There is keen recognition that the former way of doing business within the criminal justice system has not been effective or rendered the outcomes that the system initially sought. In the last decade, greater efforts have been directed to establishing thoughtful reintegration, community supervision programs that prevent formerly incarcerated individuals from rearrest and reincarceration.

Multnomah County DCJ has been on the cutting edge of employing innovative practices to reduce recidivism (prevent rearrest and continued participation in the legal justice system). As described above Multnomah County DCJ adopted EPICS.

What is EPICS?

A community supervision training/coaching model that integrates the following components: core correctional practices, principles of effective intervention, social learning theory, and cognitive behavioral therapeutic frameworks. EPICS aim is to teach community supervision officers to effectively integrate the aforementioned components into practice that translates to change. EPICS was developed by Drs. Paula Smith and Christopher Lowenkamp via the University of Ohio. EPICS is a part of the reintegration continuum and response. There was keen recognition that formerly incarcerated individuals required additional support immediately before release and post-incarceration—the supports range from continued skills building to vocation and education resources.

Core Correctional Practices (CCPs)

CCPs include the following (Dowden and Andrews 2004; Haas et al. 2007):

Appropriate use of authority: Encourages officers who are doing community supervision to employ a direct, respectful, and authoritative approach that leaves room for intermittent negotiation and engagement that moves intends to move away from shame.

Appropriate modeling and reinforcement: Officers conduct role plays to model the behaviors they seek. This is a structured learning process.

Skills building and problem-solving strategies: Through a structured cognitive behavioral therapeutic model, officer teaches specific skills like organization, planning, and communication skills, for example.

Effective use of community resources: Involves officers evaluating the need of an individual and helping to connect them to appropriate resources.

Relationship factors: Focuses on connection and empathy and acknowledges the importance of relationships.

Principles of Effective Intervention

Allow for assessment of risks based on a tool called the Level of Service Inventory—LSI. There is an adapted youth instrument called the Youth Level of Service/Case Management Inventory (Andrews and Bonta 2001, 2003). The LSI tool assesses need in ten different domains to include legal history, education/employment, financial, family/marital, accommodation, leisure/recreation, companions, alcohol/drugs, emotional/personal, and attitudes/orientation. A total score of 54 is possible. The LSI score determines the level of need and risk. Generally, the higher the need (as evidenced by a high LSI score), the higher the risk of repeating old patterns and staying entangled with the criminal justice system (Andrews and Bonta 2001, 2003). Referring back to Maslow's hierarchy of need—when needs are met risk for violence–poor physical and mental health are reduced. Needs met = lower risk. Risk of reincarceration 1 year after release is the working definition of recidivism.

Principles of effective intervention consider the relationship between risk, need, responsivity, and fidelity.

- Assessing risk and need.
- Using the data obtained from the risk/needs assessment and tailoring interventions to meet the needs and theoretically reduce the risk.
- Fidelity is concerned with how effective the interventions are.
- There are several community supervision models, like EPICS (Smith et al. 2012), that employ core correctional practices and RNR. According to studies, these models (which include core correctional practice and RNR) have demonstrated their effectiveness in reducing recidivism. Chris Trotter evaluated the following models (Trotter 1996, 2006):
  - Strategic Training Initiative in Community Supervision (STICS) (Bonta et al. 2010) and
  - Staff Training Aimed at Reducing Rearrest (STARR) (Robinson et al. 2012).

Cognitive Behavioral Therapy (CBT), practices, and approaches
A structured therapy focuses on evaluating and appropriately challenging dysfunctional automatic thoughts (personal, internal narratives), developing skills to effectively modulate emotions and behaviors, developing strategies to effectively solve problems, and strengthening problem-solving capacity.

Social Learning Theory
Social learning theory, developed by Albert Bandura (and based on prior understanding of conditioning and learning), posits that learning is a cognitive process. Further social learning theory combines cognitive behavioral and behavioral theories to suggest that individuals learn from their environment and each other through the process of observation, imitation, and modeling (Bandura 1977; Bandura and Walters 1963).

EPICS in greater detail

- Community supervision officers learn a structured way of engaging with justice-involved individuals.
- Community supervision officers are encouraged to engage with justice-involved individuals through the risks, needs, and responsivity RNR framework outlined by principles of effective intervention.
- Studies on RNR highlight the fact that justice-involved individuals are less likely to recidivate in the presence of needs (e.g., relationships, finances, education) being met.
- EPICS theoretically integrates this RNR them throughout.

Training officers in the EPICS model
There is a 3-day training led by EPICS supervisors and coaches (all parole and probation officers who have been trained in and have mastered the model). I personally went through 3 days of EPICs training, so am very familiar with the model.

In the 3-day training:

- I learned about risks, needs, and responsivity principles as outlined in the principles of effective intervention;
- Core correctional practices were taught;
- Several teaching modalities and tools were used, to include
- Role playing,
- Video presentation, and
- Group work to solidify concepts;
- Trained on how to use CBT models in sessions with justice-involved individuals; and
- Practice, practice, and practice with immediate feedback.

After the 3-day training, there is maintenance training and coaching (Labrecque and Smith 2015).

Parole and probation officers are asked to tape their individual sessions with justice-involved individuals and submit to the EPICS coaches, who review the tape and check for fidelity to the model and provide feedback for continuous improvement.

The goal of EPICS is to reduce recidivism, but the overarching goal is CHANGE.

Moving from theory to practice—what EPICS looks like with parole and probation officers and justice-involved individuals. Justice-involved individuals are expected to check-in with parole and probation officers in the community (office setting, sometimes a coffee shop). Frequency of visits is determined by the level of risk and need. Each EPICS-structured visit includes

- *Check-in*: to build rapport between justice-involved individual and officer, evaluate for any crises or immediate needs, and address and sometimes review the conditions probation and parole.
- *Review*: an opportunity for justice-involved individual to establish goals; review any referrals that were made to the community for additional support; depending on if it is the first visit or not, this is also an opportunity to review homework assignment that may have been given in a prior session.
- *Intervention*: officers work to address specific needs of the justice-involved individual; officers employ a cognitive behavioral therapeutic approach that allows the justice-involved individual to evaluate past and current behavior and consider means for maintaining a positive trajectory while reintegrating into the community.

CBT-based interventions are geared to meet the immediate needs of the justice-involved individual. For example, if an individual comes in and states that they were tempted by their peers to smoke weed and they ended up lapsing or an individual comes in and shares that they are struggling to set appropriate boundaries, interventions are conducted based on the stated need during a given session.

CBT-based interventions in the EPIC model include but are not limited:

- Behavior chain—allows for deeper analysis of behavior by breaking the issues down into smaller, palatable, understandable elements. Then it allows an individual to establish strategies for changing the smaller elements. Now the problem doesn't feel so big.

- Cognitive restructuring—involves considering narratives, appropriately challenging and reframing narratives for change.
- Cost–benefit analysis—involves weighing the cost of a behavior versus the benefit and relying on a justice-involved individual to appreciate the benefits of change.
- Skills building—there are a set of skills (some are soft skills) like communication or resolving conflict. The skills are taught, role played, and modeled in session.
- Problem-solving and graduated practice.
- *Homework:* this is an opportunity to encourage and support justice-involved individuals to take and apply the skills and problem-solving learning from supervision to their external environment. The EPICS model asks justice-involved individuals to practice, practice, practice, practice.

Again, the goal of EPICs is to reduce risks by reducing needs through addressing needs. The goal is to support sustained positive change in justice-involved individuals.

At base the EPICs, model has a solid foundation as it seeks to train officers to focus on

- Learning and employing structured cognitive therapeutic approaches to support the change they seek in justice-involved individuals,
- Developing relationships, and
- Assessing for and addressing needs.

All of these elements are critical and again have proven operative (when employed) in reducing recidivism in certain populations.

When Multnomah County DCJ performed their internal audit as a part of the quality improvement efforts, it was determined that males of color between the ages of 15 and 25 were not optimally benefiting from the EPICS model as originally designed.

A combination of factors motivated Multnomah County's desire to make a subcultural shift: (1) The internal data demanded it; and (2) emerging evidence on brain science and trauma-informed practices compelled Multnomah County DCJ to want to take a second look at whether or not the structured EPICS model was meeting the needs of all of its participants.

I was asked to work closely with seven probation/parole officers and Junior Court Counselors (JCCs) to help them reimagine the EPICS model for young men of color between the ages of 15 and 25.

Specifically, I was tasked with integrating three lenses into the EPICS model to include

- Brain development and neuroscience,
- Cultural responsivity and specificity, and
- Trauma-informed practices and approaches.

I want to reiterate that the EPICS model is a strong foundational model, and my work to integrate the three aforementioned foci was aimed at reinforcing the model for optimal change within this specific population.

Brain development and neuroscience
Important considerations:

- EPICS is a robust cognitive model that inherently mandates the engagement of the cerebral cortex (the top brain), but what if the development of this part of the brain is compromised and can't be readily accessed?
- The brain is still developing in the 15–25 year olds.

I thoughtfully questioned whether the structured EPICS model considered the brain development process and potential threats to it in this population. Further, I intentionally made the connections among fear, trauma, basic needs not being met, and attachment issues.

As discussed in prior chapters, but by the way of review, the brain develops from the bottom-up and inside-out. Brain development starts at the point of conception (when sperm meets egg) and progresses (relatively normally) from conception to about the age of 26. Research teaches us that the brain development process might be impacted even before conception, in other words, epigenetics suggest that environmental drivers can change the genetic composition of sperm and egg, which impacts subsequent brain development. As soon as sperm meets egg, it takes about 3–4 weeks for the body to develop the blueprint for the brain and spinal cord (the neural plate folds to become the neural tube). This happens during the period where most women don't know that they are pregnant. This is a critical period that is heavily impacted by environment, brain development, substance use, trauma, and poor nutrition, for example, can heavily impact the way the neural tube folds. The external environment impacts the development of the brain; for the entire 38–40 weeks, a baby is in the mother's womb. Once the baby is born, the most developed part of the brain is the bottom brain (brain stem), survival aspect of the brain. We are all born with the proclivity for survival.

Day 1 of birth to age 3 marks a critical period of growth for the brain in terms of neuronal proliferation (growth), differentiation (a neuron knowing what type of neuron it will be and what purpose it will serve), and segmentation/regionalization (a neuron knowing where they are going to go and what they will eventually become). Healthy brain development is supported by proper nutrition, decreased stress, basic needs of the child being met, and secure attachment. Healthy brain development happens when safety in the environment is created. Babies can move out of survival mode and lean toward thriving when the needs for connection, nourishment, and protection are met.

Another critical period of brain development is during adolescence when the novelty-seeking behaviors are prominent—this is a normal developmental phenomenon. Impulses are strong; adolescents are exceptionally sensitive to shame—appropriate modeling, reassurance, and conditioning in this phase are exceptionally important to help mitigate the risks of impulsivity and other unacceptable behaviors.

In the niche population, the SMART Grant focused on, males of color between the ages of 15 and 25, adverse childhood events were prevalent with a parent with a history of incarceration, a history of trauma, at some point basic needs as defined by Maslow had not been met.

***The questions I asked the Parole/Probation officers and JCCs to consider were*:**

- What happens when you did not experience secure attachment and safety wasn't created for you at birth?
- What happens when you didn't have proper nutrition and basic needs for reassurance, connection, and nourishment were not met?
- What happens when you were raised in an environment where toxic shame was passed down?
- What impact do these early insults and threats to brain development have on brain function?

Does the EPICS model account for these potential insults to brain development?

Systems change is about changing people attached to the system, so upon reviewing the science, I also tapped into the "feeling" space and asked parole/probation and JCCs to imagine the last time:

- They were hungry and how that impacted their ability to function;
- They didn't get enough sleep and how that impacted their ability to function; and
- They felt alone and how that impacted their ability to function.

The EPICS model does address needs, but it doesn't ask officers to tap into their own needs as a means of helping to meet the needs of those they seek to serve (and facilitate change in). The basic premise is that we must change in order to influence change in others.

The response to this line of inquiry:

Parole/probation officers and JCCs were able to recall a time when they were hungry, tired, and alone. Further, they were able to note their respective personal challenges with being able to function optimally in these particular scenarios. Once this level of individual engagement was demonstrated, the following question was asked:

What might it be like to be chronically tired, hungry, and alone (24–7)?

As we addressed the question, I was able to relate the understanding of brain development, potential threats to its optimal functioning, and juxtapose that with the demands of a cognitive structured model—a model that mandates functional use of the top part of the brain in population of individuals that may struggle to do so (not that they won't ever be able to do so, but may not be able in current) given their history.

Enhancement of the EPICS model by adding the lens of brain development and the 3A's

Ask—seek permission to learn more about the justice-involved individual's birth history. Ask how the justice-involved individual best learns (ask about their best learning experience).

Assess—use a tool like the MOCA to assess cognitive capacity of justice-involved individual.

Assist—use the information from the MOCA to influence shape the supervision sessions and to determine what level of support may be required outside of the supervision session.

EPICS is a strong cognitive-based model that assumes that its targeted audience are cognitively intact and can thoughtfully participate in the exercises as outlined in the model.

I respectfully challenge this assumption and simply asked the officers to move away from assumption and ask.

With the information obtained from applying the 3A's, parole officers were able to better manage their expectations in a supervision session.

Officers discovered that over 90% of their clients had some level of cognitive compromise. This then led to further assessment of why, which led to officers seeking resources to support their client in recovering some of their cognitive ability.

Change in officer's approach from considering threats to brain development in the EPICS supervision model:

- I facilitated a 4-, interactive training for officers on brain development and the potential threats to healthy development—the training mimicked the first chapter of this textbook in terms of content.
- Officers considered brain development and potential threats to it (poor nutrition, poverty, racism, protracted, and persistent exposure to trauma).
- Officers moved away from assuming that every client was cognitive intact enough to optimally participate in the model.
- Officers employed the triple A model and got more information about the justice-involved information.
- Relationship and trust built between the officer and justice-involved individual were strengthened.
- Safety was established in the context of the officer and justice-involved individual relationship.
- Referral for additional support and services were made earlier in the relationship, resulting in improved outcomes for the justice-involved individual.

In the case of males of color 15–25, when officers asked permission to engage with them it was deemed a sign of respect and probably the first time that anyone had ever treated them as if they were the experts on themselves. The change in officer's approach flowed from having to reconcile their own humanity, limitations, and proclivity for change—getting educated, then turning to self, asking critical questions, coming up close and personal with their own needs, and imagining their own behavioral response in a time when their needs were not met—this allowed officers to more thoughtfully make a shift in how they engaged 15–25-year-old males of color in community supervision at Multnomah County DCJ.

Change in officer = change in 15–25-year-old males of color. The parallel change process described throughout this text.

Cultural Responsivity and specificity

As mentioned in Chap. 2 of this textbook, culture is complex. Culture shapes the lens from which an individual views the world. To this extent, it was so critical to take officers through the exercise of considering the cultures and subcultures that have shaped them.

We walked through the exercise of automatic assumptions. Officers were given a set of images and asked to provide their initial, visceral response. Equally, they were given a set of words and asked to provide the first thought or image that came to mind. For example, they were asked what comes to mind when they think of a doctor. I wasn't interested in the politically correct answer, I wanted to know the first thought or image that came to mind. In assessing the initial thoughts and interpreting them, officers were surprised by their own initial thoughts. Digging a little deeper, we discussed how these initial thoughts are intimately connected to how we were raised, conditioned, and socialized. The environments from which we emerged shaped our collective experience and interpretation of the world.

This was, by far, one of the most powerful exercises I did with the officers.

This then led to the discussion of unconscious bias, underlying assumptions, preconceived notions, and racism. The harsh reality is that the things that we are taught (directly and indirectly) impact our behavior and how we navigate the world. If I am taught that certain individuals are scary, this changes how I engage them.

I asked officers to consider narrative and how that shaped perception. They were asked about a time that they were described in a way that didn't match up with who they actually were. In the current geopolitical milieu that we find ourselves in, officers of any kind have not been depicted in a positive light. Officers admit that this doesn't always feel good. I asked them to take this feeling and apply it to the population they sought to serve. Again, the "feeling" space is the birthplace for change.

We spent a lot of time talking about nonverbal communication and "what is not said" being just as powerful as what is spoken. Oftentimes, most human beings feel out a room to determine if it is safe enough for them to engage. Officers could agree with this sentiment. They were asked to think about a time that someone told them that they were amazing, but didn't treat them like they were amazing. They were asked to consider what had a more profound impact—what was said versus how you were made to feel? Officers were able to resonate with the "how they were made to feel" aspect of an interaction.

A few questions officers were asked to consider:

- What is more important, what you say and/or how you make people feel?
- What does it take for you (the officer) to feel safe enough in space to engage? Now apply that same principle to engaging with 15–25-year-old males of color.
- Are you aware of your unconscious thoughts, feelings, and biases that may come up in a session?
- Can you effectively serve someone you don't like and/or are afraid of?

In many ways, I have trained Multnomah County DCJ officers to be "mini-clinicians." The rapport building that we expect from parole/probation officers and JCCs is similar to the rapport building and therapeutic alliance expected in a counseling relationship. Building therapeutic rapport and alliance is the most critical element of successfully facilitating change. As cliché as this may sound: "people really don't care about how much you know until they know how much you care."

As a psychiatrist, I couldn't help but offer a psychoanalytic lens to the work. Psychoanalyst Donald Woods Winnicott wrote a piece entitled "Hate in the countertransference" (Winnicott 1994), it explores the strong, powerful emotion of hate in a therapeutic relationship and how it occupies the space between the individual who seeks to support and the individual who is seeking support. Hate and other emotions come up in sessions. Community supervision is similar to a session. Things come up for officers in a session, something can and will trigger an uncomfortable emotion and it can change the tone and tenor of the session and vice versa for the supervisee in a session. Transference is a reaction/experience from the supervisee to the officer; countertransference is a reaction/experience from the officer to the supervisee.

The bottom line is that things come up and it is important for officers to feel safe to explore the things that come up and find ways to navigate them so that it doesn't get in the way of the change they want to facilitate.

We are asking officers to have a human on human interactions. Naturally things will come up. The real question is how do you manage it when it does emerge?

Enhancement of the EPICS model by adding the lens of cultural responsivity and safe exploration of officers to consider their own biases, preconceived notions, and how this might show up in supervision with 15–25-year-old males of color

- I facilitated a 4-h, interactive training on cultural responsivity, stereotype threat, and implicit bias for officers—the training mimicked the second chapter of this textbook in terms of content.
- Officers were asked to consider how powerful narrative is.
- Officers were asked to be more aware of what they bring into a supervision session and how it may be positively or negatively impacting the session.
- A group supervision session was added to the EPIC model. The group supervision model was a safe space for parole/probation officers and JCCs to discuss some of their challenging experiences with 15–25 year olds, do some introspection, get support and feedback from their peers, and consider how to best apply the training they had received from me on implicit bias, stereotype threat, and hate in the countertransference.

Culturally specific services

There are studies that demonstrate the power of culturally specific services in improving outcomes for recipients of a service (Alcalay et al. 1999; DeLamater et al. 2000; Erickson and Al-Timimi 2001; Gillum 2009; Gondolf and Williams 2001). In the case of our work, the majority of parole/probation officers and JCCs working with males of color ages 15–25 were people of color too. When supervising officers looked like the supervisees, rapport building, creation of safety was expedited and outcomes were improved—the conditions for change were ripe. If we can't get culturally specific, the next best thing is cultural responsivity and humanity.

Change in officers' approach

Officers noted that when they felt safe (and had a safe, nonjudgmental environment) to talk about their fears, concerns, and feelings, it made it easier for them to consider the fears, concerns, and feelings of the individuals they wanted to serve and support. In the case of males of color 15–25, in a feedback session, they shared that they felt less judged and more supported in sessions with officers.

The peer group supervision model was a strong addition to the EPICS. I will talk more about the group supervision model later in this chapter and offer a framework that other systems might want to consider adopting.

Bottom line: Support begets support.

Officers felt supported and validated = 15–25-year-old males of color were being supervised felt supported and validated.

Trauma-Informed Practice and Approaches

If you were to ask three different people the meaning of trauma, you would likely get three different responses. It was important for me to establish a shared language and scientific understanding of what trauma is. I started with the connection between fear and trauma and drove home the neurobiological definition of trauma. Again, we are asking officers to have human-to-human interactions, which means, from my perspective, that officers would benefit from getting in touch with their own humanity and perhaps need for healing as (not before, but as) they were supporting supervisees with trauma and their respective healing.

The first question I posed was: "is there anyone in this space who has never been afraid?" Absolutely none of the officers raised their hand. This was what I deemed "a point of convergence"—points of convergence as defined in this textbook are shared experiences that can serve as powerful flex points for change. I pointed out that everyone had been intimate with fear at some point in their lives.

I then asked officers to consider what if felt like when they were afraid. Many of the officers were able to verbalize that they had physical discomfort (sweaty, heart rate increase, shaky), they weren't thinking straight, feeling of being in survival mode, a desire to seek safety, and limited coordination. Officers were asked if they believe that they could function at their peak capacity when they are afraid, they all answered no.

I then asked them, what part of the brain was the most active in fear-afraid state, top or bottom? They all answered, the bottom.

Shortly thereafter, officers were asked to imagine what it might feel like to be in an afraid-fear state all the time, what happens when fear doesn't turn off? They had specific answers to include that they could imagine that a person wouldn't be functioning well, a desire seek safety, some potential break down in the body might happen, survival mode all the time can be dangerous for the person experiencing it, and others subject to the person in survival mode. The answers were rather sophisticated. The connection was then made that "fear on" all the time = neurobiological definition of trauma. They got it. Some were able to identify their own trauma in some instances.

We've discussed a number of factors that contribute to trauma, threats to early brain development like adverse childhood experiences, poor nutrition, not getting basic needs met, insecure attachments, poverty, in utero substance use, houselessness, food insecurity, and other psychosocial stressors.

Officers could understand how fear could prop up in a supervisee when they are expected to come to the office for supervision sessions.

A few questions that officers were asked to consider:

- If you (the officer) can appreciate the role fear has played in your own life, how much more can you appreciate fear and fear that transitions to trauma in the lives of the persons you seek to serve?
- Can you imagine what the young men you seek to serve have been through in their lifetime and their relationship to fear (and being in survival mode) on a daily basis?
- Do you think that the young men you seek to serve are afraid when they come into your office?
- What part of the brain are your 15–25 year olds operating in when they come to see you, the top and/or bottom?

The EPICS model is a top brain, cognitive model, and it works optimally for individuals who are operating in the top part of the brain. For those who are not operating in the top part of the brain (and whom you seek to optimally benefit from the model), there is an important first step before engaging in the cognitive model—officers must create safety and reduce the fear response in their supervisees. How can an officer do this? Officers learned the scientific benefits of mindfulness—a practice that benefits the officer and the supervisee.

Enhancement of the EPICS model by adding a trauma-informed lens:

- I facilitated a 4-h, interactive training for officers on adverse childhood experiences (ACEs), the neurobiology of fear, and trauma-informed practices and approaches—the training mimicked the third chapter of this textbook in terms of content.
- Officers were asked to recall their own moments of fear as they consider the role of fear and trauma in their supervisees.
- Officers were asked to consider the fact that memory, concentration, and attention are all negatively impacted when someone is afraid, so it is less likely that a supervisee who is afraid will remember the CBT-based lessons you are trying to teach in supervision, much less the homework, unless safety is created first.
- Officers also had 2-h training on mindfulness as a self-care practice for them and as trauma-informed practice for their supervisees. They learned that mindfulness is a trauma-informed approach that reduces anxiety in the moment and creates safety, and regular, consistent practice of mindfulness can heal the brain.
- Officers were asked to practice mindfulness on regular basis for themselves and to integrate the practice of mindfulness in their supervision sessions.

Change in officer's approach

Officers were keenly aware of the role of fear, anxiety, and trauma and how ignoring in a session could compromise their ability to facilitate change.

Powerful changes include the following:

Officers began practicing mindfulness daily for themselves and even integrated mindfulness into all their administrative meetings.

Officers educated their supervisees on the benefits of mindfulness and gained permission to do mindfulness exercises before jumping into the EPICs model.

With 18-year-old supervisees, after establishing safety and establishing rapport, officers began administering the ACE survey (the LSI contains some of this information), but the 10-question ACE survey is a quick way to assess the depth of trauma.

Bottom line: When officers felt safe and taken care of it translated in supervisees feeling safe and taken care of.

Multnomah County DCJ wanted change. We covered the major change theories at the outset of this chapter, what it boiled down to me is how do we positively impact officers (attached to this system) so that they could positively impact 15–25-year-old males of color in a way they had not before.

Phase I of change (happened within the first 3 months)

Phase I of the change process with Multnomah County DCJ Parole/Probation Officers and JCCs involved training in three core areas to include brain development, cultural responsivity, and trauma-informed practices and approaches. These baseline trainings were foundational in terms of helping the group establish shared understanding and language as a team. The baseline trainings also compelled officers to see and reflect on themselves as a means of seeing and reflecting on their supervisees. They were asked to "consider and imagine" with great frequency as a means of building greater capacity for empathy. One other important aspect of the first phase of change was the intentional focus on the fears, needs, wants, and feelings of the officers. In my professional opinion, taking care of officers, tending to their basic needs, establishing rapport with officers was a way to model the type and grade of change I sought. Honestly, officers felt cared for and supported and this literally changed the way they approached their supervisees.

Changed, enlightened people can contribute to facilitating change in and enlightening others.

Systems change when people change and people change when they feel something.

Phase II of change (happened within the first 6 months)

Administrative review of policies, procedures, and practices was critical.

The most critical question in this phase was, do the policies, procedures, and practices support the type of change the system seeks?

I obtained policies and reviewed them (and their corresponding practices) with the following lenses:

Brain development—do the policies and practices account for our current scientific understanding of brain development? Moreover, do they consider that males of color between the ages of 15–25 may have emerged from conditions that didn't support healthy brain development? This is not an excuse, but an explanation and a call to action.

A working example:

15–25 year olds come to supervision without their homework or would state that they didn't do their homework.

The policy and practice suggested that not completing homework = noncompliance and interpreted as apathy.

Policies and practices with a brain development lens = assessing how the supervisee learns best, carefully and thoughtfully probing if there might be reading and/or comprehension challenges, asking what environmental barriers may have gotten in the way of them completing the homework (food insecurity, intermittent houselessness). THEN change the approach. Do the homework in session and support them doing it. DETERMINE the most effective way to teach a skill or a set of skills and how to reinforce them.

Culturally responsive—reviewed the policies with keen attention to language used. I know there are legal terms that must be used for court filings, judges, and district attorneys, however, I asked Multnomah County DCJ to consider the impact of words like "offender," "felon," and "criminal" and whether or not supervisees constantly seeing this narrative is supportive or counter to the change they sought?

The things that parole/probation officers and JCCs could change to reflect the change they sought, they did per my encouragement. Examples included

- Changing language in homework packets.
- Considering the language used in reports to the court (Imagine a supervisee who is doing really well in terms of making positive changes, they arrive at court for a check-in and a report from their supervisor is read out loud in court. Words like "offender" and "felon" keep coming up. Imagine the cognitive dissonance created in the supervisee who thought they were changing for good, but the narrative continues to keep them bound).
- Being mindful of the language used with supervisees in session—increased use of strengths-based language that built self-efficacy.
- Larger systems approach included (in Multnomah County) training judges, judicial staff, district attorneys, and public defenders on the power of narrative and trauma-informed approaches and practices.

Narrative is powerful—officers came to appreciate this. The interesting paradox here is that EPICS is a CBT-based model which inherently mandates consideration for thoughts and their impact on behavior and actions. The missing link here was making the connection between narrative and thoughts—narrative shapes thoughts. Changing narrative is critical. This type of change would be consistent with the Nudge theory change framework—making small changes and suggestions that result in impactful change.

Trauma-informed—reviewed policies with keen attention paid to practices that flowed from policies and assessed whether or not they met the goal of creating safety for supervisees and/or perpetuated trauma?

A working example: there was no specific language in the policies that asked parole/probation officers and JCCs to employ trauma-informed practices where they can—practices like mindfulness, narrative therapy, and even considering the environment in which they are conducting supervision. An important consideration in viewing anything from a trauma-informed lens is thinking about how to create trauma-informed spaces.

What is a trauma-informed space? Examples are provided in Chap. 3 of this textbook in the practical application section. In the case of Multnomah County

Parole/Probation Officers and JCCs, they were asked to reevaluate their office space and find ways to establish "safe space."

In creating a safe space, the officers were asked to consider making the following changes in their office space:

- The type of artwork they had hanging on their walls—were there pictures of guns and bulls-eye versus posters with uplifting quotes and images?
- Making sure the space was clean (is the carpet dirty and tattered? Are the chairs worn? Is your desk messy?).
- Inviting (asked them to consider adding live plants as a sign of "living" things in their office space), is the lighting was appropriate?
- A mechanism to demonstrate their desire to immediately meet the basic needs, asked officers to consider providing diapers, formula, and food.
  - Note: In response to this request, DCJ Multnomah County officers added a pantry and clothes closet in their field office for supervisees to access—very impressive stuff. Do remember that connection, belonging are basic needs too, which was emphasized.
- Asking permission to engage with supervisees in certain areas was emphasized with officers. Before going into a line of questioning that could perpetuate trauma or cause anxiety, it is helpful to ask supervisees, pinpoint the discomfort if there is any, relieve it, and then move forward.
- The example I give and gave to officers is that as a physician, I do physical exams and often use my stethoscope to listen to the lungs, heart, and abdomen. I do not touch the patient until I first explain what, where, and why?
  - **What**: I explain that I would like to listen to the heart.
  - **Where**: I explain that I would like to place the stethoscope on the left lower aspect of the chest (and state that stethoscope might be a little cold upon placement on their skin).
  - **Why**: I then explain that the area I am placing the stethoscope on the left lower aspect of the chest because that is where heart sounds are most predominant. In the process of asking permission before assessing, anxiety in the patient is reduced and capacity for creating safety and trust is increased.

Multnomah County DCJ officers have honored this what/where/why approach, and it has resulted in more judicious establishment of trust and rapport, which helps officers facilitate the change they seek in supervisees.

Phase III of change (developed over an 18-month period)

Training is an important way to disseminate information, but education doesn't always translate into practice. The original EPICS model included a training and coaching element that involved maintenance training and updates to the model and audio/tape recorded sessions scored by an EPICS coach accompanied by feedback for what the supervising officer can improve upon in future sessions. Specifically, when EPICS coaches were reviewing the audiotapes, they were listening closely to hear for adherence to the model; if there was a check-in, review, intervention, and homework covered during a session, then most boxes were checked.

The limitation in this format is that EPICS coaches can't see the interaction between the supervising officer and the supervisee—there is so much rich data that emerges from being able to see interaction. Second, the feedback is written in the original model—supervising officers are less likely to interact with written feedback. There is incredible value in being able to verbalize frustrations, vet concerns, and get real-time feedback for improvement.

Given this information, I added the following components to the original EPICS model:

- Videotaped sessions,
- Group supervision, and
- Live coaching sessions (I physically sat in sessions with supervising officers and supervisees and offered real-time feedback).

Videotaped supervision sessions with supervising officers and supervisees
This marked a major culture shift for Multnomah County DCJ officers because it required them to operate at the peak of their vulnerability. Videotaping sessions were more of public, open process compared to the audiotapes which felt more private and individual. There was much conversation about the discomforts, fear of being judged, and/or not getting something right and feeling so "out there." There was also the additional element of feeling "watched" and/or having a third party in the room and concern for the impact of this on the interaction—would the interactions be genuine and/or feel rehearsed?

The question that most officers had was, will this change the nature of the interaction between them and supervisees? The immediate and honest reply was, yes it will. Videotaping sessions as a form of quality improvement have been and are done in therapy settings. It has proven to be a powerful teaching tool in the right conditions (a safe, nonjudgmental learning environment). Videotaping provides a thoughtful (and sometimes scary) way to examine certain behaviors and explore the attachment to certain feelings (Alpert 1996).

The mechanics of videotaping, review, written, oral, and group feedback sessions:

- Officers were asked to videotape one session per week (they would have a total of four videotaped sessions per month).
- Every officer had to submit four videos per month. Review of respected officer's videos rotated on a month-to-month basis.
- Each officer presented at least five videos a piece to their peer group.
- One of the four videotaped sessions would be sent to me (subject matter expert) and the EPICS.
- I would preview the video and provide written feedback on the session from a cultural responsivity, trauma-informed, and brain development lens.
- The EPICS coach also previewed the video and provided written feedback on how well officers stuck to the fidelity of the model (did they do check-in, review, intervention, homework).

- Myself, the EPICS coach (an officer too), and the parole/probation officers and JCCs met together once per month to review the videotaped session together.
- After reviewing the video, the star of the video offered their feedback on how they through the session went. Peer officers offered their feedback, then the EPICS coach offered their feedback, and then I offered my feedback.
- Videos were recorded on company, encrypted I-phones, and sound was enhanced with a speaker attachment.

The video, group feedback sessions were deemed the richest learning experience according to the officers. Why? I created a safe learning environment.

Creating a nonjudgmental, open, safe learning environment was key. I developed a way of providing feedback that felt nonthreatening and supportive. See "*The Trauma-informed video feedback form*"

The Trauma-informed video feedback form I developed contained the following components:

Opportunity for self-reflection with these questions:

- What did you learn about yourself in this session?
- Is there anything you would change?
- Do you believe you moved toward the "change" you and your supervisee were seeking?

Opportunity to build confidence in officer and a supportive environment conducive to feedback as feedback and opportunity to grow and learn versus feedback as criticism through highlighting strengths in the session:

Strengths that I often highlighted were the officer's ability to build rapport in a session, complimented officers for employing trauma-informed, culturally responsive approaches in session. It was important to highlight when officers took their learning from the training and applied it. An example of this was noted when officers would first educate supervisees on mindfulness and then do a mindfulness exercise in session.

The strengths of the officers were myriad and sundry. I also highlighted when officers asked about birthing history and learning styles and then applied it in session.

Opportunities on "how" to grow and improve with "areas worthy of greater exploration":

Areas worthy of greater exploration were missed opportunities for change. For example, there were several occasions where supervisees would reveal to a supervising officer that they were hurting from the death of a close friend and/or depressed—in their haste to meet all of the elements of EPICS, the officers (initially) would tend to nod with this information, not address it, and move on. These moments were considered missed opportunities for greater engagement and trust building. Officers were able to more fully appreciate this phenomenon by watching themselves, and their peer officers were able to learn as well.

Opportunities to appreciate patterns and break old habits with acknowledgement and awareness of "themes":

Themes would often occur and at times compromise a session. For example, there were a few officers who would become like a parent in a session and start giving advice to the supervisee as opposed to leaving room for the supervisee to explore and take ownership of what they can do to move toward change. Being able to appreciate this phenomenon on video was important for officers.

Opportunities to learn "what" could be done to improve the interactions and move toward change with "recommendations":

Recommendations often included practical means of making changes like implementation of assessment tools, concrete community resources that could be accessed to best support the supervisee, for example.

Policy implications with videotaping EPICS sessions

Policy implications—releases of information had to be adjusted. It was explained to supervisees that the videotaping was similar to the audiotape and would be used for teaching purposes within the organization. Any uses outside of this purpose required permission/consent from the supervisee. Releases of information had an expiration of 1 year with information that the video would be on file for a specified period of time. Full disclosures were provided. Language was established around how to communicate why officers were making this shift. The short of it was that they wanted to improve in their capacity to best serve supervisees and videotaping with feedback sessions was one way to do so. Generally, supervisees were understanding, open, and appreciative of the explanation.

The missing piece

Supervising officers, EPICs coaches, and peer officers were able to co-examine the video and learn together. The piece we didn't get to, but would have been a powerful addition is to have supervising officer's review their video-recorded sessions with their supervisees. This would provide robust feedback for the supervising officer and the supervisee.

Cannot underscore this point enough: creating safety for officers in the context of this video feedback session was a way to model the kind of safety I wanted them to create for their supervisees in a session.

Group Supervision

Group supervision provides space for a shared learning experience. There are opportunities for peer support and learning that is more robust than teacher–student learning dyads (Hammer 2014). The ability to be able to meaningfully co-examine thoughts and ideas with peers builds self-efficacy and sharpens skills (Agnew et al. 2000; Reynolds 2013; Valentino et al. 2016).

In our model, officers were encouraged to share their struggles and solicit feedback from their peers. Officers often discovered that they were not alone in their struggle and the officers themselves were able to generate ways of improving and/or managing a situation moving forward. The opportunities to promote personal healing and wellness were highlighted during group supervision as well.

Officers felt supported and buoyed in these sessions.

Live coaching sessions—I physically sat in sessions with supervising officers and their supervisees

I played varsity team sports in high school and can appreciate the concept of a team and a coach. As a team member, I was expected to be in a perpetual state of openness to feedback to grow. The openness to feedback meant that I learned just as much from my teammates as I did from my coach. The coach's role was to support healthy growth. In any given year, we would lose several games, but we won the State Championship 3 consecutive years in a row. The idea of losing to win was not and is not a foreign concept. The games we lost served as our best teacher. Our coach could see the entire floor and could speak to patterns, themes, and strengths and could educate the team on how to adjust during the game. Lost games were sometimes a result of the opposing team just flat out being more prepared than we were, but there were also times that we didn't adjust to the active-live feedback from the coach during the game. In retrospect, I learned a valuable lesson about teams and coaching—we are not solely looking at one or two games, and we must keep our eye on winning the championship. When I instituted the Live Coaching model into Multnomah County's DCJ team, I had this sentiment in mind. My goal was to support officers in winning championships, and there were sure to be a few games lost, but it is about the collective and long-term commitment to win it all—and we did.

Since high school, I've read a number of books on coaching and leadership, the knowledge of which I applied with the officers. One of the most helpful books is by Peter Hawkins, author of *Leadership Team Coaching: Developing Collective Transformational Leadership.* Hawkins offers thoughts on the role of a team coach, pointing out that part of a coach's role is to provide observations and feedback, role model expectations, and educate. Hawkins also provides insight into the components of what makes an effective team to include the following areas (Hawkins 2014):

- Commissioning—a team must have a clear purpose and shared understanding of what success looks like.
- Clarifying—a team must solidify its mission and purpose. What are we working toward?
- Cocreating—team establishes ground rules for how they engage with one another, they create the subculture in which they operate, and they share in leadership and ownership of their collective success.
- Connecting—communication is critical for execution of the mission.
- Core Learning—includes coordinating information, consolidating information, reflecting on information, learning information, and integrating information.

Coaching involves tending to the developmental progression of a team and empowering and preparing the team for leadership independent of coaching. Ultimately, coaching is about facilitating change. An effective coach understands that change doesn't happen in the absence of relationship. In the end, the live coaching component was a change Multnomah DCJ officers could work with because I had established a relationship with them based on trust and safety.

Mechanics of the live coaching sessions

- Officers gained permission from their supervisees prior to me showing up to the supervision session.
- I introduced myself to the supervisee and thanked them for allowing us (the officer and me) to learn how to serve them better.
- Supervising officer and supervisee would execute a 40-min session.
- During the session, I would offer clarifications, ask follow-up questions, and ask the supervising officer to make small adjustments during the sessions (I always offered my feedback with "have or might you consider" which made it less threatening and/or off-putting).
- The live session with me, the supervising officer, and supervisee was being observed by peer officers via live video feed.
- Directly after the live session, the group including myself, the supervising officer, and peer officers would get together for a feedback session. The feedback session followed the format of the "Trauma-Informed video feedback form." The only difference in this case was that the feedback was immediate.

Live coaching with immediate feedback was deemed a useful tool by officers because they were able to make quick adjustments with their supervisees and optimize the visit. The collective feedback from officers was that they were more conscious of the thing they could be doing in any given session, and motivation for supporting change in supervisees was increased.

A critical element
I personally went through a 3-day, 24-h EPICS training with a group of new Parole/Probation Officers and JCCs. I thoroughly read through the EPCIS manual, enthusiastically participated in all of the exercises and practice sessions. It was important for me to be intimate with the model, understand its strengths and opportunities for growth. The officers appreciated the fact that we had a shared experience.

The missing link in the live coaching model, which would make for a wonderful addition:

Including the supervisee in the group feedback session directly after the live session would have enriched the model so much more.

Phase IV of change—Determining what other training was needed to support growth in officers so that they could support growth in supervisees (developed over a 24-month period)
Officers grew comfortable and confident with videotaped sessions, group feedback, live sessions, and using assessment tools in session, educating supervisees on why they were doing what they were doing. Officers appreciated improved relationships with their supervisees and change happening. When you put something into a process and the process begins to give something back to you—it feels good, it is positive reinforcement. The officers could articulate and understood that they were changed by the process of learning, practicing and integrating culturally responsive, neuroscientific and trauma-informed approaches—they could see the connection between their change and the change in the supervisees.

Officers were eager to get more training to gain more tools to support their efforts in facilitating change in supervisees. A few interesting observations, the LSI-revised tool covers a number of needs areas (as explained earlier in this chapter). Needs like mental health and substance use are covered in the assessment. Officer's experience was that they would get the assessment results and not know exactly what to do with them. With more training, coaching, and skills building, officers became better advocates and support for and to their supervisees. The LSI is an acceptable tool, but if it is not used in the way that it was intended, then it just remains a good tool. Tools are effective when they are put to use.

Multiple examples were given about mental health diagnoses and substance use disorder screens that would come up positive in the LSI, but officers didn't quite know what to do about it.

The following trainings were developed to support officers in being able to optimally use the LSI as an assessment tool. Trainings in:

- ***Substance use and the developing brain***
  Officers had a 4-h, interactive training on primary substances of abuse (cocaine, meth, opioids, alcohol, and nicotine) and their impact on the developing brain. They were provided with a quick script and a question they could ask in the context of a supervision session about substance use.
  The script went something like this: sometimes when things get hard, emotion get confused, and we may want to escape from it all. That desire to escape is understandable and can take many forms. Sometimes, people use drugs to just numb out. Has this ever been your experience? Have you ever used or are you using substances to numb out or for any reason?
  Coaching challenge: After the training, officers were asked to integrate this script about substances into their supervision sessions.
  Officer response: They were open to integrating this script into their supervision session. In video and live sessions, officers would say to their supervisee, and our subject matter expert coach has asked us to think about ways that we can best be of help to you. Supervisees were very open to support. Note the language used to explain and how it was communicated through. Officers endorsed that this addition to the session opened up meaningful conversation and allowed the officer and supervisee to partner together in obtaining appropriate resources and thoughtfully reduce a barrier/factor that contributes to recidivism when unchecked.
  Overall: Training on substance use and the developing brain heightened Officer's awareness of certain elements that (if not acknowledged and managed) can compromise the change process for the supervisee.
- ***Mental Health and its impact on the brain***
  Officers underwent a 4-h, interactive training on core mental health disorders to include psychosis, depression, and anxiety and the concomitant impact on the developing and developed brain. Officers were given greater context as to why mental health wellness management is a priority. Officers were encouraged to observe and listen for any mood changes or concerns. Officers were also encouraged to ask about any mood concerns. The script went something like this: the

world we live in can be hard, circumstances can be challenging, and our moods can change as a result. Emotions like sadness and anger while normal emotions can become concerning if we feel them daily. Has this been your experience, have you been sad or angry daily and/or for weeks on end?
Coaching challenge: Officers were asked to take their new understanding and integrate it into their supervision sessions.
Officer response: They happily integrated the script into their supervision session. Officers will share that they began to listen in a new way to their supervisees—they were more aware of what they should be listening for and were more likely to flag it and address it. They were also given community resources and became more efficient a referring supervisees out sooner, which was critical. Officers were more aware of the medication list of their supervisees and could recognize a psychotropic medication on the list, which helped them reimagine the kind of support they sought to provide to their supervisee.

- ***Understanding Structural Racism*** and its impact on the developing brain
  Officers were provided a 4-h, interactive training on structural, historical racism and how it impacts and how supervisees experience and navigate the world. Officers were asked to consider the social conditions that may shape their supervisees experience.
  This training changed the tenor of supervision—it increased the empathy in officers.
- The Psychopharmacology of Addiction
  Officers were trained on how substance use disorders are treated, standard medications, and approaches employed. Officers indicated that this was a pivotal training because they had several supervisees who struggled with substances, but didn't know exactly how to help them. Learning about addiction medicine and psychiatry opened up a more profound level of support and advocacy for their supervisees.
  Officers were excited to talk with their supervisees about what they had learned. In videotaped sessions, officers were recorded as saying things like: "you know there are community supports for that. Might I refer for you for additional support?" Supervisees were open.

The basic premise here is as the great Dr. Maya Angelou says: when we know better, we can do better.

I should note: the goal is not for officers to be specialist, the goal was to educate to raise awareness and strengthen officer's ability to advocate for their supervisees and to know when, where and how to refer.

The officer of the twenty-first century should think like a mini-clinician and should be equipped with the tools and resources accordingly.

Systems are changed by changed people.

Phase V of change—perpetuating change

The officers participating in the SMART Grant Enhanced EPICS model learned a lot and as a consequence became teachers themselves. Powerful, for sure.

Supervision sessions enhanced

Officers were using images of the brain in session to explain to supervisees what part of the brain is impacted with substance use, trauma, etc. Supervisees adopted the language and would say things like: "I was in the bottom part of my brain, but I want to get to the top."

Officer's interaction with their peers

Officers would report being in a meeting with their peers, hearing language, and encouraging their peers to reframe their narratives. Officers were also doing a fair amount of sharing the information they had learned (literally sharing power point presentations), talking about the brain and how changes in it can impact behavior.

Even more powerful, officers started employing mindfulness as practice into their lives. Soon mindfulness was being done before County meeting, and their colleagues were starting to accept and appreciate mindfulness as a useful practice for themselves and their supervisees.

Officers became better advocates

Officers found themselves in court educating Judges, Defense Attorneys, and Public Defenders about brain development and the potential threats to healthy development. The education component on behalf of the officers was not an excuse but served as an explanation for why they believed judicial officials should consider taking a different approach. Officers would have images of the brain and explain what part of the brain most of their supervisees may be operating in and how they were working to assist their supervisees with making a shift from the bottom part of the brain to the top. Officers were able to explain that the cognitive expectations placed on their supervisee may not be appropriate and they were able to suggest an alternative. An example of this was a supervisee had relapsed on a substance and the courts wanted to move in the direction of a parole violation with some incarceration time. The officer was able to provide a sound, evidence-based, and scientific rationale for why there was an increased risk for relapse in their supervisee and what they (the officer) could do in the community to help mitigate further risks (which included referral for substance use treatment and coordinated care between the officer and the treatment program). The courts listened and the outcome for this particular supervisee was vastly improved.

Officers felt confident advocating for their supervisees in the context of employment—speaking to an employer and asking them to extend a little grace to their supervisees.

In education—calling a school, speaking with administrators, and advocating for a student to stay in school. Officers often referred to the training on structural racism as one of the most helpful trainings in terms of their understanding of the oppressive potential of systems.

There are multiple examples of how officers trained in the enhanced EPICs model felt more equipped to advocate for and support their supervisees. The more inspiring aspect of this is that the officers personally felt compelled to and could appreciate the utility in advocating—this, too, represents the change the system seeks and requires.

Officers independent of the SMART Grant Team requested and received the enhanced EPICS training
Parole/Probation Officers and JCCs felt the enthusiasm, witnessed the change in approach and outcomes that their colleague receiving the enhanced EPICS training were experiencing—a request was made to open up the training to more Parole/Probation Officers and JCCs at Multnomah County DCJ. I provided over 30 additional hours of training to a total of 83 officers in trauma-informed practices/approaches, cultural responsivity, substance use and the brain, mental health and the brain, and brain development.

Phase VI of structural change
EPICS as a community supervision model is strong and in many settings, it has been effective in reducing recidivism. When Multnomah County DCJ applied for and received federal SMART Grant funding, the objective was to enhance, reinforce, and in some ways reimagine a very strong model for the purpose of optimizing its effectiveness for all populations that it served.

EPICS is anchored in cognitive behavioral theory and practice. The demands of the original EPICS model and the needs of Males of color ages 15–25 were not perfectly aligning. The question that emerged from this was: can more be done? In an effort to reconcile the data regarding males of color ages 15–25 with emerging scientific evidence on brain development, trauma, and cultural responsivity, the enhanced EPICS model was birthed.

A few structural changes were made to accommodate the enhancements:

- EPICS score sheet was amended to include consideration of brain development. An example: The question of asking supervisees how they best learn was added to the score sheet. The SMART EPICS Coach would listen for this question in the initial supervision sessions when scoring a videotaped session. Other elements were added for cultural responsivity and trauma-informed approaches as well.
- The enhancements have been codified. Officers now know that they are expected to consider these three enhanced elements in their supervision sessions.

Phase VII—the results, measuring change
Systems change when people change and people change when they feel something.

In doing this work, it was important to me to start at the person level, to teach, to comfort, to heal, to support so that they (the people) can then teach, comfort, heal, and support.

What Multnomah County DCJ wanted and every system wants is change.

They wanted to meet the goal of being able to support everyone that touches their system.

The question that everyone should be asking at this point is: did/does my working theory on systems change hold true? Do changed people, change systems?

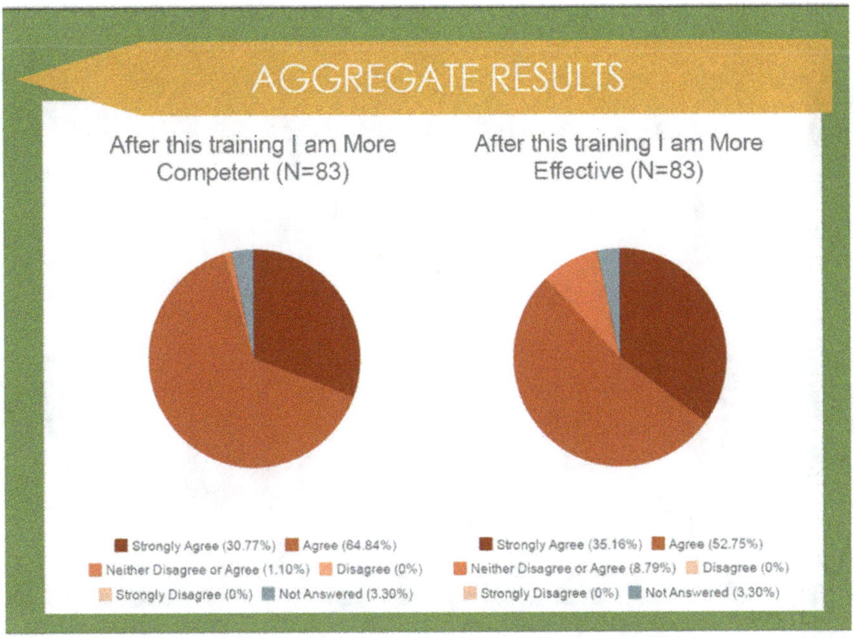

Fig. 12.1 Real data. Officers were asked about competency and effectiveness after training. N = 83. Overwhelmingly 31 and 65% indicated that they STRONGLY Agreed and/or Agreed to feeling "more competent" after training. Printed with permission. Copyright Multnomah County Department of Community Justice

Change was measured on several levels

(1) Multnomah County DCJ's internal research team measured the effectiveness of the training by providing pre- and post-training questionnaires, which I helped to develop. The pre-questionnaire asked officers to rate their knowledge on a particular subject; the post-questionnaire would assess whether or not knowledge was increased as a result of the training.
(2) Multnomah County DCJ's internal research team also captured data on officers' perception of competency in a specific subject before and after training.
(3) Other data captured included an inquiry of the likelihood of officer's taking the information they obtained in the training and apply it to their work and would assist them in making better connections with their supervisees.
(4) Lastly, there were data captured on the officer's perception of the relevance of the training material/content and whether they thought the information should be integrated into the EPICS model.

Real Results
Good Training can impact change (Fig. 12.1).

Enhanced training was deemed effective (Fig. 12.2).

Officers were asked (Fig. 12.3):

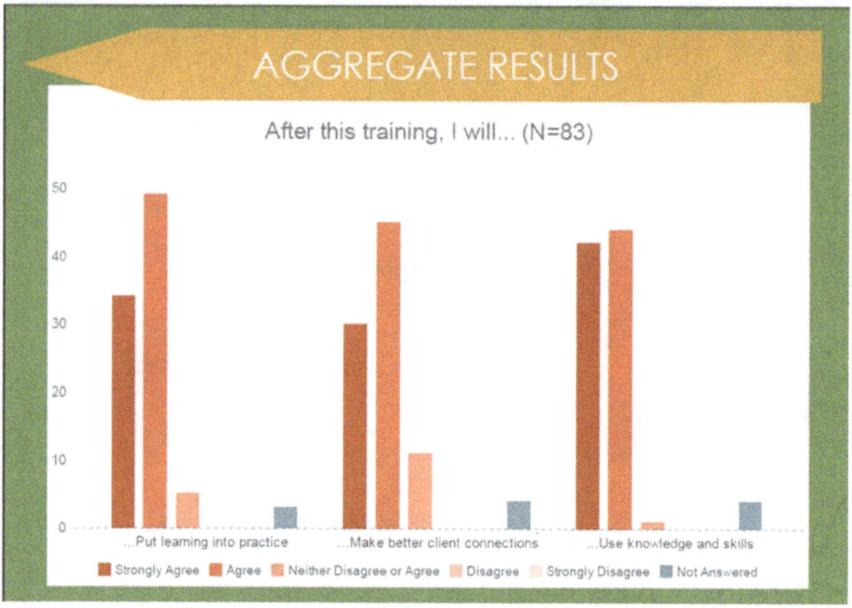

Fig. 12.2 After training, officers felt confident in their ability to apply what they had learned and improved their work with clients. Printed with permission. Copyright Multnomah County Department of Community Justice

If they would put the learning from training into practice = overwhelming they agreed.

If the training would help make better connections with their supervisees = overwhelmingly they agreed.

If they would use the knowledge and skills from the training = overwhelmingly they agreed.

Enhancements to EPICS model were deemed worthy, useful, and relevant (Fig. 12.4).

On the question of "importance of the topic", N = 72, 72% of officers rated enhanced training very important; 23% of officers rated enhanced training moderately important.

Of note, when officers were queried on how important it is to add the enhanced training into the EPICS model, N = 71, 54% responded very important and 25% responded moderately important.

The officers appreciated the different modalities employed during the training—-most of which have been included in this textbook.

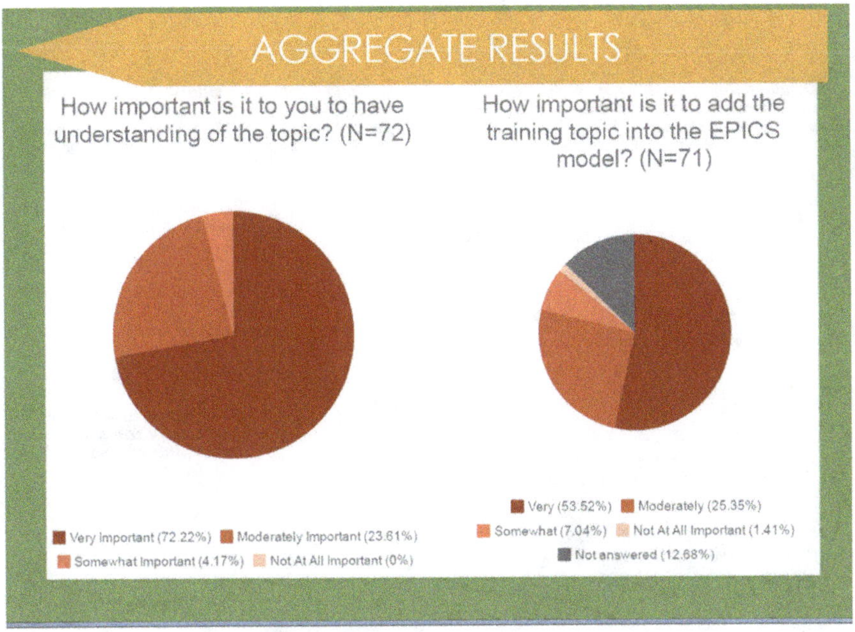

Fig. 12.3 Officers were queried on the relevance of the training topics (trauma-informed practices/approaches, cultural responsivity, brain development, substance use disorders, mental health disorders, structural racism) and overwhelmingly held the opinion that understanding these topics was important to their work. Printed with permission. Copyright Multnomah County Department of Community Justice

How did change in officers practice and behavior translate into change in supervisees?

Supervisees working with officers engaged in the enhanced EPICS model with the lenses of cultural responsivity, trauma-informed approaches/practices, and brain development applied had the following:

- Improved relationship between supervisee and officer.
- Felt the officers cared and would advocate for them and were more likely to show up for supervision sessions and be honest about their active struggles.
- Less parole violations.
- Increase in appropriate and efficient referrals for community resources.
- Increase in peer mentor support.
- Increased participation in vocational programs.
- Increased participation in education programs.
- More likely to go see someone regarding their substance use and/or mental health concerns.
- Improved decision-making.
- Increased successful completion of probation/parole and no reengagement within 6 months to a year.

COMMENTS - WHAT WAS DONE WELL

Attendees were asked "what do you think was done well?" and given an opportunity to provide open-ended comments in the post-training evaluation. There were 51 total comments. Respondents commented on the relevance, visuals, and overall structure of the trainings. They also gave positive comments on the trainer and specific training topics. Here is a selection of representative responses.

"Examples, interaction, integrating past info into current training"

"Dr. Moreland's passion"

"The presentation was good... the information and delivery were superb."

"Dr. Moreland's presentation, videos, discussion are excellent"

"Presenting study relative to criminal justice"

"Visual slides"

"I really like the Power Point examples."

"The impact and power that words can possess was explained well"

"Content was up to date/current, directly related to my work."

"Timing and use of training"

"Open and frank conversations. Ability to ask questions. Variety of materials - current events, research, videos"

"Breaking down the brain and what actions drive and promote reactions to be knowledgeable of how fear drives"

Fig. 12.4 Feedback on how the trainings were facilitated. Printed with permission. Copyright Multnomah County Department of Community Justice

Challenges in Community Supervision and how they overcome

In 2008, Bonta et al. wrote an article entitled *Exploring the black box of community supervision*. In this article, Bonta and colleagues highlighted the following (Bonta et al. 2008):

- When officers focused on the conditions of probation, recidivism rates were higher.
- When officers focused on needs over conditions, recidivism rates were lower.

Appreciating and considering Maslow's hierarchy of needs should be standard. When basic needs are met, the capacity for change increases, and unhealthy risks decrease.

Meeting needs is key.

When the needs of officers were met, the needs of supervisees were met.

When the needs of officers were met,

- Officers were able to appreciate (in their supervisees) that being afraid, anxious, hungry, and tired or having a history of trauma can compromise cognition, making it difficult for them, initially, to engage in heavy cognitive-based model.
- Officers learned the importance of creating safety as a means of optimally engaging supervisees and facilitating their change process.

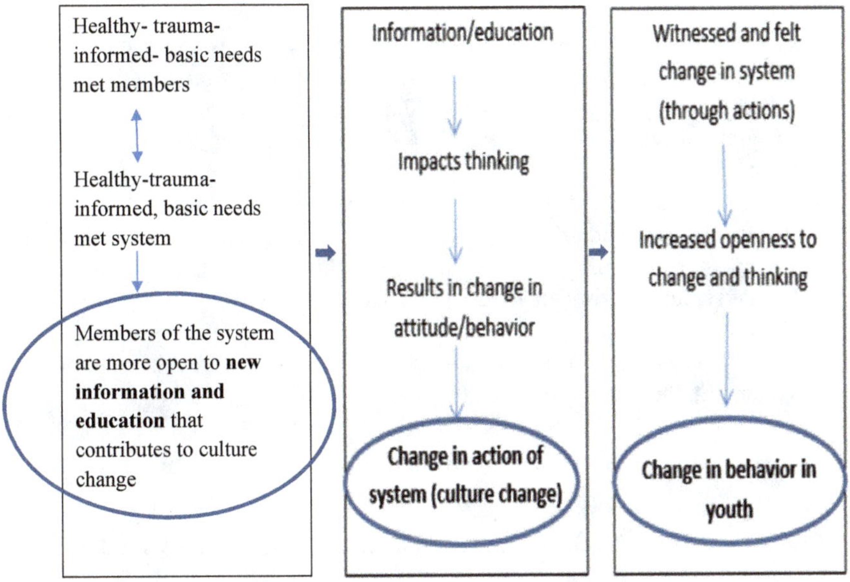

Fig. 12.5 Parallel system change. When we take care of people who work in systems, they take care of the system they work in. Printed with permission. Copyright Audrey A. Tran

- Officers became conduits for change in the system in which they worked (the examples were provided above).
- Officers became advocates for their supervisees.

I would contend that all change in a system must be parallel in order to stick. Any system committed to change should consider the model for parallel change as depicted in Fig. 12.5.

Change happens at the people level.

Quick summary

The identified challenge: EPICS, a strong cognitive model, was not as effective in meeting the goal of reducing recidivism in males of color ages 15–25 year olds.

The subtext was: Change.

My philosophical underpinning: Systems don't change if people don't change and people don't change if they don't feel something.

Steps taken to initiate the change process

- Participated in a 3-day EPICS training;
- Reviewed policies and procedures with keen focus on language and narratives and recommended changes that supported the type of change the system sought;

- Provided three <u>**core**</u> trainings (Trauma-informed practices/approaches, brain development, and cultural responsivity) with the goal of moving a group of officers (in a system) toward shared language and understanding;
- Integrated Live coaching, video recording, and coaching and group supervision;
- Trained on and provided tools for the practice of mindfulness;
- Repetition was standard in my training—each progressive training built upon one another (very much like the chapters in this textbook); and
- Created safety for officers to learn, engage, and grow

Result

The officers were themselves changed in the process and are now champions for change in the system in which they serve.

Enhanced EPICS Model as practiced by Multnomah County DCJ Officers SMART Team

1. Officer and supervisee start with 1–5 min mindfulness exercise to reduce anxiety, ***create safety*** (from the brain perspective, to reduce the activity of the amygdala and increase prefrontal cortex engagement).

2. **Check-In**: Officers inquire about substance use and mental health.
   Ask about basic needs and working to meet any needs they can while in office with supervisee and make appropriate referrals.
   Supervisees are asked about how they best learn.
   Assessments like MOCA are done as deemed appropriate—determine cognitive capacity and manage expectations appropriately for the session.

Officers are aware of and checking for their own personal biases in sessions.

3. **Review**: Officers are using images of the brain to explain trauma, substance use, and mental health impacts on the developing brain. Supervisees are appreciative of the teaching and interpret it as a sign of respect, increasing motivation for change.
4. **Intervention/Behavioral Practices**: They are adapted based on supervisees needs at the time. DCJ SMART Officers are making good use of whiteboards in their offices to help illustrate and drive home specific points. The goal is learning for change, and adaptations must be made to support the desired change.

5. **Homework**: There is flexibility around homework. Depending on the supervisee and how they indicated that they learn best, homework can be done in office during the visit. Supervisee's cognitive abilities are considered. If a supervisee indicates that they learn best by listening to music, DCJ SMART Officers integrate this into the homework portion of EPICS. The goal is changed. Change is more likely in the presence of comprehension.
6. DCJ SMART Grant Officers are now teaching their peers this enhanced model. There is now a team of beautifully trained Multnomah County DCJ officers who can support culture change and implementation of this model.

Conclusion

For 3 years, I trained and coached JCCs and POs in the areas of trauma-informed practices, cultural responsivity, and brain science. The results were phenomenal—individuals were changed and an entire system was impacted. Officers were able to see themselves as part of a system and as having agency to positively impact the system in which they served. This is what taking the "fear" out of the change process can look like. In employing the various theories on change, I focused on parole and probation officers as the main proponents of change—they (Officers) couldn't facilitate change in supervisees (in this case, young males of color ages 15–25) if they (Officers) themselves weren't change. In this case, it was noted that recidivism reduction goals were not being met. It was determined that a cultural shift had to take place in order to optimize goal attainment.

The criminal justice system can be inflexible and feel insurmountable when it comes to the subject of change. However, with the appropriate approach, lens, and engagement, change can and did happen—change happened one parole officer and Juvenile Court Counselor (JCC) at a time.

The phases of change outlined in the case study of Multnomah County DCJ Parole/Probation Officers and JCCs can be applied to and by systems (which are many) that serve youth, i.e., education, health care. As cliché as this may sound, in the words of Whitney Houston, "I believe the children are our future." I earnestly hold this conviction. There is a moral imperative to care for, support, love, engage, and help heal our youth. Systems that serve youth are uniquely positioned to fulfill this purpose. If we seek change in our youth, systems must change, which means people who work in these systems must change.

The reality is that no one wakes up poised to change because it (change) is hard and requires deep work. However, it is not impossible. The real question is how we set the conditions that make change more acceptable than the alternative (which is no change at all).

I am convinced (as demonstrated throughout this textbook) that you have to tap into the "feeling" space and effectively place a mirror in front of individuals. The change conversation cannot just be limited to "other" but must also be emphasized for "self" and in parallel.

I hope the lessons of this textbook inspire people and systems that serve youth to be trauma-informed, culturally responsive, and neuroscientifically focused.

I wish to end how I started; this textbook redefines systems by challenging individuals within any given system to consider this sentiment:

> **"Systems are intimately attached to people. Systems don't change, if people don't change. People don't change, if they don't feel something."**

"Systems are intimately attached to people. Systems don't change, if people don't change. People don't change if they don't feel something."

References

Agnew, T., Vaught, C., Getz, H., & Fortune, J. (2000). Peer group clinical supervision program fosters confidence and professionalism. *Professional School Counseling, 4,* 6–12.

Alcalay, R., Alvarado, M., Balcazar, H., Newman, E., & Heurta, E. (1999). Salud para su corazon: A community-based Latino cardiovascular disease prevention and outreach model. *Journal of Community Health, 24,* 359–379.

Alpert, M. C. (1996). Videotaping psychotherapy. *The Journal of psychotherapy practice and research, 5*(2), 93–105.

Andrews, D. A., & Bonta, J. L. (2001). *LSI-R User's Manual*. New York: MHS.

Andrews, D. A., & Bonta, James. (2003). *The Psychology of Criminal Conduct* (3rd ed., p. 260). Cincinnati: Anderson Publishing.

Bandura, A, Walters, R. (1963). Social Learning and Personality Development: New York: Holt, Rinehart and Winston.

Bandura, A. (1977). *Social learning theory*. New York: General Learning Press.

Bonta, J., Bourgon, G., Rugge, T., Scott, T., Yessine, A. K., Gutierrez, L., et al. (2010). *The strategic training initiative in community supervision: Risk-need-responsivity in the real world (User Report 2010-01)*. Ottawa, Canada: Public Safety and Emergency Preparedness.

Bonta, J., Rugge, T., Scott, T., Bourgon, G., & Yessine, A. K. (2008). Exploring the black box of community supervision. *Journal of Offender Rehabilitation, 47,* 248–270.

Bourgon, G., Bonta, J., Rugge, T., Scott, T., & Yessine, A. K. (2010). The role of program design, implementation, and evaluation in evidence-based "real world" community supervision. *Federal Probation, 74*(1), 2–15.

DeLamater, J., Wagstaff, D. A., & Havens, K. K. (2000). The impact of a culturally appropriate STD/AIDS education intervention on Black male adolescents' sexual and condom use behavior. *Health Education and Behavior, 27,* 454–470.

Devos, R. M. Lewin's Change Management Model: Understanding the three Stages of Change [internet]. Retrieved from: http://www.mindtools.com/pages/article/newPPM_94.htm.

Dowden, C., & Andrews, D. A. (2004). The importance of staff practice in delivering effective correctional treatment: a meta-analytic review of core correctional practice. *International Journal of Offender Therapy and Comparative Criminology, 48*(2), 203–214.

Erickson, C. D., & Al-Timimi, N. R. (2001). Providing mental health services to Arab Americans: Recommendations and considerations. *Cultural Diversity and Ethnic Minority Psychology, 7,* 308–327.

Gillum, T. L. (2009). Improving services to african american survivors of IPV: From the voices of recipients of culturally specific services. *Violence Against Women, 15*(1), 57–80. https://doi.org/10.1177/1077801208328375.

Gondolf, E. W., & Williams, O. J. (2001). Culturally focused batterer counseling for African American men. *Trauma, Violence, & Abuse, 2,* 283–295.

Haas, S. M., & Hamilton, C. A. (2007, May). *The use of core correctional practices in offender reentry: The delivery of service delivery and prisoner preparedness for release.* Charleston, WV: Mountain State Criminal Justice Research Services.

Hammar, C. E. (2014). Group work as an incentive for learning—students' experiences of group work. *Frontiers in psychology, 5,* 558. https://doi.org/10.3389/fpsyg.2014.00558.

Hawkins, P. (2014). *Leadership team coaching: Developing collective transformation leadership* (2nd edn.). Kogan Page Limited.

Itzchakov, G., & Kluger, A. N. (2018) The power of listening in helping people change. *Harvard Business Review*, May 17, 2018.

Kotter, J. P. (2000). What leaders really do. *The Bottom Line, 13*(1). https://doi.org/10.1108/bl.2000.17013aae.001.

Kosters, M., & der Heijden, J. V. (2015). From mechanism to virtue: Evaluating Nudge theory. *Evaluation, 21*(3), 276–291. https://doi.org/10.1177/1356389015590218.

Labrecque, Ryan M., & Smith, Paula. (2015). Does training and coaching matter? An 18-Month evaluation of a community supervision model. *Victims & Offenders, 00,* 1–20.

McFarland, W. (2012). This is your brain on organizational change. *The Harvard Business Review,* October, 16, 2012.

Mulder, P. (2013). *ADKAR model by Jeff Hiatt.* Retrieved January, 2019, from ToolsHero: https://www.toolshero.com/change-management/adkar-model/.

Ravanfar, M. M. (2015). Analyzing organizational structure based on 7S model of McKinsey. *Global Journal of Management and Business Research: An Administration and Management, 15*(10), Version 1.0 Year 2015.

Reynolds, V. (2013). Centering ethics in group supervision: Fostering cultures of critique and safety. *The International Journal of Narrative Therapy and Community Work, 4,* 1–13.

Robinson, C. R., Vanbenschoten, S., Alexander, M., & Lowenkamp, C. T. (2012). A random study of staff training aimed at reducing re-arrest (STARR): Using core correctional practices in probation interactions. *Key Issues of Science Based Supervision, 35*(2).

Sanchez, P. (2018). The secret to leading organizational is empathy. *Harvard Business Review,* December 20, 2018.

Satir, V. et. al. (1991). The Satir model: Family therapy and beyond. *Science and behavior books.* ISBN 0831400781.

Shoolin, J. S. (2010). Change management—Recommendations for successful electronic medical records implementation. *Applied Clinical Informatics, 1*(3), 286–292. https://doi.org/10.4338/ACI-2010-01-R-0001.

Shy, Y., & Mills, L. G. (2010). A critical new pathway towards change in abusive relationships: The theory of transition framework. *Clinical Social Work Journal, 38*(4), 418–425.

Smith, P., et al. (2012). Improving probation officers' supervision skills: an evaluation of the EPICS model. *Journal of Crime and Justice, 35*(2), 189–199.

Trotter, C. (1996). The impact of different supervision practices in community corrections: Cause for optimism. *Australian and New Zealand Journal of Criminology, 29,* 1–18.

Trotter, C. (2006). *Working with involuntary clients: A guide to practice* (2nd ed.). Thousand Oaks, CA: Sage.

Valentino, A. L., LeBlanc, L. A., & Sellers, T. P. (2016). The benefits of group supervision and a recommended structure for implementation. *Behavior Analysis in Practice, 9*(4), 320–328. https://doi.org/10.1007/s40617-016-0138-8.

Winnicott, D. W. (1994). Hate in the counter-transference. *The Journal of Psychotherapy Practice and Research, 3*(4), 348–356.

Index

A. Moreland-Capuia, *Training for Change*,
https://doi.org/10.1007/978-3-030-19208-2

CPSIA information can be obtained
at www.ICGtesting.com
Printed in the USA
LVHW081115280920
667286LV00002B/21

9 783030 192075